LONGSTREET HIGHROAD GUIDE
— TO THE —
CALIFORNIA COAST

BY KEN MCKOWEN

FOREWORD BY
THE CALIFORNIA STATE PARKS FOUNDATION

LONGSTREET
ATLANTA, GEORGIA

Published by
LONGSTREET PRESS, INC.
2140 Newmarket Parkway
Suite 122
Marietta, Georgia 30067

Great efforts have been made to make the information in this book as accurate as possible. However, over time trails are rerouted and signs and landmarks may change. If you find a change has occurred to a trail in the book, please let us know so we can correct future editions. *A word of caution:* Outdoor recreation by its nature is potentially hazardous. All participants in such activities must assume all responsibility for their own actions and safety. The scope of this book does not cover all potential hazards and risks involved in outdoor recreation activities.

Printed by RR Donnelley & Sons, Harrisonburg, VA

1st printing 2000

Library of Congress Catalog Number 00-104187

ISBN: 1-56352-594-1

Book editing, design, and cartography by Lenz Design & Communications, Inc., Decatur, Georgia. www.lenzdesign.org. Online version: www.sherpaguides.com

Cover illustration by R. Swain Gifford, *Picturesque America*, 1872

Cover design by Richard J. Lenz, Decatur, Georgia

Illustrations by Danny Woodard, Loganville, Georgia

Photographs by Ken McKowen

The flashing and golden pageant of California,
The sudden and gorgeous drama, the sunny and ample lands,
The long and varied stretch from Puget sound to Colorado south,
Lands bathed in sweeter, rarer, healthier air, valleys and mountain cliffs,
The fields of Nature long prepared and fallow, the silent, cyclic chemistry,
The slow and steady ages plodding, the unoccupied surface ripening,
the rich ores forming beneath;
At last the New arriving, assuming, taking possession,
A swarming and busy race settling and organizing everywhere,
Ships coming in from the whole round world, and going out to the whole world,
To India and China and Australia and the thousand island paradises of the Pacific,
Populous cities, the latest inventions, the steamers on the rivers, the railroads, with
many a thrifty farm, with machinery,
And wool and wheat and the grape, and diggings of yellow gold.

—Walt Whitman, *Song of the Redwood-Tree, 1891-92*

Contents

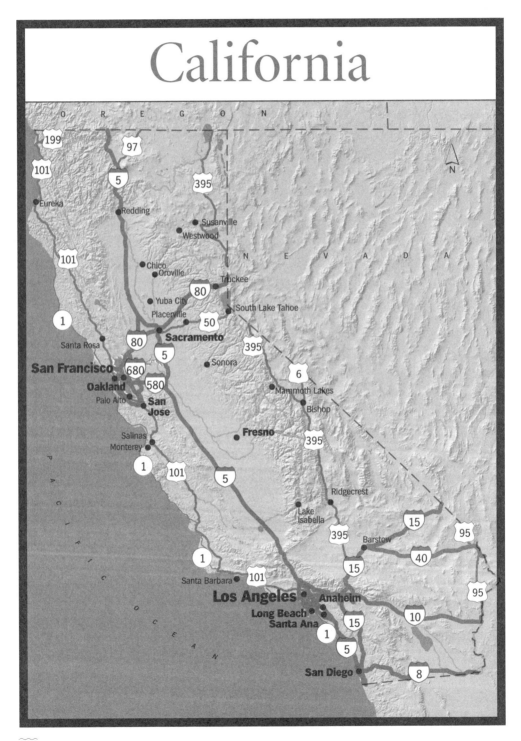

California

How Your Highroad Guide is Organized

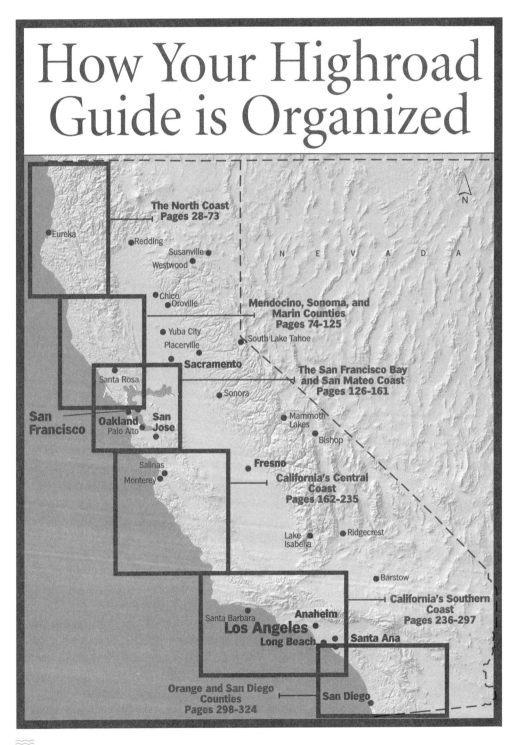

The North Coast
Pages 28-73

Eureka

Redding

Susanville

Westwood

NEVADA

Chico
Oroville

Mendocino, Sonoma, and
Marin Counties
Pages 74-125

Yuba City
Placerville

South Lake Tahoe

Sacramento

Santa Rosa

Sonora

The San Francisco Bay
and San Mateo Coast
Pages 126-161

San
Francisco

Oakland
Palo Alto

San
Jose

Mammoth
Lakes

Bishop

Salinas

Monterey

Fresno

California's Central
Coast
Pages 162-235

Lake
Isabella

Ridgecrest

Barstow

California's Southern
Coast
Pages 236-297

Santa Barbara

Los Angeles

Anaheim

Long Beach

Santa Ana

Orange and San Diego
Counties
Pages 298-324

San Diego

How To Use Your Longstreet Highroad Guide

The *Longstreet Highroad Guide to the California Coast* includes a wealth of detailed information on the best of what the coast has to offer, including hiking, camping, fishing, scenic driving, and boating. The Longstreet Highroad Guide also presents interesting information on the natural history, flora, and fauna of the coast, giving readers a starting point to learn more about what makes this part of California so special.

The coast is divided into six major sections beginning in Northern California and moving south, and each section is covered in its own chapter. There is also an introduction to the natural history of the California coast.

The maps in the book are keyed by figure numbers and referenced in the text. These maps are intended to help orient both casual and expert coastal enthusiasts. Below is a legend to explain symbols used on the maps. Remember that hiking trails frequently change as they fall into disuse or new trails are created. Serious hikers may want to purchase additional maps from the U.S. Geological Service before they set out on a long hike. Sources are listed on the maps.

A word of caution: Coastal waters can be dangerous for swimming, fishing, and boating. California has powerful and frequently changing tides, and wild animals can act in unexpected ways. Be aware of your surroundings and make safe decisions so all your memories will be happy ones.

Legend

Amphitheater	Camping	Ranger Station
Parking	Bathroom	Misc. Special Areas
Telephone	Wheelchair Accessible	Town or City
Information	First Aid Station	Physiographic Region/ Misc. Boundary
Picnicking	Picnic Shelter	Regular Trail
Dumping Station	Shower	State Boundary
Swimming	Biking	
Fishing	Comfort/Rest Station	70 Interstate
Interpretive Trail	Park Boundary	522 U.S. Route
Good Diving	Good Snorkeling	643 State Highway

Foreword

For more than 30 years the California State Parks Foundation has pursued its vital mission of protecting and enhancing many of California's natural, historic, and cultural treasures—California's 265 state parks. *The Longstreet Highroad Guide to the California Coast* describes many of these special places—the best that California has to offer.

In 1969, the late William Penn Mott, former director of both the California State and National Park Systems, envisioned an organization that could do all the things that government couldn't do when it came to acquiring and protecting California's parklands. Since this visionary beginning, the California State Parks Foundation has funded critical parkland acquisitions, vital preservation and restoration projects, and environmental education programs that benefit all Californians. But what continues to make the foundation so successful are the people of California who will not compromise their own nor their children's natural or cultural legacy and who support our work to protect and enhance these special places.

Each of California's beaches, parks, wildlife reserves, and museums is a gem. I encourage you to read this book and then strike out and discover parts of California you never knew existed. Your newly found understanding of the natural forces that created our 1,100-mile coast is certain to enhance your appreciation of what lies around the next bend in the trail.

—Susan Smartt, President, California State Parks Foundation

HARBOR SEAL
(Phoca vitulina)
Harbor seals can swim to depths of 300 feet and stay underwater for nearly 30 minutes.

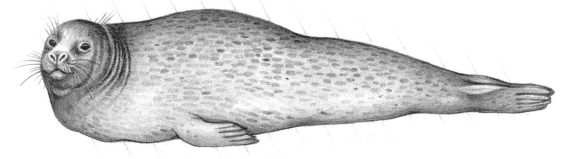

Preface

Some say that California is as much a state of mind as it is a state of the Union. Perhaps. But no human mind could possibly have competed with the hand of nature to create all that is found here. Writing this book gave me a wonderful opportunity to revisit many of California's most breathtaking coastal treasures and to discover works of nature I'd somehow overlooked during more than 25 years of traveling the state's 1,100 miles of coast.

This book was also an interesting challenge. Having previously spent many years writing about California's coastal parks I didn't wish to simply rehash old material, but instead I wanted to take a new look at everything I could. And I did. I walked on beaches I had never before seen and down trails I'd never traveled. I also wandered through my favorite old haunts in the northern redwoods, along the Big Sur coast, and in the Santa Monica Mountains.

Sometimes an old place turned out to be a new and wonderful experience. The only previous time that I'd hiked the trail to the Pygmy Forest at Jughandle State Reserve rain poured down and mushrooms sprouted everywhere I looked. This time there was fog at the beach that opened to a bright blue sky by the time I made it to the top of the last ancient marine terrace where the diminutive trees struggle for survival.

RIVER OTTER
(Lutra canadensis)
A shy, water-loving mammal seen in coastal rivers and occasionally in marsh areas.

RACCOON
(Procyon lotor)
This highly adaptable
animal feeds on crabs in
California's salt marsh.

Hiking in Sinkyone Wilderness one evening I found myself standing between two bull elk, one with his harem peacefully grazing behind him and the second intent on having his way with the harem's cows. Rutting season makes bull elk kind of crazy. With my heart pounding from both trepidation and excitement, I took refuge of questionable worth behind the only nearby tree hoping the loser wouldn't work out his frustration on little me. I then enjoyed the sight and sounds of the bulls' challenges and counter challenges.

As my travels and writing for this project drew to a close I wanted to be sure I had included the best of California's coast from among so many thousands of choices. I think that I have succeeded on two levels. If you're new to California's coast, this book will prove to be an invaluable time-saving guide that can quickly lead you to the highlights of this magnificent, 1,100-mile coast. And, if you're a seasoned visitor, it's likely you've not seen everything—and even if you have, there may be an unexpected bull elk in your future travels.

—Ken McKowen

Acknowledgments

Writing an informative guidebook requires the author to collect, evaluate, and interpret a massive volume of information that is solicited from untold numbers of experts, discovered in libraries, or found in one's own reference materials. But, before all the planning and research begins, someone must have the vision for the book, in this case the entire Longstreet Highroad Guides series, and that was Longstreet Press. So, I first thank Longstreet Press for creating a truly wonderful series of informative guides.

To acknowledge all those who helped my writing effort to reach fruition is nearly impossible. But, the most important person I must thank is Longstreet Press' Director of Development Marge McDonald for finding me and trusting that I could continue the excellent work of the authors who wrote the previous Highroad Guides. To thank everyone who contributed to my ability to write this book, I'd have to reach back more than 20 years to the park rangers and naturalists whom I have known and worked with and who have shared their own favorite places and their life-long love of nature and history. Many of those personal treasures I have included in these writings.

More recently, John Arnold, an information officer at California State Parks

NORTHERN ROCK
BARNACLES
(Balanus balanoides)

headquarters in Sacramento, provided an invaluable pile of park brochures. Hayden Sohm, a park superintendent in the Santa Monica Mountains, and the district's office staff willingly provided both written information and their own ideas about where to go. A volunteer living part time in the Sinkyone Wilderness inadvertently guided me to what turned out to be a center stage seat for a bull elk confrontation; the national park staff at their Orick visitor center not only provided great trail information, but also offered insight into the area's non-native invasive plants.

GREEN SEA URCHIN
(Strongylocentrotus drowbachiensis)

Tom Moss, a resource ecologist in Monterey District State Parks, helped clarify several issues regarding plant species and communities. I must thank Lorena Wainer, the workshops coordinator for the Tijuana River National Estuarine Reserve, for sending me a significant amount of material at the last minute after Southern California's first and worst storm of the year caused me to miss my long-sought return trip there. Then there was the woman, whose name I missed, at the Don Edwards San Francisco Bay National Wildlife Refuge visitor center, which I discovered is closed on Mondays, the day I was there. She kindly allowed me inside the visitor center to look around while she gathered publications that significantly aided my writing.

As deadlines loomed and time quickly passed, long-time friend and fellow writer Dahlynn Shiflet provided invaluable editing of my very rough first drafts of the last half of the book. Dahlynn's efforts certainly made Pam Holliday's work easier. Pam, working with Richard Lenz at Lenz Design & Communications, is an editor of extraordinary skill who caught my inconsistencies, questioned my occasional vagueness, and helped hone my words into succinct clarity. Thanks to Chip Evans at Lenz Design for his skill in making the best maps possible.

And finally, I must thank my wife Denise and the dozens of friends and relatives who smiled their understanding of my need to spend so many days on the road and the long, solitary hours writing.

—Ken McKowen

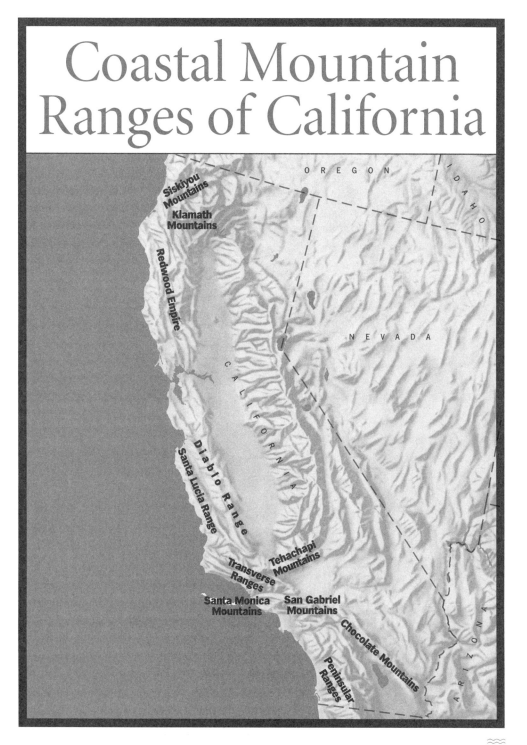

Coastal Mountain Ranges of California

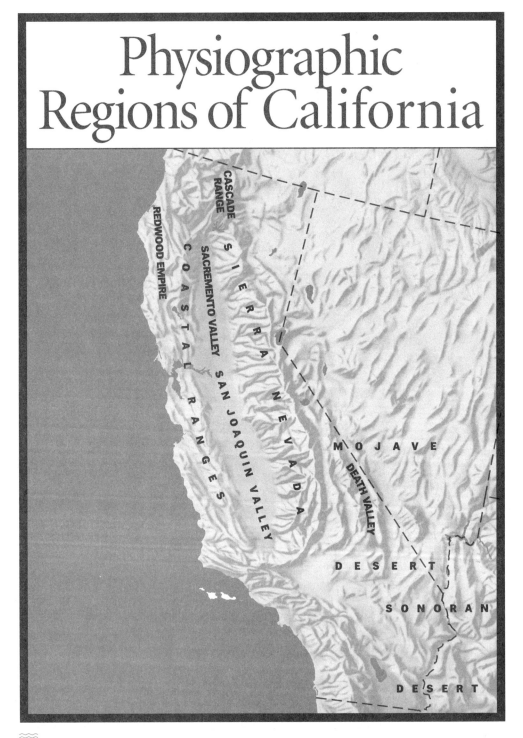

Physiographic Regions of California

The Natural History of California

The natural history of California is as varied and dynamic as the 34 million people who call the Golden State their home. And California's borders are just as varied as her citizens, with the forests of Oregon to the north, the deserts of Nevada to the east, and a foreign nation to the south. But it's California's western boundary that holds most people's attention. The boundary is constantly changing as beach sands shift, cliffs collapse, and rivers deposit millions of tons of silt at their mouths every year. This constant geologic activity is coupled with the Pacific Ocean's pounding waves and changing currents to create 1,100 miles of sand-covered beaches and steep, jagged cliffs. Add the geologic changes that two battling tectonic plates have created, and the result is an extraordinarily rugged and beautiful coast.

The sometimes violent but most often subtle forces of nature have molded California's coast, and in turn have created plant communities that range from

[*Above:* Seaside daisies (*Erigeron glaucus*) in Wilder Ranch State Park]

Geologic Time Scale

Era	System & Period	Series & Epoch	Some Distinctive Features	Years Before Present
CENOZOIC	Quaternary	Recent	Modern man.	11,000
		Pleistocene	Early man; northern glaciation.	1/2 to 2 million
	Tertiary	Pliocene	Large carnivores.	13 + 1 million
		Miocene	First abundant grazing mammals.	25 + 1 million
		Oligocene	Large running mammals.	36 + 2 million
		Eocene	Many modern types of mammals.	58 + 2 million
		Paleocene	First placental mammals.	63 + 2 million
MESOZOIC	Cretaceous		First flowering plants; climax of dinosaurs and ammonites, followed by Cretaceous-Tertiary extinction.	135 + 5 million
	Jurassic		First birds, first mammals dinosaurs and ammonites abundant.	181 + 5 million
	Triassic		First dinosaurs. Abundant cycads and conifers.	230 + 10 million
PALEOZOIC	Permian		Extinction of most kinds of marine animals, including trilobites. Southern glaciation.	280 + 10 million
	Carboniferous	Pennsylvanian	Great coal forests, conifers. First reptiles.	310 + 10 million
		Mississippian	Sharks and amphibians abundant. Large and numerous scale trees and seed ferns.	345 + 10 million
	Devonian		First amphibians; ammonites; fishes abundant.	405 + 10 million
	Silurian		First terrestrial plants and animals.	425 + 10 million
	Ordovician		First fishes; invertebrates dominant.	500 + 10 million
	Cambrian		First abundant record of marine life; trilobites dominant.	600 + 50 million
	Precambrian		Fossils extremely rare, consisting of primitive aquatic plants. Evidence of glaciation. Oldest dated algae, over 2,600 million years; oldest dated meteorites 4,500 million years.	

towering redwoods in the north to the low chaparral along the central coast and desert scrub in the south. Even though California experiences what is often described as a Mediterranean climate—mild, rainy winters and warm, dry summers—its rainy season can produce over 100 inches of precipitation in Humboldt County while dropping less than 6 inches in San Diego County. These climatic differences help to support 54 of the West's 73 cone-bearing trees, with 21 being endemic to California.

People have joked for years that one of California's infamous earthquakes might one day drop much of the state into the ocean. Several million years ago, much of California lay beneath the blue waters of an ancient sea. Look carefully at many of the coastal cliffs and their skewed layers of ancient, metamorphosed ocean bottom mud, and you will discover the fossilized remains of small sea creatures. Come inland 100 miles or more, crossing the coastal mountains and the Central Valley, and once again these same fossils and their ancient sea floor home can be found in cliff faces of the uplifted lower Sierra Nevada foothills. But the joke about the catastrophic earthquake is not too far off. Although it won't happen in one sudden, giant jolt, geologists tell us that a large portion of California's coast will not remain with us forever. As the leading edge of the giant Pacific tectonic plate continues to dive beneath the North American plate, it is also moving north at the rate of about 1 inch each year, and it will continue to do so.

Geologic History

What seventeenth century nautical map makers first noticed from the outlines of their crude maps, and twentieth century scientists now believe through their use of modern technology, is that the earth is made up of a series of seven massive and numerous smaller plates. Study a map of Africa and Europe and compare their western coastlines with the eastern coasts of the American continents. The shape of their outlines, if pressed back together, match remarkably like correct puzzle pieces snapping into place. The widely separated modern continents also share many of the same types of rock, minerals, and fossils along the matching areas of their coasts.

These plates are essentially massive, broken pieces of the earth's crust that vary in thickness from 3 miles to 35 miles. They slip across the earth's surface on the under-lying 1,800-mile-thick mantle, although at something much slower than a snail's pace. It is theorized that some 200 million years ago there was but one continent. For reasons that may never be known, the original plates began pulling apart, gradually forming our modern continents and much of the California we know today. Return here following the passage of another 60 million years, and it's likely you'd not recognize a much changed California coast where two massive tectonic plates continue grinding into one another.

Two major plates, the North American plate and the Pacific plate, create most of the excitement for Californians. Through the eons, several smaller plates, such as the Farralon and the Juan de Fuca, have also contributed to this complex puzzle, pushing through and leaving behind minerals that don't always match those found in the two primary plates that we see today.

As the significantly smaller Farralon and the Juan de Fuca plates were making their way north and out of the geologic picture, except for the mineral scrapings they left behind, the massive Pacific plate moved east colliding with the huge North American plate. To visualize what occurred over the next 60 million years, slowly push a vertically held white spatula across thickly-piled chocolate frosting on a chocolate cake. As the cake passes beneath, the frosting will pile up and over the spatula, remaining much thicker and higher where the spatula finally stops its progress. Similarly, as the heavy, basalt-laden (darker, iron and magnesium-rich) Pacific plate, which covers much of the Pacific Ocean, moved east, it dove into a subduction zone, essentially beneath its own scraping spatula, which was the North American plate's much more complex geologic mix of lighter elements and minerals. What the disappearing Pacific plate left behind was the scraped and piled layers of ocean bottom, mostly the sedimentary mud, that makes up much of today's Coastal Mountains.

About 25 million years ago the Pacific plate began sliding in a more northerly direction. Over this time, the changed movement along the San Andreas fault has transported portions of what had originally been Baja, Mexico, to the California central coast. South of what appears to be a beak that juts into the Pacific Ocean from Santa Barbara, this northward moving landmass compressed part of the earth's crust into the 5-million-year-old Transverse Ranges, the only east-west aligned mountain range in the state. Curiously, because of where the two great plates meet along the edge of California, Los Angeles is built on the Pacific plate and San Francisco on the North American plate. At the Pacific plate's current rate of northerly movement, return here in 10 million years and Los Angeles will be directly west of San Francisco.

This phenomenon of plate tectonics creates several notable consequences, especially for California. What comes to mind most often are the earthquakes that shake the state along the infamous 800-mile-long San Andreas fault and along several other less famous, but equally active and dangerous faults. And California experiences hundreds of earthquakes every day, albeit most are very minor and seldom noticed. But periodically much more destructive earthquakes strike, such as the temblor that destroyed San Francisco in 1906 and another, not quite as strong, that did a reasonable replay in the fall of 1989.

Researchers have come to better understand earthquakes and why they occur by studying the complex San Andreas and other fault systems. Unfortunately scientists haven't yet learned to predict either earthquakes' frequency or their intensity with any level of accuracy. For example, the Northridge earthquake that struck

Los Angeles surprised seismologists when a previously unknown and deeply buried blind thrust fault finally gave way.

California's earthquakes are not going away soon. As the great plates continue to move and grind against one another, the rocks deep underground bend under the forces, occasionally giving slightly. Each day these temporary stress reductions create dozens of barely perceptible small earthquakes throughout much of California. Problems arise when these small slippages don't occur as often as they should, and after much longer build-ups of pressure, the faults release suddenly and with more power, producing temblors that knock food off grocery store shelves and occasionally level buildings and freeways.

It doesn't take feeling the unsettling rolling of the quaking ground to experience first-hand the power of an earthquake. Spend much time traveling through the vast stretches of California's open lands along the coastal hills and you might begin to wonder why some of the ranch and farm country fences that trail off for miles into the distance have sudden jogs in them. They weren't made crooked by a drunken cowboy fence builder, but by the action of a strike slip fault, also called a horizontal motion strike slip fault.

Different types of earthquake faults create differing kinds of problems for California's cities and towns, freeways and roads, and even simple country fences and powerlines. With a normal fault, also called a vertical motion dip slip fault, one side drops anywhere from several inches to several feet in relation to its opposite side, which may actually be pushed upward. Equally descriptive names are given to other types of faults, including lateral left and right, oblique, and reverse faults. More important than their names is the fact that they all can and do cause earthquakes.

Climate and Weather

Those fortunate enough to live along California's northern and central coasts are often fond of quoting what Mark Twain supposedly mumbled: "The coldest winter I ever spent was a summer in San Francisco." The remark is most often spoken by coastal residents, followed by a knowing chuckle, when summer tourists escaping 100-plus degree Fahrenheit interior valley temperatures and clad only in T-shirts and shorts stream to coastal resorts and are greeted by bone-chilling 55-degree fog-shrouded evenings and mornings.

Summer fog extends along much of California's coast, although as one nears Los Angeles and San Diego and their warmer water temperatures, summer's gray blanket of morning moisture, when it forms, tends to be thinner and burns off more quickly. While inland air temperature differences, changing ocean currents and temperatures, jutting landmasses and landform orientations, and numerous other factors are responsible for where coastal summer fog may be found, there is a general cycle that it follows.

During summer when warm, moisture-laden air crosses the cold, upwelled ocean waters offshore it condenses into fog. It's then drawn inland by a pressure difference created by the air rising from the heated landmass. Generally each day's rising sun evaporates or "burns off" the fog. On good weather days, the fog remains well offshore and the winds that bring it over coastal landmasses never develop. But more often summer fog does arrive, and it settles in for the night, dropping anything from a light veil of translucent white to a shroud of nearly impenetrable gray over the landscape.

Not every summer day or every location along California's coast experiences the same degree of fog. For example, on a particularly gray day along the shores of Monterey Bay in the city of Monterey, where the temperature struggles to reach 65 degrees Fahrenheit, Santa Cruz (just across the bay) may be 75 degrees and sunny with no fog; and while Monterey may be foggy in the early morning and evening and 75 degrees in midafternoon, a thick, drippy fog may engulf adjacent Pacific Grove all day and the temperature may never reach 60 degrees.

Certainly, the Pacific Ocean plays the key role in California's climate. The coldest winter storms begin in the Pacific, generally up near the Aleutian Islands, and track southeastward, bringing with them varying amounts of rain. Tropical storms, most generally associated with spring, form in the western Pacific, then sweep in from near the Hawaiian Islands or even from farther south. These storms tend to be warmer and bring with them significant amounts of precipitation. While these rains initially may cause some local flooding along the coastal lowlands, most of the damage is usually done in the higher Sierra and Central Valley as the warm, spring rains quickly melt the winter snowpack, which in turn raises river levels to flood stages. These rivers, in turn, carry huge amounts of sediment to their mouths at the coast.

OCEAN CURRENTS

California's climate is the result of numerous worldwide, ongoing natural events, and understanding ocean currents is key to gaining a better understanding of the state's entire climatic picture. Wade into the warm waters splashing ashore along one of San Diego's beaches and you will be standing in water that months earlier was probably passing offshore from Alaska and before that, Japan. Worldwide, ocean currents, and in the case of California, several linked currents, move water in giant circular patterns called gyres. A Pacific Ocean gyre circulates huge amounts of surface water that help regulate California's climate. The southward moving California Current moves warm water into the westward moving North Equatorial Current, which in turn pushes the surface water northward into the Kurishio Current that flows along the east coast of Japan. From there, the North Pacific Current picks up this now cooling water and, moving eastward, further cools its huge mass, where the California Current once again pulls it south and the cycle begins anew.

It's these southern-flowing cold waters that make California's north coast beaches

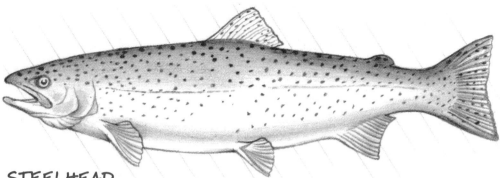

STEELHEAD
(Oncorhynchus mykiss)
Steelhead are rainbow trout that migrate to the sea. They average 10 pounds and can grow as large as 42 pounds.

much too chilly to swim in, at least without a wetsuit. They also help to moderate much of California's coastal temperatures so that the beach at Malibu may be a comfortable 75 degrees Fahrenheit on an August afternoon. Same day, same time, but directly inland 30 miles, the temperature has climbed to 90 degrees, while inland another 80 miles the temperature is hovering at a sweltering 115 degrees.

A second and equally important type of ocean water movement is the thermohaline current. This is a deep water current, primarily driven by temperature and salinity differences, friction, and the forces of gravity. The current acts as a continuously moving conveyor belt, transporting and mixing deep, cold waters from the poles with waters from the warmer equatorial zones and from ocean to ocean. This constant movement is vital to moderating worldwide water temperature extremes.

Other factors affect not just California's coastal weather, but weather around the world. A slight increase or decrease in the earth's current 23.5-degree tilt on its axis in relationship to its orbit around the sun can have dramatic effects on weather. Increases or decreases in the make-up of the earth's atmospheric gasses, especially carbon dioxide, can impact weather. Many of these factors, such as the earth's tilt or orbit, change only over tens of thousands of years. Others, such as levels of carbon dioxide, can change within a century or two. Significantly more short-term, and therefore of more immediate concern, are the periodic and dramatic changes in the Pacific Ocean's surface water temperatures.

EL NIÑO AND LA NIÑA

There is no doubt about the dramatic effects that El Niño and La Niña have on weather, not only in California, but also around the world. Although cycles and intensities vary, about every four years El Niño brings extended periods of heavy rain to northern California and tends to leave normally dry southern California even drier. Central California gets caught in the middle, with either a very dry winter or with heavy rains that begin in November and don't slow until late spring, inundating roads, homes, and farmlands and causing massive landslides along the coast. El Niño provided California's with warm, water-driven weather during the winters of 1985-86, 1991-92, 1993-94. During the 1997-98 winter, the latest El Niño event, scientists recorded the warmest ocean water temperatures ever off some parts of Northern California's coast. While anglers in Central California that winter enjoyed catching fish species generally found no farther north than San Diego, two years later many areas of the state were still repairing damage from the record-setting rains.

It is thought that fishermen off the coast of South America coined the term El Niño because of the periodic warming of the ocean waters that began about Christmas every few years. *El Niño* is Spanish for Little Boy or Christ Child. *La Niña*, or Little Girl, creates the opposite effect.

During non-El Niño conditions, the trade winds blowing west across the tropical Pacific Ocean push warm water toward Indonesia and leave nutrient-rich, cooler waters off Ecuador, greatly enhancing the fishing success of that country's fishermen. As the trade winds begin to slow, as happens during El Niño years, the situation changes. Ecuadorian water temperatures warm, the upwelling of nutrient-rich colder water slows, and the ocean's surface temperature rises 14 degrees Fahrenheit or more. This, in turn, triggers rainfall as the air rises over the warming waters. It's when these warmer Pacific waters push northward that they begin to interfere with California's normally moderate weather patterns.

Natural Processes

Beyond the inevitable changes that the earth's restless tectonic plates bring, including the earthquakes that occasionally send quivers through portions of California, numerous other forces of nature have greatly assisted in molding the look and feel of the coast. These forces place their individual footprints on the land, whether that land lies 1,500 feet above sea level or 2 miles below the ocean's surface.

WATER AND EROSION

Water serves as one of the greatest forces of change. By freezing and thawing it can break large rocks into smaller stones and ultimately grind stones into sand. Water can very quickly transport massive amounts of soil and sand from inland valleys and mountains to coastal river mouths. Ultimately, most of California's winter rain and snowfall that doesn't sink into underground aquifers or evaporate into the atmosphere, cascades over vertical cliff faces, tumbles down steep mountain canyons, and meanders through wide valleys, ceaselessly moving small pieces of the earth with it.

Water, especially large quantities of fast-moving water, is capable of transporting huge quantities of sand and larger earthen rubble great distances. Sometimes water simply penetrates deeply into already unstable soils and acts as an amazingly effective lubricant assisting gravity in doing what it does best—moving things on higher levels to lower levels. Southern California's coastal cliffs are probably some of the best-known places for seeing this phenomena. Not only have people built their homes and businesses on already unstable hillsides, but in many places bulldozers and wildfires have removed stabilizing plants and trees. The result is that during especially wet winters, television news crews generally capture numerous examples of houses or entire neighborhoods sliding downhill or hillsides sliding down onto houses.

While it may take eons for a water medium to reduce big rocks to smaller rocks, once the sand is light enough for water transport, it tends to accumulate at the mouths of rivers creating bars and dams. During the slow flows of summer, these dams can effectively prevent the stream's water from flowing directly into the ocean. Winter's increased water flows generally break through the sand dams allowing fish and other wildlife to once again move freely from fresh water to salt water.

Fast-running rivers are not the only vehicles of erosion. Ocean waves have a tremendous impact on the changing shape of California's coastal zone. The size of waves is related directly to the strength of the winds that drive them and the distance they are pushed. Waves work untiringly, whether it's summer's gentle rollers or the spectacular and dangerous giants that a winter storm front can smash against coastal rocks, sending plumes of white water dozens of feet into the air. While waves serve a good purpose in aiding the mixing of the ocean's warm and cold surface waters, when combined with high tides, powerful winter waves can be especially damaging, washing dozens of feet of coastal cliffs into the ocean during short periods of time.

UPLIFT AND MARINE TERRACES

California's coast, like many of the world's coastlines over the past several million years, has seen relatively dramatic rises and falls in the level of the oceans in relationship to the shore. As with manmade inland reservoirs where fluctuating water levels create small terraces around the shoreline, several ice ages and weather changes, along with tectonic plate movements, have created expansive marine terraces along California's coast. Often they are difficult or impossible to distinguish, having been eroded or filled or covered by vegetation. But there are a few areas along the coast where such geologic formations are relatively easy to identify.

One of the easiest places to explore an ancient marine terrace is along the Mendocino Coast, where the land pushed upward approximately 100 feet every 100,000 years. If it were possible to create a side view of the rising mountain beginning at the ocean's edge and moving inland about 3 miles, there would be five distinct terraces, each about 100 feet higher in elevation than the last. Each terrace is composed of a deep base of Graywacke Sandstone, and the sandstone is covered with up to 20 feet of ancient beach deposits. Above the beach sand and gravel lies from 1 to 3 feet of more recently deposited soil of varying compositions. In Southern California's Los Angeles County, the Palos Verdes Hills exhibit 13 terraces that rise a total of about 1,300 feet above sea level.

California's coast offers a first-hand look at the past 60 million years of the state's complex and very confusing geologic past. Study a geologic map of California and the profusion of colors representing rock types is quite phenomenal. The abrupt and variety of changes in rock types found along the coast generally coincide with the presence of the numerous parallel faults. Most coastal alluvial deposits are marine sedimentary in nature, a result of the North American plate scraping a layer of marine soils off the Pacific plate as it dives beneath the North American plate and into the coastal subduction zone. As a result, only a few continental (North American plate) sedimentary rocks and alluvial deposits are present along California's coast.

Near Cape Mendocino, where a relatively short, 50-mile-long fault exists, late Mesozoic eugeosynclinal rocks of the Franciscan Formation lie adjacent to Cenozoic marine sedimentary rocks, and fronting those are Cenozoic nonmarine (North American plate) sedimentary rocks and alluvial deposits. And while Cenozoic volcanic rocks are extremely common in northeast California and in the Mojave Desert in the southeast, they are rare along the coast, except on Santa Cruz Island, in a small area north of Los Angeles, and in the coastal mountains of Sonoma County.

While marine sedimentary rocks dominate the coast, occasional intrusive igneous rocks are present, primarily Mesozoic age granitic rocks similar to those that make up much of the Sierra Nevada and Southern California's Peninsular Ranges. These granitic rocks are a result of the remaking of the Pacific plate. As the continental shelf forces the Pacific plate's heavy basalt deeper toward the earth's mantel, it is heated to a state of magma, becoming lighter and more buoyant. The magma then rises toward the surface, melting lighter North American plate minerals as it rises. Where it reaches the surface, its silicon-and aluminum-rich content, mixed with other minerals, solidifies as granitic rock.

TIDES, CURRENTS, AND LITTORAL SAND MOVEMENT

That narrow band of land that lies between the low and high tides, the littoral zone, is an area of constant change. Over time rivers transport millions of cubic yards of sand from mountains, hills, and valleys to river mouths where it is washed into the ocean. Ocean currents moving laterally to the shore deposit sand along beaches and tide pools. Winter's strong wave actions erode bluffs and further add to the growing collection of transportable sand. It's generally summer's more gentle wave action that rebuilds the sandy beaches, replenishing sand lost to wind, tide, and storm actions. The result is that much of California's coast experiences wide and sandy beaches during summer where just months earlier only beaches of large cobbles existed. But even the cobbles have their own special attraction as they clatter up and down the beach to the rhythm of winter's crashing waves.

The Pacific Ocean's tides have created their own unique worlds in and near the coastal littoral zones. The plants and animals that cling tenuously to life in this hostile environment have spent eons evolving so they can survive alternating periods of wet and dry, pounding surf and desiccating sun. They experience two high tides and two low tides each 24 hours and 50 minutes, with sea levels varying widely, driven by the gravitational pulls of the moon and the sun.

To better understand tides is to understand the synchronized movements of the sun and the moon and the changing power of their respective gravitational pulls on the earth's oceans as the three heavenly bodies pass around one another. The moon's diminutive size is more than compensated for by its nearness to earth in its battle for gravitational control of the oceans. It closeness gives it about twice the gravitational pull as the sun.

The sun and moon's gravitational pulls, along with centrifugal force created by the earth's rotation, simultaneously stretch and contract portions of our oceans' elastic and contiguous surface. Place the moon and sun in alignment, either with the moon between the earth and sun as during a new moon, or with the earth between the moon and sun as during a full moon, and together they stretch the ocean's surfaces nearest them, creating the highest tides. When the moon lies at a right angle to the alignment of the earth and sun, as during the first quarter and third quarter moons, the high tides, called neap tides, are much lower. Each day's two high tides are offset by two low tides where the moon and sun's gravitational pulls are at their minimums.

Printed tide tables are good for giving general predictions for the tides in specific areas of California's coast, as tide levels and their times can be significantly different in northern and southern parts of the state. This is especially true when considering that the coastal city of San Diego is located well east of Reno, Nevada, a mostly desert state that people generally think of as lying east of California. The result is that the moon's gravitational pull will change the ocean's level near San Diego well before it impacts the tides in Eureka. What tide tables can't accurately predict is the local changes that winter storm surges or local coastal geography can cause.

STRIPED SKUNK
(Mephitis mephitis)

Natural Communities

The orientation of California's shoreline in relation to the south-trending ocean currents has also helped define the look of the state's seashore. From the Oregon border south about two-thirds of the way to the Mexican border, the coast tends to follow a gentle southeast line. But near Point Conception, it turns much more abruptly to the southeast, swinging inward as though a giant bite has been removed, and not moving back to its more gentle southeast line until reaching San Diego. This change in orientation to the prevailing ocean currents, combined with a different angle that faces attacking winter storms whose fury is further blunted by eight large off-shore islands, has helped to create and maintain southern California's many broad sandy beaches.

Within or near California's generally rocky north and central coast and the sandy beaches of the south coast are several other important terrain features: streams and rivers and their sometimes accompanying wetlands, coastal dunes, bluffs and head-lands, marine terraces, coastal mountains, rocky intertidal zones, nearshore waters, offshore islands, and open ocean. Each zone supports unique and fascinating species of plants and animals, each with specific attributes that allow for survival and propagation in a very hostile environment.

OPEN WATERS

California's coast, unlike that of the Gulf and Atlantic states, tends to drop off into very deep water very quickly, which helps explain why California's many rivers have never built the broad flat deltas found at the mouths of such rivers as the Mississippi. The continental shelf that runs the length of the state and lies about 25 miles from the coast at San Francisco has moved to within 10 miles of shore in Monterey Bay. Deep underwater valleys slash their way from the deep Pacific and into the shallow, but steep, continental shelf at several locations. The most famous of these underwater valleys is the Monterey Canyon. Within just a few miles of Monterey's harbor and shoreline, the canyon's bottom has dropped 4,300 feet, the same distance as from the Grand Canyon's South Rim down to the Colorado River. Another few miles offshore the canyon's depth reaches 2 miles.

These deep waters with great currents and changing temperatures bring an abundance of underwater life close to California's shoreline. The most obvious to anyone who comes to the coast during January and February is the great southern migration of gray whales. From vantage points along shore or standing on the deck of a charter whale-watching boat, it's possible to see dozens of these graceful creatures in a single day. Coming back from the brink of extinction, gray whales (*Eschrichtius robustus*) are now near their historic numbers before uncontrolled whaling began.

KELP FORESTS

A great forest lies just offshore along much of California's coast, a forest that supports an incredibly rich and diverse underwater and surface world of life. Seen from the beaches and cliffs, the canopy of these great beds of giant kelp (*Macrocystis pyrifera*) rides upon the swell of waves outside the surf zone, held afloat by small hollow float structures that grow among the kelp's leaf-like blades. Another species, generally less prolific, but still common within or near the giant kelp forests, is bull kelp (*Nereocystis luetkeana*). Both are forms of algae and prolific growers. During summer's long days and full sunlight, kelp can grow up to 18 inches per day.

Sea otters (*Enhydra lutris nereis)* frolic on the floating beds of yellow-brown kelp fronds that undulate slowly with the rhythm of the waves. In between their near constant preening sessions, the otters dive for abalone or other food, then float almost casually on their backs on the water's surface, using small stones to pound the succulent meat free, as gulls swarm nearby hoping to glean small bits of leftovers. Beneath the surface the long stalks of kelp may be 100 feet or more in length, reaching the bottom where they are secured to rocks with a holdfast structure rather than a root system. Winter storms often tear free holdfasts that aren't well secured to solid bottom structures and toss piles of kelp on the beaches.

Beneath the surface the long fronds create a dense forest that serves as both shelter and a food source for numerous species such as blue rockfish (*Sebastes mystinus*), brown turban snails (*Tegula brunnea*), Pacific sardines (*Sardinops sagax*), and leopard sharks (*Triakis semifasciata*). Mostly they feed on one another or on other creatures that inhabit the kelp forests. Few actually feed on the kelp, with the exception of sea urchins (*Strongylocentrotus* spp.) and abalone (*Haliotis* spp.), both of which can consume large quantities. Fortunately, sea otters enjoy eating both urchins and abalone, helping maintain the delicate balance of plant and animal.

GIANT KELP
(Macrocystis pyrifera)
This long, brown seaweed grows secured to rocks in deep water.

THE SEASHORE

Washed by tides, dried by the sun, and pounded by waves, California's seashore is a place of contradictions. Within its boundaries much of the life that's present and dependent upon the ocean's waters for survival are left dry twice each day as the tides reach their lowest points. Other creatures, such as bacteria and diatoms, survive on the higher rocks, those splashed with life-giving ocean waters only during the highest of tides or when storm-driven waves splash well above the mean high tide level. Scattered across these rocks, acorn barnacles (*Chthamalus* and *Balanus* spp.) open their trap-like doors to feed and reproduce when life-giving seawater finally splashes across them. A few feet lower into the splash zone, powerful winter waves unmercifully pound the animals and small plants that cling tenaciously to the rocky shore. Many animals that inhabit the shoreline. California sea lions (*Zalophus californianus*), sea otters (*Enhydra lutris*), harbor seals (*Phoca vitulina*), and many species of birds are able to move to more agreeable surroundings when water conditions no longer meet their needs, but many of the animals here are significantly less mobile.

One of the most common seashore creatures is the mussel (*Mytilus* spp.). Mussels thrive in one of the most hostile of environments in the splash zone, surviving the force of tons of crashing water by attaching themselves to rocks in tight bunches with the sharp edges of their shells pointed so as to divert the water's force. Having tough, fibrous, byssal threads of glue that bind them to the rocks also helps to keep them in place, at least until they are ready to move.

The best time to explore the shoreline is at low tide when the ocean recedes revealing the secrets of the tide pools. Animals scramble about, either coming out to secure food in the absence of crashing waves, or to follow the receding waters where food and safety from predators are most easily found. Sculpins (*Clinocottus* spp.) search for food and lay their eggs in the shallow tide pools. Black shelled turban snails (*Tegula funebralis*) scrape algae from the rocks, while others such as dogwinkle snails (*Nucella* spp.) eat just about any other creature that happens into their territories.

Probe a little deeper and more of a tide pool's magic comes to life. Coralline algae, which looks like tiny reddish fingers of coral, bend at their numerous joints as water moves over them. Most people's favorites, sea stars, such as the ochre star (*Pisaster ochraceus*), can release a telltale scent in the water as they travel about searching for food, allowing the quicker animals to escape their deadly grasp. Sea stars use their powerful sucking action to peel less mobile creatures, such as mussels, from their safe and secure rock perches. Even when one of its own arms becomes lunch for a passing sea otter, the unlucky sea star simply finds a safe haven where it can stay until its missing arm regrows.

Anemones (*Anthopleura elegantissima*), soft, puffy-looking creatures with short tentacles, shrink themselves in size and reveal sticky little bumps that help keep them from drying out when tides recede. Often the many individuals in a colony of anemones appear identical. This results because they reproduce by splitting in half, then

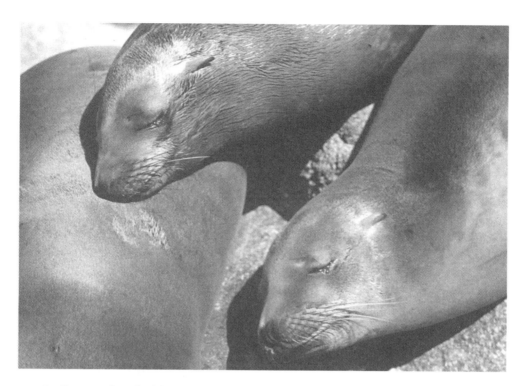

Sea lions spend much of the day basking on land and feed mainly at night on mollusks and fish.

the twins do the same, and so on. Other animals, such as hermit crabs (*Pagurus* spp.), take up residence inside the shells of dead turban snails, discarding smaller shells for larger ones as they grow. Since they can live as long as three decades, they can go through numerous stolen houses. Mixed into these tide pool menageries are spiny sea urchins (*Strongylocentrotus* spp.) that are able to grasp tide pool rocks with their hundreds of tube-like feet, while using their upper tentacles to grab food that the constantly moving water currents float past.

While healthy tide pools are rich with life, even richer are the areas that lie just slightly farther offshore, which can only be revealed to the drying air by the lowest of tides. Hundreds of species of plants and animals inhabit this rich zone, among them slimy waves of green surf grass (*Phyllospadix* spp.). The thick blankets of surf grass serve as both homes and food for sea stars and other creatures, such as seaweed limpets (*Discurria insessa*). Surf grass is a true flowering plant, not an algae as are so many of its neighbors. It clings to the rocks and boulders where the sea keeps it wet. Blades of surf grass serve as homes for crustose coralline algae (*Melobesia mediocris*) and food for bat stars (*Asterina* spp.). Nearby, different species of sponges, each sporting its own brilliant color, along with surfgrass limpets (*Tectura paleacea*), thrive in this oxygen-rich environment. This same coastal area also serves as a crucial transition zone for animals that must move between the open ocean and the estuaries and wetlands where they feed and reproduce.

SANDY BEACHES

California's southern beaches are famous around the world, thanks in part to the songs of the Beach Boys during the 1960s. But what most people take for granted—miles of white sand beaches, crowded with surfers and sunbathers—is really a complex sand transport system that we have, in times past, completely disrupted in our efforts to meet our own needs. Fortunately for Southern California, its shoreline faces the Pacific Ocean's storms at a different angle than central and Northern California. And with the Channel Islands breaking up some of each storm's strength before it can strike the mainland, less sand is washed from the shoreline at Huntington State Beach each winter than from the beaches in Northern California. Many of Northern and Central California's summer sand beaches are washed away during winter, leaving only pebbles and stones. They won't be covered again by sand until winter's high surf fades into summer's much less powerful waves.

Most of the sand that accumulates on California's shoreline begins its journey from the interior mountains, washed to the sea by rivers and streams. Significantly smaller amounts of sand come from coastal cliff and rock erosion and from sand washed ashore from ancient and submerged, nearshore dunes. All of this sand is caught in a series of conveyer belt-like littoral currents that slide down California's coast. In the natural process, as the conveyor belt removes old sand from a beach, it drops newer sand as a replacement, maintaining a delicate balance. Only during winter storms is more sand removed than is replaced, but mostly in Northern and Central California. Sand is also lost along its way down the coast, dropped off the conveyor belts into the dozens of marine canyons that cut laterally into the coastal shelf. Once in these marine canyons, the sand is swept downward and lost to the deeper parts of the ocean, often well offshore.

Well-meaning efforts to improve some of California's harbors have often resulted in costly and unforeseen circumstances. In the 1920s, Santa Barbara built a breakwater to create a protected harbor. The breakwater caused huge amounts of sand to accumulate on one side, while on the harbor side, there suddenly was no sand available to replace that which continued to be removed by the ocean currents. A series of heavy winter storms cut away up to 150 feet of shoreline from some beaches. Santa Barbara is not the only community to make such a mistake. Those cities that followed Santa Barbara's breakwater construction actions often continue to spend millions of dollars every few years to keep their harbors dredged free of sand and their beaches replenished with sand.

WETLANDS: ESTUARIES AND SLOUGHS

A variety of wetlands are wedged into the few areas of California's coast not already covered by steep cliffs or broad expanses of open sand or cobbles. Within the broad category of wetlands lie the coastal sloughs. These narrow and winding waterways can be filled with salt water or fresh water, seasonally or year-round, and their shorelines are primarily mud and marshy soils. They may or may not have a year-round connection to the open ocean.

A different kind of wetland is the estuary, which lies inland beyond the reach of the ocean's waves, but within the influence of the tides and the ocean's salt water. It depends on a flow of fresh water to mix with the salt water. The flow of fresh water may be a continual flow, such as where the Sacramento and San Joaquin rivers create permanent estuaries around San Francisco Bay, or a seasonal, rain-fed steam that flows into the estuary at Elkhorn Slough on the edge of Monterey Bay.

Salt marshes are those areas within the estuaries or sloughs where high tides inundate large flats, creating extremely hostile conditions for all but the most specialized plants. Yet, in spite of such an apparently inhospitable environment, salt marshes are amazingly productive, its plants creating much more oxygen and carbohydrates per acre than a wheat field. Such a rich food source also creates an equally rich and diverse food chain.

In those areas of California where wetlands still remain, they are most often made up of broad mud flats and estuarine salt marshes. San Francisco Bay, itself significantly reduced in size following more than a century of being filled and developed, contains nearly 90 percent of California's remaining salt marshes. There are only about two dozen other smaller salt marshes along California's coast. Most of the marshes were drained, filled, and developed during those early years before their true importance was fully recognized and protective legislation passed.

The brackish waters of California's remaining coastal wetlands support an incredibly rich palette of life. In this natural community that experiences periodic inundations from daily tides and seasonal rises in rivers and creeks that drain nearby hills and mountains, aquatic and terrestrial life finds refuge. The Pacific Flyway also brings an autumn rush of not only ducks and geese, but also many dozens of other species of smaller birds escaping the cold northern winters for the temperate climate of coastal California. Then there's the spring rush north again to their nesting grounds.

The plants that live in the brackish waters of these estuarine wetlands have developed special morphological and physiological traits for surviving in a world that would be deadly for any normal terrestrial plant. Some plant species such as saltwort (*Batis maritima*) and pickleweed (*Salicornia bigelovii*) are highly tolerant to these hypersaline conditions. Some, such as cordgrass (*Spartina foliosa*), have specialized their adaptations so much that they can grow only where tidal flows come regularly year-round. Cordgrass is not found farther inland or where fresh water flows are more prevalent. One of the critical adaptations that these salt-tolerant plants have

BROWN PELICAN
(Pelecanus occidentalis)

developed is a mechanism for excreting the excessive amounts of salt that they ingest as they take water into their stems and leaves. Salt excreted from many of these plants forms as small crystals on the leaves and stems and is finally washed or falls away in the wind or rain.

The most obvious residents and visitors to California's wetlands are birds that come to feed on the rich bounty of food that thrives in this diverse habitat. In the deeper waters, birds that share their time between the sloughs and the open ocean waters rest and feed. Cormorants (*Phalacrocorax* spp.) and loons (*Gavia* spp.) dive for fish, while the once nearly extinct brown pelicans (*Pelecanus occidentalis*) cruise just above the water's surface or circle above and dive headfirst into the brackish waters hoping to come to the surface with lunch. The great Pacific Flyway brings a winter flood of waterfowl, including mallards (*Anas platyrhynchos*), American widgeons (*Anas americana*), and numerous other species of ducks into the calm waters. And while great blue herons (*Ardea herodias*) and snowy egrets (*Egretta thula*) wade in shallow water mud flats hunting small fish, a marsh hawk (*Circus cyaneus*) glides low over the nearby drier grasslands searching for unsuspecting birds and mice. Sea otters (*Enhydra lutris*), harbor seals (*Phoca vitulina*), and sea lions (*Zalophus californianus*) enter the canals and waterways, while songbirds add their own touch of color and melodies to the constant movement of estuary life.

COASTAL DUNES

Rivers, streams, ocean currents, and wave action deposit sand onto open beaches, but it takes wind to constantly move and mold the tons of tiny sand grains into dunes. It is rare for enough of those ingredients to exist in the right amounts in the same place, so dunes occupy only a few small areas of California's coast. Where dunes exist, their shifting sands, devoid of nutrients and unable to retain moisture, are inhospitable to most plant and animal life. Yet, there are a few, hardy pioneering plants and animals that are capable of existing in this hostile and changing environment and provide the first footholds in the long road to dune stabilization.

Dunes begin life as sand that blows freely across a beach until a protrusion, such as a rocky outcropping or a changing shoreline orientation, rocks, driftwood, clumps of kelp, or existing plants, prohibits its passage. The sand accumulates, finally to a point above the water's surface where small dune plants are able to establish a foothold, the beginning of dune stabilization. As the life cycle of dunes continues, the more recently built foredunes afford protection for the older dunes behind them, enabling the older dunes to support larger forms of vegetation, which act to further stabilize the sand. Some of California's coastal dunes were formed more than 18,000 years ago. Dunes that old, long since stabilized by vegetation, can be found inland a mile or more from the shoreline, often covered by houses or forests, making them difficult to identify.

The plants that are able to establish a tenuous toehold in the shifting dune sands are generally low growing, in order to escape the wind. They are deep-rooted so they can reach as much life-giving water as possible because moisture very quickly percolates through the porous sand. Plants such as beach strawberry (*Fragaria chiloensis*), yellow sand verbena (*Abronia latifolia*), Menzies wallflower (*Erysimum menziesii*), and beach primrose (*Oenothera cheiranthifolia*), in addition to being able to establish themselves on bare dunes, also provide food and cover for a variety of insects and small animals.

COASTAL CLIFFS

Crashing waves have stamped their own unique mark on California's varied geography, carving spectacular coastal bluffs from the steep mountain faces that have risen from the sea. Waves, especially powerful winter waves that have already removed the buffering sand beaches, can quickly, efficiently, and violently erode the relatively soft, steep mountain faces. Composed mostly of sedimentary rocks such as shale and sandstone, cliffs quickly succumb to wave action and are washed away, exposing more cliff face. Often, softer, unconsolidated alluvial soils lie on top of the crumbly sandstone, providing even less defense against the attacking ocean.

While such erosion is a normal part of nature, it causes great inconvenience for the people who try to contend with or choose to ignore its consequences. As these erosion-prone soils, often made up of small grains of quartz, mica, and feldspars, become saturated, either by wave action or by rain, their structure tends to collapse. For most people, the consequences of building homes on such geologically unstable ground don't come as any surprise. What is surprising is that so many property owners don't believe that their homes, constructed on such sites, inevitably will become floating ocean debris, some much sooner than others.

COASTAL MOUNTAINS

California's coastal mountains are actually comprised of three separate ranges, with a fourth, the Klamath Range paralleling a narrow strip of the Coast Range in the

DOUGLAS FIR
(Pseudotsuga menziesii)

far northwest corner of the state. The Coast Ranges, totaling 600 miles in length, are separated at about the midpoint by San Francisco Bay. They begin at the Oregon border and extend south to the Santa Ynez River near Point Arguello where they meet the Transverse Ranges. The Transverse Ranges, one of North America's few primarily east-west oriented mountain ranges, extends east about 320 miles to the mountains near Joshua Tree National Monument in the Mojave Desert and south along the California coast only about 60 miles, from near Los Angeles to the Mexican border.

For the most part, the mountains of all the ranges reach to the seashore. In many areas along the coast, Highway 1 offers breathtaking views over precipitous drops of 600 feet or more to the ocean on the west side of its often narrow ribbon of asphalt, and equally precipitous mountain rises on the east side. One of the most dramatic stretches of Highway 1 is in the southern portion of the Coastal Ranges through the Santa Lucia Mountains. Here, some of the steepest mountain rises are found. Just 4 miles inland, Cone Peak rises 5,155 feet. But it's the northern coastal mountains that hold the highest peaks. Solomon Peak in the Trinity Mountains rises 7,581 feet above sea level.

Besides differences in the types of rocks found, what is most obvious to anyone traveling the length of California's coast is the mosaic of vegetation found in the coastal mountains. The wet northern reaches of the coastal mountains support large stands of coast redwoods (*Sequoia sempervirens*) and Douglas fir (*Pseudotsuga menziesii*) and understory plants such as California bay (*Umbellularia californica*) and madrone (*Arbutus menziesii*). Move farther south where the rains come slightly less often, and the redwoods retreat to more isolated and protected canyons, and a different kind of conifer comes on the scene. Often referred to as fire pines, several trees such as the generally twisted and picturesque Monterey pine (*Pinus radiata*) and knobcone pine (*Pinus attenuata*) grow in thick groves or stand in open spaces. Prevailing ocean winds often press and form the pines' crowns low and flat as they patiently await the heat of fire to release their seeds and drop them to the newly burned, bare mineral soil. Still farther south, scattered oaks (*Quercus* spp.) join sprawling sycamores (*Platanus racemosa*) through canyons as coastal scrub covers much of the open hillsides.

OFFSHORE ISLANDS

Lying offshore between Santa Barbara and San Pedro, the closer of the eight Channel Islands appear as faint, slightly dark mounds in the distance. The islands are remnant eroded peaks of the Santa Monica Mountains, which are part of the Transverse Ranges. The mountain range's alignment runs east and west, against the grain of all other California mountain ranges. The Transverse Ranges extend inland to Joshua Tree National Monument.

The geology of the Channel Islands is complex and not fully understood. As the submerged western tip of the Transverse Ranges, many of the islands were once connected during the last Ice Age, although probably not to the mainland. A variety of rock types exist on the islands. Mesozoic granite and late Jurassic and Cretaceous Franciscan Formation rocks are found on tourist-popular Santa Catalina. San Clemente Island, located south of Santa Catalina, and Santa Cruz Island, to Santa Catalina's northwest, are made up of Cenozoic volcanic rocks, with Cenozoic marine sedimentary rocks also covering parts of Santa Cruz Island.

A half million years of isolation from the mainland has done much to protect the rich variety of wildlife that inhabit the islands and the waters that surround them. More than a century of livestock grazing has significantly impacted the native grasses and other plants that Chumash Indians once wandered among, and introduced species, especially African ice plant, have further reduced or eliminated many native plants.

Five of the eight islands, San Miguel, Anacapa, Santa Barbara, Santa Rosa, and Santa Cruz, are part of the Channel Islands National Park, while San Nicolas, Santa Catalina, and San Clemente islands remain primarily in private hands. San Miguel Island serves as a seasonal home to more species of pinnipeds than any other equal-sized location in the world. Bulbous-nosed elephant seals (*Mirounga angustirostris*) and California sea lions (*Zalophus californicus*) are common along the islands' beaches where they haul out for resting, mating, and birthing their young.

CALIFORNIA BLACK OAK
(*Quercus kelloggii*)
The ellipsoidal, 1-inch-long acorn of the California black oak was once a staple food of California Indians.

Native Americans

California's coast provided a rich and varied source of food for the Native Americans who lived here for thousands of years. With their primary need for sustenance so easily met, the dozens of different tribes that inhabited this land were able develop rich and distinct cultures. Textiles, weapons, money, boats, woven and clay pottery, and even musical instruments were everyday parts of the lives of California's Indians.

It is thought that California's first inhabitants arrived during the last Ice Age, probably 25,000 years ago or earlier. It's unknown how many of these early travelers crossed over the Bering Strait from Asia, but once in California, their numbers likely increased. Many experts have attempted to estimate the pre-European, Native American population of what we call California. Their estimates have ranged from as many as 750,000 to as few as 125,000, with the real number lost forever. A reasonable estimate would place their original population near 250,000. Few of California's 250,000 Indians belonged to anything resembling the strong tribal political units that are so well known in the central and eastern United States. They spoke hundreds of dialects based on several families of languages. Some, such as Athabascan and Algonkin, were also spoken in one form or another in the eastern U.S. Tolowa, Hupa, Yana, Pomo, Costanoan, Modoc, Maidu, and Miwok are some of the better known tribes, but within each there were often several subtribes. Within each of those there could be numerous villages, none of which maintained political allegiance to their neighbors.

Like all Indians in the New World, California's natives had no natural immunities to introduced European diseases such as smallpox and measles. For thousands of Indians, the diseases were deadly, quickly decimating their populations. It is unfortunate that the Native Americans had no formal written language, or that the Spanish padres had little desire or need to document aboriginal populations or their rich cultural heritage.

Much of what we know about California's native cultures is based on mostly nineteenth and early twentieth century anthropological and archeological studies. Even by 1900, when many of the more serious researchers realized what was being rapidly lost, far too many of those Indians old enough to remember life before the Gold Rush had nothing left but faded childhood memories. Fortunately, there is a growing resurgence of interest in Indian history among the remaining ancestors of California's original settlers, as well as in the academic world, which is helping to increase an overall understanding of California's native cultures.

Spanish and Mexican Periods

The great riches that Garcí Ordóñez de Montalvo attributed to a paradise he called California originally were both mystical and mythical, creations for his book published in 1510. When Hernando Cortés began plundering Mexico's riches in the sixteenth century, his soldiers used the name California to describe what is today Baja California. Yet, in spite of the rumors of such great wealth, the Spanish were very slow in exploring and developing the lands that lay beyond their colonial empire in Mexico.

The Mission Santa Barbara, founded in 1786, is the 10th of California's 21 missions.

It wasn't until 1542 that Juan Rodríquez Cabrillo, a Portuguese navigator, while sailing under the flag of the Spanish Crown, discovered and claimed the lands from San Diego to Monterey. But without the obvious golden treasures plundered in Central America and Mexico, combined with long and difficult sailing against winds and currents along the Baja and Alta California coasts, Spain did nothing with the new lands that Cabrillo had claimed. Sixty years later, in 1602, another Spaniard, Sebastian Vizcaíno, rediscovered both San Diego and Monterey bays and once again claimed these lands for Spain. And again, Spain ignored the lands that would become known as California. Finally, in the late 1760s, Spain began taking serious interest in its claimed but unsettled lands in the wilds of California. Still, it wasn't the promise of easy riches to help fill the Spanish Crown's treasury that brought the change. It was the perceived need for a protective buffer between its established colonies in Mexico and the rapid expansion of Russian settlements and trading outposts spreading down the West Coast of North America.

While permanent Russian settlements came no further south than the Mendocino Coast at Fort Ross, Spain implemented a successful program that was designed to greatly expand its control of California. In March 1869, some 200 Spaniards began moving north from Mexico under the command of Gaspar de Portola and stopped in what would become San Diego.

Spain had charged Fray (Father) Junipero Serra with the responsibility of building a series of missions that would help establish Spain's control of these new lands. Already 56 years old, Serra established the first mission, San Diego de Alcalá in today's San Diego. Each of Serra's settlements included three integral parts. The mission or church served the religious needs of its small Spanish pueblo or village, while focusing much of its energies on eliminating the native culture and converting the Indians to Spanish-speaking, tax-paying citizens. A presidio or military fort was created near each mission and pueblo as a means for protecting the settlers and missions and for keeping the Indians under control.

In just 53 years, the padres built twenty-one missions, each placed roughly a day's walk apart, and spread some 600 miles from San Diego in the south to Sonoma and Mission San Francisco Solano in the north. Under the padres' direction, Indian labor built and operated the missions, and California's natives also provided the labor that grew the grain and raised the cattle needed to support themselves and the accompanying civilians and military personnel who lived in the pueblos and manned the presidios.

The work of the missionaries, and particularly that of Father Serra, helped Spain expand its tenuous grip on California, but only temporarily. During the early nineteenth century, foreign wars in Europe consumed much of Spain's financial resources, reducing the Crown's already minimal support to its New World empire. As new generations of Spanish citizens were born in California, often of mixed blood and never knowing the old country, their yearning for independence developed. These Californios, as they were called, tired quickly of Spain's arbitrary laws and of those sent to enforce the country's dictates. Their yearning for freedom culminated with Mexico, including their Mexican controlled portion of California, becoming the Republic of Mexico in 1824.

Mexico's independence from Spain did not end troubles in California. Internal conflicts between the missions, Mexican authorities, and the general populace led to secularization of the missions in 1835. The lands and the missions' Indian laborers were liberated from the missionaries, leaving the churches on their own. Under the new laws, Indians were supposed to receive back at least part of their lands. Unfortunately, the Californios and some of the early European and American settlers who more educated and knowledgeable in the ways of markets, incentives, the law, and fraud were able to gain control of Indian lands.

It was during the ensuing years that California's newest land barons created their great ranchos. In addition to Indian lands, the Mexican government granted huge tracts of land to its governors, military leaders, and other prominent citizens. From the early 1820s until 1846, when United States citizens began entering Mexican California in force, the non-native population expanded relatively quickly, from about 3,700 people to nearly 8,000. But the pastoral setting where Californios raised cattle and traded hides and tallow to the growing numbers of trade ships that plied California's Pacific coast was being assaulted from several directions.

RUSSIANS AND THE FUR TRADE

California's large population of cute and cuddly sea otters offered opportunities for Americans, Russians and the British to make large profits in the fur trade. Iron products and other necessities were traded to the settlers along the California and

Pacific Northwest coast for otter pelts, which were taken to China and traded for tea, spices, and silk. These and other highly prized goods were then taken by ship to England, Europe, and to the East Coast of the United States and sold, creating substantial profits for ship owners and their captains.

In defiance of powerless Spanish claims and threats, the Russians established Fort Ross on an ocean bluff along the Sonoma coast, just north of the Russian River. It served as an outpost that supplied Russian pelt hunters who came down from the Aleutian Islands. The Russians finally abandoned Fort Ross when John Sutter, after acquiring a Mexican land grant and establishing New Helvetia (today's Sacramento), purchased the outpost. Sutter never realized any substantial or long-lasting financial gain from his land and other business dealings. A poor head for business, coupled with the Gold Rush, led to his economic downfall and subsequent loss of his land holdings.

THE EARLY AMERICANS

In 1846, there were probably no more than 700 Americans and a handful of British subjects living in California. Some of the more ambitious foreigners assumed Mexican citizenship, married Mexican women, started businesses that prospered, and ultimately became leading citizens of their communities. Essentially isolated from Mexico by distance, politics, and economics, neither the old Californios' families nor many of the new Mexican citizens felt any particular loyalty to their mother government, its Alta California (Mexican-controlled California) appointees, or their policies.

The California Bear Flag Revolt was one of those anomalies of history that has been difficult to explain. It seems that a rag-tag group of recent American immigrants, some also Mexican citizens (but only for land acquisition purposes), feared that the Mexican government was planning to take their property and expel them from California. As a questionable preventative measure, they stole a small herd of horses that a Mexican military officer was moving from Sonoma to Monterey. Probably under the influence of too much brandy, and attempting to better justify their actions, they deemed their horse-thieving as the beginning of a revolution. On June 14, 1846, they marched on Sonoma where General Mariano Guadalupe Vallejo immediately surrendered his command and welcomed the conquerors into his home. Vallejo soon found himself under arrest and jailed at Sutter's Fort, and the Bear Flaggers created a flag for their newfound republic. It featured a crudely drawn grizzly bear that more accurately resembled a pig, with the words "California Republic" emblazoned below. While the original design remains on the state flag, albeit with a more honorable appearing grizzly bear, the new republic lasted only about two weeks.

When real war finally broke out between Mexico and the United States on May 13, 1846, the initial and heaviest fighting was along the Texas-Mexico border.

In California, the U.S. Navy was under standing orders to take and occupy California as soon as war was declared. This was done as much to firmly eliminate Mexico's control of the western side of the continent as to keep the English and Russians at bay, each very much aware of the riches in furs and timber that California held. On July 7, 1846, with his U.S. Pacific fleet anchored in Monterey Bay, Commodore John D. Sloat came ashore, peacefully lowered the Mexican Flag from beside the Custom House, and raised the Stars and Stripes, declaring California under U.S. control. While Monterey surrendered immediately and peacefully, U.S. military forces in California soon fought several battles with Californios, not always emerging victorious.

With the signing of the Treaty of Guadalupe-Hidalgo on February 2, 1848, peace returned to California. California, along with most of the land that would become the other western states, now belonged to the United States. And, unknown to most everyone, just nine days earlier James Marshall had discovered gold in the American River, about 200 miles northeast of Monterey.

The Environmental Movement

The environmental movement has many of its roots buried deeply in the West. In California there was an early group of visionaries who pushed the original idea that not all federal lands should be given away for people to develop and exploit, but that special areas should instead be protected. Yosemite and California's coast redwoods served as the catalysts for many of these early environmentalists and the organizations that they created. Frederick Law Olmsted, a well-known writer and the principal designer of New York's Central Park, became one of the pioneers of the movement, especially after he moved to California. Once here he helped to push the Yosemite park idea, becoming an early lobbyist who enlisted the support of architects and artists, photographers, and others who could help promote the importance of saving Yosemite. John Muir was another of those whose articulate and persuasive writings about the wonders of nature, and of Yosemite in particular, helped turn the tide.

Finally, in 1864, as the Civil War raged, President Lincoln signed a bill that set aside Yosemite Valley as California's first state park, although Yosemite ultimately reverted to federal control. With the vision firmly in place and a single victory under their collective belts, a number of individuals continued the fight.

While there were some limited efforts to protect the Sierra's giant sequoias (*Sequoiadendron giganteum*), little was being done for the coast redwoods (*Sequoia sempervirens*). That began to change in 1899, after Andrew Hill brought back photos of a private grove of coast redwoods that a European magazine had commissioned him to take. Soon afterward, Hill brought a group of prominent politicians and community leaders to the redwood groves in Big Basin where they decided to create an organization that could help preserve these grand trees. On May 18, 1899, collecting $32, they chose officers for the newly formed Sempervirens Club.

It took a couple of years, numerous uphill battles, and broadened public, political, and academic support, but finally legislation was introduced and passed that provided funding for acquisition of redwood lands, which became Big Basin Redwoods State Park. As lumbermen eyed other prime old growth redwood groves, California's citizens heightened their efforts to purchase and protect them, but successes were few and slow in coming. Another organization, Save-the-Redwoods League, was also actively raising money and purchasing redwood property, but it wasn't until 1921 when the organization began its memorial grove program that significant amounts of acreage began to be purchased.

With timber interests and conservationists now vying for redwood lands and the legislature taking little positive action to help save groves of 2,000-year-old trees, additional people, including William Crocker, president of Crocker National Bank in San Francisco, and John D. Rockefeller Jr. became involved. In 1927, a $6 million bond issue for park acquisition was approved for the ballot. The following year, in November, 1928, voters passed what had been dubbed Proposition 4 by a nearly three-to-one majority. The modern California State Park System was born. Today, there are 265 state parks encompassing over 1.4 million acres.

CITIZENS AND THE COASTAL ACT

With 85 percent of Californians living within 30 miles of the ocean, the demand for control of and access to coastal property has been increasing each year. For too many years the result of this insatiable demand was that much of the coast was being turned into private havens for the rich at the exclusion of everyone else. Hotels and other structures began blocking public views of the ocean and bays, and wetlands were being filled and dammed in alarming numbers. Finally, in 1972, the people of California, tired of inaction by their state legislators to protect one of their state's greatest assets and reminiscent of struggles earlier in the century, took things into their own hands. Through the initiative process, which allowed private citizens to bypass lethargic state lawmakers, Proposition 20, The Coastal Conservation Initiative, was placed on the statewide ballot.

Proposition 20 passed and with its passage came the establishment of the California Coastal Commission. With extensive public input, the commission developed a coastal plan designed to ensure the protection of critical coastal resources, and just as importantly, the plan guaranteed continued public access to the coast.

Today, the Coastal Commission continues its watchdog role. Coastal development is still allowed, but on a more limited and much more sane basis. Continued public access to beaches and protection for wetlands and endangered plant communities are always the primary considerations.

The North Coast

More than 150 years after the first redwood forests were harvested, second-growth trees are approaching the habitat values of their parent groves.

FIGURE NUMBERS

7	North Coast Side Trips
8	Prairie Creek Redwoods State Park
9	Redwood National Park
10	Patrick's Point State Park
11	Arcata Area
12	Eureka
13	Humboldt Redwoods State Park
14	Lost Coast Area
15	Sinkyone Wilderness State Park

California's North Coast

Rain is taken for granted in California's north coast. The forests that grow the world's tallest trees, lush green meadows, fern-covered forest floors, and rivers filled with migrating salmon and steelhead, all depend on the 60 to 100 inches or more of annual rainfall. These rain-enriched resources allowed California's Indians to live full lives and to develop exceptionally rich cultures. And, these were the same resources that attracted the first Europeans, the Russians, and finally the Americans. While each had specific economic interests, often based on which commodity from nature was most profitable at the time, few countries had any problems crossing vague and rarely defended colonial boundaries during California's eighteenth and nineteenth centuries. Within Spain's claimed lands of Alta, or upper California, the English hunted whales, the Russians trapped furs, and the Americans came for it all, including lumber from the redwood forests.

[*Above:* Rockefeller Forest in Humboldt Redwoods State Park holds magnificent old-growth trees]

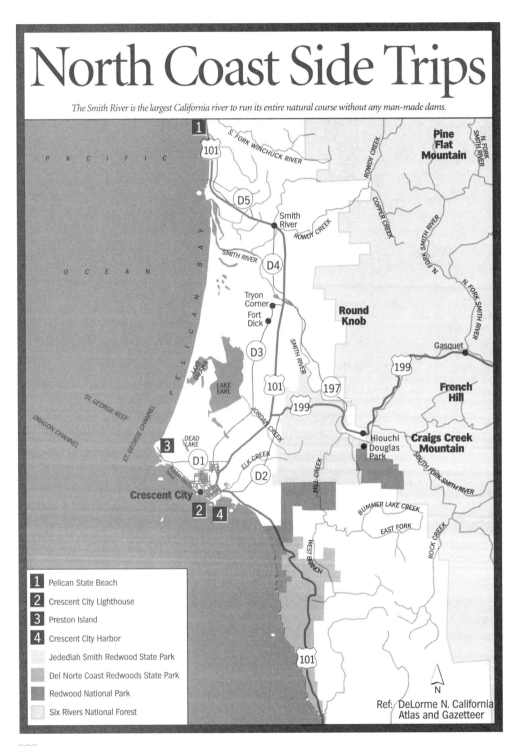

North Coast Side Trips

The Smith River is the largest California river to run its entire natural course without any man-made dams.

PACIFIC

OCEAN

PELICAN BAY

S. FORK WINCHUCK RIVER

101

D5

Smith River

ROWDY CREEK

ROWDY CREEK

SMITH RIVER

D4

Tryon Corner

Fort Dick

D3

LAKE TALAWA

LAKE EARL

SMITH RIVER

101

JORDAN CREEK

ST. GEORGE REEF

DRAGON CHANNEL

ST. GEORGE CHANNEL

DEAD LAKE

3

D1

ELK CREEK

D2

Pebble Beach Drive

Crescent City

2   4

COPPER CREEK

N. FORK SMITH RIVER

ROWDY CREEK

Pine Flat Mountain

N. FORK SMITH RIVER

N. FORK SMITH RIVER

Round Knob

Gasquet

199

French Hill

197

199

Hiouchi
Douglas Park

Craigs Creek Mountain

SOUTH FORK SMITH RIVER

MILL CREEK

BUMMER LAKE CREEK

EAST FORK

ROCK CREEK

WEST BRANCH

101

1 Pelican State Beach

2 Crescent City Lighthouse

3 Preston Island

4 Crescent City Harbor

Jedediah Smith Redwood State Park

Del Norte Coast Redwoods State Park

Redwood National Park

Six Rivers National Forest

N

Ref: DeLorme N. California Atlas and Gazetteer

More than 150 years following the Americanization of California, most of the old-growth redwood forests have been harvested and the salmon and steelhead runs have been reduced significantly. But with new, more enlightened attitudes, many of California's north coast natural resources are returning. State and national parks protect most of the remaining old-growth redwoods, and now, more than 150 years after the first redwood and Douglas fir forests were harvested, second-growth trees have created replacement forests that in some areas are approaching the habitat values of their parent groves. Legislated protections have allowed the numbers of California otters, hunted to near extinction in the nineteenth century, to return to near their historic population levels. The same types of protections, along with help from scientists and their ongoing monitoring programs, are helping restore salmon and steelhead runs to many rivers and creeks where they once were found in unimaginable numbers.

Major north coast rivers, such as the Klamath, Mad, Eel, and Smith, along with their numerous forks and the hundreds of small creeks that feed them, add to the appeal of the north coast for visitors. Each year kayaks become more numerous on many of the rivers, and drift boats carrying fishing enthusiasts have always been popular. Many other people enjoy the great opportunities for bird-watching that rivers afford, swimming or wading in some of the calmer pools, or simply walking along their shorelines.

Much of northern California's breathtaking coastal lands remain as private property holdovers from the nineteenth century when lumber barons, farmers, and cattlemen gained control of thousands of acres of Indian lands. Today, pockets of public property, mostly state and national parks, acquired through purchases or gifts, punctuate the private lands, protecting old-growth redwoods and providing access to ocean beaches. But whether publicly or privately held, even today, most of Del Norte and Humboldt counties remain wild, with steep mountain trails, dense forests, and meandering rivers always worth exploration.

Crescent City

[Fig. 7] The city's crescent-shaped bay and harbor are home to lumber docks for loading ocean freighters, several fish processing plants that handle the catch from local fishing trawlers, public boat slips, a launch ramp, and the U.S. Coast Guard headquarters. It's a relatively small town, but it boasts a great beach at its southern end, directly adjacent to US 101. When the surf is decent, you can watch wetsuit-clad surfers riding the breaking waves.

As trade increased significantly along California's rugged coast, especially with the Gold Rush, maritime safety became a significant issue along the rugged coastline. Dangerous winds and currents drove numerous wooden sailing ships into the rocky shoreline, often with significant loss of life in the cold, churning waters. In response

Tsunamis

When giant, unpredictable waves strike coastal areas, far too often the media mistakenly describes them as tidal waves. *Tsunami* is a Japanese word that much more accurately describes this great underwater disturbance: a series of higher than normal waves caused by sudden movements of the ocean floor. Earthquakes are the most common cause of the largest tsunamis, but underwater volcanic eruptions can also trigger this destructive phenomenon.

The waves, generally several hundred miles long and as much as 75 feet high, are hardly noticeable in the open ocean, but as they approach the shallow coastal waters they begin to rise rapidly. The 1964 Anchorage, Alaska earthquake generated a relatively small tsunami that struck Crescent City, California with a wave 12 feet high. The wave surged inland 1,600 feet and destroyed most of the city's central business district.

Even though high, destructive tsunamis are rare, warning sirens have been installed along some of the populated, low-lying areas of the far northern California and the Oregon coasts. The sirens sound when a tsunami threatens the area, hopefully giving as many people as possible time to reach higher ground before it strikes.

to these growing tragedies, the United States began building lighthouses, first near some of the busier and more difficult-to-access and busiest harbors, and later along the more dangerous stretches of the coast.

The **Crescent City Lighthouse** [Fig. 7(2)] was constructed in 1856 near the mouth of the bay. The lighthouse is accessible to the public, generally Wednesday through Sunday, from April through September, and when tides are low enough to get across the rocks from the mainland. The lighthouse contains a museum that is devoted to early maritime history and holds a collection of Tolowa Indian artifacts. Phone (707) 464-3089.

Pebble Beach Drive [Fig. 7] connects with Seventh Street in downtown, then parallels the coast as it heads north along the bluffs overlooking the Pacific. There are several pull-outs along the road and stairways to the beach area below.

Preston Island [Fig. 7(3)] lies on the north end of Crescent City and really isn't an island, but a spit. There's a paved road off Pebble Beach Drive that leads to the island-spit, where great views and picnic tables await.

The masts of boats in the **Crescent City Harbor** [Fig. 7(4)] are visible from adjacent US 101, at the south end of town. The public wharf portion of the harbor was originally constructed in 1950, and then rebuilt in 1987. During fogless evenings, the wharf is a great place to enjoy beautiful sunsets.

Directions: Crescent City is located on US 101, about 20 miles south of the Oregon border.

For more information: Crescent City/Del Norte Chamber of Commerce, 1001 Front Street, Crescent City, CA 95531. Phone (707) 464-3174.

🦝 NORTH COAST SIDE TRIPS

[Fig. 7(1)] **Pelican State Beach** is situated on the California and Oregon border, about 21 miles north of Crescent City and just off US 101. It is a secluded, 5-acre park that sits on a bluff overlooking the Pacific Ocean. Surf fishing from the beach can be quite good, especially considering that only about 5,000 people visit the park each year, and most come to enjoy the views or walk the beach, not to fish. Phone (707) 445-6547.

Lakes Earl and Tolowa [Fig. 7], located not far from California's infamous Pelican Bay State Prison, are integral parts of a large wetland that provides refuge for tens of thousands of waterfowl and other birds, especially during the fall migration. The lakes mark the culmination of the Smith River after it drops down through the mountains and enters the flat and open delta where fresh water mixes with the Pacific Ocean. It's a marshy land, with scattered ponds and dunes surrounding the lakes. There are only a couple of access points, and they can be a challenge to find, since there are few directional signs to the lakes. The area parallels US 101, north of Crescent City. Take Lake Earl Drive, then turn west on Lower Lake Road and enter the park by turning west on Kellogg or Pala Road. Phone (707) 464-6161, ext. 5151.

🦝 THE KLAMATH RIVER

The Klamath River is California's second largest river and drains much of the state's northwest corner, which includes some of its most rain-drenched mountains. The river's lower portion, below the Iron Gate Dam, was designated a Wild and Scenic River in 1981. When some of the Klamath's tributaries are included, such as portions of the Salmon River and Wooley Creek, there are 12 miles of river classified as wild, 24 miles that are scenic, and another 250 miles that are classified as recreational. As many visitors drive across the US 101, Klamath River bridge, all they see are the golden grizzly bear statues that stand guard at each end. But the Klamath River is a major salmon fishery for coho (*Oncorhynchus kisutch*) and chinook (*Oncorhynchus tshawytscha*) salmon that migrate upriver annually, heading to their spawning grounds.

The river's mouth can change each winter as the large sand and gravel bar is eroded, moved, and redeposited. Roads off US 101 parallel both the north and south sides of the river. On each side, there are places where boats can be launched. During summer, the relatively calm river area that lies inland from the mouth has become a popular kayaking area. There's plenty of shoreline to explore and it's a great place to see many bird species, including raptors.

Directions: The Klamath River is located 21 miles south of Crescent City on US 101.

Redwood State Parks

🖾 JEDEDIAH SMITH REDWOODS STATE PARK

[Fig. 7] Giant, ancient redwoods, a lazy flowing river, and trails that wind through waist-tall forests of ferns make this park extremely popular. It's a combination of isolation, good fishing, and the opportunity to be well away from civilization that attracts most people. Many families have been coming here each year, some for generations.

This most northern of California's major redwood state parks was named after a famous early American explorer who traveled through this area. In 1822, a time when America's frontier West began at the banks of the Missouri River, Jedediah Strong Smith was 23 years old and just beginning his fur trapping career that would soon bring him to California. Five years later, Smith and 19 other men were herding 250 horses from Red Bluff in the northern Sacramento Valley over the mountains to the coast near Crescent City, and then on to Oregon. By this time, Smith had experience surviving violent encounters with Indians. On this trip, several weeks after the group had camped on Elk Creek, in what is now a part of Jedediah Smith State Park, Smith's party moved north and soon clashed with the Kelawatset Indians near Oregon's Umpqua River. Only Smith and three of his men survived. Three years later, Smith's luck ran out. Comanches killed him while he was trapping on the Cimarron River in Kansas.

During his short lifetime Jedediah Smith was credited with being the first Euro-American to visit the redwood coast; he rediscovered South Pass, one of the easier and more popular routes over the Rockies; and he was the first to reach the Mexican settlements in California via the Great Salt Lake, a trip that got him tossed in jail for having entered the country illegally. He was the first to cross the Sierra Nevada Mountains and to travel the length of California and he was the first to reach the Pacific Ocean from the upper Sacramento Valley.

While the history attributed to Jedediah Smith is certainly fascinating, it's the redwoods and his namesake river that attract most people to this secluded redwood park. The Smith River begins life in the Siskiyou Mountains to the east and flows freely all the way to the ocean, bisecting the park. It is the largest California river to run its entire natural course without at least one man-made diversion dam used either for water storage, flood control, or hydroelectric power, or all three.

For the geological origins of the Smith River, wander back in time some 200 million years to when erosion was washing sediments into the Pacific Ocean that settled on what was known as the Gorda plate. The Gorda plate, like the much larger Pacific plate, slid under the North American plate. The North American plate scraped the thick, ancient sediments off the top of the diving Gorda plate, leaving them back on shore once again as mountains to be eroded and carried back to the sea. The

Smith River Basin resulted from all of this tectonic activity.

As the Smith River drops down through the Klamath Mountains, it enters what is called the Franciscan Assemblage, an area made up of those ancient, softer, ocean sediment scrapings. It's within these more easily erodible rocks that the river channel widens into the alluvial flats that support the park's giant redwoods.

The gravel bars at the edges of the river are great places to relax on inner tubes and air mattresses or to wet a fishing line. The Smith River also supports fall runs of steelhead (*Oncorhynchus mykiss*) and salmon (*Oncorhynchus* sp.), while Mill Creek, a major tributary, provides valuable gravel spawning beds for both species.

The Smith River's riparian zone is home for willows (*Silex* sp.) that grow quickly and profusely. Big leaf maples (*Acer macrophyllum*) and red alders (*Alnus ruba*) thrive in the shade created by the redwood forest. In addition to the extensive groves of old-growth redwoods, the park's 10,000 acres also support sitka spruce (*Picea sitchensis*), Port Orford cedar (*Chamaecyparis lawsoniana*), Douglas fir (*Pseudotsuga menziesii*), and western hemlock (*Tsuga heterophylla*).

While wandering through the forest and along the river, it's always exciting to spot some of the less commonly seen birds such as the bald eagle, pileated woodpecker (*Dryocopus pileatus*), endangered spotted owl (*Strix occidentalis*), and marbled murrelet (*Brachyramphus marmoratus*), the last two being small birds that have brought huge changes to the timber harvesting industry throughout the Pacific Northwest. There's also a chance of running into black bears (*Ursus americanus*), coyotes (*Canis latrans*), and black-tailed deer (*Odocoileus hemionius columbianus*).

Directions: From Crescent City and US 101, take Highway 199 east, 9 miles to the park.

Activities: Fishing, camping, hiking, swimming (no lifeguard).

Facilities: Campground, picnic facilities, group campground.

Dates: Open year-round.

Fees: There are fees for camping and day-use.

Closest town: Crescent City, 9 miles.

For more information: Jedediah Smith Redwoods State Park, 1375 Elk Valley Road, Crescent City, CA 95531. Phone (707) 464-6101 ext. 5112 during summer (ext. 5101 off-season). For camping reservations phone (800) 444-7275.

DEL NORTE COAST REDWOODS STATE PARK

[Fig. 7] Del Norte Coast Redwoods State Park is fairly typical of most of California's north coast redwood parks. Hike the trails beneath the redwoods and where there are breaks in the stands, especially in that half of the 6,400 acres that was logged before it could be protected as a park, an intermixed woodland thick with madrone (*Arbutus menziesii*), red alder (*Alnus rubra*), big leaf maple (*Acer macrophyllum*), and the ever-present tanoak (*Lithocarpus densiflora*) grows profusely. But the redwoods will ultimately win the battle. Nearer to the second-growth redwoods

Prairie Creek Redwoods State Park

California's gold fever brought miners to the beach at Gold Bluffs in 1851.

8 Requa Road

KLAMATH RIVER

To Crescent City

N

Ref: Six Rivers Nat. Forest
Forest Service Map

HOPPAW CREEK

TURWAR CREEK

Del Ponte Ridge

D8

101

Klamath

169

Klamath Glen

Klamath Beach Road

RICHARDSON CREEK

7

SAUGER CREEK

K L A M A T H   R I V E R

WAUKELL CREEK

Coastal Drive

MCGARVEY CREEK

TARUP CREEK

Starwein Flat

TARUP CREEK

KLAMATH RIVER

P A C I F I C

OMAGER CREEK

O C E A N

OSSAGER CREEK

101

N. FORK AH PAH CREEK

1

4

KLAMATH RIVER

Newton B Drury Scenic Parkway

PRAIRIE CREEK

BOAT CREEK

5

Fern Canyon

HOME CREEK

6

PRAIRIE CREEK

S. FORK

KLAMATH RIVER

SQUASHAN CREEK

GODWOOD CREEK

Coil Barrel Road

S. FORK

1

2

101

7

3

To Patricks Point

SURPUR CREEK

1	Gold Bluffs Beach
2	Revelation Trail
3	West Ridge Trail
4	Butler Creek Trail
5	Fern Canyon Trail
6	James Irving Trail
7	Coastal Trail
8	Klamath River Overlook

Prairie Creek Redwoods State Park

Redwood National Park

Trail

that are slowly reclaiming their original boundaries, the woodland forest struggles for what little light escapes through the spread of the overstory redwood branches.

Mill Creek carves its way through a portion of the park, where forest land ranges in elevation from the ocean shore to 1,277 feet above sea level. Mill Creek serves as an important spawning stream for both salmon and steelhead. The creek also is home to dippers (*Cinclus mexicanus*), curious little birds that hop along the stream banks and among the rocks, then disappear for several seconds underwater as they swim after insects. Great blue herons (*Ardea herodias*) also search the shallow waters looking for fish and crustaceans, while the more terrestrial birds, varied thrushes (*Ixoreus naevius*), steller's jays (*Cyanocitta stelleri*), and a variety of hawks, are found throughout much of the park.

Much of the coast within the park is extremely mountainous and generally too steep to be safe. There is a 0.5-mile-long sandy beach known as Wilson Beach and False Klamath Cove, that allows access to tide pools during low tides. The beach is steep, the water very cold, and currents much too dangerous for swimming.

Directions: The park is adjacent to US 101, about 7 miles south of Crescent City.

Activities: Hiking, camping, fishing, beachcombing.

Facilities: Campground.

Dates: Open year-round.

Fees: There is a fee for camping and day-use. Camping reservations are generally required during summer (800-444-7275).

Closest town: Crescent City.

For more information: Del Norte Coast Redwoods State Park, Sector Office, 1375 Elk Valley Road, Crescent City, CA 95531. Phone (707) 464-6101, ext. 5120.

PRAIRIE CREEK REDWOODS STATE PARK

[Fig. 8] Several years ago, a new freeway bypass diverted large trucks and fast-driving travelers off of the original, narrow and twisting two-lane US 101 that passed through the center of the park. The abandoned section of highway was renamed Newton B. Drury Scenic Parkway. Today, the 8-mile-long parkway allows visitors to enjoy a much slower and more appropriately paced drive through the spectacular redwood forest that borders the old highway.

Besides the redwood forest, there is one additional highlight that brings people here, many year after year—the Roosevelt elk (*Cervus canadensis roosevelti*). The park boasts a large population, actually several small herds, of elk. One of the easiest places to view the elk is just off the side of the parkway at the small coastal prairie, the large meadow near the entrance to one of the park's campgrounds and the visitor center. There are almost always elk, either bedded down or munching the grass, at the edges of the open grassland and the forest border.

As with many parks, the visitor center is generally a good place to begin your visit. Prairie Creek's visitor center, in addition to its small gift shop, which offers a great

Redwood National and State Parks

[Fig. 9] The dense redwood and Douglas fir forests of the north coast thrive on 60, 70, or more inches of rain each year. But the north coast, like most of California, is a land of rainy winters and dry summers. Swirling clouds of heavy, summer fog often envelope the great forests of the north coast and provide critical moisture and humidity to the shallow-rooted trees, which helps them to survive until the winter rains return. But, today, it takes more than nature's hand for the remaining old-growth redwoods to survive.

When Redwood National Park (*see* page 43) was established in 1968, it marked a renewed commitment to an ongoing land acquisition program. Added to the long-established redwood state parks, the new land was designed to save the relatively few old-growth trees that still remained on private lands and to implement conservation efforts that would better protect the previously logged upland watersheds. That protection included purchasing logged-over mountains and replanting the areas in order to reduce flooding, erosion, and the resulting mud that clogged the spawning gravels of salmon and steelhead.

When Congress established Redwood National Park, it included three, long-established California state parks within its boundary, although the state parks continued to be managed by California's Department of Parks and Recreation. As the national park continued to expand, it became evident that having two separate public landowners managing adjacent lands with policies that could potentially impact one another, was not an efficient way to operate. Today, Redwood National Park and the three contiguous state parks, Jedediah Smith Redwoods (*see* page 34), Del Norte Coast Redwoods (*see* page 35), and Prairie Creek Redwoods (*see* page 37), work together on planning for such things as maintenance, resource management, and interpretive programs.

selection of publications, features numerous natural history exhibits. Here, visitors can discover the names of the many wildflowers and birds most often seen in the park.

Prairie Creek State Park has two campgrounds, the first of which is located at the south end of what is called Elk Prairie. The second is another very popular campground on **Gold Bluffs Beach** [Fig. 8(1)]. It requires a much more adventurous drive to find. To get there, about 3 miles north of Orick, Davison Road heads west from US 101. The first 200 yards or so, in the meadow that borders both sides of the road, is often a good place to see another of the elk herds. The road soon turns to dirt and heads upward into the forest where it winds for several miles, finally dropping down and emerging at Gold Bluffs Beach. Be warned, the road is narrow and many of the turns tight enough that vehicles over 8 feet wide and 24 feet long are prohibited. The beach campground is about 2 miles down the road, which hugs the tall bluff. Once again, elk can generally be seen near the road, often in the low dunes between the road and the beach.

Gold Bluffs Beach was aptly named. In 1851, California's gold fever spilled over from the mines of the Sierra foothills' Mother Lode and the Trinity River area to these bluffs. Thousands of miners flooded the area and filled the large camp that was established along the base of the bluffs. There was, and remains, gold in the bluffs, but the early miners could never manage to extract large enough quantities to make the operation economically viable. While the name of the bluffs is a reminder of its history, most first-time visitors probably believe the name is for the gold color of the bluffs' crumbly rock.

Directions: Prairie Creek Redwoods State Park headquarters and visitor center are located about 6 miles north of Orick and the Redwood State and National Parks Visitor Center. Driving north from Orick on US 101, take the Newton B. Drury Scenic Parkway. Exit to the park headquarters.

Activities: Camping, backpacking, fishing, picnicking, hiking.

Facilities: Campground, backcountry camps, and a visitor center. There are showers in Elk Prairie Campground and solar showers in the Gold Bluffs Beach Campground.

Dates: Open daily. Camping reservations are advised during summer. Phone (800) 444-7275 to make camping reservations.

Fees: There are day-use and camping fees.

Closest town: Orick, 6 miles south.

For more information: Prairie Creek State Park, 127011 Newton B. Drury Scenic Parkway, Orick, CA 9555. Phone (707) 464-6101, ext. 5064 or ext. 5301.

TRAILS

Revelation Trail: [Fig. 8(2)] Near the visitor center, a short, 0.3-mile, very level and easy trail loops into the redwoods. As its name implies, the trail provides revelations about the nature of the redwood forest, not only for those able to see and hear normally, but also for those who may have physical impairments. The trail's many stopping points are designed to relate the same information to those who may be sight- or hearing-impaired.

West Ridge Trail: [Fig. 8(3)] At 6.1 miles, this trail is the park's longest. It follows the ridgeline that lies about 500 to 600 feet above and about 2 miles east of the ocean. The trail is only moderately difficult, remaining relatively level. It begins near the park's visitor center and heads north, ending on Newton B. Drury Scenic Parkway. Many hikers head west just before the trail's end and take the **Butler Creek Trail** (1.8 miles) [Fig. 8(4)] down to the beach.

Fern Canyon Trail: [Fig. 8(5)] This is one of the most popular destinations in Prairie Creek Redwoods State Park. It's a very easy, 0.7-mile trail that begins at the north end of the Gold Bluffs Beach. The short, level walk offers a look at the geologic history of this part of the north coast. Following in the bed of the shallow creek, the trail meanders through a carved, sheer-walled canyon, revealing the nearby Klamath River's 4 million-year-old gravel deposits.

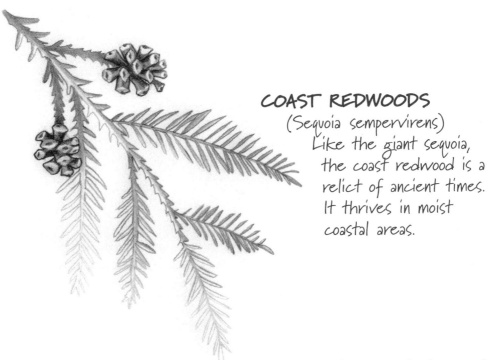

COAST REDWOODS
(Sequoia sempervirens)
Like the giant sequoia,
the coast redwood is a
relict of ancient times.
It thrives in moist
coastal areas.

The narrow canyon walls rise 50 feet or more and are almost completely covered by thick mats of bright green ferns. Five-finger fern (*Adianthum pedatum*), lady fern (*Athyrium felix-femina*), and sword fern (*Polystichum munitum*) are the most common. Orange-colored salmon berries (*Rubus spectabilis*) ripen during June and July, and they're edible, but oenanthe (*Oenanthe sarmontosa*), which is related to carrots, is poisonous. Another berry popular with anyone hiking up the canyon is the thimbleberry (*Rubus parviflorus*), similar to the salmon berry. Pull the delicate red berry from its stem and it looks somewhat like a thimble. It has a very enjoyable flavor.

It seems nearly impossible that this small stream and its narrow canyon are home to so many animals, especially during late summer when the water is so shallow. Coastal cutthroat trout (*Salmo clarkii clarkii*) come upstream in early spring and spawn, and rare and endangered species, such as the red-legged frog (*Rana aurora*) and the Pacific giant salamander (*Dicamptodon ensatus*) also live in this moist refuge.

The trail heads upstream, then rises to the top of the bluff and loops back to the parking lot. It also connects with the **James Irving Trail** [Fig. 8(6)] that leads back across the coastal hills to the visitor center (4.2 miles). The best time to visit the Fern Canyon Trail is during the summer when the water is low and the small footbridges are in place.

Coastal Trail: [Fig. 8(7)] Six noncontiguous sections make up the coastal trail that leads hikers through Redwood National and State Parks. It meanders, primarily along the coast, but occasionally detours inland, such as in Del Norte Coast

Redwoods State Park. One of the gaps in the trail is at the mouth of the Klamath River. Hikers must turn inland to the US 101 highway bridge to get across the river. The trail begins near the end of Enderts Beach Road, just north of Del Norte Coast Redwoods State Park and ends in the south, about 1.5 miles north of Orick at US 101. Camping is allowed in the established enroute campsites on a first-come, first-served basis. Camp-sites on the national park lands are free. The Butler Creek primitive camp in Prairie Creek Redwoods State Park requires a permit, which can be obtained at the park office. For more informa-tion on this trail, contact Redwood National and State Parks, 1111 Second Street, Crescent City, CA 05531-4198. Phone (707) 464-6101.

Coast Redwoods

Coast redwoods (*Sequoia sempervirens*) are the tallest trees in the world and some of the oldest living things. They covered much of the northern hemisphere 140 million years ago, but that range has been significantly reduced by global climate changes. Dependent on winter rains and foggy summers, today the coast redwood is restricted to a narrow, discontinuous 500-mile strip of coastline from north of the California border into lower Oregon, and south to the Big Sur coast.

There are two other related redwoods. The giant sequoia (*Sequoiadendron giganteum*) is found only in a few places along the Sierra Nevada's western slopes. The dawn redwood (*Metasequoia glyptostroboides*) grows naturally only in a remote area of China. The dawn redwood, unlike its California cousins, is deciduous, losing its leaf-like needles each autumn.

The world's tallest redwood title is transferred as the trees grow, die, or lose part of their tops to high winds or lightning strikes. In 1963, the tallest tree was thought to be in Redwood National Park. In 1999, another report placed a 600- to 800-year-old redwood in 700-acre Montgomery Woods State Reserve as the tallest tree, at 367.5 feet tall. The Montgomery Woods tree measurement was confirmed by the Guinness Book of World Records. The reserve is located west of US 101, near the hot springs resort of Orrs Spring, 11 miles northwest of Ukiah on Comptche Road. Phone (707) 937-5804.

NORTH COAST SIDE TRIPS

Cal Barrell Road: [Fig. 8] While this is a very narrow dirt road that can be driven, it can also be walked. The road is about 0.5 mile north of the Prairie Creek Redwoods State Park headquarters entrance and on the east side of the Newton B. Drury Scenic Parkway. Spring is the best time to head up the road because scattered among the towering redwoods are colorful clusters of wild rhododendrons (*Rhododendron macrophyllum*). Their pink and white blossoms beautifully accent the deep, red bark of the redwoods, especially on those days when the light filters softly through light fog or cloud cover.

Redwood National Park Area

Redwood National Park was established in 1968 in an effort to protect old-growth redwoods.

1 DeMartin Section, Coastal Trail
2 Dolason Prairie Trail
3 Lady Bird Johnson Grove Trail
4 Redwood Creek Trail
  Redwood National Park
  Humboldt Lagoons State Park
  Prairie Creek State Park
  Trail

To Crescent City

101

PRAIRIE CREEK

Newton B. Drury Scenic Parkway

MAY CREEK

SURPUR CREEK

Davidson Road

1

SKUNK CABBAGE CREEK

PRAIRIE CREEK

Berry Glenn

LITTLE LOST MAN CREEK

LOST MAN CREEK

Lady Bird Johnson Grove

4

3

Bald Hills Road

REDWOOD CREEK

101

Orick

TECTAH CREEK

P A C I F I C
O C E A N

MCARTHUR CREEK

ELAM CREEK

Old State Hwy.

STONE LAGOON

Tall Trees Access Road

BOND CREEK

2

Bald Hills Road

Tall Trees Grove

Dolason Prairie

REDWOOD CREEK

MCDONALD CREEK

TOM-MCDONALD CREEK

TOM CREEK

BIG LAGOON

BRIDGE CREEK

N

DIAMOND CREEK

PITCHER CREEK

Ref: DeLorme N. California Atlas and Gazetteer

101

Coastal Drive: [Fig. 8] On the south side of the Klamath River, take the Klamath Beach Road to Coastal Drive. This dirt and gravel road offers a great view of the mouth of the Klamath River and wonderful ocean views along much of its 7.5-mile length. Along the road, which takes about 45 minutes to drive and connects with Newton B. Drury Scenic Parkway, watch for a structure that resembles an old farmhouse and barn; it was actually a World War II radar station. Its farmhouse look was a disguise to protect it from a possible Japanese attack.

Klamath River Overlook: [Fig. 8] From US 101, cross to the north side of the Klamath River and turn west onto Requa Road, which winds to the top of another river mouth and coastal overlook. On warm, sunny days, this is a great place to sit at one of the picnic tables and enjoy a little wine and cheese and a spectacular view of the north coast.

Humboldt Lagoons State Park: [Fig. 9] Dry Lagoon and nearby Stone Lagoon are areas where resource management programs have begun to reverse the effects that pioneer farmers and dairy ranchers created by draining wetlands. Today, the two lagoons adjacent to US 101, 40 miles north of Eureka, teem with wildlife, especially birds that thrive in the restored marshy areas. Just off the highway, between the two lagoons, there is a small visitor center (open summer only) that once was part of a motel and restaurant. Boating, hiking, and fishing are popular in the park. There are a few boat-in and undeveloped environmental campsites. For information about access to the campsites, phone (707) 488-2041.

Redwood National Park

[Fig. 7, Fig. 8, Fig. 9, Fig. 10] Redwood National Park shares many stretches of its meandering boundary with three state parks—Prairie Creek Redwoods, Del Norte Coast Redwoods, and Jedediah Smith Redwoods. Together the state and national parks form a World Heritage Site and International Biosphere Reserve, a worldwide recognition of their environmental significance.

Redwood National Park was created in 1968, several decades after the state parks were established to protect old-growth redwoods. Although much of the forest within the national park contains second-growth redwoods, the park plays a crucial role in protecting the old-growth trees that remain. The National Park Service is actively rehabilitating the logged lands, eliminating exotic plant species that have taken over many hillsides, and planting native trees such as redwoods and Douglas firs. With thousands of acres of watershed now protected from the unavoidable damage created by logging activities, especially during the early, unregulated years of the industry, flooding is much less prevalent. The ongoing efforts also help protect the stream and river gravels needed by spawning steelhead and salmon.

The coast portion of Redwood National Park is a relatively unspoiled meeting of land and sea that stretches from Stone Lagoon, directly parallel with US 101, just

Northern Spotted Owl

Probably no single animal species has caused more court battles, demonstrations, and forced changes in human behavior than the northern spotted owl (*Strix occidentalis*). Its need to nest primarily in old-growth redwood and Douglas fir forests, and its use as an indicator species that is able to gauge the relative health of a forest environment, has stopped numerous major logging operations. The government recognizes the small owls as a *threatened* species, which generally makes the removal of their nesting habitat in the old-growth forests illegal, or at best, extremely difficult to justify, even on private lands.

south of Orick, north to Crescent City. Most of it is accessible only by way of hiking trails, and there are several popular access points. One of the longest stretches of easily accessible beach is between Stone Lagoon and the Redwood Information Center in Orick. The long pull-off between the highway and the beach is a very popular day-use and overnight area for motor homes and trailers willing to forego anything in the way of amenities, except for the beautiful ocean beach view.

A walk along the beach is likely to bring sightings of numerous shorebirds chasing the ebb and flow of the slapping waves and searching the sand for insects, tiny crustaceans, and anything else that fills their bills. The rocky tidepools are a rich zone for exploration. Mussels, anemones, sea stars, and snails are among the dozens of very different animal species that are dependent upon the swirl of fresh, clean salt water for survival. Double-crested cormorants (*Phalacrocorax auritus*) and brown pelicans (*Pelecanus occidentalis*) glide low and elegantly above the water, or rise high and dive below the surface to feed.

The Prairie Creek Visitor Center, located just south of Orick, provides exhibits and a large assortment of publications about the area's cultural and natural history, as well as maps, permits for backcountry camping, and general information about both the state and national parks found in the area.

Directions: Redwood National Park lies along various portions of US 101, between approximately Trinidad on the south and Crescent City to the north.

Activities: Hiking, backpacking, fishing, camping.

Facilities: Campgrounds, visitor center, trails.

Dates: Open daily except Thanksgiving, Christmas, and New Year's Day.

Fees: Camping fees are charged in some areas.

Closest town: Crescent City, Orick, and Trinidad.

For more information: Redwood National and State Parks Information Center, 1111 Second Street, Crescent City, CA. 95531-4198. Phone (707) 464-6101.

TRAILS

Many of the trails in Redwood National Park, such as the Coastal Trail (*see* page 40), connect with trails in the adjacent state parks. Bears are occasionally encountered on the mountain trails. If you come across a bear, make plenty of noise and back away from it slowly, and it shouldn't bother you.

DeMartin Section, Coastal Trail: [Fig. 9(1)] This 10-mile round-trip hike heads into the backcountry, through forests of old-growth redwoods, western hemlock (*Tsuga heterophylla*), and Douglas fir (*Pseudotsuga menziesii*). While there are several grades, some relatively steep, this all-day hike is only moderately difficult. Pick up the trail south of Crescent City. Look for milepost marker 15.6 along US 101 and the signpost marked, "CT." Park off the road.

Dolason Prairie Trail: [Fig. 9(2)] Here's an opportunity to see elk up close, just not too close. This moderately difficult hike weaves through prairies and oaks as it switchbacks down to Redwood Creek. You can either hike back out on the same trail, or connect with the Redwood Creek Trail that follows the canyon back toward Orick. Take Bald Hills Road about 1.5 miles north of Orick, then drive 3 miles to the Dolason Prairie picnic area, which is located past the Redwood Creek Overlook picnic area.

Lady Bird Johnson Grove Trail: [Fig. 9(3)] This is an easy, 1-mile walk that leads through to the redwood grove where Lady Bird Johnson dedicated Redwood National Park in 1968. The grove trailhead is located on Bald Hills Road, about 3 miles east from US 101 and Orick. Phone (707) 464-6101, ext. 5265.

Redwood Creek Trail: [Fig. 9(4)] This is a summer hike because seasonal bridges are removed during winter's high water. It's an 8.5-mile walk along the creek to Tall Trees Grove. While some people hike the trail in one day, others consider it much easier to backpack in. There are some restrictions, such as not camping within 0.25 mile of the Tall Trees Grove. It's best to check at the Redwood National Park Information Center in Orick for the most updated information. Phone (707) 464-6101, ext. 5265.

Tall Trees Grove: [Fig. 9] For those unable to hike the 8.5 miles up Redwood Creek to visit the Tall Trees Grove, a few permits are issued daily for vehicle access via Bald Hills Road, off US 101 and Orick. The free permits allow vehicles access to the

NORTHERN SPOTTED OWL (Strix occidentalis) The spotted owl is identified by its large, dark eyes and white spots on the head, back, and underparts.

Patrick's Point State Park Area

Patrick's Point State Park lies on a bluff 100 feet above the ocean with trails that lead to the water.

Ref: DeLorme N. California Atlas and Gazetteer

N

101

BIG LAGOON

DIAMOND CREEK

PITCHER CREEK

GRAY CREEK

NORTH FORK MAPLE CREEK

Patricks Point

101

Patricks Point Dr

Candy Mountain

MAPLE CREEK

NORTH FORK MAPLE CREEK

BURRIS CREEK

MAPLE CREEK

The Gap

MAPLE CREEK

Stagecoach Rd

MILL CREEK

M LINE CREEK

BEACH CREEK

Twentyone Rock

NORTH FORK

Trinidad

Trinidad Head

Trinidad Scenic Dr

LUFFENHOLTZ CREEK

RAILROAD CREEK

Westhaven

Moonstone

LITTLE RIVER

101

Tip Top Ridge

Crannell

LITTLE RIVER

P A C I F I C   O C E A N

1	Rim Trail
2	Agate Beach Trail
3	Octopus Trees Trail
	Patricks Point State Park
	Redwood National Park
······	Trail

Tall Trees Access Road. From the drive-in trailhead, the Tall Trees Grove is only a 1.3-mile hike each way, with an 800-foot drop in elevation to the grove. Bald Hills Road is steep and winding, and trailers and motor homes are not allowed. Either stop in or phone the Redwood National Park Information Center in Orick for permit information. Phone (707) 464-6101, ext. 5265.

Trinidad Area

PATRICK'S POINT STATE PARK

[Fig. 10] Tectonic plate movements, geologic uplifting, and many thousands of years of erosion have combined forces and created headlands along the length of California. Patrick's Point is one of the more prominent of the headlands that separate rocky cliffs and long sandy beaches. One of the favorite destinations at Patrick's Point is Agate Beach. The waves wash a constant supply of small, semiprecious agates into the beach gravels. Access to the beach can be a challenge for many and may be impossible for those unable to negotiate the steep wooden stairs that drop from the top of the bluff trail to the sandy beach below.

Sightings of black-tailed deer (*Odocoileus hemionius columbianus*) are common, especially along the bluff and in the open meadow near Ceremonial Rock, which is actually an ancient sea stack that was left high and dry following the rising of the land. It's located near the center of the park. Another ancient sea stack, Lookout Rock, is located just off Rim Trail, near the hike and bike campground.

A good place to begin a quick, single-day exploration of some of the park's more prominent features is at the new visitor center, which is located near the park entrance. Exhibits and information are available that will enhance anyone's visit, including how to identify the agates on Agate Beach.

Sumêg Village, just a short walk from the visitor center, is a reconstruction of a Yurok Indian village. The Yurok's redwood shelters played critical roles in their lives. They believed that the redwood planks were spirits and that their shelters actually lived. The Yuroks gave their houses names, and each family's loyalty was to its home, rather than to the tribe.

In 1990, in much the same traditional manner as it was done for thousands of years, local Yurok Indians used stone mauls and wedges to split the redwood planks for the reconstructed village. Inside the low-built homes, the Yuroks dug pits 4- to 5-feet deep to increase the living space. Today, the village is used for special Yurok ceremonies and events, but it is open daily for anyone to wander through.

The Yurok maintained a distinctive class system within the tribe. The aristocrats of a Yurok village, depending upon their level of wealth, maintained larger collections of fine clothing. They would generally provide the special clothing or regalia worn by all the tribal dancers at many ceremonies. Displayed wealth included clothing adorned with various shells seen as valuable to the culture, such as olivella, (*Olivella biplicata*), butter clam (various genera), cockles (various genera), dentalliam (*Dentallium* sp.), and red abalone (*Haliotis rufescens*). Even more rare and valuable were the dresses made from the skins of albino deer.

Like most public and private lands throughout northwest California, black bear and raccoons are always present, even though they may not often be seen. Exceptions to their natural shyness are too often found in campgrounds where these animals have learned that people too often leave ice chests full of food unsecured.

Along the park's rocky, southern shoreline, tidepools are a cold, inviting haven for dozens of different animal species, from mussels and oysters to sea stars and anemones. California sea lions, once prey for Yurok hunters, bark their incessant calls from the offshore rocks. If you're interested in fishing, there's plenty of both rocky and sandy shoreline to be found within the park. During certain times of the year various fish species migrate in close to shore toward their spawning areas, offering anglers the opportunity to regularly catch lingcod (*Ophiodon elongatus*), kelp greenlings (*Hexagrammos decagrammus*), sea trout or steelhead (*Oncorhynchus mykiss*), and cabezone (*Scorpaenichthys marmoratus*).

The park's 65 inches of annual rain provides plenty of moisture for a tremendous variety of plants. Sword ferns and redwoods are common and easily identified, but spruce, hemlock, and Douglas fir are also prevalent within the park's boundaries. In the open meadows and along the forest trails, spring and summer bring a plethora of wildflowers, such as Douglas iris (*Iris douglasiana*), rhododendrons (*Rhododendron macrophyllum*), false lilies-of-the-valley (*Maiantheumum dilatatum*), and the ever-present berries—blackberries (*Rubus ursinus*), salmon berries (*Rubus spectabilis*), thimbleberries (*Rubus parviflorus*), and huckleberries (*Vaccinium ovatum*).

ROOSEVELT ELK

(*Cervus canadensis roosevelti*)

During the elks' fall mating season, bulls challenge each other with loud snorting and bugling, and with short, false charges. Their occasional battles produce the loud sounds of colliding antlers.

Directions: From the town of Trinidad, drive 6 miles north on US 101 and take the Patrick's Point Drive Exit and follow the road to the park entrance. As an alternative, Patrick's Point Drive parallels the west side of the US 101 freeway from Trinidad.

Activities: Camping, hiking, fishing, beachcombing.

Facilities: Campground, visitor center.

Dates: Open year-round.

Fees: Camping and day-use fees.

Closest town: Trinidad, 6 miles.

For more information: Patrick's Point State Park, 4150 Patrick's Point Dr., Trinidad, CA 95570. Phone (707) 677-3570.

TRAILS

Patrick's Point State Park has several miles of trails that connect the coastal beach on this small peninsula with inland areas, including park headquarters, the visitor center, Ceremonial Rock, and several campground loops.

Rim Trail: [Fig. 10(1)] Most of Patrick's Point State Park lies on a bluff 100 feet above the ocean beach. The Rim Trail leads around the park's coastal perimeter and has six steep but negotiable, 0.25-mile side trails that lead to the water's edge. The coastal views are great nearly anywhere along the trail, which leads hikers to such special places as Wedding Rock, Patrick's Point, and Palmer's Point. Abalone Point, another side trail, is one of the more popular places to watch gray whales during winter. It's also a place to wander among the jagged coastal rocks and piles of driftwood that winter storms deposit along the shore. The Rim Trail begins near Palmer's Point on the south end of the park, and after about 2 miles ends at the Agate Beach parking lot on the north end of the park.

Agate Beach Trail: [Fig. 10(2)] This 0.25-mile-long trail, with its last portion being a steep stairway, leads to very popular Agate Beach. The beach is long and wide

Roosevelt Elk

Walking along a trail and suddenly coming upon a 1,200-pound bull Roosevelt elk (*Cervus canadensis roosevelti*) can be somewhat unsettling, especially during the fall rutting season when bulls are very aggressive. Fortunately, most of the time elk are relatively benign, as long as people keep a safe distance. During much of the year the small herds of maybe a dozen or more cows are easily located as they lazily graze in the meadows, or lie resting in the tall grasses, often with only their heads visible. It's common most of the year to see the cows and bulls in their own separate groups. The fall mating season usually finds bulls challenging other bulls with their loud snorting and bugling, but also with short, false charges. Their occasional battles produce the loud sounds of colliding antlers that echo across the meadows and through the forests. All this late summer and early autumn posturing, bluffing, and fighting determines which of the biggest and strongest bulls get the right to mate with the cows, which leads to calves being born in May and June.

Mountain Lions

Sighting a mountain lion or cougar (*Felis concolor*) in the wild can be both exciting and frightening. Mountain lions range throughout most of California, but the secretive cats are seldom seen by humans. Whenever hiking in mountain lion country, which includes most of California's undeveloped coast, it's best to travel with others. Always keep smaller children nearby and don't allow them to run down the trail by themselves.

Cougar Country Hiker Safety Tips

- If you encounter a mountain lion, never run. They are likely to assume that you are fleeing prey and give chase. You can neither outrun nor hide from a mountain lion.
- Stand tall and wave your arms or a jacket, trying to appear as large as possible. Throw sticks or stones, but try to bend down as little as possible while picking them up.
- If the lion does not move away first, move back away slowly while facing the lion.
- If you have small children with you, pick them up, bending over as little as possible.
- In the unlikely event that you are attacked, face the cat and fight back. Mountain lions will attempt to bite the back of your neck and head.
- Report any lion sightings to a ranger immediately. Phone (707) 464-6101 or stop by park information centers in Orick, or in Crescent City at 1111 Second Street.

and is a great place to explore and look for small agates. The ocean waves constantly move the semiprecious gems on and off the sandy beaches, polishing the stones and making them wonderful finds. As always, use caution whenever exploring near the surf line, especially if there are high waves. The water is cold and the rip currents can be extremely strong. Rogue waves have been known to sweep unsuspecting people off the rocks or from the beach.

Octopus Trees Trail: [Fig. 10(3)] This 0.25-mile loop trail leads to a stand of sitka spruce (*Picea sitchensis*) where, over the years, many of the trees' roots have grown over fallen logs, most of which have since rotted and disappeared back into the soil. What's left are tentacle-like roots that loop away from their trunks.

TRINIDAD

[Fig. 10] The tiny community of Trinidad is a popular destination for many who visit Patrick's Point State Park. It's also a wonderful stopover for anyone traveling US 101 and who is in need of a short diversion. Spanish mariner Captain Bruno Hezeta discovered the site and named it for the day that he landed here, Trinity Sunday, 1775. It was another 75 years before the town was actually founded, and then only because it offered a well-protected harbor where gold miners and their equipment and supplies could be unloaded. Mining operations first took place inland in the Trinity mines and later at Gold Bluffs Beach to the north.

Today, the tiny community provides a multitude of services, including a few

Black Bears

Black bears (*Ursus americanus*) are common in redwood country. In many areas where people congregate, bears can become nuisances or even more dangerous than normal. Always remember that all bears are wild and that their primary goal is to eat. Wildlife managers generally must destroy bears that make a habit of wandering into campgrounds, ripping open car doors and breaking apart ice chests for food. They can smell food odors even inside cars.

Do not make food available to bears or any wild animal. If camping, store food in airtight containers locked in your car's trunk or in bear-proof storage lockers. If backpacking, store food over tall tree branches out of their reach. And always dispose of garbage in bear-proof trashcans. REMEMBER: A FED bear is a DEAD bear.

shops, several bed and breakfast inns, small motels, and restaurants. About two blocks off the main road through town is a well-marked turn-off to the **Trinidad State Beach**. The beach parking lot sits about 120 feet above the ocean, so it's a short walk across the open meadow area and down through the trees to get to the beach. Two small streams empty into the Pacific here, making it a fairly popular place to fish.

The main street through town hooks around to a replica of the old lighthouse. The overlook offers a great view of Trinidad's small harbor. The road continues down to the harbor and wharf where there's boat launching, a pier for fishing, fishing trips, and a restaurant. There's also a beach that's popular in summer.

Directions: Trinidad and Trinidad State Beach are located just off US 101, 19 miles north of Eureka.

Activities: Shopping, hiking, picnicking, fishing, boating.

Facilities: The town of Trinidad offers groceries, gas stations, fishing, picnicking, and restaurants.

Dates: Open year-round. Fishing trips from the pier are available seasonally.

Fees: Trinidad State Beach is free.

Closest town: Eureka, 19 miles.

For more information: Trinidad Chamber of Commerce, PO Box 356, Trinidad, CA 95570. Phone (707) 677-1610. For Trinidad State Park contact Patrick's Point State Park, 4150 Patrick's Point Dr., Trinidad, CA 95570. Phone (707) 677-3570.

MOUNTAIN LION
(*Felis concolor*)

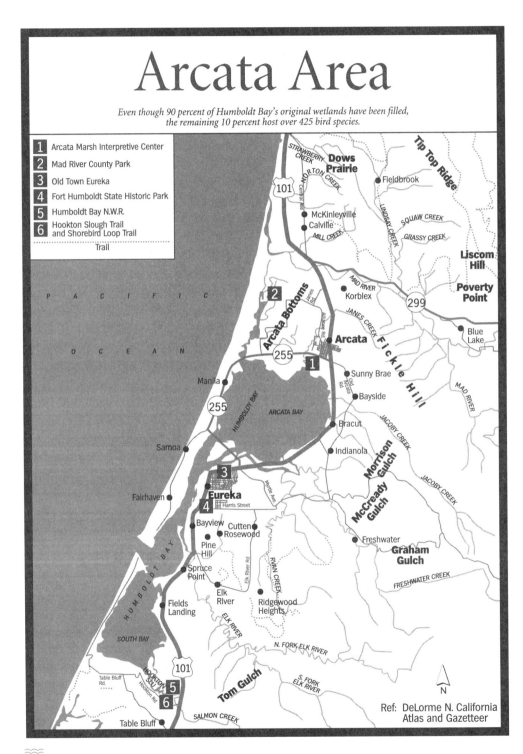

Arcata Area

Even though 90 percent of Humboldt Bay's original wetlands have been filled, the remaining 10 percent host over 425 bird species.

1 Arcata Marsh Interpretive Center
2 Mad River County Park
3 Old Town Eureka
4 Fort Humboldt State Historic Park
5 Humboldt Bay N.W.R.
6 Hookton Slough Trail and Shorebird Loop Trail
···· Trail

Ref: DeLorme N. California Atlas and Gazetteer

Arcata

[Fig. 11] The city of Arcata, a close neighbor of Eureka, located on the northern end of Humboldt Bay, is home to numerous wildlife viewing areas. Even though 90 percent of the original wetlands around Humboldt Bay have been filled, the remaining 10 percent play host to over 425 bird species. While waterfowl are common, especially during the fall migration, it's equally reasonable to expect that a gray jay, ruffed grouse, rock sandpiper, or even a peregrine falcon (*Falco peregrinus*) might end up on the far side of a pair of binoculars or spotting scope.

The **Arcata Marsh Interpretive Center** is the perfect starting place to gather information about the surrounding wetlands, view numerous exhibits about the wildlife, learn about special efforts to restore the wetlands, or maybe join a guided nature walk. Just outside the interpretive center there is a trail that meanders for 4.5 miles through 154 acres of restored marsh. This entire area was originally part of the wetland, but it was filled and turned into an industrial and timber processing area. Even today, old and rotted wood pilings mark the locations of buildings and warehouses from an earlier era. Much of the marsh has been restored in what began as a test project designed to naturally treat up to 5 million gallons of the city's raw sewage each day.

The incoming sewage circulates through a series of ponds, marshes, chlorinating facilities, and an aquaculture project, allowing algae, fungi, bacteria, and microorganisms attached to plant roots to filter and transform the solids. All this may sound pretty ugly, but thousands of birds have found new homes in this restored wetland. Mallards, cinnamon teal (*Anas cyanoptera*), golden crowned sparrows (*Zonotrichia atricapilla*), palm warblers (*Dendroica palmarum*), and Thayer's gulls (*Larus thayeri*) are only a small sampling of the birds that can be found in the area. For some, black-crowned night herons (*Nycticorax nycticorax*), great blue herons (*Ardea herodias*), American bitterns (*Botaurus lentiginosus*), and an occasional green heron (*Butorides striatus*) provide more interesting sights.

While Arcata's South G Street runs along the east side of the marshes, South I Street bisects a portion of the area and ends at a parking lot where the only concrete boat launch on the north end of Humboldt Bay is located.

Besides being a birder's paradise, the Arcata Marsh is also a perfect place for the amateur or professional botanist. Trails lead past areas thick with shrubs and trees such as big leaf maples (*Acer macrophyllum*), coast willow (*Salix hookeriana*), transplanted Monterey pine (*Pinus radiata*), red alder (*Alnus rubra*), wax myrtle (*Myrica californica*), and coyote bush (*Baccharis pilularis*), one of the more common shrubs found around the fringes of the marsh. Add bulrush (*Scirpus acutus*), broadleaf cattail (*Typha latifolia*), marsh pennywort (*Hydrocotyle ranunculoides*), and pickleweed (*Salicornia virginica*) to the list of plants that create this rich, biotic plant community.

Scattered around the trail that winds throughout the marsh are interpretive signs that help tell the story of this successful restoration. There are also bird blinds for

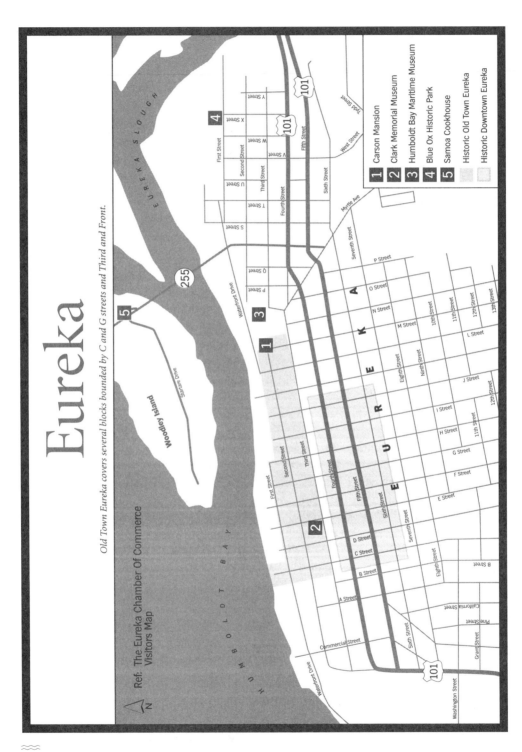

Eureka

Old Town Eureka covers several blocks bounded by C and G streets and Third and Front.

Ref. The Eureka Chamber Of Commerce
Visitors Map

N

1	Carson Mansion
2	Clark Memorial Museum
3	Humboldt Bay Maritime Museum
4	Blue Ox Historic Park
5	Samoa Cookhouse
	Historic Old Town Eureka
	Historic Downtown Eureka

anyone wishing to simply sit and wait for the birds to come to them.

Directions: Arcata Marsh Visitor Center is located on South G Street in Arcata. From US 101, take the Samoa Boulevard (Highway 255) Exit west. Turn left (south) onto South G Street and drive about 0.5 mile to the center, which is on the right.

Activities: Walks and information.

Facilities: Exhibits, trails.

Dates: Arcata Marsh is open daily. Visitor center is generally open in the afternoon.

Fees: None, but there is a jar for donations.

Closest town: Arcata.

For more information: Arcata Marsh Interpretive Center, 569 South G Street, Arcata, CA 95521. Phone (707) 826-2359.

MAD RIVER COUNTY PARK

[Fig. 11(2)] Mad River County Park is a slightly out-of-the-way secret that lies in an area known as the Arcata and Mad River Bottoms. The lands that surround the mouth of the Mad River, where it empties into the Pacific Ocean just north of Arcata, are primarily agricultural. The bottomlands host more bird species than anywhere else in the area, which is a significant number considering the rich habitat provided by Humboldt Bay. During winter, raptors and shorebirds are relatively common when the fields flood. In the fall, the skies and the fields fill with the sound and sights of migrating birds. Lesser yellowlegs (*Tringa flavipes*) become common here and mallards (*Anas platyrhynchos*), northern shovelers (*Anas clypeata*), pintails (*Anas acuta*), gadwalls (*Anas strepera*), and American widgeons (*Anas americana*) swim the edges of the river as it rises with the first winter rains. More rarely seen is the occasional prairie falcon or rough-legged hawk (*Buteo lagopus*). At night, short-eared owls (*Asio flammeus*) replace the raptors, hunting mice and other small nocturnal mammals.

One of the best ways to enjoy the avian and water world is by boat, but only small boats can navigate the shallow river. Canoes and kayaks are common and considered the best way to slide silently along the shoreline habitat that many birds favor. When the winter rains finally come, the river's flow can rise dramatically very quickly, making boating quite dangerous.

Directions: This popular birding and boating area can be reached by taking the Samoa Boulevard Exit from US 101 in Arcata. Drive about 5 blocks, turning right (north) on K Street. Continue on K Street, which turns into Alliance Road. Continue north, past Stromberg Avenue, turning left (west) onto Spear Avenue. Follow Spear Avenue around the wide bend that passes near the Aracata Bottoms, turning left onto Upper Bay Road, then right onto Mad River Road, which leads to Mad River Beach and boat launch.

Activities: Birding, boating (small boats), kayaking, fishing.

Closest town: Arcata.

For more information: Eureka Humboldt County Convention and Visitors Bureau, 1034 Second Street, Eureka, CA 95501. Phone (800) 346-3482.

Eureka

It may be difficult to imagine how the rush for California's Sierra foothill gold in 1850 could possibly have created the town of Eureka, so far north and on the coast. As the prospectors spread out from the central Mother Lode in the Sierra foothills, they found gold in many places throughout California. One of those early discoveries was along the Trinity River, near what today is the small, historic town of Shasta, in the northern part of the Sacramento Valley. These early miners also discovered that getting supplies was much easier if they were hauled by ship up the coast, landed at Humboldt Bay, then packed over the Trinity Alps, rather than being hauled by wagon or horseback up the often wet and swampy Sacramento Valley.

Eureka's position near the entrance to Humboldt Bay assured its continuing success even as the gold petered out. It was timber, giant redwoods, and Douglas fir that drove Eureka's continued growth and created millionaires of some of its citizens. One of those early lumber barons was William Carson. A grand and beautiful reminder of Carson's wealth remains today. The **Carson Mansion**, [Fig. 12(1)] a whimsical, three-story Victorian, was constructed in the 1880s and includes elaborate scrollwork, gingerbread, and other embellishments that help make it one of the most photographed Victorians in the country. It's located near the waterfront, at Second and M streets in Old Town Eureka. Unfortunately, the mansion cannot be toured, only photographed from the street, from outside the fence.

Old Town Eureka [Fig. 11(3)] covers several blocks near the waterfront, bounded by C and G streets and Third and Front. Many of the old buildings, including several Victorians that have graced the waterfront area since the latter half of the nineteenth century, have been restored and are now filled with a wonderful and eclectic collection of shops and restaurants.

One such gem is the **Clark Memorial Museum**, [Fig. 12(2)] located in the historic, Roman Renaissance-style Bank of Eureka building at Third and E streets. Among its treasures from Eureka and Humboldt County's histories is one of the largest collections of Northwest Indian basketry, some 1,200 pieces. Phone (707) 443-1947.

Humboldt Bay Maritime Museum [Fig. 12(3)] is one of the many relatively small maritime museums found in the historic towns along the Pacific Northwest coast, from California to Washington. Eureka's maritime museum, which is open daily, boasts ship models and other maritime artifacts both inside and outside the building. The museum is at 1410 Second Street, behind the Carson Mansion. Phone (707) 444-9440.

Blue Ox Historic Park, [Fig. 12(4)] along with its small museum, is a wonderful place to watch modern-day craftsmen working with nineteenth and early twentieth century woodworking hand and power tools to create all the beautiful and intricate gingerbread that adorns Victorian homes. Private builders and restorers of famous historic homes from around the country place orders here for replacement architectural millwork, from balustrades to turned porch columns. There's a small fee to tour the complex, but it's well worth a visit to the millworks and museum. For those so inclined, Blue Ox also offers classes in woodworking, blacksmithing, and pottery. The Blue Ox is located at 1 X Street in Eureka. Phone (800) 248-4259.

The **Samoa Cookhouse** [Fig. 12(5)] is one of the more enjoyable places to eat in all of Eureka. This is the last surviving lumber mill cookhouse in all of California. Lumberjacks no longer eat here, but its long and fascinating history is captured in the old photos that cover all of the walls and the displayed artifacts, from the first chain saws to some of the cookhouse's first stoves.

This is a great place to bring those teenagers or other big eaters who never seem to get enough food. The cookhouse serves three meals each day in a family-style setting, and the cook determines what is being served. Breakfast generally includes pancakes, scrambled eggs, bacon, sausage, juice, and coffee, and it's all you can eat, as are all the meals. Dinner generally offers two main types of meat such as steak and ham. The prices are pre-set, and they are quite reasonable, considering that you get to enjoy your meal seated at long, picnic-style tables and can eat as much as the lumberjacks.

Directions: The cookhouse is just off Route 255 in Eureka. From US 101 near the north end of Eureka, cross the prominent Samoa Bridge (there are directional signs to the bridge along US 101), which dead-ends into Route 255. Turn left onto Route 255, and the Samoa Cookhouse is easy to find by following the signs a couple of hundred yards down the road. Phone (707) 442-1659.

Directions: Eureka is located on US 101, about 278 miles north of San Francisco.

Activities: Shopping, sight-seeing, fishing, boating, bird-watching.

For more information: Eureka Humboldt County Convention & Visitors Bureau, 1034 Second Street, Eureka, CA 95501. Phone (800) 346-3482.

EUREKA LODGING

Eureka is the largest town in Humboldt County, so there are plenty of hotels and motels to choose from. But, since the town is noted for its grand, nineteenth century architecture, staying at one of the many historic homes that have been converted to bed and breakfast inns is a great alternative.

An Elegant Victorian Mansion B&B Inn. 1406 C Street, Eureka. The home was built in 1888 and has since been completely renovated. *Moderate to expensive. Phone (707) 444-3144.*

Eagle House Victorian Inn. 139 Second Street, Eureka. This historical landmark was originally built in 1880 as a Victorian-style hotel with 24 rooms. It is in the heart of Old Eureka. *Moderate to expensive. Phone (707) 444-3344.*

A Weaver's Inn. 1440 B Street, Eureka. The inn features beautiful woodwork and tiled fireplaces that enhance its Queen Anne Victorian architecture. *Moderate to expensive. Phone (707) 443-8119.*

Abigail's Elegant Victorian Mansion. 1406 C Street, Eureka. The B&B is well known for the French gourmet breakfast served to its guests who, while dining, can enjoy the opulent Victorian furnishings and interiors in this 1888 National Historic Landmark building. Experience history by playing gramophones, touring in antique cars and coaches, playing croquet, watching silent movies (videos), and browsing 1900-era books and magazines. *Moderate to expensive. Phone (707) 444-3144. www. eureka-california.com.*

Eureka Inn. 518 Seventh Street, Eureka. While this is not a B&B, it's on the National Register of Historic Places and is a member of the Historic Hotels of America. The inn's English Tudor architecture will make any stay memorable. *Moderate to expensive. Phone (707) 442-6441.*

FORT HUMBOLDT STATE HISTORIC PARK

[Fig. 11(4)] The fort wasn't constructed until 1854, the year after Brevet Lt. Colonel Robert C. Buchanan and his troops arrived to quell the problems settlers were having with the Hoopa Indians. Indians were killing white settlers who, since 1848, had been taking over Indian villages and hunting lands, while killing any Native who resisted. Buchanan constructed Fort Humboldt on a bluff overlooking the bay, and included a large and open parade field surrounded by more than a dozen buildings. Everything needed to support his troops was built of wood, including the officers' quarters, which just so happened to house a young officer named Ulysses S. Grant.

While too many soldiers used alcohol to excess as a way of dealing with the boredom, Grant apparently wasn't so disposed. Yet he couldn't escape the boredom. He became so depressed with his assignment this far outside the fringes of civilization that after four months he resigned his commission, writing to his wife, "Whoever hears of me in ten years will hear of a well-to-do old Missouri farmer."

The Indian wars continued for another 10 years, although isolated skirmishes were much more common than major battles and campaigns. Often it was the settlers who took action when they weren't satisfied that the army had done enough. In 1863, Governor Leland Stanford authorized establishment of the volunteer "Mountain Battalion." It soon forced the Hoopa Indians into accepting lands in Hoopa Valley along the Trinity River. Within another half dozen years, the army abandoned the fort and sold the property.

The old Fort Humboldt became a state historic park in 1955, and many of the original buildings that had long since disappeared were reconstructed. What's been added is equally interesting. With this part of the north coast better known for its logging industry than for its Indian wars, a large collection of historic logging equipment is displayed in sheds and in the open. The equipment includes locomotives and steam donkeys, including a Washington slack-line steam donkey. Loggers used this marvel of late nineteenth century technology to haul huge redwood logs on overhead lines to the locomotive loading areas, sometimes as much as a 0.5 mile away. There is a self-guided trail through the outdoor exhibit area.

During Fort Humboldt's periodic living history days, logging demonstrations are popular, especially when the steam donkey is fired up.

Directions: The park is located at the south end of Eureka, just off US 101, off Highland Avenue.

Activities: Picnicking, strolling through exhibits.

Facilities: Exhibits, visitor center.

Dates: Open daily.

Fees: There is a day-use fee.

Closest town: Eureka.

For more information: Fort Humboldt State Historic Park, 3431 Fort Ave., Eureka, CA 95503. Phone (707) 445-6567.

HUMBOLDT BAY NATIONAL WILDLIFE REFUGE

[Fig. 11(5)] As a winter stopover point for migrating birds, Humboldt Bay National Wildlife Refuge is critical to hundreds of thousands of birds annually. More than 200 bird species either live or pass through the refuge. For many of the winged visitors, the nutritious eelgrass that grows so prolifically in the shallow waters and the mud flats is the prime attraction. The diversity of habitat found in the tideland ecosystem also contributes to its attractiveness to birds, including several endangered species.

Humboldt Bay is a long and narrow body of water that lies between two moderately large towns, Arcata and Eureka. The refuge covers 2,200 acres, and the U.S. Fish and Wildlife Service continues acquiring and restoring wetlands and related wildlife habitat areas including sandspits, brackish marsh, and freshwater marsh areas. The goal is to reach 9,000 acres of restored wetlands.

The largest part of the refuge is around South Humboldt Bay, with several smaller parcels located in North Humboldt Bay. The habitat restoration program is designed to provide additional sites, not only for the winter visits by migratory geese and ducks, but also for endangered species like the peregrine falcon (*Falco peregrinus*), western snowy plover (*Charadrius alexandrinus nivosus*), Aleutian Canada goose (*Branta canadensis leucopareia*), and California brown pelican (*Pelicanus occidentalis*).

Because of the extensive eelgrass beds, the refuge is also a primary home for black brant (*Branta bernicla*). More than 30,000 of these small geese can be seen on the 14-mile-long Humboldt Bay during their fall migration. They use the bay as a staging area in spring for the trip to their northern nesting sites in Alaska, Russia, and Canada.

A good way to view the wildlife is from a boat. The most accessible boat launch is at the marina, below the Samoa Bridge in Eureka. There's a county boat ramp on the Samoa Peninsula, near the historic community of Samoa, just west of Eureka. Winds and tides can be treacherous for small craft here, especially for kayaks and canoes, so always check weather forecasts and tide tables before heading out.

Directions: The refuge is located at Humboldt Bay. The largest section of the refuge and the office are located just west of and adjacent to US 101, at the Hookton Road Exit.

Activities: Bird-watching, fishing, hunting in season in specified areas, hiking, and boating.

Facilities: Boat launch, trails.

Dates: Most of the refuge is open daily from sunrise to sunset. The Triangle Marsh/Shorebird Loop Trail is open only from Oct. through May.

Fees: None, except in the hunting area during waterfowl hunting seasons.

Closest town: Eureka, about 12 miles north.

For more information: Humboldt Bay National Wildlife Refuge, 1020 Ranch Road, Loleta, CA 95551. (707) 733-5406.

TRAILS

Hookton Slough Trail: [Fig. 11(6)] The trail follows Hookton Slough for about 1.5 miles to where South Humboldt Bay begins to widen. The trail is open during daylight hours and passes through grasslands, freshwater marsh, open mud flats, and the open water of the bay. From US 101 south of Eureka, take the Hookton Road Exit and drive west for 1.2 miles, and follow the signs to the trailhead parking area.

Shorebird Loop Trail: [Fig. 11(6)] This is probably the best trail in the refuge for viewing shorebirds. This 1.75-mile loop is also relatively level, making it an easy walk. There's a short spur trail that leads to Long Pond, the largest of the refuge's freshwater ponds. Expect to see shorebirds and waterfowl, especially during winter, and the ever-present herons and egrets nearly any time of year. Look more closely to see treefrogs and river otters that live along the waterways. The trailhead parking area is reached via the Hookton Road Exit from US 101. There's a refuge entry gate on the northwest side of the freeway near the exit. The trail is only open on weekdays from October through May.

Ferndale

[Fig. 13] Just off US 101 there's a two-lane country road that crosses the Eel River, not far from its mouth, then meanders west through open farm and dairy land. The road finally enters a most intriguing historic Danish dairy town just before heading into the steep, coastal mountains of the Lost Coast to the west.

Ferndale's concentration of grand Victorians, so many of them restored to their original colorful grandeur, were built by prosperous Danish dairy farmers who settled this rich bottomland in the nineteenth century. The farms remain prosperous, but today, it's the thousands of tourists who visit the town each year who have helped spur the restoration of the elegant old homes, which originally were referred to as "butterfat palaces."

The town's main street is a kaleidoscope of colorful buildings that have been transformed into a wonderful collection of gift shops and antique dealers, restaurants and bakeries. The **Ferndale Museum**, located at 515 Shaw Street, has exhibits of early farm machinery, logging tools, furniture, and clothing.

One of the more intriguing museums to be found anywhere is the **Kinetic Sculpture Museum**, located at 580 Main Street. Inside, there are dozens of the human-powered contraptions that serve as the race vehicles in the Arcata to Ferndale Kinetic Sculpture Race. This annual three-day event, begun in 1969 by two Ferndale artists, requires individuals or teams to race their human-powered "sculptures" over land, sand, mud, and water. Some of the devices look like contorted combinations of bikes, boats, and giant caterpillars.

For those with several more hours to kill and a willingness to drive a narrow, mostly one-lane road, Main Street through Ferndale turns into Mattole Road and heads west into the forest and mountains. It ultimately emerges at the mouth of the Mattole River and Cape Mendocino, the northern end of an area called the Lost Coast, and the westernmost point in California.

Directions: About 14 miles south of Eureka, on US 101, turn south onto Mattole Road. It first crosses the historic Fern Bridge, then continues for about 5 miles to the town of Ferndale.

Activities: Shopping, walking, photography.

Facilities: Museums, bed and breakfast inns, restaurants.

Closest town: Eureka, 19 miles north.

For more information: Ferndale Chamber of Commerce, PO Box 325, Ferndale, CA 95536. Phone (707) 786-4477.

PEREGRINE FALCON
(Falco peregrinus)
An extremely fast flier, the peregrine falcon feeds on ducks and other water birds.

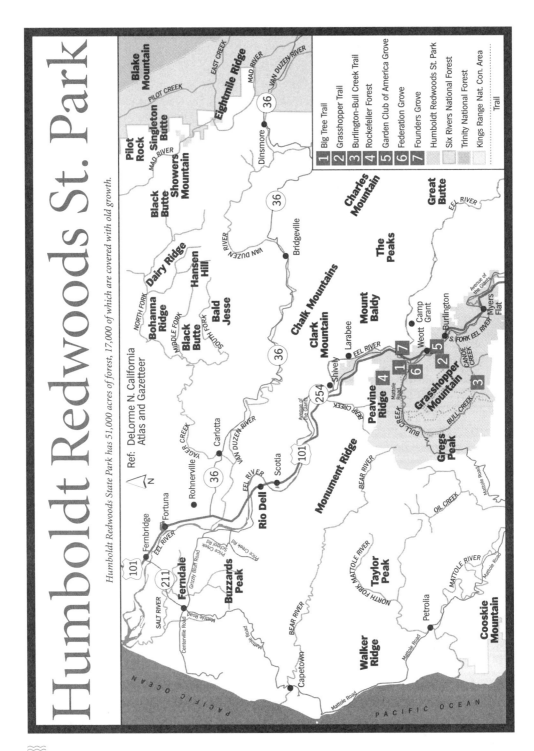

Humboldt Redwoods St. Park

Humboldt Redwoods State Park has 51,000 acres of forest, 17,000 of which are covered with old growth.

Ref: DeLorme N. California Atlas and Gazetteer

1	Big Tree Trail
2	Grasshopper Trail
3	Burlington-Bull Creek Trail
4	Rockefeller Forest
5	Garden Club of America Grove
6	Federation Grove
7	Founders Grove
	Humboldt Redwoods St. Park
	Six Rivers National Forest
	Trinity National Forest
	Kings Range Nat. Con. Area
	Trail

Humboldt Redwoods State Park

[Fig. 13] For two centuries writers have attempted to adequately describe the ancient redwood forests. Most nineteenth century readers scoffed at the earliest writers' obviously exaggerated claims about the size and age of these trees, believing that nothing of such proportions could possibly exist. Even today, books, travel articles, and photographs fail to do justice to the old-growth forest in Humboldt Redwoods State Park.

Of the park's 51,000 acres of forest and rivers, 17,000 acres are covered with old-growth forest. The trees must be experienced in person, at least by driving along the Avenue of the Giants, the meandering, two-lane road that passes near some of the largest and oldest trees. Much better than driving is to walk among trees that top 300 feet in height and range from 500 years to 2,000 years of age. Wandering among the ancient forests is like entering a magnificent, centuries-old cathedral.

Humboldt Redwoods State Park lies in the center of prime redwood country. Plenty of water and moderate temperatures are the keys to creating thriving redwood forests. The giant trees have very shallow root systems, requiring significant amounts of surface water, which comes primarily in the form of winter rains. The trees survive California's dry summers as banks of fog form along the coast, keeping the tree needles moist and the air humid.

The best place to begin any visit is on the Avenue of the Giants. The visitor center and park headquarters provides exhibits, publications, and lots of great information about camping, hiking, and backpacking in the park. Its hours are limited during winter when nearly constant rain brings visitation to the park, except by fishermen, to a trickle.

The first people to live here among the great trees and along the shores of the Eel River were the Sinkyone Indians. They used the redwoods for shelter, fashioning plank-like strips of the heavy, stringy bark into lodges for protection from rain, as well as for their religious ceremonies. Considering the massive size of a mature redwood, the tiny seeds found in its cones, which are not much larger than golf balls, did not serve as a food source. For that the Indians depended on the salmon and steelhead that ran up the rivers and streams throughout the area. Redwood logs did provide the raw material for their canoes. Using fire and mostly stone and antler tools, the great logs were hollowed and formed into very serviceable boats.

It was California's gold that lured the first outsiders into the remote rivers and forests of the Humboldt area. In 1850, a group of miners chose the Eel River route from the Trinity gold fields when they headed back to San Francisco. The group's leader had the unfortunate experience of running into a grizzly bear. He barely survived the encounter, but when he finally reached civilization, the secret of the redwoods was out. Fortunately, it was another 25 years before the first settler, Tosaldo Johnson, homesteaded 160 acres near today's Albee Creek campground.

Even the first few American settlers could do little to harm much of the great redwood forests. It took the expansion of roads and railroads into the area to open the great forests for exploitation. In 1914, a railroad was constructed into the area, and eight years later the original Redwood Highway was completed. Thus began the era of large-scale commercial logging. It wasn't long before technology was clearing entire mountainsides of the ancient redwoods and shipping the trees to mills. While some of the more visionary lumber companies could see that there was indeed an end to the supply of old-growth trees and began replanting their harvested acres, other companies ignored warnings that they were courting ecological disaster and a certain end to their own livelihoods.

During the winters of 1955, and again in 1964, heavy rains washed untold tons of sand and gravel down bare hillsides, filling rivers and streams, flooding cities and highways, and toppling hundreds of ancient redwoods that once grew on the rich alluvial soils near the Eel River. The gravel beds that salmon and steelhead needed for spawning were clogged with silt, preventing the fish eggs from hatching and the fry from surviving and returning the ocean. To this day, restoration work continues, not only in the stream beds but also on the timber-harvested lands, especially in the Bull Creek watershed that now lies within the park.

Redwood forests are often distinguished by the obvious absence of other trees and shrubs, especially in the largest groves found along the alluvial flats near rivers. The thick redwood canopy tends to shade out competition, allowing only an occasional tall and spindly white alder (*Alnus rhombifolia*), tanoak (*Lithocarpus densiflorus*), or big leaf maple (*Acer macrophyllum*) to grow. Periodic flooding tends to deposit silt along the forest floor, causing the redwoods to develop new lateral root systems closer to the surface, while further discouraging understory plant competition. Wander on most of the forest trails beneath the great trees where sword ferns (*Polystichum* sp.) are generally the most conspicuous plant; but wildflowers also have their moments. The three white petals of trillium (*Trillium ovatum*) and the flower clusters of red clintonia (*Clintonia andrewsiana*) offer special surprises for hikers.

Avenue of the Giants [Fig. 13] is a US 101 bypass road that provides an up-close look at the redwoods for those who may be unable to spend too much time wandering on foot among the giants. Depending upon the starting location, the Avenue of the Giants is 32 miles long. It begins on the south, about 6 miles north of Garberville. There's a marked exit off US 101. At the north end, heading south, the first exit is about 4 miles south of the old lumbering community of Scotia. The grandest portion of the drive is found between the towns of Myers Flat and Dyerville. As the Avenue of the Giants meanders through the forest and along the South Fork of the Eel River, there are numerous pullouts and short trails that lead into the trees or to the river.

Rockefeller Forest [Fig. 13(4)] is in the densely forested and less traveled northwestern portion of Humboldt Redwoods State Park. The dirt and gravel Mattole Road passes through the forest, which received its name from John D. Rockefeller, who in 1930 provided the Save-the-Redwoods League with its largest donation up to that time. His gift of $2 million allowed the league and the State of California to purchase 10,000 acres along Bull Creek that Pacific Lumber Company had earmarked for harvesting. It was a major addition to the fledgling California State Park System. Rockefeller Forest holds some of the most magnificent of the park's old-growth trees.

The **Williams Grove** is located about 1 mile north of Myers Flat, adjacent to the Avenue of the Giants. The **Garden Club of America Grove** [Fig. 13(5)] is another mile farther north, and the **Federation Grove** [Fig. 13(6)] is located near where Bull Creek enters the South Fork of the Eel River. One of the most popular stops is the **Founders Grove**, [Fig. 13(7)] located another mile north at the end of a short road off the Avenue of the Giant. The groves are identified along the Avenue of the Giants and are easy to find.

The **Eel River** and the **South Fork of the Eel River** [Fig. 13] combine their flows in the park, and generally, following the first rains in October, salmon and steelhead are the reasons most fall and winter visitors flock here. Drift boats by the dozens are in the more popular areas of the river, while shore anglers often have just as much good luck. Fishing success can be even more unpredictable on the Eel River as flows can change quickly, going from too little water for the salmon to high, unfishable, silt-laden waters, to perfect conditions within a couple of days. During low water conditions that sometimes accompany California's periodic droughts, fishing may be prohibited temporarily. Before fishing, it's always a good idea to check the regulations and to call the California Department of Fish and Game's north coast information center. Phone (707) 442-4502.

Most of the thousands of people who stay at Humboldt Redwoods State Park each year camp in one of the several campgrounds found in the park. While Burlington Campground seems to be very popular, perhaps because of its central location in the park, its nearness to the visitor center, and the fact that it has only 56 campsites, Hidden Springs Campground is equally attractive. It's much larger, with 154 campsites.

Albee Campground, located on Mattole Road, 5 miles west of US 101 and the Avenue of the Giants, has 38 campsites. There are also hike and bike, group, and equestrian campsites, along with several trail camps in the park. During summer, reservations are generally needed at Hidden Springs Campground (phone 800-444-7275), while the other campgrounds are available on a first-come, first-served basis.

Directions: Humboldt Redwoods State Park is located 30 miles south of Eureka and 6 miles north of Garberville, on the Avenue of the Giants, just off one of several marked exits along US 101.

Activities: Hiking, mountain biking, horseback riding, fishing, camping, nature study, ranger-led hikes.

Facilities: Campgrounds, visitor center, picnic areas.

Dates: Park is open year-round. Some campgrounds closed during winter.

Fees: There are moderate camping fees.

Closest town: Garberville, 6 miles from park's southern boundary; Scotia, 3 miles from northern boundary.

For more information: Humboldt Redwoods State Park, PO Box 100, Weott, CA 95571. Phone (707) 946-2409.

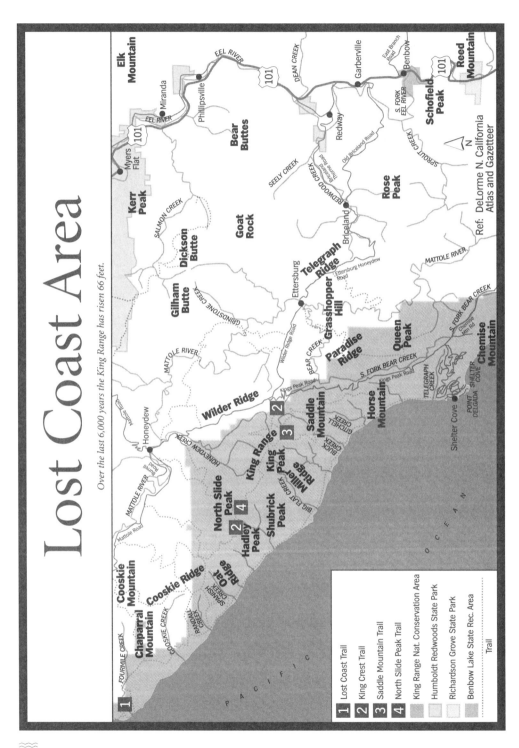

Lost Coast Area

Over the last 6,000 years the King Range has risen 66 feet.

Ref: DeLorme N. California Atlas and Gazetteer

Elk Mountain

Reed Mountain

Schofield Peak

Kerr Peak

Bear Buttes

Rose Peak

Dickson Butte

Goat Rock

Gilham Butte

Telegraph Ridge

Grasshopper Hill

Queen Peak

Paradise Ridge

Chemise Mountain

Wilder Ridge

Saddle Mountain

Horse Mountain

King Range

King Peak

Miller Ridge

North Slide Peak

Shubrick Peak

Hadley Peak

Oat Ridge

Cooskie Mountain

Cooskie Ridge

Chaparral Mountain

Miranda
Phillipsville
Myers Flat
Honeydew
Ettersburg
Briceland
Redway
Garberville
Benbow
Shelter Cove

EEL RIVER
DEAN CREEK
S. FORK EEL RIVER
SEELY CREEK
SPROUT CREEK
SALMON CREEK
REDWOOD CREEK
MATTOLE RIVER
GRINDSTONE CREEK
BEAR CREEK
S. FORK BEAR CREEK
N. FORK BEAR CREEK
MITCHELL CREEK
BUCK CREEK
BIG FLAT CREEK
HONEYDEW CREEK
SPANISH CREEK
RANDAL CREEK
COOSKIE CREEK
FOURMILE CREEK
TELEGRAPH CREEK

Mattole Road
Kings Peak Road
Wilder Ridge Road
Ettersburg Honeydew Road
Old Briceland Road
Thorne Road
Briceland Thorne Road
East Branch Road
Chemise Mtn Rd

POINT DELGADA
SHELTER COVE

101

PACIFIC OCEAN

Legend

1 Lost Coast Trail
2 King Crest Trail
3 Saddle Mountain Trail
4 North Slide Peak Trail

King Range Nat. Conservation Area
Humboldt Redwoods State Park
Richardson Grove State Park
Benbow Lake State Rec. Area

Trail

TRAILS

With over 100 miles of trails in the park, there is something for everybody. Some trails, primarily those at least 5 feet wide, are open to mountain bike use, and many are also open for horseback riding. Stop in the visitor center or park office and get a copy of the park map to find out which trails are open for what kinds of uses.

Big Tree Trail [Fig. 13(1)] provides a bit more adventure for park visitors. The trail begins at Founders Grove and follows Bull Creek for 4.5 miles to the Big Tree Area, which includes the Giant Tree and the Flat Iron Tree. **Grasshopper Trail** [Fig. 13(2)] connects the Garden Club of America Grove, one of many redwood groves adjacent to the Avenue of the Giants, with the Grasshopper Trail Camp. The camp is about 5 miles away, and the trail has a 3,000-foot elevation gain. The **Burlington-Bull Creek Trail** [Fig. 13(3)] offers a popular and relatively level hike that follows the South Fork of the Eel River, connecting the heavily used Burlington Campground with Decker Creek to its north and Canoe Creek to the south. The trail is 4 miles long.

For those who are unable to enjoy long hikes, there are short trails that lead through several of the named redwood groves, many of which have small picnic areas and are located directly adjacent to the Avenue of the Giants.

The Lost Coast

California's Lost Coast is an area of only a few, narrow paved roads, a few more miles of dirt roads that in places create challenges for anything less than four-wheel-drive vehicles, and many more miles of hiking trails. It includes the incredibly rugged King Mountains, essentially isolated on a piece of coastline that bulges out into the Pacific, west of Garberville and US 101. The San Andreas fault lies just offshore, marking the rift that separates the Pacific plate and the North American plate. The ancient and continuing tectonic movements also make the Lost Coast's mountains some of the most geologically active in the country. During the past 6,000 years the King Range has risen 66 feet.

The mountains aren't the only things active here. The Lost Coast can receive 100 inches of rain during "dry" winters and twice that amount during "wet" winters. All this rain running down streams and rivers has severely cut the mountains, creating steep cliffs, lots of sliding slopes, and thick forests.

There is little private property, especially within the thousands of acres that stretch down the coast. The most notable nonpublic land is the small town of Shelter Cove, which effectively separates the King Range National Conservation Area on the north from Sinkyone Wilderness State Park and 3,800 acres of Trust for Public Land property on the south.

But, even though the Lost Coast is a relatively wild area free of human inhabitants today, this has not always been the case. In the 1850s, probably 6,000 years after the first Indians arrived here, American settlers entered the mountains, bringing sheep and cattle to graze in the meadows and forests. They were soon followed by men looking for oil and who were successful in finding it. Although not a high-profit operation, they drilled California's first oil well here in 1865.

During this same period, the centers of industry required a continuous supply of leather belts needed to run steam-powered factory equipment. Harvesters came to the mountains of the Lost Coast to strip the bark from tanoaks, which was needed in the leather harvesting process. Commercial fishing, based in Shelter Cove, followed, and then the loggers came. Even though logging continued in some areas of the Lost Coast as late as the 1960s, scattered forests of old-growth Douglas fir and redwoods remain.

For a few years, a railroad was operated from Bear Harbor. The rugged mountains of the Lost Coast were not the best choice for such a venture. The Bear Harbor and Eel River Railroad was designed to transport logs from the coastal mountains to Piercy, which lies on the Eel River. The beginning portion of the route from Bear Harbor was so steep that a winch was required to raise and lower the locomotive and cars during the initial leg of the trip. A storm destroyed the harbor's pier in 1899, hampering the rail operation, and the railroad's owner died in an accident in 1905. One year later, the great San Francisco earthquake severely damaged trestles and stretches of track, ending the railroad's use. A few of the old rails remain today, rusting in the damp, salt air.

SHELTER COVE

[Fig. 14] The easiest and fastest route into the Lost Coast is to drive west out of Garberville, through Redway to Shelter Cove. Shelter Cove Road is paved but narrow as it winds through the forest and over the coastal mountains. Dropping down from the summit into the surprisingly large community of Shelter Cove, it offers wonderful views of the rugged mountains that surround the aptly named town. There is a miniature maze of subdivision-like streets that wind around the area and a substantial number of mostly vacation homes scattered along the hillsides and across the flat meadows that once fed cattle and sheep and served as staging areas for harvested timber.

In the main cove at the end of Machi Road, there is a public beach with restrooms and a boat launch facility. Little Black Sand Beach is another popular spot and is located on the north side of the Shelter Cover community, off Beach Road. But many people who come to the Lost Coast are looking for more of a wilderness experience, and that's easy enough to find in both the King Range National Conservation Area and in Sinkyone Wilderness.

Directions: From Garberville/Redway follow the signs west to the Shelter Cove/King Range National Conservation Area. Although the road is paved, it is narrow and twisting. Expect the 22-mile trip to take about 45 minutes.

Activities: Hiking, camping, fishing, boating, backpacking, beach exploration.

Facilities: Boat launch, marina, store, picnic area.

Dates: Open daily.
Closest town: Garberville, about 22 miles.
For more information: Shelter Cove Information Bureau, phone (707) 986-7069.

KING RANGE NATIONAL CONSERVATION AREA

[Fig. 13, Fig. 14] The conservation area ranges in elevation from sea level to the top of King's Peak at 4,087 feet, the King Range's highest mountain. The conservation area stretches for 35 miles, from the mouth of the Mattole River in the north to Sinkyone Wilderness State Park in the south, and ranges inland about 4 miles at its widest point.

Congress established the King Range National Conservation Area in 1970 and placed it under the control of the Bureau of Land Management. Within the conservation area's 60,000 acres, old-growth Douglas fir forest serves as home to Cooper's hawks (*Accipiter cooperii*) and bald eagles. Endangered spotted owls (*Strix occidentalis*) live in the canopy, while on the forest floor elk, black bears, and black-tailed deer feed on the grasses and shrubs.

In an earlier time, Mattole and Sinkyone Indians lived throughout the area, but they were forced to give up much of their traditional way of life when American settlers began arriving in relatively large numbers. During the 1850s, white settlers first came to graze cattle and sheep and were soon followed by the commercial fishing industry and finally by the timber harvesters. The lands were logged for decades, with some of the most intense logging activity occurring during the 1950s and 1960s. When the steep and unstable mountainsides were clear-cut, they eroded easily, creating massive land slides that choked the Mattole River and other waterways in the area. Now, major restoration programs are beginning to return forests to the once-stripped mountainsides.

The King Range offers an opportunity for both car camping and backpacking. There are campsites at the Mattole River mouth, which are the only drive-in sites on or near the beach. To reach the **Mouth of the Mattole Recreation Site,** from US 101, take the Ferndale Exit and drive 5 miles to the town of Ferndale. Continue on the same road through town and follow the signs to Petrolia. One mile past Petrolia, turn right on Lighthouse Road and follow it until it ends. It's about 45 miles total, which will take about 1.25 hours to drive. The remaining car-accessible campsites are reachable via Mattole Road, which winds along the eastern side of the conservation area, generally following the Mattole River. They include **A.W. Way County Park**, which will accommodate tents and trailers along the Mattole River, and is located about 8 miles north of Honeydew, and **Honeydew Creek**, which has several creekside campsites for tents and trailers and is located about 1 mile south of Honeydew.

Most of the camping done in the King Range National Conservation Area is in trail camps or in the **coast camps** which are undesignated sites on or near the beach. Some of the more popular areas are near Cooksie Creek, Randall Creek, Big Creek, Big Flat Creek, Buck Creek, and Gitchell Creek. Each of the creeks crosses the Lost

Sinkyone Wilderness State Park

Sinkyone Wilderness consists of nearly 7,400 acres with an adjacent 3,000 acres owned by the Trust for Public Land.

Ref: DeLorme N. California Atlas and Gazetteer

N

BEAR CREEK

Telegraph Ridge

Ettersburg Honeydew Road

Briceland Thornroad

Briceland Thorn Road

Redwood Drive

REDWOOD CREEK

Briceland

4

Alderpoint Road

Garberville **Little Buck Mountain**

Bell Springs Road

2

MATTOLE RIVER

Rose Peak

S. FORK EEL RIVER

SPROUT CREEK

101

Queen Peak

Thorn Junction

WEST FORK SPROUT CREEK

E. BRANCH S. FORK EEL RIVER

5 Benbow

Shelter Cove Road

Schofield Peak

Reed Mountain

TOM LONG CREEK

Bell Springs Road

Chemise Mountain Road

BRICELAND THORN ROAD

MATTOLE RIVER

6

Cooks Valley

Briceland Road

INDIAN CREEK

Chemise Mountain

3

Bear Road

Andersonia

Piercy

E. BRANCH S. FORK EEL RIVER

Red Mountain

PACIFIC OCEAN

Usal Road

STANDLEY CREEK

S. FORK EEL RIVER

RED MOUNTAIN CREEK

7

101

HIGH TIP

Bear Harbor **1**

BEAR HARBOR

Jackass Ridge

USAL CREEK

8

CEDAR CREEK

Chimney Rock

Usal Road

9

Leggett

Little Red Mountain

TIMBER POINT

S. FORK USAL CREEK

1 **208**

S. FORK EEL RIVER

101

Usal Road

HOLLOW TREE CREEK

S. FORK EEL RIVER

208 Hales Grove

1

BOND CREEK

Elkhorn Ridge

Coast Trail (*see* below) between the Mattole River in the north and Shelter Cove near the south end of the conservation area.

Directions: There are three access routes into the King Range National Conservation Area. From US 101, take the Ferndale Exit, and continue driving through Ferndale, following the signs to Petrolia. Lighthouse Road, which leads to the mouth of the Mattole River (5 miles), is 1 mile past Petrolia. Honeydew can be reached by taking the South Fork/Honeydew Exit from US 101. Follow the signs for about 23 miles to Honeydew, then bear left 1 mile to the Honeydew Creek Recreation Site. Plan on it taking at least 1 hour to travel the 24 miles. The southern access is from Garberville/Redway to Shelter Cove. Although the road is paved, the 22-mile trip will take about 45 minutes.

Activities: Hiking, camping, fishing, backpacking, beach exploration.

Facilities: Some campsites with picnic tables and pit toilets, trails.

Dates: Open daily.

Fees: There are camping fees.

Closest town: Ferndale, about 32 miles to the north and Garberville, 22 miles to the southeast, and Shelter Cove, which lies on the coast, adjacent to the conservation area in the south.

For more information: Bureau of Land Management Office, Arcata Field Office, 1695 Heindon Road, Arcata, CA 95521-4573. Phone (707) 825-2300.

TRAILS

There are more than 70 miles of trails lacing this mostly roadless land. With so many interconnecting trails, it is critical to have a topographic trail map of the area. An excellent map is available from Wilderness Press, 2440 Bancroft Way, Berkeley, CA 94704. Phone (800) 443-7227, fax (510) 548-1355. The map also is sold at numerous stores and visitor centers throughout the north coast, including Sinkyone Wilderness State Park, PO Box 245, Whitethorn, CA 95489 (phone 707-986-7711), and Arcata Resource Area, US Bureau of Land Management, 1695 Heindon Road, Arcata, CA 95521. Phone (707) 824-2300.

The **Lost Coast Trail** [Fig. 14(1), Fig. 15(1)] begins near the mouth of the Mattole River, then meanders inland and south for 3.2 miles, reaching the coast at the Punta Gorda lighthouse. From Punta Gorda the trail follows the beach reaching Spanish Flat after 5.2 miles and Big Flat in 7.5 additional miles. It's another 14.1 miles before the conservation area portion of the trail connects with the Sinkyone Wilderness trail at Whale Gulch.

The **King Crest Trail** [Fig. 14(2)] is 10.5 miles long, with the top of King's Peak located at about the midway point. The trail begins in the north at the **Smith Etter Jeep Road** and **North Slide Peak Trail** [Fig. 14(4)]. It passes the **Saddle Mountain Trailhead** [Fig. 14(3)] near the south end, which leads back to Honeydew Creek tent camping area. The King Crest Trail's southernmost trailhead begins at the **King Peak Road**, which leads to Shelter Cove.

🏵 SINKYONE WILDERNESS STATE PARK

[Fig. 15(3)] One of only a few wilderness areas within California's State Park System, Sinkyone's nearly 7,400 acres, with an adjacent 3,000 acres owned by the Trust for Public Land, offer numerous trails, backpacking camp areas, and a wild coast accessible only on foot.

For thousands of years before the first Europeans arrived, the Sinkyone Indians lived on this part of the coast. They occupied permanent villages alongside streams and rivers and moved out in family groups to hunt and forage in the hills during the summer. They spent time along the coast fishing, gathering seaweed and shellfish, hunting seals and sea lions, and harvesting the occasional dead whale that washed ashore. Fish were an important source of food during the winter. All kinds of fish were caught, but the seasonal salmon run was especially important, because once the fish were dried, they provided food for many months.

From the late nineteenth century and well into the twentieth century, human activities stripped the land of natural resources. Grazing and logging were the two most common and popular practices. Game trails that once allowed elk and deer to reach fresh feeding areas were turned into rough roadways for horse-drawn wagons and pack mules, and later for logging trucks. Open marine terraces and inland meadows were filled with grazing sheep and cattle or turned into farmland. Bear Harbor became the main shipping transportation point.

Logging operations had the most impact on the area. Well into the twentieth century timber was shipped to makeshift port facilities via narrow gauge railroads constructed throughout the area. Today, areas that appear to be modern jeep trails are actually abandoned railroad right-of-ways from a past era. Several of the accessible coastal bluffs, where lumber schooners could safely anchor close enough to shore, were once used as temporary loading facilities. Steel cables or "wire chutes" were stretched between the schooners and the bluff to haul logs out to the ships. The block and tackle cable chute built in 1875 at Northport was one of the first to be used in California. The timber companies developed similar loading areas at Needle Rock, Anderson's Landing, and Bear Harbor.

The park's visitor center, which is located in a century-old ranch house at Needle Rock, should be one of the first stops visitors make in the park. Actually, it's very near the end of the primary road into the area. The center is staffed by volunteer camp hosts, many of whom return regularly and have become extremely knowledgeable about the park and its miles of trails. There are also exhibits in the visitor center, along with a table filled with related books and maps that are for sale.

Camping is allowed only in the designated backcountry campsites. Some, such as the Railroad Creek and Orchard Creek camps, can be reached by a short, 0.25-mile walk from the roadside parking area. The Bear Harbor Cove sites, which are located near the edge of a meadow at the ocean's edge, are a 0.4-mile, relatively level walk away. The trail passes through an area frequented by elk, so watch for them, especially during the fall rutting season when some of the big bulls can become a bit cantankerous—and dangerous if you're not paying attention.

For those not into backpacking, there are two rooms for rent, each of which will sleep four people, in one of the old buildings at Needle Rock. All bedding must be provided by the renters, who must also clean up the rooms before leaving. There is no smoking, pets, or alcohol permitted. Most people who bear the rather arduous drive over a very rough dirt road and spend time here are looking to escape as many people and traces of civilization as possible. Advance reservations can be made through the park.

Directions: There are two primary entrances into the wilderness. To reach the northern end of the wilderness area, from US 101 take the Garberville or Redway Exit and head to Redway, located about 3 miles north of Garberville on Business 101. Turn west on Briceland Road (Mendocino County Road 435), and drive 12 miles, where you'll take the left fork to Whitethorn. Continue another 3.5 miles to what is called Four Corners. At the intersection, continue straight ahead on a rough road filled with huge potholes. The road is narrow, steep, and twisting. Drive 3.5 miles to the visitor center. The last 3.5-mile section is generally not passable, especially for two-wheel-drive vehicles, when raining.

To reach the southern entrance to the park at Usal Beach, take Highway 1, 3 miles north of Rockport. Turn northwest on Mendocino County Road 431 and drive 6 miles on the unpaved road to the Usal Campground.

Activities: Hiking, fishing, backpacking.

Facilities: Visitor center, campsites with picnic tables, and pit toilets.

Dates: Open daily.

Fees: There are camping fees.

Closest town: Garberville, about 20 miles.

For more information: State Parks Management District, North Coast Redwoods, PO Box 245, Whitethorn, CA 95489. Phone (707) 986-7711 (recorded message).

TRAILS

There are numerous trails within the wilderness, most of which run north and south along the length of the park. The **Lost Coast Trail** [Fig. 14(1), Fig. 15(1)], as it runs from Usal at the south end of the wilderness area, north to Bear Harbor, is not a trail for beginners. The trail is only 16.3 miles, but it generally takes the better part of three days and two nights of difficult hiking to negotiate its mountain valleys and passes. Taking a longer time to complete the trail is better than trying to rush along its pathway because on those clear summer days, when the fog remains far offshore, there is a plethora of incredible sights, including ocean views and redwood groves. Portions of the trail stay on the lower, western sides of the mountains, ranging up to about 1,000 feet above sea level, but much of it is along the coastal bluff, perhaps 250 to 500 feet above the pounding surf. The Lost Coast Trail continues north from Bear Harbor another 5.3 miles, through Orchard Creek and Needle Rock to Whale Gulch.

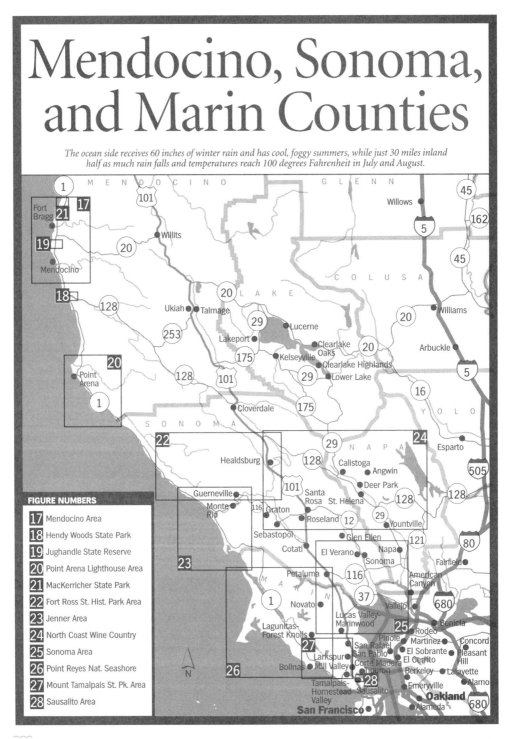

Mendocino, Sonoma, and Marin Counties

The ocean side receives 60 inches of winter rain and has cool, foggy summers, while just 30 miles inland half as much rain falls and temperatures reach 100 degrees Fahrenheit in July and August.

FIGURE NUMBERS

17 Mendocino Area
18 Hendy Woods State Park
19 Jughandle State Reserve
20 Point Arena Lighthouse Area
21 MacKerricher State Park
22 Fort Ross St. Hist. Park Area
23 Jenner Area
24 North Coast Wine Country
25 Sonoma Area
26 Point Reyes Nat. Seashore
27 Mount Tamalpais St. Pk. Area
28 Sausalito Area

Mendocino, Sonoma, and Marin Counties

The Mendocino Coast is a favorite escape from the traffic, confusion, and the often frantic pace that most people face who live in California's urban areas. Most of Highway 1 along this portion of the coast is a twisting, two-lane road that forces sometimes agonizingly slow and careful driving, especially when stuck following a large motor home or truck. But it's also not a highway that most people care to drive too quickly. The scenery and the special places hidden along many of the side roads make for great exploring.

Equally as rugged and beautiful as Mendocino's coastline, the Sonoma coast begins to show the subtle transition from the great redwood and Douglas fir forests of the far north that grow nearly to the ocean's edge, to the coastal scrub and mostly treeless exposed mountains of the central coast. A relatively low mountain range, at least by California standards, separates the coast from the inland valleys. In spite of

[*Above:* The rocky shoreline of Mendocino Headlands State Park]

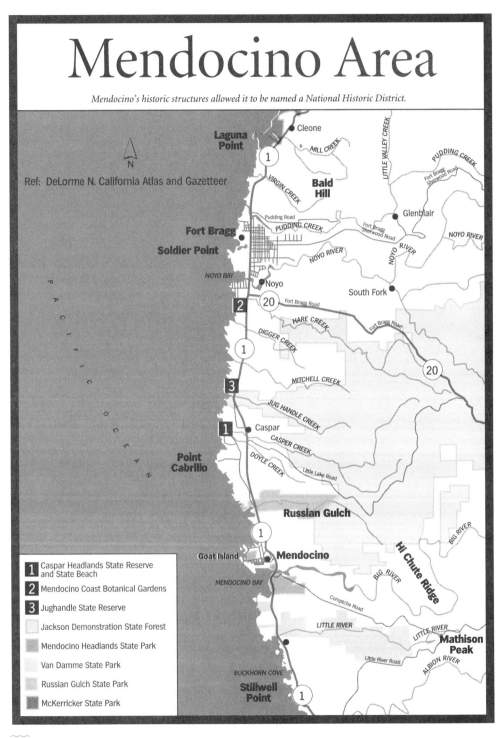

Mendocino Area

Mendocino's historic structures allowed it to be named a National Historic District.

Cleone

MILL CREEK

LITTLE VALLEY CREEK

PUDDING CREEK

Laguna Point

1

Fort Bragg Sherwood Road

N

Ref: DeLorme N. California Atlas and Gazetteer

VIRGIN CREEK

Bald Hill

Glenblair

Pudding Road

PUDDING CREEK

Fort Bragg Sherwood Road

NOYO RIVER

Fort Bragg

Soldier Point

NOYO RIVER

NOYO RIVER

RIVER

NOYO BAY

Noyo

South Fork

P

2

20

Fort Bragg Road

A

1

HARE CREEK

Fort Bragg Road

C

DIGGER CREEK

I

3

MITCHELL CREEK

20

F

JUG HANDLE CREEK

I

1

Caspar

CASPER CREEK

C

DOYLE CREEK

Point Cabrillo

Little Lake Road

O

C

Russian Gulch

BIG RIVER

E

1

Hi Chute Ridge

A

Goat Island

Mendocino

BIG RIVER

N

MENDOCINO BAY

1 Caspar Headlands State Reserve and State Beach

Comptche Road

2 Mendocino Coast Botanical Gardens

LITTLE RIVER

3 Jughandle State Reserve

LITTLE RIVER

Jackson Demonstration State Forest

Mathison Peak

Mendocino Headlands State Park

Little River Road

ALBION RIVER

Van Damme State Park

Russian Gulch State Park

BUCKHORN COVE

McKerricker State Park

Stillwell Point

1

Tidepool Exploring

California's tidepools, especially along the lesser-visited north coast, support a large and diverse group of plants and animals that are readily visible. Most of the animals are protected by fish and game regulations, at least during certain times of the year. But they can be enjoyed during any month of the year by tidepool explorers.

A few words of caution: Winter is generally not a good time for exploring tidepools because of the often dangerous high surf. Even summer can be dangerous when hopping on the sharp and slippery rocks above the cold and surging waters. Be very careful and never turn your back on the ocean.

A most peculiar plant is the sea palm (*Postelsia palmaeformis*), which looks very much like a miniature palm tree clinging tenaciously to the rocks in the surf zone. It's actually an alga that is able to attach itself with holdfasts to the rocks and withstand the constant ebb and flow of the powerful wave action.

Perhaps the most commonly seen animal is a simple creature called the black turban snail (*Tegula funebralis*), so named because of the shape and color of its shell. The biggest are usually no larger than a walnut and are black or deep purple in color. The surprise comes when one of the shells suddenly sprouts longer legs, rather than its normal, boneless snail foot, and scrambles quickly across the bottom of a stranded pool of water during low tide. It is very common for hermit crabs (*Pagurus samuelis*), which aren't true crabs, partly because they have no shell of their own, to take up residence inside an abandoned black turban snail shell.

While giant green anemones (*Anthopleura xanthogrammica*), ochre stars (*Pisaster ochraceous*), often called starfish, and purple urchins (*Strongyloncentrotus purpuratus*) live well in the changing tides by seeking protective hiding places, the odd-looking goose-neck barnacle (*Pollicipes polymerus*) fights off the waves in a different manner. It uses one of the strongest natural glues known to stick itself to the rocks in the mid-to-low tide zones where the wave action is most powerful. As tons of water washes over them, they turn their plate-like, somewhat pointed heads toward the incoming wave, then swivel around to strain plankton and absorb oxygen from the less powerful retreating wave. Goose-neck barnacles often live on rocks among colonies of California mussels (*Mytilus californianus*).

their lack of height, the mountains create vastly different climates within a short distance. On the ocean side there is 60 inches of winter rain and cool, foggy summers. Just 30 miles inland half as much rain falls and thermometers edge toward the century mark in July and August.

By California standards, the Marin coast is not long, stretching from near the center of Bodega Bay to the Golden Gate. While much of the inland and especially the southern portion of the county is developed, nearly all of the coast remains in public ownership, most as part of several parks. Point Reyes National Seashore,

Golden Gate National Recreation Area, and Mount Tamalpais State Park provide coastal access and inland trails, along with many recreational opportunities. As with its neighboring counties to the north, Marin County has a diverse coast line, with high cliffs and long sandy beaches, rich estuaries and protected bays.

Travel across the coastal mountains and into the inland reaches of Mendocino and Sonoma counties, and coastal forests and scrub are replaced by rolling hills of vineyards that grow some of the world's finest wine grapes. Hundreds of wineries turn those crops into millions of bottles of wine each year, with dozens of award-winning vintages being shipped to restaurants and retail outlets around the world.

The vast majority of the Mendocino, Sonoma, and Marin county coastlines remain as wild and rugged as they were 200 years ago. Most of the tiny communities that managed to establish footholds along this stretch of coast were originally logging camps and have seen the boom and bust of the timber industry. Today they depend on tourism and with good reason.

During the nineteenth century, shipwrecks were common along much of California's coast. Jerome B. Ford was with a search party looking for survivors of a China-bound trading ship when he reported the presence of the great redwood forests to Henry Meiggs, the owner of a sawmill at Bodega Bay to the south. Meiggs quickly established another mill on the Mendocino headland, placing Ford in charge. Two years later, in 1854, Ford sailed to Connecticut to marry 23 year-old Martha Hayes, leaving orders that a house be built in his absence for himself and his new wife. When the newly wed couple returned, Martha loved the beautiful views from the house's main and second floors, but disliked the kitchen and dining room. They had been placed in the basement. A remodeling effort was soon underway to correct the design flaw on their new home, which was only the second house that had been constructed in the town of Mendocino.

While the timber industry thrived long after Ford's time, it did begin to slow in the 1950s and 1960s. Fortunately, it was about this same time that artists and others came seeking the solitude and creative inspiration they couldn't find in the big cities. The new arrivals began repairing and caring for many of the old Victorians and other buildings that were strikingly reminiscent of a nineteenth century New England fishing village. Artists' studios, shops, restaurants, B&Bs, and museums slowly began to fill the 100-year-old-buildings along the quaint downtown area, which sits on an ancient coastal terrace above the Pacific Ocean. It's the collection of these historic structures, without the intrusion of modern-day fast food restaurants, chain bookstores, and hotels that has allowed the town of Mendocino to be named a National Preservation District.

The town of Mendocino is only several square blocks that lie on part of a point of land that juts west from Highway 1. West from the clustered shops and homes of Mendocino, the marine terrace merges into **Mendocino Headlands State Park** [Fig. 17]. There are parking areas off Heeser Drive and a trail that meanders around most of the 2 miles of the spectacular coastal bluffs. Paths and a stairway allow access down the steep bluffs to the beach. Be cautious during and after winter storms, when high surf and tides can make the beaches and the trails to them dangerous.

The **Mendocino Headlands State Park Visitor Center** is located in the historic **Ford House,** which is situated on the bluff along Main Street. The historic home overlooks the small but enticing Mendocino Bay. It is managed by state park volunteers and houses exhibits about historic Mendocino, a small bookstore, and art exhibits by local artists.

The **Kelley House Museum,** located at 45007 Albion Street (which is up one block and parallels Main Street), is another historic house that has become a museum. Originally built in 1861, today it houses photos related to the logging and shipping heydays of Mendocino. Its hours of operation can be sporadic. Phone (707) 937-5791.

The **Big River** enters Mendocino Bay and the Pacific Ocean on the south side of town. A wide sand beach is accessible from North Big River Road, which is located on the east side of Highway 1, between the Main Street turn-off into Mendocino and the bridge that crosses the Big River.

Directions: Mendocino is located along Highway 1, about 11 miles south of Fort Bragg.

Activities: Picnicking, fishing, hiking, shopping.

Facilities: The state park offers only a visitor center in town. Mendocino has restuarants, shops, and overnight accommodations, mostly Victorian bed and breakfast inns.

Dates: State park visitor center is open daily.

Fees: None at Mendocino Headlands State Park. The visitor center asks for a donation. There is a small entrance fee at the Kelley House Museum.

Closest town: Fort Bragg, 11 miles north.

For more information: For general information about the town of Mendocino contact the Fort Bragg-Mendocino Coast Chamber of Commerce at 322 N. Main, Fort Bragg, CA 95437. Phone (707) 961-6300. For information about Mendocino Headlands State Park, contact Russian Gulch State Park, Hwy 1, PO Box 440, Mendocino, CA 95460. Phone (707) 937-5804.

MENDOCINO COAST SIDE TRIPS

Driving on Highway 1, along the Mendocino County coast, it is impossible to drive more than a few miles without passing a sign that identifies a public coastal access, and generally those access points are state or regional parks and beaches. The only problem in visiting most of these areas is that it's so easy for planned short visits to inadvertently stretch into an hour or more of pure enjoyment.

Westport-Union Landing State Beach is 19 miles north of Fort Bragg and offers campsites on a bluff above the ocean. This is a popular spot for surf fishing, abalone diving, and spearfishing. Contact Mendocino Coast State Parks. Phone (707) 937-5804.

Caspar Headlands State Reserve and State Beach [Fig. 17(1)] only covers about 6 acres, surrounded by private housing, but it offers an opportunity to enjoy sculpted rocks, eroded fissures, and a sand beach. A permit, available at nearby Russian Gulch State Park (Hwy. 1, Mendocino) is required to enter the area. Contact Mendocino Coast State Parks. Phone (707) 937-5804.

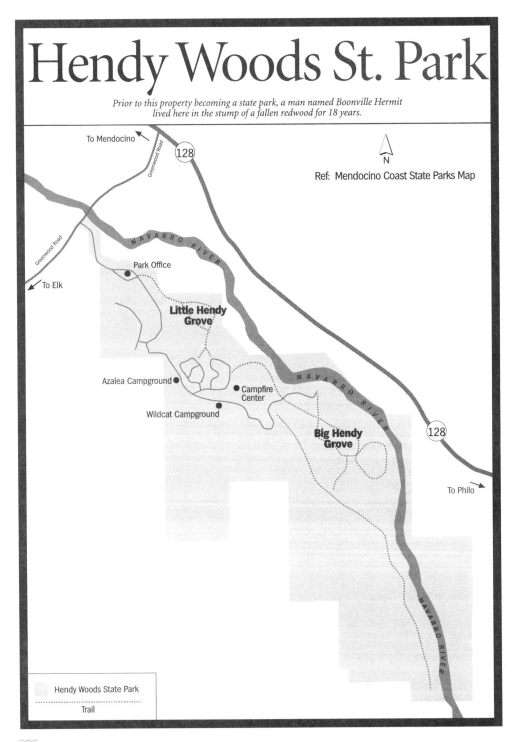

Hendy Woods St. Park

*Prior to this property becoming a state park, a man named Boonville Hermit
lived here in the stump of a fallen redwood for 18 years.*

To Mendocino

Greenwood Road

128

N

Ref: Mendocino Coast State Parks Map

Greenwood Road

To Elk

NAVARRO RIVER

Park Office

Little Hendy Grove

Azalea Campground

Campfire Center

Wildcat Campground

NAVARRO RIVER

Big Hendy Grove

128

To Philo

NAVARRO RIVER

Hendy Woods State Park

Trail

Mendocino Coast Botanical Gardens [Fig. 17(2)] features 3 miles of trails through 47 acres of wonderful gardens filled with hybrid rhododendrons, heathers, fuchsias, dwarf conifers, heritage roses, camellias, and dahlias. The gardens are located 2 miles south of Fort Bragg and 7 miles north of Mendocino at 18220 N. Highway 1. Phone (707) 964-4352.

Van Damme State Park [Fig. 17] is located 3 miles south of Mendocino, off Highway 1, and is one of the most popular abalone diving locations on the north coast. The park is much larger than its coastal frontage, extending inland along the Little River about 4 miles. The park has developed campsites, along with trails that lead to a small bog with unique plants and to a Pygmy forest similar to the one in nearby Jughandle State Reserve. Contact Mendocino Coast State Parks. Phone (707) 937-5804.

Hendy Woods State Park [Fig. 18] is one of those inland redwood parks that is somewhat drier than its coastal neighbors. Prior to the property becoming a state park, a man known as the Boonville Hermit lived here for 18 years in the stump of a fallen redwood. He's now gone. The Navarro River that flows through the park offers good steelhead fishing during the fall run, and swimming, kayaking, and canoeing during the warm summer months. The park is located 8 miles northwest of Boonville and 0.5 mile south of Highway 128, on Philo Greenwood Road. Contact Mendocino Coast State Parks. Phone (707) 937-5804.

Schooner Gulch State Beach [Fig. 20(3)] is a beach and headlands that offers wonderful ocean sunset views and access to beaches for fishing, exploring, surfing, and diving. It's located 3 miles south of Point Arena, where Schooner Gulch Beach crosses Highway 1. Contact Mendocino Coast State Parks. Phone (707) 937-5804.

Gualala River Regional Park [Fig. 20(2)] straddles both sides of Highway 1. The park offers a quiet, forested campground set beside the easy flowing Gualala River on the east side of the highway and on the west side there's a day-use beach where the river empties into the Pacific Ocean. Approaching from the south, the turn-off comes up quickly on the left for the day-use area where picnic tables and a visitor center await. There is another access road to the beach area, located on the north side of the river, just off the west side of Highway 1. The park is located about 14.6 miles south of Point Arena.

WESTERN PINE BEETLE
(Dendroctonus brevicomis)
In 1917 and 1943, this beetle destroyed about 25 billion board feet of ponderosa pine along the Pacific coast, an amount of devastation that is seldom matched by any pest.

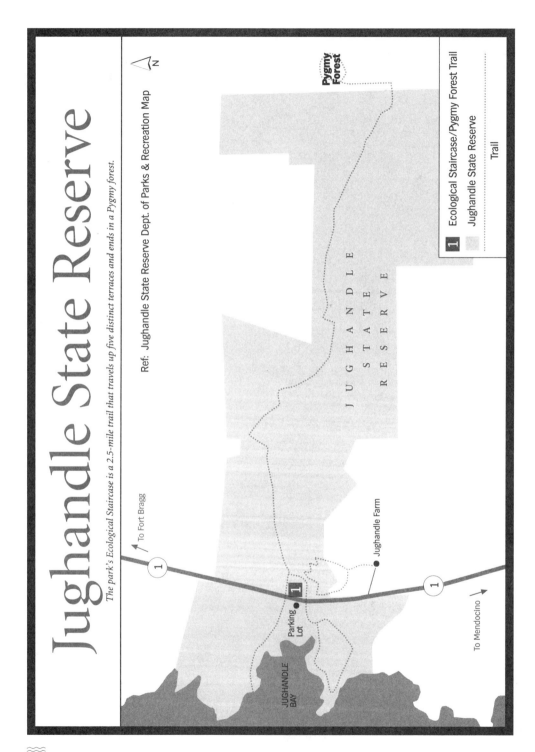

Jughandle State Reserve

The park's Ecological Staircase is a 2.5-mile trail that travels up five distinct terraces and ends in a Pygmy forest.

Ref: Jughandle State Reserve Dept. of Parks & Recreation Map

N

Pygmy Forest

JUGHANDLE STATE RESERVE

To Fort Bragg

1

Parking Lot

1

Jughandle Farm

1

To Mendocino

JUGHANDLE BAY

1 Ecological Staircase/Pygmy Forest Trail

Jughandle State Reserve

Trail

JUGHANDLE STATE RESERVE

[Fig. 17(3), Fig. 19] When most people pull off Highway 1 and into the small parking lot located about halfway between Mendocino and Fort Bragg, their intent is most often to take the short walk out to Caspar Point and view the craggy cliffs and pounding surf. During winter this is a great place to watch for gray whales spouting as they pass near just offshore. Visitors are often surprised by the small, secluded beach that is tucked into those same cliffs at the mouth of Jughandle Creek. But the real treat here is the trail that ducks back under the highway bridge and heads up the forested hillsides to the east.

One of the most prominent, yet unrecognized geological features along much of California's coast is the terracing that has taken place over the past 500,000 years. The combination of a rising land mass, forced upward by the collision of the Pacific and North American plates, and the changing ocean level, caused by the combination of warming temperatures and melting ice caps, has created coastal shelves that are quite obvious in some places, especially once they are pointed out. Jughandle State Reserve is one of those places where the terraces are easily identified, in spite of the covering forest and tens of thousands of years of erosion and change.

The park's **Ecological Staircase** [Fig. 19(1)] is a 2.5-mile trail (5 miles round-trip) that heads out from the parking lot, travels up five distinct terraces, which you'll feel as you hike, stopping finally at what is termed a Pygmy forest because of the severely stunted trees that fight to survive in the poor, thin soils. Approximately 150 feet in height and 100,000 years separate the tops of each of the terraces.

As the trail leads from the bottom of the canyon of Jughandle Creek it passes through thick walls of willows (*Salix* sp.), alders (*Alnus* sp.), thimbleberry (*Rubus parviflorus*), blackberry (*Rubus ursinus*), bracken fern (*Pteridium aquilinum*), and the unsuspecting hiker's nemesis, stinging nettles (*Urtica dioica*). Approaching the first terrace, the riparian habitat changes to bishop pine (*Pinus muricata*) and Monterey pine (*Pinus radiata*), which was introduced here from its native central California habitat.

Hiking between some of the terraces, many of the changes that the pioneer farmers made are difficult to identify, as nature has slowly reclaimed the cleared, tilled, and grazed land. By the second terrace, grand fir, sitka spruce (*Picea sitchensis*), and western hemlock (*Tsuga heterophylla*) have added their presence to the growing collection of conifers. This terrace is also a good place to begin noticing the soil. The grayish podsol, Russian for "ash soil," has been leached of all its alkaline nutrients, making it highly acidic.

Still higher up the hillside, Douglas fir (*Pseudotsugo menziesii*) and redwoods begin to be seen in growing numbers and many of the shrubs, such as rhododendron (*Rhododendron macrophyllum*) and tanoak (*Lithocarpus densiflora*), begin to appear. But what most people hike this trail for is the Pygmy forest, which lies just ahead. As the soil becomes poorer, the final stage of podsolization occurs when the leached acids mix with quartz below the surface and form into an impervious hardpan. The result is that plants are severely stunted because their roots are unable to reach the nutrients and water they need.

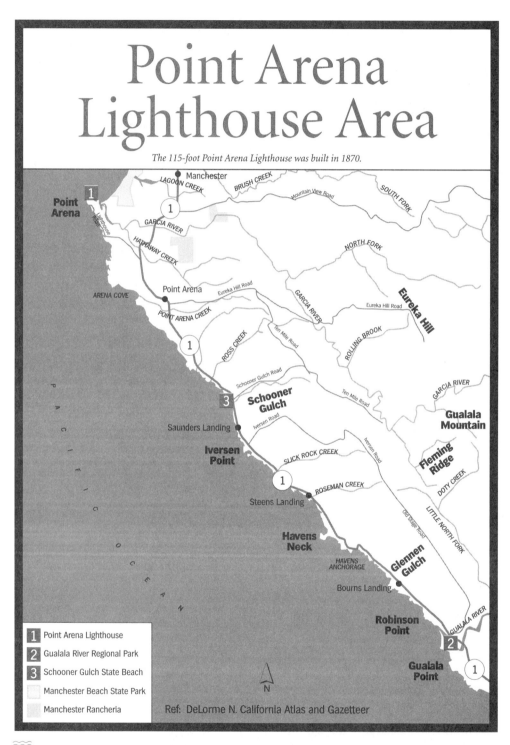

Point Arena Lighthouse Area

The 115-foot Point Arena Lighthouse was built in 1870.

Manchester

LAGOON CREEK

BRUSH CREEK

Mountain View Road

SOUTH FORK

Point Arena

Lighthouse Road

1

GARCIA RIVER

HATHAWAY CREEK

NORTH FORK

Point Arena

Eureka Hill Road

GARCIA RIVER

Eureka Hill Road

Eureka Hill

ARENA COVE

POINT ARENA CREEK

1

ROSS CREEK

Ten Mile Road

ROLLING BROOK

GARCIA RIVER

Schooner Gulch Road

3

Schooner Gulch

Ten Mile Road

Gualala Mountain

Saunders Landing

Iversen Road

Iversen Point

SLICK ROCK CREEK

Iversen Road

Fleming Ridge

DOTY CREEK

1

ROSEMAN CREEK

LITTLE NORTH FORK

Steens Landing

Old Stage Road

Havens Neck

HAVENS ANCHORAGE

Glennen Gulch

Bourns Landing

GUALALA RIVER

Robinson Point

2

P A C I F I C   O C E A N

Gualala Point

1

1 Point Arena Lighthouse
2 Gualala River Regional Park
3 Schooner Gulch State Beach
☐ Manchester Beach State Park
☐ Manchester Rancheria

N

Ref: DeLorme N. California Atlas and Gazetteer

On the upper terrace, the State Reserve merges with the Jackson State Forest. The trail first connects with a wider road that quickly crosses another road serving as a fire break. Perhaps 100 yards past the "fire break" road, there is a boardwalk trail that cuts into the Pygmy forest on the right. The boardwalk, along with interpretive panels, leads through a portion of the trees in a short loop trail. It's the perfect way to see these Bolander pines (*Pinus bolanderi* ssp.) and rare pygmy cypresses that may be 50 years old, but are only from 2- to 5-feet tall.

There is no other trail back to the parking lot, but the return hike provides a perfect opportunity to see some of the park's wildlife, such as yellow-bellied sapsuckers, and if it's been raining much, an incredible assortment of mushrooms can sprout, seemingly overnight.

Directions: The park is located just off Highway 1, about 6 miles south of Fort Bragg.

Activities: Hiking, bird watching, whale watching, fishing.

Facilities: None.

Dates: Open daily.

Fees: None.

Closest town: Fort Bragg, 6 miles north.

For more information: Mendocino Coast State Parks, Hwy. 1, PO Box 440, Mendocino, CA 95460. Phone (707) 937-5804.

FORT BRAGG

[Fig. 17] Elegant Victorian homes and early twentieth century Craftsmen style buildings can easily recreate images of the old days. But in the old days, Fort Bragg went through many changes, not the least of which was complete destruction when the earthquake that destroyed most of San Francisco in 1906 did essentially the same in Fort Bragg.

The Pomo Indians had inhabited this land of ocean and redwoods for thousands of years by the time the United States acquired California in 1846. Four years later American maritime traders discovered this area's potentially profitable redwood forests when *The Frolic* crashed on the coastal rocks and scavengers came to salvage what they could. The Bureau of Indian Affairs soon arrived, and their goal was to place the Pomo Indians on a 25,000-acre reservation. In spite of the bureau's efforts, the Indians remained hostile to the American intruders. The army was brought in the following year to establish a fort that was designed to help subdue the Indians and ensure peace in the area.

After the fort was abandoned in 1864, the growing community depended upon logging redwoods to provide for their support. The many small lumber companies that formed during those early years were soon dwarfed when C.R. Johnson founded the Redwood Lumber Company in 1885. Fighting back, in 1891, many of the smaller mills joined forces, forming the Union Lumber Company.

Johnson was elected the first mayor of Fort Bragg when the city was incorporated in 1889. Its name honored Colonel Braxton Bragg, the man whose name was also later given to Fort Bragg, North Carolina. San Francisco's 1906 earthquake destroyed

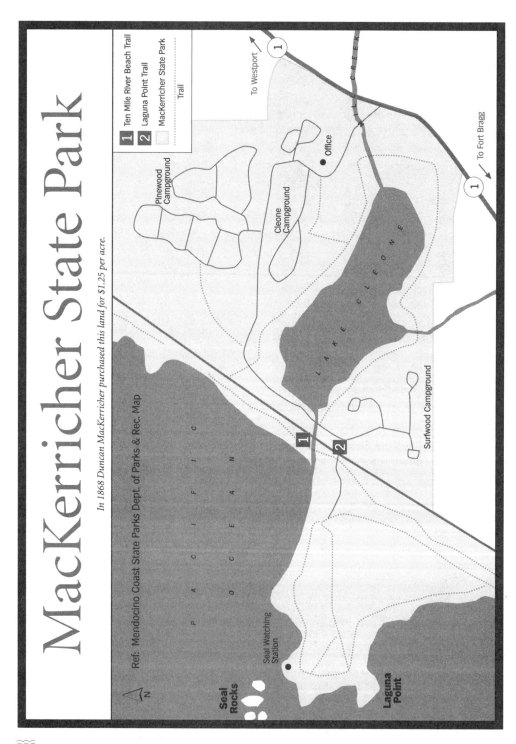

MacKerricher State Park

In 1868 Duncan MacKerricher purchased this land for $1.25 per acre.

Ref: Mendocino Coast State Parks Dept. of Parks & Rec. Map

Legend
1 — Ten Mile River Beach Trail
2 — Laguna Point Trail
— MacKerricher State Park
······· Trail

To Westport

To Fort Bragg

Office

Pinewood Campground

Cleone Campground

LAKE CLEONE

Surfwood Campground

PACIFIC OCEAN

Seal Rocks

Seal Watching Station

Laguna Point

N

most of the town's buildings, but the mills were soon producing the thousands of board feet of lumber needed to rebuild itself and San Francisco.

Guest House Museum is located on Main Street (Highway 1), between Redwood and Laurel streets, and offers a glimpse into Fort Bragg's logging history. C.R. Johnson had the Victorian constructed as his home in 1892. Union Lumber Company acquired the property, and in 1912, used it as a guesthouse for friends and customers. Georgia Pacific, another large lumber company, purchased the house in 1973 and donated it to the city in 1986.

Fort Building is a small structure just north of City Hall, located on Franklin, between Pine and Laurel streets. It is significant because it is the last remaining vestige of the original Fort Bragg. Originally, it was the fort's quartermaster, storehouse, and commissary. Today it's a small museum, with photos, an old cannon, and a model of the original fort.

Noyo River and Harbor crosses under Highway 1, near the south end of Fort Bragg. Although tiny when compared with San Francisco, or even with many of California's other smaller port towns, it is extremely busy. Fort Bragg's commercial and sport fishing operations keep boats active on a regular basis, and with its marina and boat ramp, a large number of anglers launch their own boats at the well-protected harbor.

The Wharf Restaurant (phone 707-964-4283), located in Noyo Harbor and overlooking the river, is always popular with its good food and great views.

The **Skunk Train**, in spite of its name, draws thousands of people each year for the train ride from the coast to the valley. The train passes through redwood forests and over open meadows, offering a relaxing and different way to enjoy the coastal mountains. California Western Railroad, Inc. operates the several locomotives, including steam-powered locomotives, more modern diesel-electric locomotives, and several real "skunks," which are quite rare gasoline motorcars. Equipment and schedules vary, so contact either the Fort Bragg Depot (phone 707-964-6371) or the Willits Depot (phone 707-459-5248) for additional information about the varying schedules, prices, and types of equipment running.

Several sport-fishing boats and charter companies call Fort Bragg their home port, including the *Patty-C* (phone 707-964-0669) and Anchor Charters (phone 707-964-4550 or 707-964-3854).

Directions: Fort Bragg is located about 6 miles north of Mendocino and about 180 miles north of San Francisco, on Highway 1.

Activities: Fishing, shopping, whale watching.

For more information: Fort Bragg-Mendocino Coast Chamber of Commerce, 332 North Main Street, Fort Bragg, CA 95437. Phone (707) 961-6300 or (800) 726-2780.

MACKERRICHER STATE PARK

[Fig. 21] The park's main entrance is quite intriguing. Near the entrance kiosk and a small visitor center and store, there is a skeleton of a moderately sized gray whale pieced together. Inside the visitor center, several additional skeletons, including those of a sea otter and a sea lion, hang from the ceiling.

It is Scottish immigrant Duncan MacKerricher whose name is attached to the park. In 1868 he purchased what had been an Indian reservation for $1.25 per acre. MacKerricher and his heirs worked the former *El Rancho de la Laguna* until 1949, when it became a state park. Over the years, most of the area was heavily logged, especially the north end of the ranch, near Ten Mile River. The remnants of an old railway that transported logs from Ten Mile River to the Union Lumber Company in Fort Bragg still remain. Today, a road passes between the ocean and Lake Cleone, once a tidal lagoon that was cutoff from the ocean waters. The far north end of the park, which is about 5 miles from Lake Cleone, includes a long stretch of dunes.

Directions: The park is located on the west side of Highway 1, about 3 miles north of Fort Bragg.

Activities: Camping, fishing, hiking, picnicking, bird-watching, beach and tidepool exploration, and coastal whale watching.

Facilities: Visitor center with small gift shop, campground, day-use facilities.

Dates: Open daily.

Fees: Camping fee.

Closest town: Fort Bragg, 3 miles north.

For more information: Russian River/Mendocino State Parks, PO Box 123, CA 95430. Phone (707) 865-2391 or (707) 937-5804.

BELTED KINGFISHER
(*Megaceryle alcyon*)

TRAILS

Ten Mile River Beach Trail: [Fig. 21(1)] The 10-mile round-trip hike along Ten Mile Beach follows an old logging road part of the way. Ten Mile River got its name not because it's a 10-mile round-trip hike from Lake Cleone, but because it's located 10 miles south of the Noyo River in Fort Bragg.

The trail passes dunes and two wet, marshy areas, Sand Hill Lake and Inglenook Fen, that are off limits to all but researchers. They support such rare and intriguing plants as marsh pennywort (*Hydrocotyle verticillata*) and bog orchid (*Platanthera leucostachys*). The trail heads inland as it approaches the marshy mouth of Ten Mile River. There is an opportunity to see other wildflowers such as columbine (*Aquilegia* sp.) and larkspur (*Delphinium* sp.), and to watch belted kingfishers (*Megaceryle alcyon*) dive into the calm river waters and come out with small minnows.

Laguna Point Trail: [Fig. 21(2)] The trail begins just past Lake Cleone on a coastal terrace, 20 to 30 feet above the ocean and the narrow strip of beach and rocky shoreline. The 0.3-mile boardwalk trail is located at the northwest corner of the parking lot that is located a short distance past the lake. The level boardwalk trail leads through the woods and along the coast to Laguna Point, where there is a great view of the rocky coast.

POINT ARENA LIGHTHOUSE

[Fig. 20(1)] The lighthouse was built in 1870, and its 2-ton Fresnel lens was a powerful beacon of safety along the rugged north coast. Now, the old, hand-polished lens that served as a vital aid to navigation for the hundreds of ships that plied the coastal waters has been replaced by an electronic beacon maintained by the U.S. Coast Guard. While it may not be as romantic, the electronic beacon is certainly more dependable, at least in the absence of the dedicated, on-site lighthouse keepers.

The 115-foot tower sits near the end of a long and narrow point of ancient coastal terrace that someday will lose its battle against the crashing waves. The drive out to the lighthouse from Highway 1 takes only a few minutes as the two-lane country road leads out across the open cattle country. Visitors must park outside the gate to the complex and walk the 0.5 mile to the lighthouse. Docents offer tours of the lighthouse and fog signal room.

Three of the former lighthouse keeper houses on the grounds are available as vacation rentals throughout the year, but reservations are required.

Directions: From Highway 1, about 2 miles north of the town of Point Arena, take Lighthouse Road to its end, approximately 2 miles.

Activities: Sight-seeing.

Facilities: Museum, vacation rental historic houses.

Dates: Open daily, with seasonal changes in hours.

Fees: There is a fee for tours.

Closest town: Point Arena, 4 miles.

For more information: Point Arena Lighthouse, phone (707) 882-2777.

COLUMBINE
(*Aquilegia* sp.)

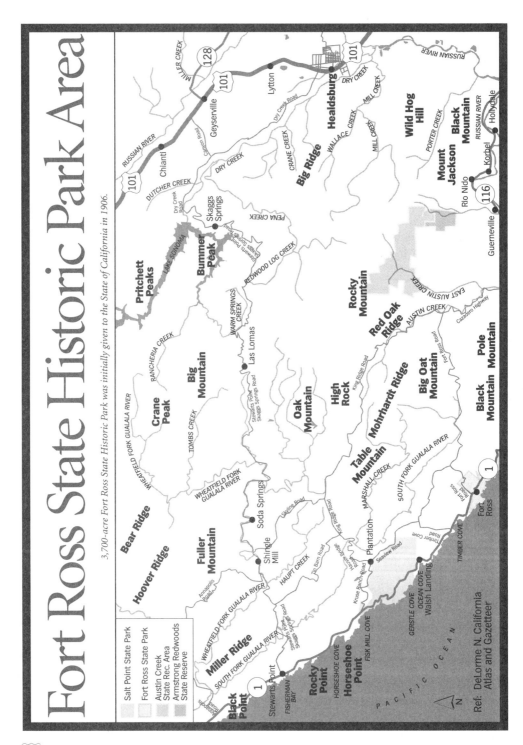

Fort Ross State Historic Park Area

3,700-acre Fort Ross State Historic Park was initially given to the State of California in 1906.

Sonoma County

SALT POINT STATE PARK

[Fig. 22] The park offers a little something for just about everyone. Vegetation ranges from coastal scrub on some of the more open hillsides to forests of Bishop pine (*Pinus muricata*), Douglas fir, and second-growth redwoods, with scatterings of tanoak (*Lithocarpus densiflora*) and madrone (*Arbutus menziesii*). Hike up the mountain above the coast and there's a Pygmy forest where stunted versions of redwoods, cypress, and Bishop pine grow slowly in the nutrient-depleted hardpan soil.

The park's coastal bluffs and isolated beaches provide great fishing and diving. One of the most popular scuba diving spots is Gerstle Cove, a portion of which is an underwater reserve. Within the reserve's boundaries, divers and fishermen aren't allowed to take or disturb any of the animal or plant life. But outside the underwater reserve, surf fishing and underwater spearfishing is allowed, within the bounds of fish and game regulations. During the relatively short season, the parking lot near Gerstle Cove, as well as some of the other coastal access points in the park, serve as staging areas for abalone divers.

Highway 1 runs between the coast and the higher ridgeline of the park, and there is a campground on each side. The developed portions of the park, where the campgrounds and day-use picnic areas are located, are centered near the southern end of the park. From the campgrounds, several trails meander through the park, with the most popular hike leading through the prairie to the Pygmy forest. The hike is about 2 miles long, depending on the starting point.

Directions: The park is located about 18 miles north of Jenner, on Highway 1.

Activities: Camping, hiking, scuba diving, picnicking, and fishing.

Facilities: Campground and picnic area.

Dates: Open daily.

Fees: There are camping and day-use fees. Camping reservations are recommended for summer camping. Phone (800) 444-7275.

Closest town: Jenner, 18 miles north.

For more information: Salt Point State Park, 25050 Coast Highway 1, Jenner, CA 95450 Phone (707) 847-3286 or (707) 865-2391.

FORT ROSS STATE HISTORIC PARK

[Fig. 22] The Spanish discovered that attempting to keep other countries from intruding into lands in the New World that they had claimed for themselves was not an easy task. As early as the mid-eighteenth century, Russian trappers had been following seal and sea otter populations down the West Coast from Alaska. Spain countered by pushing its mission settlements farther north into Alta, or northern

California. Unfortunately, Spain never settled much farther north than San Francisco, and in numbers so small so as not to make any difference. Thus, it probably wasn't much of a surprise when California's Spanish government discovered that in March, 1812, a large group of Russians and their Alaskan laborers had landed just north of the Russian River and had begun building a very substantial wooden fort.

One of the Russians' first forays into this part of California's coast resulted in their returning to Mother Russia with over 1,000 sea otter pelts. They soon returned with intentions of staying and farming the land, in addition to hunting sea otters. After the Russians established their permanent settlement, within a short eight years they had hunted the sea otters to near extinction. Although the Russians desired to trade both pelts and agricultural products with the Spanish settlements to the south, Spain remained nervous about her Russian neighbors as well as the American ships also sailing California's coastal waters. Once the sea otters were gone, the Russian settlement began to fail. Agriculture was not particularly successful on the cold and foggy north coast.

Anxious to leave, in 1841 the Russians finally found an interested buyer named John Sutter, an immigrant who already had established Sutter's Fort in what would become Sacramento. Sutter's only real interest was in obtaining the livestock and supplies the Russians were leaving behind. The fort and surrounding land was largely abandoned until George Call acquired it as part of his 15,000 acre ranch in 1873. He used the somewhat sheltered anchorage below the coastal fort as a loading area for timber harvested from his land. The fort and its 3-acre site were given to the State of California in 1906, and since that time over 3, 270 acres have been added. Significant restoration work has been completed on the fort.

A museum and visitor center acts as the entrance to the fort. Exhibits range from Native Americans to the Russian presence in the area. Through the back door of the visitor center there is a short trail that leads to the fort, passing a vegetable garden along the way. The fort's stout vertical timbers are impressive, even today, as are the cannon muzzles that point out of the gun ports in the corner towers or blockhouses. The interior of the fort is largely open, with only four buildings, in addition to the two corner towers. They include the chapel, reconstructed after the first chapel burned, the manager's house, the officials' quarters, and the Russian employee barracks. There is another short trail that provides access to the small beach at the base of the bluff below the fort.

For hikers who like to wander, most of Fort Ross State Historic Park's 3,700 acres are located on the east side of Highway 1, which bisects the park. It consists of open meadows and redwood forests. Since there are no established trails, the area is open to wandering, mostly uphill. The mountains on the east side of Highway 1 rise to 1,400 feet above sea level. Since the Russians were the first people in California to do extensive logging of redwoods, the park has California's oldest second-growth redwood trees.

Directions: The park is located about 11 miles north of the town of Jenner and the mouth of the Russian River, just off Highway 1.

Activities: Hiking, beach exploration, whale watching from shore.

Facilities: Visitor center, small gift shop.

Dates: Open daily, except Thanksgiving, Christmas, and New Year's Day.

Fees: There is a day-use and museum fee.

Closest town: Jenner, 11 miles north.

For more information: Fort Ross State Historic Park, 19005 Coast Highway, Jenner, CA 95450. Phone (707) 847-3286.

JENNER

[Fig. 23] Tucked into the hillside above the Russian River, Jenner is a good place to stop along Highway 1 and view wildlife, mostly birds, but occasionally harbor seals (*Phoca vitulina*). Near the middle of the small, coastal community, a state park visitor center juts out into the edge of the river. Even if the center is closed, it has interpretive panels outside that tell a little about the natural history of the area. At the north end of Jenner, there's a parking area on the ocean side of Highway 1, soon after the road begins to climb and head north out of town. This promontory provides a panoramic view of the Russian River's mouth and the Pacific Ocean.

The town was originally known as Jenner Gulch and was settled primarily by workers from the nearby lumber mills. During the mid-nineteenth century a ferry operated across the Russian River. It ran until the early twentieth century, transporting passenger vehicles between the ends of the coast highway that stopped on either side of the river.

The river's mouth, like many of California coastal rivers, does not always flow into the ocean. During the summer months, large sand accumulations can block or severely restrict the river's ability to reach the Pacific. Winter storms generally change

BEAVER
(*Castor canadensis*)

Jenner Area

Jenner, originally known as Jenner Gulch, was primarily settled by workers from nearby lumber mills.

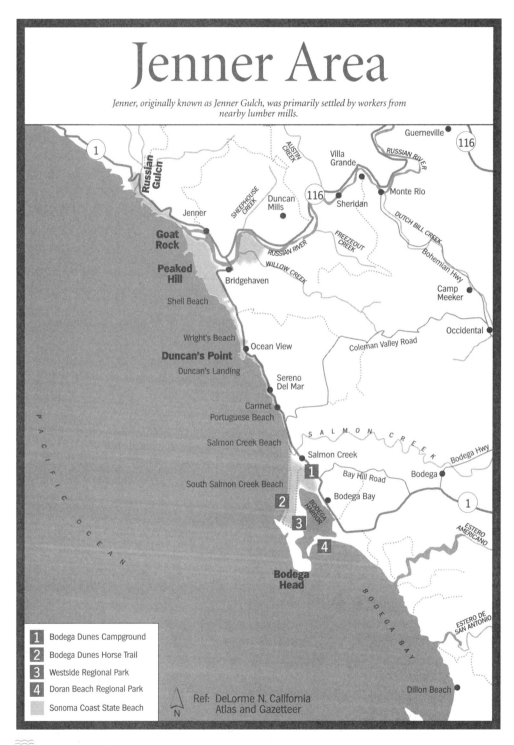

Bodega Dunes Campground

Bodega Dunes Horse Trail

Westside Regional Park

Doran Beach Regional Park

Sonoma Coast State Beach

Ref: DeLorme N. California
Atlas and Gazetteer

N

that. High, crashing waves and significant increases in river runoff tend to scour out its mouth. During spring and early summer this promontory is a great place to view harbor seals and their newly born pups that bask on the sandy beach and frolic in the water near the river's mouth.

This portion of the California coast is also free of the San Andreas fault, which lies offshore. The coast between Bodega Bay to the south and Fort Ross to the north is made up of nearly all Franciscan rocks, the result of the scraping off of the ocean's surface at the subduction zone. The relatively rare blueschist is found combined with serpentinites in road cuts south of Jenner. Blueschist is one of those rocks found only in subduction zones. It is created under high pressure, but at relatively cool temperatures, being expelled upward before its temperature can be raised to that of the adjoining minerals and its content metamorphosed into a different form.

SONOMA COAST STATE BEACH

[Fig. 23] While this stretch of Sonoma County's coastline is referred to as a single state beach, it's actually 16 miles of secluded, sandy beaches, dunes, rocky headlands, and natural bridges carved from ancient headlands. The public beach begins 2.5 miles north of Jenner at the mouth of the Russian River at **Russian Gulch**, a small creek. There's a parking lot and a trail to the large beach area.

This entire stretch of coast is a great place to watch for migrating gray whales during winter and for several different species of gulls during the changing seasons of the year. Telling the difference between what most people simply call "sea gulls" can be challenging, even for experts. Gulls go through several color variations during the first few years of their lives, making immature birds especially difficult to identify. Heermann's gull (*Larus heermanni*), California gull (*Larus californicus*), ring billed gull (*Larus delawarensis*), and the western gull (*Larus occidentalis*) are the most commonly seen. Equally easy to view, but much easier to identify are some of the other birds such as Pelagic cormorants (*Phalacrocorax pelagicus*), and western grebes (*Aechmophorus occidentalis*) which are often seen swimming in the waters just offshore. Common during summer is the brown pelican (*Pelecanus occidentalis*), a large, graceful flier that once teetered on the brink of extinction due primarily to the use of the insecticide DDT.

Goat Rock is a very prominent and popular stop for travelers along Highway 1, as well as for locals who like to fish along the beaches in the area. Rather than hiking down long and steep trails from the Highway, there's a road that winds down to beach level from Highway 1, about 0.75 miles south of the Russian River bridge. The miniature peninsula has a parking area and restroom.

Be cautious about getting too close to the ocean when hiking along the beach, especially during winter. The beach is fairly steep, and sleeper waves are relatively common. Every year these large, periodic, and completely unpredictable waves sweep people from areas they thought were safe into the cold Pacific waters.

Duncan's Landing is 1.5 miles north of Bodega Bay, just off Highway 1. It once served as a loading point for ships picking up lumber and other products produced along this area of the coast. Today it provides a great show during times of high waves, when the surf can actually crash up over the roadway that circles the area. And that makes getting too close to the lower cliffs very dangerous. During spring and early summer, the open coastal terrace is alive with wildflowers that contrast beautifully with the blue Pacific in the background.

Wright's Beach is probably the most popular part of Sonoma State Beach, primarily because of the 30-site campground that is situated on the beach, at the base of the coastal bluff. A thick hedgerow of shrubbery around the campsites acts as a partial barrier against the ever-present winds that come off the water and can be quite cold most of the year, even during summer. The wide beach is a great place for exploring, fishing, or simply watching sunsets.

Bodega Dunes Campground [Fig. 23(1)] is much more protected from ocean winds, although the summer fog that is common along all of California's coast can still make tents and anything else left in the open very wet. Bodega Dunes has the advantage over Wright's Beach in offering both open coastline, where the Pacific's pounding surf can be experienced, and the more protected waters and tidal flats of Bodega Bay. Although the campground doesn't actually bound the bay, it's a short walk out the back of the campground and across Bay Flat Road to the water's edge.

Bodega Head lies at the end of Bay Flat Road and overlooks the entrance into Bodega Harbor. At the parking area there are several short trails that lead along the rocky bluff. It is often windy and cold on the exposed bluff, so dress adequately. There are a few steep trails that lead down to sand and gravel beaches at the water's edge along the head. Take Bay Flat Road from Highway 1, past Bodega Bay's harbor.

Bodega Dunes Horse Trail [Fig. 23(2)] has its staging area just off Bay Flat Road, behind the Bodega Dunes Campground. Horses are allowed on the beach, for a total of about 5 miles of accessible trail. It's best to check at the Salmon Creek headquarters (1.25 miles north of Bodega Bay on Highway 1), for specific rules regarding restricted areas.

Directions: Sonoma Coast State Beach stretches from Bodega Bay, north along Highway 1 to just north of the Russian River.

Activities: Hiking, fishing, beachcombing, horseback riding, camping.

Facilities: Two family campgrounds, Wright's Beach and Bodega Dunes.

Dates: Open year-round. From May through Sept., advance reservations are almost always required. Phone (800) 444-7275.

Fees: Moderate camping fees. Most day-use areas are free, with the exception of Wright's Beach and Bodega Dunes, which charge day-use fees.

Closest town: Bodega Bay on the south and Jenner on the north end of the park.

For more information: Russian River/Mendocino State Parks, PO Box 123 Duncans Mills, CA 95430. Phone (707) 865-2391 or Sonoma Coast State Beach, phone (707) 875-3483.

BODEGA BAY

[Fig. 23] While the Miwok and Pomo Indians were the first to settle this part of California's coast, the town of Bay was founded by Firmin Candelot in the late 1800s. The name wasn't expanded to Bodega Bay until 1941. In 1843, Captain Stephen Smith claimed much of the surrounding land, naming it Rancho Bodega, probably after Lt. Juan Francisco de la Bodega y Quadra who had sailed his ship *Sonoma* into the south end of the bay in 1775. Smith constructed the first steam-powered sawmill in California and the bay served him well as a port for shipping his lumber products to distant markets.

Historic Bodega

People old enough to remember Alfred Hitchcock and his film *The Birds* still come to the nearby inland community of Bodega to see the old Potter School House and St. Theresa's Church, where part of the filming was done. Bodega is located 5 miles southeast of Bodega Bay along Highway 1, then approximately 1 mile east on the Bodega Highway.

Even today, Bodega Bay remains relatively undeveloped along much of its shoreline to which Highway 1 clings. A few old houses, some dilapidated fishing piers, and falling-down buildings long past their prime, especially along the southern portion of the bay, are the most visually intriguing. There are a few newer structures and they begin to increase in numbers and concentrations as Highway 1 continues north toward the harbor area.

Bodega Bay Harbor, with its small, picturesque community on its northeastern shore, has the largest and busiest harbor between San Francisco and Fort Bragg to the north. The community offers numerous hotels and restaurants and there are plenty of opportunities to try your hand at fishing. Besides the state campground at its north end, the bay is surrounded by mostly regional or county parklands including **Westside Regional Park** (phone 707-875-3540) [Fig. 23(3)] and **Doran Beach Regional Park** (phone 707-875-3540) [Fig. 23(4)], which lies at the end of the long spit marking the south shoreline of Bodega Harbor. There are numerous private facilities surrounding the harbor, including boat launching areas and ocean sport fishing opportunities such as with **Wil's Fishing Adventure** (phone 707-875-2323) or **The Boathouse** (phone 707-875-3495). The fishing trips can be especially productive, and depending upon the season, can bring in salmon, halibut, rockcod, lingcod, albacore, and even Dungeness crab.

For a change of pace in overnight accommodations, the **Chanslor Guest Ranch & Stables** (phone 707-875-9008) in Bodega Bay offers comfortable rooms with mountain and ocean views, along with horseback rides through the hills and along the beach. There's a special ride into a wetlands preserve that is easy enough for younger children (about age 8) and offers a close look at a different habitat.

Directions: Bodega Bay is located along Highway 1, about 70 miles north of San Francisco.

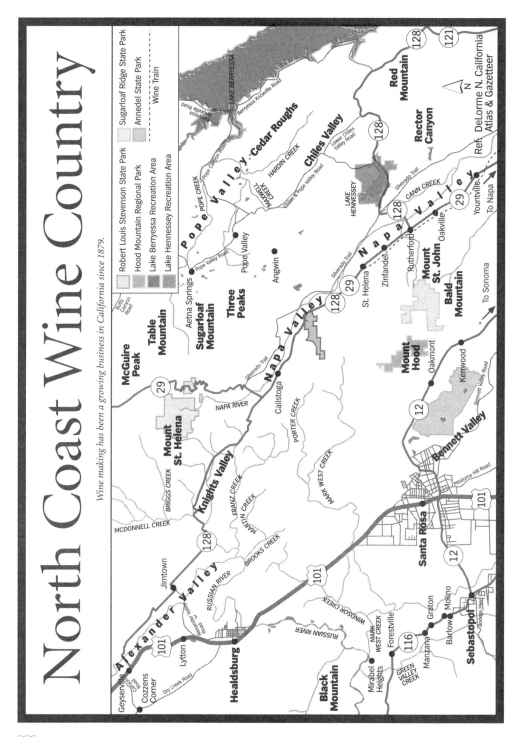

North Coast Wine Country

Wine making has been a growing business in California since 1879.

Activities: Hiking, fishing, horseback riding, beachcombing, camping.

Facilities: Hotels, grocery stores, restaurants, fishing and boating supplies, campgrounds.

For more information: Sonoma Coast Visitors Center, 575 Coast Highway 1, Bodega Bay, CA 94923. Phone (707) 875-3422.

NORTH COAST WINE COUNTRY

[Fig. 24] Within a relatively small area of California, three counties, Napa, Sonoma, and Mendocino, produce most of the state's best-known and award-winning wines. Wine making has been a growing business since it began well over 100 years ago. Louis Finne established Mendocino County's first winery in 1879, near today's town of Hopland. Europeans who originally came for the Gold Rush settled in the coastal mountains and valleys and many planted grapes to remind them of their homelands.

The growers built their own wineries and produced jug or bulk wines. Today, California's wine industry has matured significantly, with hundreds of wineries and thousands of acres devoted to vineyards. Each year, the number of acres planted in grapes continues to grow, while new wineries, many of them small, family-owned businesses, add to California's reputation for producing great wines at affordable prices.

If you're traveling on Highway 1 along the coast and get the urge to do a little wine tasting, a good way into prime wine-making country is Highway 116, where it connects with Highway 1 near the mouth of the Russian River. This is one of a handful of roads that leads from Highway 1, crossing eastward over the coastal mountains and ultimately connecting with US 101. As an added bonus, parts of Highway 116 also follow the wanderings of the Russian River. As the road heads east, it passes through several different valleys, each having its own microclimate and soil type that provides optimum growing conditions for different grapes.

The Russian River valley is a cooler growing area where chardonnay and pinot noir wines are produced. It's also where more *methode champenoise*, or sparkling wine, is produced than anywhere else in California. Dry Creek Valley is best known for its zinfandel and petite sirah, while its neighboring Alexander Valley produces grapes that are transformed into just about

WESTERN
TANAGER
(*Prianga
ludoviciana*)

everything, including chardonnay, sauvignon blanc, cabernet sauvignon, merlot, and zinfandel.

All this is good news for wine aficionados, because there are plenty of opportunities for tasting the wonderful products of California's master wine makers. Simply pick a town and nearby you're likely to find several wineries, some of which offer tours, or, at the very least, tasting rooms. Also note many of the wineries have begun charging small fees for their wine tastings, while others still offer tastings of some of their wines without charge to visitors.

There are three primary ways to enjoy touring the wine country, and each has its advantages. The most popular is by private car. Most people choose a specific area of the wine country, such as near the towns of Napa or Sonoma, and drive from winery to winery, or from tasting room to tasting room, which are often only a few hundred yards apart. Just be aware of how much you're drinking, or better yet, appoint a designated driver. The roads can get extremely crowded on busy summer weekends.

Another always popular approach is to bicycle through the wine country. It's best that you choose the flatter routes, rather than getting into the coastal hills, which can get very steep. One route you might try is the 18 miles one-way along Highway 29, between Napa, Yountville, and St. Helena. You'll pass nearly 25 wineries or tasting rooms, which will offer plenty of opportunities to find excuses for riding only part of the distance.

That particular route is also taken by the famed and very popular **Napa Valley Wine Train** (phone 707-253-2111 or 800-427-4124). Samuel Brannan, a man who made his first fortune in California's gold fields, started the original railroad in 1864. Southern Pacific Railroad Company purchased it in 1885, and then, 102 years later, sold it to the owner of today's Napa Valley Wine Train, Inc. Many of its Pullman carriages are from the early twentieth century and have been lavishly restored. The train runs several times each day, serving brunch, lunch, and dinner. Men are requested to wear jackets for dinner. The trips cost from about $30 to around $100, the highest price being for the monthly Murder Mystery Dinner Theatre. The train station is located in downtown Napa at 1275 McKinstry Street.

The small town of Geyserville, just off US 101, is home to the hugely popular **Chateau Souverain**, which has a tasting room and a café. Other well known wine producers in the area are **Geyser Peak** (phone 707-939-6277), which was founded in 1880 and is located at 14301 Arnold Drive, and **J. Pedroncelli Vineyards** (phone 707-857-3531), located at 1220 Canyon Road. Both are open daily.

Simi Winery is one of many special places to visit. The winery, started by two Italian brothers in 1876, is now owned by Moet-Hennessy and Louis Vuitton. It produces primarily Bordeaux varietals and chardonnay. Wine tasting and tours are offered daily. It's located at 16275 Healdsburg Avenue, Healdsburg. Phone (707) 433-6981.

For sauvignon blanc-lovers, **Canyon Road Winery** (phone 707-857-3417) is the place to do tastings. Their 1997 vintage won more medals than any other American sauvignon blanc. They also have fine cabernet, merlot, and chardonnay. It is in Geyserville at 19550 Geyserville Avenue and is open daily.

Domaine Chandon (phone 707-944-2892) appears more as a beautiful park than a winery. There is a world-class restaurant featuring French cuisine that complements the wonderful wines. Its champagne-style wines are excellent, as are the winery's many other varietals. It is open Wednesday through Sunday for lunch and dinner. Reservations are suggested. The winery is at One California Drive, Yountville.

Merryvale Vineyards (phone 707-963-7777) offers a unique experience for anyone wanting to learn more about wines. Seminars are offered Fridays, Saturdays, and Sundays discussing the essential components of wine making and how perfectly balanced wines are produced. The vineyard's wines are tasted, allowing participants to learn to judge wine types and qualities. There is a small fee and reservations are suggested. The vineyard tasting room is at 1000 Main Street, St. Helena. It's also open for daily wine tasting.

Sutter Home (phone 707-963-3104) is the nation's sixth largest winery, yet it has remained a family operation since 1947. The visitor center is located in the original winery site. Tours are offered. There are also limited accommodations on the grounds. It is located at 277 St. Helena Highway (Highway 29), South St. Helena.

For further information: Mendocino Winegrowers Alliance, PO Box 1409, Ukiah, CA 95482-1409. Phone (707) 468-9886. The Sonoma County Wine & Visitor Center in Rhonert Park, just off US 101, showcases over 100 wineries with video seminars and a model working winery. Phone (707) 875-3866.

SONOMA

[Fig. 25] The Franciscans first came here in 1823 and constructed the last and most northerly of their missions. Mission San Francisco Solano de Sonoma served the religious needs of the citizens and the nearby Sonoma Barracks housed the troops of General Mariano Vallejo. There were varying efforts to establish a pueblo, but the local Indians weren't particularly cooperative in allowing a village of Mexican citizens on their land, at least any distance from the protection of the Mexican soldiers at the barracks. But things would soon change.

As the Americans continued to push their way into California during the 1840s, Mexican control was quickly slipping. Soon after a rag-tag band of Americans stole a bunch of Mexican army horses, they quickly decided they should escalate their actions to a full revolution. The Americans seized General Vallejo at his home, with the general not objecting or attempting to convince the Americans that what they were doing was a bad idea. The Bear Flag Revolt, as it became known, was short-lived, lasting only a few weeks. It ended when the Americans landed in force in Monterey on July 6, 1846 as part of the war against Mexico.

Today, the Mexican soldiers' barracks and several of the other historic buildings in

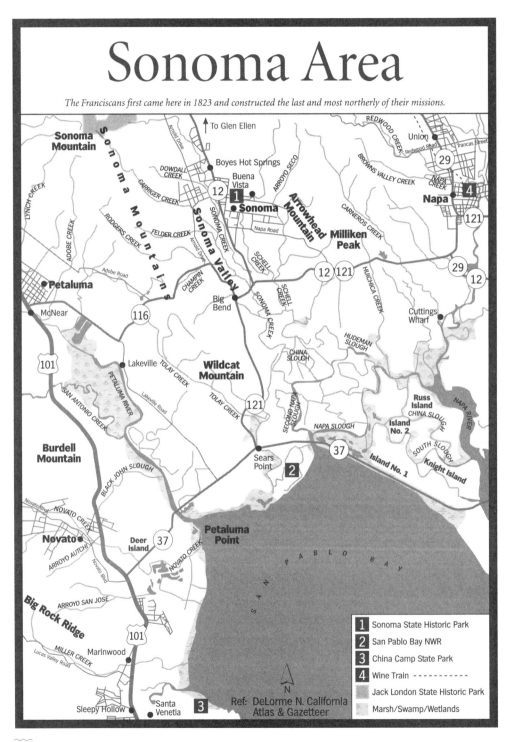

Sonoma Area

The Franciscans first came here in 1823 and constructed the last and most northerly of their missions.

To Glen Ellen

Sonoma Mountain

Union

Redwood Creek

Redwood Road

Trancas Street

Boyes Hot Springs

Browns Valley Creek

29

Dowdall Creek

Buena Vista

Arroyo Seco

Napa Creek

Carriger Creek

12

Sonoma Mountains

Arnold Drive

Sonoma Creek

Sonoma Valley

Felder Creek

Lynch Creek

Napa Road

Napa

4

121

1 Sonoma

Arrowhead Mountain

Carneros Creek

Milliken Peak

Adobe Creek

Rodgers Creek

Schell Creek

12 121

Huichica Creek

29

12

Petaluma

Adobe Road

Champlin Creek

Big Bend

Schell Creek

Cuttings Wharf

McNear

116

Sonoma Creek

Hudeman Slough

China Slough

Lakeville

Tolay Creek

Wildcat Mountain

Petaluma River

San Antonio Creek

Lakeville Road

Tolay Creek

121

Second Napa Slough

Napa Slough

Russ Island

China Slough

Napa River

Island No. 2

South Slough

Knight Island

101

Burdell Mountain

Black John Slough

Sears Point

2

37

Island No. 1

Novato Blvd

Novato Creek

Deer Island

37

Petaluma Point

Novato

Arroyo Autchi

Novato Blvd

Novato Creek

SAN PABLO BAY

Big Rock Ridge

Arroyo San Jose

101

Miller Creek

Marinwood

Lucas Valley Road

1 Sonoma State Historic Park

2 San Pablo Bay NWR

3 China Camp State Park

4 Wine Train - - - - - - - - - -

Jack London State Historic Park

Marsh/Swamp/Wetlands

Sleepy Hollow

Santa Venetia

3

N

Ref: DeLorme N. California Atlas & Gazetteer

the small town are part of **Sonoma State Historic Park** [Fig. 25(1)]. La Casa Grande, Vallejo's Sonoma home and the Blue Wing Inn, the first building north of San Francisco constructed specifically as a hotel, are only a few pieces of the town's historic fabric. Within the barracks, now a museum and visitor center, are restored rooms and a small theater.

The center of Sonoma is a plaza park, surrounded by Sonoma Barracks, shops, and restaurants. The **Sonoma Valley Visitors Center** is also located across the street from the plaza, on the opposite side of the barracks. It's a good place to get information about wineries in the area.

Directions: The town of Sonoma is located about 22 miles south of Santa Rosa and US 101, on Highway 12.

Activities: Hiking, picnicking.

Facilities: Museums, restaurants, hotels.

Dates: Open year-round.

Fees: There is a fee at Sonoma State Historic Park.

For more information: Sonoma State Historic Park, phone (707) 938-1519, or the Sonoma Valley Visitors Bureau, 453 First Street East, Sonoma, CA 95476. Phone (707) 996-1090.

JACK LONDON STATE HISTORIC PARK

[Fig. 25] Even if you have no interest in Jack London's life or his work, wandering the trails among oaks and pines is a great way to spend a day exploring this 800-acre park. There's a 0.75 mile walk that leads to a dam, lake, and bathhouse built by London, and bicycling and horseback riding are permitted on some of the park's trails. But most people come here lured by a curiosity to visit the home of one of America's most prolific and best-loved writers.

Jack London's adventure novels, *Call of the Wild* (1903) and *The Sea Wolf* (1904), made him famous and provided the income for him to begin living life as he wanted. But his output did not stop there. London tried to write at least 1,000 words each day, a feat that allowed him to complete more than 50 fiction and nonfiction books from 1900 to 1916, along with hundreds of magazine articles and short stories. Some of his works have been translated into more than 70 different languages.

One of Jack London's dreams was to sail around the world in his custom-built sailing ship, the *Snark*. While he and his second wife, Charmain, made it only to Australia, the 1906-07 voyage provided background material for years to come. Another dream was to operate a modern farm. Seeking an escape from his home in Oakland, he purchased land just outside the small community of Glen Ellen, near Sonoma. Here, living in a small ranch house on what he called his Beauty Ranch, he continued his writing to support himself and his wife, operated his modern farm, and began construction of his new home, Wolf House. He also managed to spend two tours as a war correspondent, travel extensively, and entertain a near constant stream

Point Reyes National Seashore

Sir Francis Drake first came to Point Reyes in 1579 seeking new lands for England.

BODEGA BAY

STEMPLE CREEK

Bodega Ave

PETALUMA RIVER

Dillon Beach

Dillon Beach Road

Tomales

Tomales Petaluma Road

Tomales Point

Petaluma

Chileno Valley Road

Ocean Roar

Hamlet

CHILENO CREEK

Chileno Valley

LAGUNA LAKE

Chileno Valley Road

SAN ANTONIO CREEK

Blakes Landing

WALKER CREEK

Antonio Mountain

TOMALES POINT TRAIL

1

7

Bolinas Ridge

Pierce Point Road

Marshall

SALMON CREEK

Marshall Petaluma Road

Reynolds

Marconi

TOMALES BAY

ARROYO SAUSAL

Red Hill

Novato Blvd

Three Peaks

Hicks Mountain

Point Reyes Petaluma Road

ABBOTTS LAGOON

Millerton

STAFFORD LAKE

PACIFIC OCEAN

Seahaven

Inverness

Bivalve

Nicasio Valley Road

Sir Francis Drake Blvd

St Francis Drake Blvd

NICASIO RESERVOIR

Redwood Canyon

4

SCHOONER BAY

TOMS BAY

Point Reyes Station

6

Tocaloma

Nicasio

Lucas Valley Road

4

DRAKES ESTERO

ESTERO DE LIMANTOUR

Limantour Road

Bear Valley Visitor Center

Bear Valley Road

Barnabe Mountain

St Francis Drake Blvd

Nicasio Valley Road

Forest Knoll

Lagunitas

3

2

Coast Trail

OLEMA CREEK

Bear Valley

Bolinas Ridge

DRAKES BAY

San Andreas Rift Zone

KENT LAKE

Pine Mountain

5

WILDCAT LAKE

PINE GULCH CREEK

Ref: DeLorme N. California Atlas and Gazetteer

N

CRYSTAL LAKE
PELICAN LAKE

ALPINE LAKE

BOLINAS LAGOON

Bolinas

BOLINAS BAY

1	Tule Elk Reserve/ Pierce Point Ranch	7	Tomales Point Trail
2	Limantour Beach		Point Reyes Nat. Seashore
3	Drakes Beach		Tomales Bay State Park
4	Point Reyes Beach North & South		Samuel P. Taylor State Park
5	Point Reyes Lighthouse		Audubon Canyon Ranch
6	Bear Valley Trail, Earthquake Trail, Kule Loklo Trail		Trail

of guests, all in addition to spending plenty of time in local bars, drinking and debating other locals.

London's Wolf House, a mansion that cost more than $80,000 in 1913, burned to the ground just a few days before he and Charmain were planning to move in. Some of the stone and concrete walls are all that remained following the fire and still remain today. Even after his depression eased over the loss of his house, London did not remain healthy. He worked longer hours writing, trying to make the money he needed to support his farm and other projects. Finally, on November 22, 1916, London's lifestyle caught up with him and he died at the age of 40 from gastrointestinal uremic poisoning. Jack London's ashes were scattered on a hill not far from Wolf House, next to the graves of two pioneer children.

Today, the ranch house where he did much of his writing has been restored and is open to the public. Many of the other structures, including the remnant stone walls of his Wolf House, can be seen. His widow, Charmain, had another house built in 1919-20, somewhat similar to the nearby Wolf House. Following her death in 1955 at age 84, it became a visitor center and museum dedicated to her late husband. It houses photographs and mementos of their world travels, as well as many of Jack London's personal possessions, including his roll-top desk and dictaphone.

There are several miles of trails that lead to London's sherry barn, stone manure pit, the winery ruins, distillery building, pig palace, the 40-foot tall concrete silos, and the 5-acre lake.

Directions: From Sonoma, take Highway 12 to London Ranch Road, just outside the town of Glen Ellen.

Activities: Hiking, picnicking.

Facilities: Museum, visitor center, trails.

Dates: Open year-round.

Fees: There is a day-use fee.

Closest town: Glen Ellen.

For more information: Jack London State Historic Park, 2400 London Ranch Road, Glen Ellen, CA 95442. Phone (707) 938-5216.

Point Reyes National Seashore

[Fig. 26] Miwok Indians were the first to inhabit this land, probably attracted by the abundant food supplies and moderate climate. The first hint that their idyllic life was going to change came in 1579, when Francis Drake, seeking new lands for England's Queen Elizabeth I, sailed his ship, the *Golden Hind*, into Drakes Estero, where he stayed for more than a month making repairs to his ship. The friendly Miwoks provided additional food to the English crew. During their stay, his crew had opportunities to explore the area, discovering a rich land that certainly reminded some of them of home. Before continuing on his around-the-world journey, Drake named the land *Nova Albion*, or New England.

Although a few other maritime explorers either passed by or landed near Point Reyes, including Don Sebastian Vizcaino in 1603, it took nearly 200 more years before there was any serious attempt to settle these lands. By the time the Americans had won Point Reyes and the rest of California from Mexico, who had taken it from Spain, the Miwok had disappeared from the land. During Mexico's control, three men, collectively known as the Lords of Point Reyes, controlled the peninsula through land grants. Soon after it came under American control, a San Francisco law firm obtained the property and divided it into a series of ranches for beef and dairy cattle. Cattle continue to graze throughout the peninsula grasslands today.

For first-time visitors, the **Bear Valley Visitor Center** is the best place to begin. It's located just a few hundred yards down Bear Valley Road, off Highway 1 in the community of Olema. The visitor center, besides offering maps, camping permits, a museum, and bookshop, serves as a starting point for numerous trails that reach all parts of Point Reyes.

With so many working ranches still on the Point Reyes Peninsula**, Pierce Point Ranch** [Fig. 26(1)] offers a chance to see what went into a historic dairy operation. The ranch offers an opportunity to see a turn-of-the-century ranch house and many of the outbuildings needed for the dairy operation, including the milking barns where the cows were herded each day. Interpretive panels explain the dairy operation and the incredible attention that was paid to cleanliness. After all, the Pierce Point Ranch produced some of the finest butter and other dairy products for markets in San Francisco and beyond. The ranch is at the end of Pierce Point Road, which connects with Sir Francis Drake Boulevard, about 7 miles from the Bear Valley Visitor Center.

As the park's Pierce Point Road nears the Pierce Point Ranch, it passes through the **Tule Elk Reserve** [Fig. 26(1)]. Within the reserve, tule elk (*Cervus canadensis nannodes*) graze and bed down on the open grasslands. Before nineteenth century meat hunters decimated their population, thousands of elk once roamed these hills. Today, a program is in place to restore tule elk to the open lands of Point Reyes National Seashore, although they are being restricted to this small part of the park so they don't compete with the cattle ranches still operating here. **Do not approach the elk. They are wild animals and can be very dangerous.**

Directions: To reach the Bear Valley Visitor Center, take Highway 1 to Olema. Turn west on Bear Valley Road and drive about 1 mile to the entrance road.

Activities: Hiking, camping, fishing, bird-watching, beachcombing.

Facilities: Visitor centers, historic buildings. Camping in the park is limited to four, hike-in campgrounds. There is no car camping in the park. Permits are required to use the hike-in campgrounds and may be obtained at the Bear Valley Visitor Center. Reservations are suggested due to the popularity of camping at Point Reyes.

Phone (415) 663-8054, Monday through Friday, or make reservations in person at the Bear Valley Visitor Center, seven days a week. Reservation requests may also be faxed, (415) 663-1597.

Dates: Park is open daily. Hours vary for visitor centers and historic buildings.

Fees: There is a fee for camping.

Closest town: Olema, 1 mile.

For more information: Point Reyes National Seashore, Point Reyes Station, CA 94956-9799. Phone (415) 663-1092.

POINT REYES BEACHES

With so much shoreline, the beaches of Point Reyes attract nearly everyone, but it's always important to be aware of the dangers that accompany high waves and cold water. The most popular beaches are those easily reached by car or by short walks.

Limantour Beach [Fig. 26(2)] is one of the more popular beaches at Point Reyes, partly because it can be reached by driving, has a beautiful beach (but no lifeguard service), and it's near Estero de Limantour. There's a short trail that goes out onto Limantour spit, providing a perfect place to view birds on Drakes Bay, on the open ocean, and in the Estero de Limantour wetlands.

Drakes Beach, [Fig. 26(3)] near the Kenneth C. Patrick Visitor Center, offers one of the safer beaches for sunbathers, swimmers, and beachcombers. Even though the waves are smaller here than other places around the park, it can still be dangerous. Lifeguards are not available, so use with caution.

Point Reyes Beach North and South [Fig. 26(4)] both face the open Pacific Ocean and are subject to dangerously heavy surf and strong rip currents. They are great to explore and on the occasional sunny day, sunbathe, but entering the water for any reason should be avoided. The beaches are off Sir Francis Drake Boulevard, 13.2 and 15.7 miles respectively, from the Bear Valley Visitor Center.

POINT REYES LIGHTHOUSE

[Fig. 26(5)] The drive out to the lighthouse is more like a drive back in history, when cattle ranches reigned over the open lands of the peninsula, producing beef and some of the finest dairy products available anywhere. Cattle still graze on the grass-lands and are herded across the roads, stopping traffic. The ranch houses, barns, and corrals needed for ranching operations are still scattered throughout the low, rolling hills.

When you reach the small parking lot, there is a 0.4-mile walk to the small museum and visitor center. As you walk toward the lightstation facilities, check the roadcut on the left. On the shady, moist face of the rocks, a couple of different plants color their surfaces. The furry rock violet is *Alga trentephohlia*, an alga that contains green chlorophyll, but its red pigments predominate. Pale green lichen also grow on the rocks. It is made up of both algae and fungi. The fungi secure the plant to the

Townsend's Big-Eared Bat

Point Reyes National Seashore hosts two of the Pacific coast's largest maternity colonies of Townsend's big-eared bats (*Plecotus townsendii*), an animal species that the California Department of Fish and Game lists as being of special concern. With so much of their natural habitat having been removed for farming and the widespread use of pesticides that poison the insects they normally feed on, the small bat has seen better times.

With the National Park Service's policy of preserving both cultural and natural resources, some of the old, abandoned buildings have become primary bat maternity sites, in addition to the more natural hollows found in bay trees. Monitoring and protection programs are continuing, assuring that a healthy population of these very beneficial animals remain at Point Reyes.

rock surface and absorb moisture, while the algae produce food for both.

From the visitor center a stairway leads down to the lighthouse that sits on the small point of land. It's 308 steps down, and for some, a very difficult 308 steps back up to the museum and visitor center. If the fog hasn't enveloped the point, there are excellent views down the coast and out across the open Pacific Ocean. It's a good viewpoint for watching gray whales during their winter migration. There is no fee to tour the lighthouse.

Directions: To reach the Lighthouse, take Highway 1 to Point Reyes Station. Turn west on Sir Francis Drake Boulevard and drive 20.5 miles to the lighthouse parking area.

Activities: Hiking, bird-watching.

Facilities: Visitor center.

Dates: The Lighthouse and visitor center is open Thursday through Monday.

Fees: None.

Closest town: Point Reyes, 20.5 miles.

For more information: Point Reyes National Seashore, Point Reyes Station, CA 94956-9799. Phone (415) 663-1092.

TRAILS

There are many miles of trails inside Point Reyes National Seashore. While they are well marked and well used, it's a good idea to get a map from the Bear Valley Visitor Center before hiking in the park. It's also important to go prepared for very changeable weather. A warm, sunny afternoon can change to bone-chilling, wind-driven fog, often within an hour or less. Winters can bring warm sunshine or heavy rain, along with extremely high and dangerous surf. The surf can be extremely hazardous at anytime of the year, especially on the more northerly facing beaches and bluffs.

Bear Valley Trail: [Fig. 26(6)] Beginning at the Bear Valley Visitor Center, this trail is 4.1 miles of rolling hills to Arch Rock. This popular landmark is located at the mouth of Coast Creek, which is at the north end of Wildcat Beach. At the beach, the trail connects with the Coast Trail.

Earthquake Trail: [Fig. 26(6)] This 0.7-mile trail leads from the visitor center to the nearby San Andreas fault. This trail offers an opportunity to stand on one of the most unstable pieces of real estate in California.

Kule Loklo Trail: [Fig. 26(6)] This is also a 0.7-mile trail that leaves from the visitor center parking lot and heads up a short hill through a woodlands area, then a eucalyptus grove, and finally ends at an open meadow where Native Americans and other volunteers have constructed a replica of a Miwok Indian village.

Tomales Point Trail: [Fig. 26(7)] There are two trails that begin at the Pierce Point Ranch. The first is a quick, 0.5-mile walk to the beach. The second follows the ridge, mostly on the Pacific Ocean side of the narrowing peninsula, out to Tomales Point. The hike offers great views of the ocean and of Tomales Bay to the east.

Coast Trail: [Fig. 26] The trail meanders about half the length of Drakes Bay, turning inland near Limantour Spit. To reach the south trailhead, from Highway 1 at the north end of Bolinas Lagoon, take Olema-Bolinas Road and turn right on Mesa Road. The trail begins at the Palomarin trailhead, which is at the end of Mesa Road.

POINT REYES LODGING

Point Reyes National Seashore offers little in the way of overnight lodging, except for those willing to hike into one of the campgrounds. But just outside the park in some of the small towns there are numerous choices for overnight accommodations. Following are a few of the cottages, small inns, and hotels listed by their towns that can meet most people's needs.

Blackthorne Inn. 266 Vallejo Avenue, Inverness. The inn resembles a giant tree house. *Expensive. Phone (415) 663-8621.*

TOWNSEND'S BIG-EARED BAT
(Plecotus townsendii)
During the winter, these bats hibernate in caves and keep their large ears folded back. If the bats are disturbed, they unfold their ears and move them in circles like antennae.

Hotel Inverness. 25 Park Avenue, Inverness. The attractive and comfortable hotel was built in 1906. *Expensive. Phone (415) 669-7393.*

Olema Inn. 10,000 Sir Francis Drake Boulevard, Olema. Originally built as an inn around 1876, today it offers first-class accommodations surrounded by antique furnishings. *Moderate to expensive. Phone (800) 532-9252.*

For more information: Point Reyes Lodging, PO Box 878, Point Reyes, CA 94956. Phone (800) 539-1872 or (415) 663-1872.

Marin County

TOMALES BAY STATE PARK

[Fig. 26] Long and narrow, Tomales Bay marks one of California's ongoing major geologic events. The San Andreas fault runs through the middle of the bay, effectively separating the westward-moving North American plate from the Pacific plate that is driving downward and more slowly to the northwest as the two grind together. Each

Oysters

Many people consider oysters to be a delicacy, while others gag at the thought of eating one of these popular little slimy mollusks. There are several species of oysters but only a couple of any commercial interest. The California oyster (*Ostrea lurida*) is the native bivalve found in muddy bay and estuary bottoms. But a larger and more prolific introduced species called *Crassostrea gigas*, which sports several common names including Pacific oyster and Japanese oyster, is the choice of most growers.

Johnson's Drakes Bay Oysters, located near the shore of Drakes Estero at Point Reyes, grows, harvests, and sells fresh Pacific oysters in three sizes. While Drakes Bay is too cold for oysters to spawn naturally, it does allow them to be harvested year-round. Spawning takes place in a lab where millions of microscopic larvae and water are added to tanks filled with old oyster shells. After the larvae attach or set themselves on shells, bags of the shells are hung in the bay for about two months. After this initial period of growth, the shells are strung to 8-foot-long wires and returned to the water where they remain for another 18 to 24 months. Suspended above the bottom mud where their native cousins live, the maturing oysters are protected from predators such as crabs and sea stars.

Like the other oyster companies near Point Reyes and Tamales Bay, Johnson's Drakes Bay Oysters harvests only a set number of oysters each day, so if you want fresh oysters, call a day or two ahead and place your order. The small operation is located on Point Reyes, on a short, dirt side road just off Sir Francis Drake Boulevard, about 10 miles west of the Big Bear Visitor Center near Olema. Phone (415) 669-1149.

year, the land on the western side, primarily Point Reyes National Seashore, moves approximately 2 inches. During the 1906 San Francisco earthquake, which was centered near the park, the two plates shifted 20 feet within a few seconds. It's the combination of these movements that over thousands of years has moved the landmass of Point Reyes from its point of origin as part of the Tehachapi Mountains, to its current location more than 300 miles south.

The fact that there are two colliding tectonic plates separated by a flooded valley provides an opportunity to compare the different rocks found on each side. On the east side of the lagoon, the outcroppings are mostly Franciscan rock, sandstones scraped from the top of the Pacific plate as it moves under the North American plate. Rocks on the west side of the bay are part of the Salinian block, with its granite outcroppings as evidence of its one-time connection to rock formations in southern California. Much of the lower areas are buried under sedimentary rocks that were laid down when the granite was still beneath the sea, 10 to 20 million years ago.

GIANT PACIFIC OYSTER
(*Crassostrea gigas*)
This species is a native of Japan but it is the oyster of choice for growers in California.

Tomales Bay State Park spans a small portion of the land on both sides of the bay. The largest part of the park is on the western side, running into Inverness Ridge. The surrounding hills offer forests and woodlands to explore, while the main focus for many who visit is the park's beach access. There are also a couple of short trails, including one that identifies the plants along its route. The park also has one of the last remaining virgin bishop pine (*Pinus muricata*) forests.

Directions: From Highway 1 at Point Reyes Station, turn west onto Francis Drake Boulevard for about 7 miles. Turn right on Pierce Point Road. The park entrance is about 1 mile on the right.

Activities: Hiking, swimming, picnicking, fishing, beachcombing.

Facilities: Picnic areas, six walk-in/bike campsites.

Dates: Open daily.

Fees: There is a small day-use fee.

Closest town: Inverness.

For more information: Tomales Bay State Park, Star Route, Inverness, CA 94937. Phone (415) 669-1140.

BOLINAS LAGOON PRESERVE

[Fig. 27(1)] Nature has created the perfect habitat for wildlife in Bolinas Lagoon. With its open, protected waters and shallow tidelands, along with surrounding hillsides of grasses, chaparral, and woodlands, there is ample food and shelter for hundreds of animal species. While pulling to the side of the road that follows the east side of the lagoon is an option for viewing the water birds, visiting Audubon Canyon Ranch's Bolinas Lagoon Preserve is a better choice.

The preserve is home to one of California's largest great blue heron rookeries, with at least 100 pairs of great blue herons (*Ardea herodias*) and generally a few pairs of snowy egrets joining in the nesting efforts each year. The herons arrive in January and within a month begin their very elaborate courtship activities, which are followed by nesting in the tops of the redwood trees in February. Together, the male and female herons incubate their two to five eggs for about 28 days until they hatch, then share in feeding the chicks until they are able to fledge in 10 to 12 weeks.

Directions: The Bolinas Lagoon Preserve is located on Highway 1, 3 miles north of Stinson Beach and 15 miles south of Point Reyes Station.

Activities: Hiking, interpretive programs, picnicking.

Facilities: Picnic area, bookstore, and display hall.

Dates: Open to the general public from mid-Mar. to mid-July, on weekends and holidays only. It's also open to schools and groups by appointment.

Fees: None, but a donation is requested to help support the preserve's operation.

Closest town: Stinson Beach, 3 miles.

For more information: Audubon Canyon Ranch Headquarters, 4900 Highway 1, Stinson Beach, CA 94970. Phone (415) 868-9244.

TRAILS

The only way to really enjoy the full viewing benefits that the reserve has to offer is by spending time on some of the 8 miles of trails. Since most of the trails lead into the wooded hills above the lagoon, another benefit of walking is the opportunity to see some of the other wildlife. It's not all that unusual to catch a passing glimpse of black-tailed deer (*Odocoileus hemionus*), bobcats (*Felis rufus*), badgers (*Taxidea taxus*), raccoons (*Procyon lotor*), and brush rabbits (*Sylvilagus hachmani*).

The Overlook: It's a 0.5-mile climb up this most popular trail that leads to an overlook offering an unbeatable bird's-eye view of the great blue heron and great egrets (*Casmerodius albus*) in their tree-top homes. Audubon naturalists are often on-site to interpret the life cycles and needs of the breeding birds.

Self-Guided Nature Trail: It's a gentle 0.75-mile loop trail that leads into the canyon, with about a 200-foot elevation gain.

STINSON BEACH

[Fig. 27(2)] Stinson Beach is operated by the National Park Service as part of Golden Gate National Recreation Area. It's also the name of the small community that grew up around the beach. Located just south of Bolinas Lagoon, the town of Stinson Beach is a curious collection of old and new homes, a few B&Bs, cafés and restaurants. In many ways, it appears as one of several holdover refuges for some of those who have never quite given up on the 1960s.

It's fun, it's quaint, it's a quiet refuge… except on warm summer weekends when the beach portion of Stinson Beach fills with people. It's one of the more popular and car-accessible beaches for many miles, easily reached by people living in Marin County. The beach is one of only a few along the north coast with summer lifeguard service. There's a small visitor center in the park.

Directions: Stinson Beach is located on Highway 1, about 11 miles north of the Highway 1 and US 101 junction, north of the Golden Gate Bridge.

Activities: Swimming, beachcombing, fishing.

Facilities: Seasonally-operated visitor center.

Dates: Open daily.

Fees: None.

Closest town: Stinson Beach.

For more information: Stinson Beach Ranger Station is operated only during summer. Phone (415) 868-0942 or (415) 868-0734 during summer. At other times contact National Park Service, Fort Mason, San Francisco, CA 94123. Phone (415) 331-1540.

MOUNT TAMALPAIS STATE PARK

[Fig. 27] Commonly referred to as Mount Tam, the 6,300-acre park rises from sea level to the top of the 2,571-foot-high peak that gives this meeting of coast and mountains its name. Spanish explorers originally named the mountain *La Sierra de Nuestro Padre de San Francisco*, which was later changed to Tamalpais, the Coast Miwok Indians' name for the promontory.

This is an incredibly popular park with "Bay Area" hikers and anyone who simply wishes to go for a drive on the park's winding roads that meander along the coast and up to the mountain's many majestic overlooks. On clear days you can see the Farallon Islands 25 miles away and incredible views across the inland delta, San Francisco Bay, Mount Diablo, and occasionally, even the snow-capped Sierra Nevada, nearly 200 miles east.

The mountain is part of the Coast Range and is therefore essentially the layer of ancient mud and other materials that were scraped off the ancient ocean floor as the

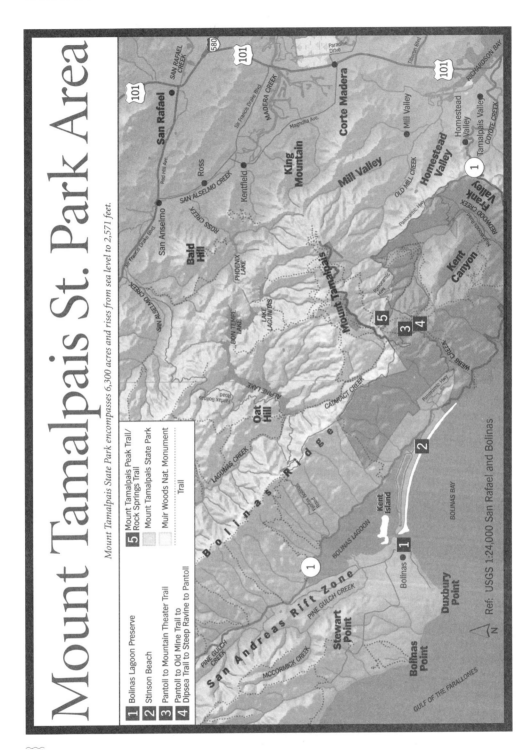

Mount Tamalpais St. Park Area

Mount Tamalpais State Park encompasses 6,300 acres and rises from sea level to 2,571 feet.

1 Bolinas Lagoon Preserve
2 Stinson Beach
3 Pantoll to Mountain Theater Trail
4 Pantoll to Old Mine Trail to Dipsea Trail to Steep Ravine to Pantoll

5 Mount Tamalpais Peak Trail/ Rock Springs Trail

Mount Tamalpais State Park

Muir Woods Nat. Monument Trail

Ref: USGS 1:24,000 San Rafael and Bolinas

Pacific plate plunged into the subduction zone along the eastern side of the San Andreas fault. The remnant scraped and uplifted piles of metamorphic rock, including sandstone, shale, greenstone, chert, and serpentine, are the most common on the mountain that has been rising higher for the past one million years.

The different mineral types, combined with a million years of weathering, have created a wide range of habitats and microclimates that today support over 750 different plant species. Rolling grasslands, hillside chaparral, oak woodlands, and dense stands of Douglas fir and coast redwoods are found beside the 50 miles of hiking trails inside the park. Spring is an absolutely glorious time to visit, as brightly colored wildflowers cover entire hillsides. California poppies (*Eschscholzia californica*), golden fields (*Lasthenia* sp.), white-spotted coral root (*Corrallorhiza maculata*), Calypso orchid, (*Calypso bulbosa*), Douglas iris (*Iris douglasiana*), and shooting stars (*Dodecatheon* sp.) join dozens of other species for their annual show.

With such plant diversity comes an equally diversified animal community. Bobcats (*Lynx rufus*), black-tailed deer (*Odocoileus hemionius columbianus*), raccoons (*Procyon lotor*), gray foxes (*Urocyon cinereoargenteus*), and even an occasional mountain lion (*Felis concolor*) call the park home. Ranchers and others who feared,

Tomales Bay Boating

The seemingly calm waters of Tomales Bay can appear to be a boater's delight, and they usually are. It's a great place to cruise quietly in a kayak or canoe, or head out in a small boat to do a little fishing. Be aware: The changes between high and low tides can be very strong, especially at the mouth of the bay. Low tides can leave unaware boaters stranded on shallow mud flats. Winds can pick up very quickly, so check weather predictions before heading out. Although rare, there were two white shark attacks at the mouth of Tomales Bay several years ago, a popular seal haul-out area. Also, the water is cold, 50-55 degrees Fahrenheit, so hypothermia should always be a concern if you accidentally capsize.

Many of the bay's animals are protected, such as harbor seals, California sea lions, and the endangered brown pelican. If your approach makes them begin to act nervously, or makes birds take flight, you need to back away. You're too close. Keep back at least 100 to 200 feet. Some areas of the bay, such as Hog Island and Pelican Point, are closed to public use because of the wildlife that frequent them.

Boat-in camping is allowed only on National Park beaches on the west side of Tomales Bay, north of Indian Beach at Tomales Bay State Park. There are a limited number of sites and they may be reserved in advance. For reservations, phone (415) 663-8054, Monday through Friday. There are other limitations, so call in advance. Reservation requests may also be faxed, (415) 663-1597. They can be made seven days a week at the Bear Valley Visitor Center in Olema.

Sausalito Area

Sausalito was originally named Saucito, which means "little willow," because of little willows that grow along nearby streams.

N

Ref: Sausalito Chamber of Commerce
Visitor's Guide Map

RICHARDSON BAY

Liberty Ship Way

6 Bridgeway Blvd

Easterby Street

To San Rafael

Napa Street

Pine Street

Caledonia Street

Locust Street

Litho Street

Turney Street

Pine Street

Johnson Street

Bridgeway Blvd

Humboldt Ave.

3

2

Solmaker Drive

Park Street

1

Visitor Information Center

Bulkey Ave.

Princess Street

5

Bridgeway Blvd

Bulkey Ave.

To San Rafael

S A U S A L I T O

1 101

4

Second Street

Alexander Ave.

To US 101
and San Francisco

1	Plaza Vina Del Mar And Gene Hiller Building
2	Sausalito Yacht Harbor
3	Arc Row
4	Chart House, Walhalla, Valhalla
5	Castle
6	San Francisco Bay-Delta Model
	Golden Gate National Rec. Area
	Dunphy Park
	Gabrielson Park
- - - -	Scenic Walk
———	Trail

1 101

To San Francisco and
Golden Gate Bridge

misunderstood, or saw economic gain, hunted some of the original wild inhabitants, including the bear and elk, into localized extinction.

Birds are especially prolific in the park. Red-tailed hawks (*Buteo jamaicensis*), turkey vultures (*Cathartes aura*), great horned owls (*Bubo virginianus*), screech owls (*Otus asio*), and the pileated woodpeckers (*Dryocopus pileatus*) are relatively common in the park, although none are seen as often as the sometimes obnoxious-acting steller's jays (Cyanocitta stelleri) and ravens (*Corvus corax*).

A feature found in no other state park in California is an amphitheater that the Civilian Conservation Corps built during the Depression of the 1930s. The natural stone theater seats 3,750 people and often fills for its annual Mountain Play, which has been performed each spring since 1913. Pantoll Road, which will get you to the Mountain Theater, also intersects with Ridgecrest Boulevard, leading the remainder of the way to a parking lot and visitor center located near the 2,571-foot summit of Mount Tamalpais.

Camping in the park is limited to just 16 developed campsites at Pantoll Campground, which is available on a first-come, first-served basis. The Rocky Point—Steep Ravine Environmental Campground has six walk-in campsites that sit on a knoll overlooking the Pacific Ocean. In the same area ten rustic cabins, each equipped with wooden bunks, a table, and a wood stove, occupy the opposite side of the same knoll, with gorgeous views that look north toward Stinson Beach. There is access to a rocky beach below the cabins. You have to bring your own firewood, cooking equipment, and sleeping bags. Water is provided from outside faucets. Also found outside the cabins are shared primitive toilet facilities. The cabins are incredibly popular and generally require reservations well in advance. For reservations, phone (800) 444-7275.

Directions: North of the Golden Gate Bridge, from US 101, take Highway 1 to the Stinson Beach Exit and follow the signs up the mountain to the Pantoll Ranger Station.

Activities: Hiking, fishing, picnicking, camping, and theater during spring and summer.

Dates: Open daily. Top of the mountain closes at sunset.

Fees: There are fees for camping and day-use in designated areas.

Closest town: Stinson Beach, less than 1 mile from the park's northwest boundary, along Highway 1.

For more information: Mount Tamalpais State Park, 801 Panoramic Highway, Mill Valley, CA 94941. Phone (415) 388-2070.

TRAILS

There are over 50 miles of extensively used trails within the park and some of them connect with 700 miles of surrounding trails on adjacent public lands. Many of the trails are short, but connect with so many other trails along the way that you can easily plan much longer hikes. The park's Pantoll Ranger Station is an excellent place to obtain maps and directions to trailheads.

Pantoll to Mountain Theater Trail [Fig. 27(3)] offers a 2-mile loop that begins at the Pantoll Ranger Station parking lot and winds up the ridge for 1 mile, with a 600-foot elevation gain to the CCC-era Mountain Theater. The trail provides excellent views of the Pacific Ocean, toward Stinson Beach. The trail loops back down the **Old Mine Trail** to the parking lot, affording views of the San Francisco Bay and Mount Tamalpais.

Pantoll to Old Mine Trail to Dipsea Trail to Steep Ravine to Pantoll [Fig. 27(4)] is a 3.5-mile loop that requires more of a workout, but also includes passages through a redwood canyon. It offers many coastal viewpoints during its 1,000-foot elevation change, beginning from the Pantoll Ranger Station.

Mount Tamalpais Peak Trail [Fig. 27(5)] is actually made up of a series of trails. It begins at the Pantoll Ranger Station and initially climbs 600 feet and 1 mile to the Mountain Theater. From here, take the **Rock Springs Trail** across the south-facing serpentine slope to the old right-of-way for what was known as "The Crookedest Railroad in the World," an early nineteenth century tourist transport to the mountain's summit. Follow the old track bed to the top of the 2,571-foot-high mountain. It's an 8.5-mile round trip.

SAUSALITO

[Fig. 28] This is one of several small towns often overlooked by travelers, whose focus is generally on San Francisco. Sausalito is a wonderfully quaint town filled with shops and restaurants along its main street, which parallels the waterfront.

Dig more than a few inches below today's sidewalks, paved roads, and parking lots and Indian middens, ancient mounds of buried shells and artifacts, are reminders of the Coast Miwok who first inhabited this entire region. The Indians' name for this area was *Lewan Helowah*, or West Wind. When the Spanish arrived in 1775, they saw the abundance of clams, abalone, shrimp, and salmon, along with deer, elk, and bear, and immediately considered this to be a paradise. The Spanish called the area *Saucito* (Little Willow) because of all the small willows that grew along the nearby streams. The name was slowly Americanized to Sausalito.

William Richardson, an English seaman, married a Mexican citizen, the daughter of the Commandante of the San Francisco Presidio. It was common for English and American men to marry Mexican women during Mexico's control of California. As a result of his marriage, Richardson was given a 20,000-acre land grant in today's Marin County, where he built his home near Sausalito's present downtown. He lost his land holdings in poor business deals, helped along by dishonest lawyers. In 1868 the land was sold to the Sausalito Land & Ferry Company, which laid out streets and subdivided the central waterfront into view lots. The ferry service was soon replaced by a rail line that attracted even more people to what had become a major transportation hub.

Even at this early date, Sausalito was becoming a community for San Francisco's rich elite who built beautiful summer homes on the hillsides and moored their yachts in the harbor yacht clubs. Their elegant lifestyles contrasted sharply with the working class who lived on the town's outskirts or in the cheap boarding houses. Portuguese boatbuilders and fisherman, Italian and German merchants, and Chinese railroad workers made Sausalito a vibrant, lively town.

When workers completed the Golden Gate Bridge in 1937 and the town's train and ferry services folded, Sausalito's importance as a transportation hub for goods and people moved to San Francisco. Seemingly doomed to obscurity, Sausalito bounced back to life with War II's need for construction of Liberty ships. Its Marin shipyard closed on September 18, 1945, having launched 93 vessels.

With world peace declared, the town returned to its pre-war size. As the 1950s descended on Sausalito, the creative element of society—the writers, artists, and philosophers—discovered this retreat, with its low rent and warm climate. Some people claim there remains a bohemian aura among the small colony of artists and writers. Today, those creative intellects who call Sausalito home have been joined by urban escapees, software developers, bankers, and Hollywood stars.

Bridgeway, the town's main street, follows the shoreline of the bay as it winds along the base of the high bluff on the west. Driving, or better yet, walking its several blocks, is the best way to enjoy most of what Sausalito has to offer. Near the south end of the marina, near **Plaza Viña del Mar**, [Fig. 28(1)] there is a small visitor center where maps and other information can be obtained. There is a walking tour guide available that is worth purchasing.

Across the street from Viña del Mar, is the **Gene Hiller** building, [Fig. 28(1)] constructed in 1894 originally as a bakery, but later as the Bank of Sausalito. It also served for some 50 years as the Old City Hall, when during city council meetings a rowdy drunk might be escorted down the aisle to the small cell behind the council podium.

The **Sausalito Yacht Harbor** [Fig. 28(2)] is one of the most intriguing such facilities anywhere. Tied here are watercraft ranging from ocean-going yachts worth millions to remarkably luxurious houseboats that serve as permanent homes for their owners. One easily noticed yacht is a splendid replica of the Taj Mahal.

Ark Row [Fig. 28(3)] is just a half-block west from the yacht harbor and a short walk down a wooden footpath. The small, flat-bottomed bungalows along the shore, some dating from the nineteenth century, were used as floating, year-round homes by artists and writers. Others, generally more elaborate than these that remain today, were used as floating summer vacation homes and winter duck hunting blinds by the rich. When not in use, especially during winter, they were dragged onto shore.

At the south end of town, near the corner of Bridgeway and Second Street, is the **Chart House**. [Fig. 28(4)] It was originally the **Walhalla**, a German beer garden in 1893. During Prohibition, it was rumored that bootleg whiskey was smuggled up from under its pier supports through a trap door behind the bar. In 1950, a well-known San Francisco madam looking for a more acceptable line of work transformed the old edifice into an elaborate Victorian structure she named the **Valhalla**. It soon became a well-respected restaurant and bar for the Bay area elite.

Salmon

Coho salmon (*Oncorhynchus kisutch*) and steelhead (*Oncorhynchus mykiss*) are anadromous fish, meaning that they return each year to spawn in Redwood Creek and other small streams along the Pacific Coast. Their life cycles begin when fertilized eggs hatch from 30 to 45 days after their deposit and fertilization in the gravels of oxygen-enriched, coastal-draining streams and rivers. Even after hatching, the fish remain in the protection of the gravel beds, subsisting on their own yolk sacks until large enough to emerge and feed on their own. The juvenile salmon, or fry, initially swim in protective schools, but soon disperse into more protected and solitary pools where they continue to feed and grow for their first year of life.

When winter rains again fall, high water allows streams to break through summer's sand dams created at their mouths. At the same time, the one-year-old salmon undergo "smoltification," the beginning of their transformation from solitary, freshwater-living fingerlings to schooling, sea-going salmon. Following about two years in the ocean, feeding and growing much larger, the salmon and steelhead return to the streams of their birth where they repeat their egg-laying and fertilization rituals.

A major difference between the salmon and steelhead is that the salmon will defend their redds (pockets of fertilized eggs) for a week or so and then die. Steelhead will generally return to the ocean and repeat their egg-laying cycles several times during their lives.

The salmon that migrate up Redwood Creek in Muir Woods are unique in California. They are the last truly wild, genetically distinct coho population in the state, having never been mixed with hatchery fish. Coho are generally found in the creek from November through January, while the steelhead are seen from January through April.

On the hillside above Bridgeway, about halfway between Valhalla and the visitor center, is the remains of a never-completed **Castle**. [Fig. 28(5)] William Randolph Hearst purchased the property and began construction on a grand mansion, but his plans were thwarted by townspeople. Apparently, they disapproved of his mistress and refused to grant Hearst's request that Water Street be rerouted in order to accommodate his grand design. After abandoning the project, Hearst put most of his mansion-building energies into San Simeon, soon to be known as Hearst Castle.

Most of the structures along Bridgeway are historic, with their own stories to tell. Today, the old buildings are being used as restaurants and shops and all are a joy to explore.

Directions: From US 101/Highway 1, take either the Bridge Boulevard Exit (north end of town), the Rodeo Avenue Exit, Spencer Avenue Exit, or the Alexander Avenue Exit (south end of town nearest Golden Gate Bridge). Follow any of the exits east toward the waterfront. An alternative, if in San Francisco, is to take the Blue and

Gold ferry service from San Francisco's Fisherman's Wharf.

Activities: Shopping, kayaking, fishing, bicycling, boating.

For more information: Sausalito Chamber of Commerce, PO Box 566, Sausalito, CA 94966. Phone (415) 331-7262. Sausalito Visitors Center, phone (415) 332-0505. For ferry service schedules, phone (415) 773-1188.

SAN FRANCISCO BAY-DELTA MODEL

[Fig. 28(6)] The streams and rivers that merge and finally empty into San Francisco Bay drain 40 percent of all California's fresh water. The intricate web of wetlands, estuaries, deltas, bays, tidal, and river flow rates are intimately connected, so much so that a single change in one area can have significant effects elsewhere, not always for the best.

In an effort to better understand how this massive water system interacts, the U.S. Army Corps of Engineers constructed a scale model. It's not your typical model because this one covers a full 1.5 acres, all inside a World War II-era building used during the Liberty ship construction. The model can track river flows, tidal differences, and how changes, such as water diversions, bottom dredging, or wetland fill projects can affect other parts of the system.

Even though most of this geographic area is commonly referred to as San Francisco Bay, it's actually a collection of three bays and the Golden Gate, and at 72,000 acres, the largest remaining tidal wetland in California. As large of an area as the bays cover—some 350 square miles total—only about 20 percent is more than 30 feet deep, with the deepest being the Carquinez Strait that connects San Pablo and Suisun bays, at 110 feet. Most are less than 15 feet deep, with much of the shallowness created during the late nineteenth century when hydraulic gold mining in the Sierra washed millions of cubic yards of silt down the rivers, filling about 30 percent of the bay. Each tidal cycle brings about 1.5 million acre-feet of saltwater in and out of the Golden Gate, while 50,000

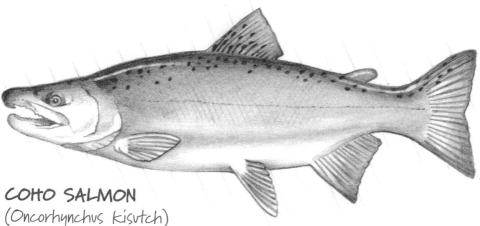

COHO SALMON
(Oncorhynchus kisutch)
Also called silver salmon, this anadromous fish generally ranges from Point Hope, Alaska to Monterey Bay, California.

acre-feet of fresh water flows in from the rivers. An acre-foot is equal to 43,560 cubic feet or the amount of water it takes to fill an acre to a depth of one foot.

The facility tour is self-guided, with a short introduction video available at the start of the tour. Walkways allow easy viewing of the different parts of the model, which is constructed in a horizontal scale of 1 foot = 1000 feet and a vertical scale of 1 foot = 100 feet. During water-flow experiments, the difference between the vertical and horizontal scales is compensated for with small copper tabs strategically placed to slow the water's movement. It's a fascinating look at a very complex natural system.

Directions: From US 101, north of the Golden Gate Bridge, take any of the Sausalito exits and drive east toward the water's edge to Bridgeway. The Bay Model Visitor Center is located at 2100 Bridgeway, Sausalito. There are directional signs along Bridgeway.

Dates: Open Tuesdays through Saturdays.

Fees: None.

Closest town: Sausalito

For more information: Bay Model Visitor Center, 2100 Bridgeway, Sausalito, CA 94965. Phone (415) 332-3871.

SAN PABLO BAY NATIONAL WILDLIFE REFUGE

[Fig. 25(2)] San Pablo Bay shares much of the same history with its more glamorous neighbor, San Francisco Bay, but also has its own stories to tell. Its rich waters, surrounding wetlands, and feeding rivers once provided refuge for untold millions of waterfowl, fish, and mammals, many of which are no longer found here. Today, San Pablo Bay serves as a major recreation area for boating and fishing enthusiasts, in addition to serving maritime trade. The following was written by an early visitor to the area:

The deer, antelope and noble elk...were numerous beyond all parallel. In herds of many hundreds, they might be met, so tame that they would hardly move to open the way for the traveler to pass. They were seen lying or grazing, in immense herds, on the sunny side of every hill, and their young, like lambs, were frolicking in all directions. The wild geese, and every species of waterfowl darkened the surface of every bay and firth, and upon the land, in flocks of millions they wandered in quest of insects, and cropping the wild oats which grew there in richest abundance. When disturbed they arose to fly, the sound of their wings was like that of distant thunder. The rivers were literally crowded with salmon.... It was literally a land of plenty, and such a climate as no other land can boast of.—George C. Yount, 1833.

As Congress makes funding available and appropriate private properties are placed on the market, wetland acreage is added to San Pablo Bay National Wildlife Refuge. The goal is to complete the originally authorized 20,000-acre refuge designed for protecting and restoring suitable habitat for migrating waterfowl. Wetlands, originally reclaimed for agricultural uses more than a century ago, are now being converted back to seasonal or tidal wetlands, both critical habitat for resident and migratory birds.

The combination of San Pablo Bay's open waters, wetlands, and mud flats make this a great bird-watching spot. Brewer's (*Euphagus cyanocphalus*) and red-winged (*Agelaius phoeniceus*) blackbirds fly in and out of the thick rows of tules that line the highway. Northern harriers (*Circus cyaneus*) fly low over the open lands searching for squirrels, mice, rabbits, or small birds. They compete with gopher snakes (*Pituophis melanoleucus*) for the same live prey, while turkey vultures (*Cathartes aura*) soar high overhead looking for many of the same animals, but only when they are dead. Cinnamon teal (*Anas cyanoptera*), mallards (*Anas platyrhynchos*), northern pintail (*Anas acuta*), and northern shovelers (*Anas clypeata*) are only a few of the migrating waterfowl that spend time feeding and resting in the refuge.

Directions: Take either US 101 or Interstate 80 to Highway 37. Follow Highway 37 east to 0.25 mile from Highway 121. The public gate is on the south shoulder of Highway 37. Park here and walk through the gate along the east bank of Tolay Creek.

Activities: Bird-watching, photography, seasonal waterfowl hunting.

Facilities: None.

Dates: Open year-round.

Fees: None.

For more information: San Pablo Bay National Wildlife Refuge, PO Box 2012, Vallejo, CA 94592. Phone (510) 792-0222.

CHINA CAMP STATE PARK

[Fig. 25(3)] This is one of those out-of-the-way places that few people except Bay Area locals ever get far enough off the US 101 freeway to see. It sits on the southwest edge of San Pablo Bay and in addition to its fascinating and sad history, it offers more than 1,600 acres of undeveloped hills, one of which offers a 360-degree view of the bay and several north bay counties. On clear days, of which there are many because of the protecting hills that generally keep out the fog that invades neighboring San Francisco Bay, Mount Diablo, Angel Island, and Mount Tamalpais are also visible.

There are 15 miles of trails in the park and many offer short walks to salt marshes, mud flats, meadows, and up the hills into oak woodlands and a small redwood grove. The park protects the largest, undisturbed watershed in this very developed portion of Marin County.

China Camp State Park is home to numerous animals. Deer, fox, and squirrels live and feed on the hillsides, while large populations of shorebirds search the wetlands for food. The park is also popular for fishing. Striped bass (*Morone saxatilis*) and white sturgeon (*Acipenser transmontanus*) can both be caught when the tide is in.

This land passed through the hands of the Coast Miwok Indians when the Spanish established their missions here in the nineteenth century. Timoteo Murphy acquired Rancho San Pedro, Santa Margarita y las Gallinas as a land grant. Following his death, the property was subdivided and in 1868 John and George McNear purchased the land now occupied by the park. The McNears grazed cattle, manufactured bricks, and quarried basalt, shipping their products by barge throughout the area.

The park gained its name from the Chinese fishermen who settled here, creating more than 20 villages along the bay. They came to California from the maritime province of Kwantung, China, looking for the golden riches that every immigrant expected during the mid-nineteenth century. On San Pablo Bay the Chinese began harvesting grass shrimp, a business that they were so successful and profitable in that non-Chinese fishermen pushed for passage of legislation that, when passed in 1911, outlawed the efficient Chinese bag nets.

During their prosperous early years, the Chinese dried the majority of their catches on the hillsides behind the camps and shipped most to either China or to other Chinese communities in the United States. Within China Camp State Park, remnants of some of the early buildings remain and a small museum exhibit explains the history of the Chinese here.

Directions: From US 101 in San Rafael, take the North San Pedro Road Exit and drive east for 5 miles until the road enters the park.

Activities: Bird-watching, fishing, swimming, hiking, picnicking, camping. There are 30 walk-in campsites. Reservations are advised during summer. Phone (800) 444-7275.

Dates: Open daily.

Fees: There are day use and camping fees.

For more information: China Camp State Park, Route 1, Box 244, San Rafael, CA 94901. Phone (415) 456-0766.

MUIR WOODS NATIONAL MONUMENT

[Fig. 27] This relatively small, 560-acre park is very popular with summer tourists, especially those driving from San Francisco, who want to experience a redwood forest. Anytime of the year is a good time to visit, with spring bringing its profusion of wildflowers, including the large, white blooms of the California buckeye tree (*Aesculus californica*). It's always nice to see the showy leaves of the bigleaf maple (*Acer macrophyllum*) open in spring because it is a reminder that in the fall they will add wonderful splashes of brilliant yellow to the forest.

What the park is best known for is its redwoods. The largest trees, both in height and diameter, grow in the Cathedral and Bohemian groves. At 14 feet across, 250 feet tall, and 1,000 years old, they are impressive, but are only babies compared with their cousins in the redwood groves farther north in Humboldt County.

Among the redwoods, Douglas fir, and other trees, many animals find homes, although, except for chipmunks and squirrels, few are seen by visitors. Black-tailed mule deer (*Odocoileus hemionus*) and spotted owls (*Strix occidentalis*) are rarely seen, while numerous species of butterflies, including migrating monarchs (*Danaus plexippus*) and the acmon blue butterfly (*Icaricia acmon*) are much more numerous and visible.

The national monument was created in 1905, when Congressman William Kent and his wife Elizabeth purchased the property because it contained some of the last remaining uncut old-growth redwoods in the Bay Area. They paid $45,000 for the original 295 acres, then donated the land to the federal government in order to assure its continued protection from logging. In 1908, President Theodore Roosevelt declared the property a national monument and wanted to name it after Kent. Kent had another idea, preferring that it bear the name of one of the country's leading preservationists of the time, John Muir.

On summer weekends, when up to 10,000 people may visit the park in a single day, it's good to get here early because parking is limited. The small parking lot and the roadside shoulders fill quickly. There are no picnicking or camping facilities in the park.

Directions: After crossing the Golden Gate Bridge heading north from San Francisco on US 101, take the Highway 1 Exit and continue north on Highway 1. Turn right on the Muir Woods road and drive about 3 miles to the park entrance. The roads to the park are steep and winding. Vehicles over 35 feet long are prohibited.

Activities: Hiking, bird-watching.

Facilities: Visitor center, paved walking trail.

Dates: Open daily.

Fees: There is a small entry fee.

Closest town: Mill Valley, 3 miles.

For more information: Muir Woods National Monument, Mill Valley, CA 94941. Phone (415) 388-2595.

John Muir

Philosopher, scientist, and author John Muir was born on April 21, 1838 in Dunbar, Scotland. His family emigrated to the United States in 1849, finally settling near Portage, Wisconsin. Muir developed an early interest in nature and following three years at the University of Wisconsin he left, preferring instead to enter what he called "the University of the Wilderness."

He traveled extensively around the world, including a 1,000-mile walk from Indianapolis to the Gulf of Mexico, always spending time alone, contemplating nature and man. In 1868, he walked across the San Joaquin Valley, later writing: "Then it seemed to me the Sierra should be called not the Nevada, or Snowy Range, but the Range of Light...the most divinely beautiful of all the mountain chains I have ever seen." This love affair with the Sierra would never waver and he returned there often.

His prolific writings and unbounded love of nature helped create Yosemite National Park in 1890. In 1892, Muir and others founded the Sierra Club to "do something for wilderness and make the mountains glad." Muir's reputation also attracted the attention of President Theodore Roosevelt. Muir and Roosevelt traveled to Yosemite in 1903 and lay beneath the trees where they discussed and planned the essentials of many of Roosevelt's future conservation programs. Muir also helped in the creation of Mount Rainier, Sequoia, and Grand Canyon national parks. Muir remained an active conservationist and president of the Sierra Club until his death in 1914.

The San Francisco Bay and San Mateo Coast

San Francisco Bay attracts 70 percent of the millions of waterfowl and shorebirds that migrate up and down the Pacific Flyway each spring and fall.

M A R I N

S O L A N O

C O N T R A   C O S T A

A L A M E D A

S A N   M A T E O

S A N T A   C R U Z

S A N T A   C L A R A

N

San Francisco

101 37 80 680 12 160 1 4 4 580 92 1 35 280 35 1 17 152 1 101

Novato
San Anselmo
San Rafael
Larkspur
San Pablo
Mill Valley
Vallejo
Benicia
Pinole
Martinez
El Sobrante
Richmond
El Cerrito
Orinda
Albany
Berkeley
Piedmont
Pittsburg
Antioch
Concord
Pleasant Hill
Walnut Creek
Lafayette
Moraga Town
Danville
Oakland
Alameda
San Ramon
San Leandro
Castro Valley
Dublin
San Lorenzo
Ashland
Hayward
Pleasanton
Daly City
San Bruno
Millbrae
Burlingame
Hillsborough
San Mateo
Foster City
Belmont
North Fair Oaks
Fremont
Newark
Union City
San Carlos
Redwood City
Menlo Park
Stanford
Palo Alto
Milpitas
Mountain View
Sunnyvale
Alum Rock
Los Altos
Santa Clara
Cupertino
San Jose
Saratoga
Campbell
Los Gatos
Live Oak
Santa Cruz
Watsonville
24

FIGURE NUMBERS

30	Marin Headlands
31	The Presidio of San Francisco
32	San Francisco Bay's Islands
33	City of San Francisco
34	Metro San Francisco
35	San Francisco Bay Area

San Francisco Bay Area and San Mateo Coast

T he pastoral setting that marks most of lands north of San Francisco Bay instantly disappears as you pass through the tollbooths at the south end of the Golden Gate Bridge. Yet among the museums, skyscrapers, shops, and restaurants that fill the city, there are parks filled with gardens and forests and miles of open beaches. San Francisco's streets that traverse breathtakingly steep hills are legendary, as are the streetcars and Fisherman's Wharf.

Continue driving on Highway 1 as it heads south out of San Francisco and the businesses and homes that crowded to the edges of the freeway near the city soon give way to open mountains and craggy cliffs that drop directly into the Pacific Ocean. Highway 1 follows the coastline very closely here, with only a few small towns to mark the open lands used mostly for cattle grazing, when it is usable at all.

[*Above:* Walking the Golden Gate Bridge, a 3.2-mile round trip, is a popular activity]

Marin Headlands

The Marin Headlands block came into existence 100 million years ago in the depths of the Pacific Ocean and slowly moved along the San Andreas fault to its present location.

Ref: Golden Gate N.R.A. N.P.S. Map

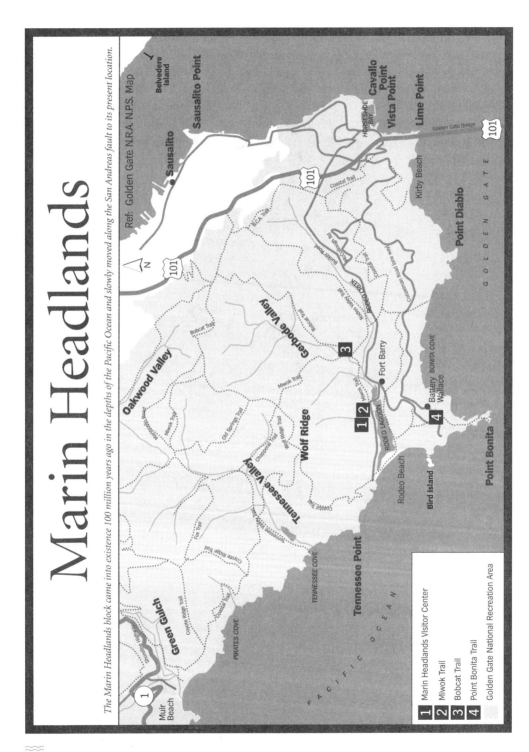

Muir Beach

Green Gulch

Shoreline Highway

Coyote Ridge Trail

Coastal Trail

PIRATES COVE

Northwoods Road

Miwok Trail

Oakwood Valley

Old Springs Trail

Chappeval Trail

Fox Trail

Coyote Ridge Trail

Tennessee Valley Trail

Tennessee Valley

TENNESSEE COVE

Tennessee Point

Bobcat Trail

Miwok Trail

Gerbode Valley

Bobcat Trail

Wolf Ridge Trail

Wolf Ridge

Coastal Trail

RODEO LAGOON

Rodeo Beach

Rodeo Valley Trail

Miwok Trail

Fort Barry

Coastal Trail

Bird Island

Battery Wallace

BONITA COVE

Point Bonita

Bunker Road

McCullough Rd

Conzelman Road (one way)

Coastal Trail

RODEO CREEK

BONITA COVE

Point Diablo

GOLDEN GATE

Kirby Beach

Golden Gate Bridge

101

101

Coastal Trail

BCA Trail

101

N

Sausalito

Belvedere Island

Sausalito Point

HORSESHOE BAY

Cavallo Point

Vista Point

Lime Point

PACIFIC OCEAN

1 Marin Headlands Visitor Center

2 Miwok Trail

3 Bobcat Trail

4 Point Bonita Trail

Golden Gate National Recreation Area

Farallan National Wildlife Refuge

The refuge is the largest seabird rookery along the eastern Pacific Ocean, south of Alaska. Each spring and summer, a quarter million seabirds visit the Farallan Islands' steep cliffs and rocky outcroppings, lying just 27 miles west of the Golden Gate. Pigeon guillemots (*Cepphus columba*), rhinoceros auklets (*Cerohinca monocerata*), tufted puffins (*Lunda cirrhata*), common murres (*Uria aalge*), cormorants (*Phalacro-corax* sp.), and oystercatchers (*Haematopus* sp.) are some of the more common birds seen. Jaegers (*Stercorarius* sp.), shearwaters (*Puffinus* sp.), and albatross (*Diomedea* sp.) join birds that can be seen during boat trips around the islands. California sea lions (*Zalophus californicus*), northern elephant seals (*Mirounga angustirostris*), steller's sea lions (*Eumetopias jubatus*), and harbor seals (*Phoca vitulina*) haul out on the narrow beaches and lower rocks or swim in the area, as do several species of marine turtles.

Many trips to the island include whale sightings, with blue whales and humpbacks being the most commonly observed during spring and summer. It's also a thrill when pods of Dall's (*Phocoenoides dalli*), Risso's (*Grampus griseus*), or Pacific white-sided dolphins (*Lagenorhynchus obliquidens*) begin riding the boat's bow wake.

The islands are off limits to visitors. The only way to view the islands' wildlife is from a charter tour boat or a private boat.

For more information: Gulf of the Farallones National Marine Sanctuary, Fort Mason, Building 201, San Francisco, CA 94123. Phone (415) 561-6622. Oceanic Society Expeditions, Fort Mason Center, Bldg. E., San Francisco, CA 94123. Phone (415) 474-3385.

Golden Gate's Migrating Birds of Prey

Like many bird species, raptors also migrate when changing weather reduces their food supplies below acceptable limits. Each fall, as temperatures drop and the days grow shorter in the higher mountains to the east and north and smaller prey animals slip into hibernation, thousands of raptors begin their southerly migrations to warmer climates.

Most raptors are terrestrial hunters and prefer not to fly over large bodies of water. Therefore, as they migrate down California's coast, the Pacific Ocean forces them to stay inland. As they approach Marin, they are squeezed to the west by the sprawling open waters and wetlands of San Pablo Bay. The result is that thousands of hawks, turkey vultures, and a few eagles are funneled over the Marin Headlands before they cross San Francisco Bay at its narrowest opening near the Golden Gate.

The migration season runs roughly from September through November and during those three months over 20,000 birds of prey will pass through this very narrow corridor. Red-tailed hawks (*Buteo jamaicensis*) make up the largest number of birds, with an average of nearly 7,000 passing overhead. Sharp-shinned hawks (*Accipiter striatus*), Cooper's hawks (*Accipiter cooperii*), and turkey vultures (*Cathartes aura*) also pass in large numbers. American kestrels (*Falco sparverius*), prairie falcons (*Falco mexicanus*), red-shouldered hawks (*Buteo lineagtus*), broad-winged hawks (*Buteo platypterus*), and a few ferruginous hawks (*Buteo regalis*) also are seen. Sightings of golden eagles (*Aquila chrysaetos*) are more rare, with only an occasional bald eagle (*Haliaeetus leucocephalus*) crossing at the Golden Gate.

During September and October, Golden Gate Raptor Observatory docents give free public programs on weekend afternoons at Hawk Hill.

Directions: To reach Hawk Hill from near the north end of the Golden Gate Bridge off US 101, drive west on Conzelman Road for 1.8 miles. Look for the brown and white "Hawk Hill" sign. Park on the side of the road before it becomes one-way, then walk the few hundred feet up the ocean side of Hawk Hill to the flat summit.

Closest town: San Francisco, 4 miles south or Sausalito, 2 miles to the northeast.

For more information: Golden Gate Raptor Observatory, Building 201, Fort Mason, San Francisco, CA 94123. Phone (415) 331-0730. Raptor hotline recording, phone (415) 561-3030, ext. 2500.

Golden Gate National Recreation Area

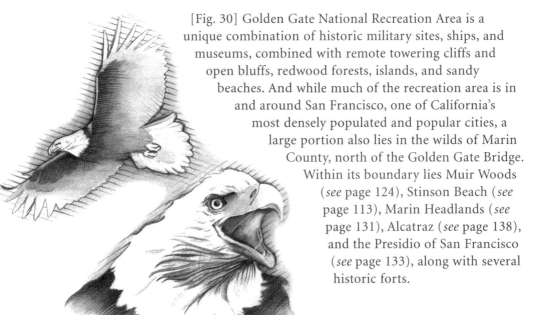

[Fig. 30] Golden Gate National Recreation Area is a unique combination of historic military sites, ships, and museums, combined with remote towering cliffs and open bluffs, redwood forests, islands, and sandy beaches. And while much of the recreation area is in and around San Francisco, one of California's most densely populated and popular cities, a large portion also lies in the wilds of Marin County, north of the Golden Gate Bridge. Within its boundary lies Muir Woods (*see* page 124), Stinson Beach (*see* page 113), Marin Headlands (*see* page 131), Alcatraz (*see* page 138), and the Presidio of San Francisco (*see* page 133), along with several historic forts.

BALD EAGLE
(Haliaeetus leucocephalus)

The national recreation area protects over 76,000 acres, 1,250 historic structures, and 27 rare and endangered species, while serving 20 million visitors each year. With the Golden Gate Bridge connecting its north and south parts, anyone can hike a remote trail in the morning and view migrating hawks and grazing elk in the afternoon, and in the evening dine in some of the world's finest restaurants.

MARIN HEADLANDS

[Fig. 30] From a distance the Marin Headlands and the lands behind them appear as reddish-brown hills, essentially devoid of plant life, except for a few small pockets of green. Nothing could be farther from the truth. The headlands' geology is laid open for inspection and that story helps explain its modern appearance. The Marin Headlands block began its existence 100 million years ago in the depths of the Pacific Ocean, far to the south. It has slowly moved to its present location, sliding along the San Andreas fault.

At the north end of the Golden Gate Bridge from San Francisco, take the first exit, which swings under the freeway and back onto the west side of the bridge onto Conzieman Road. There's a pullout at Battery Spencer and additional pullouts farther down the road that offer spectacular views back across the Golden Gate toward San Francisco, at least on clear, fogless days.

Check the roadcuts or hike down to Rodeo Cove or Tennessee Cove and look closely at the reddish rock formations. Through a hand lens or strong magnifier, the remnants of small, one-celled organisms that lived in the ancient ocean are visible. These radiolarians, now transformed into radiolarian chert, were originally laid down with layers of equally ancient mud, but over millions of years have been severely contorted by tremendous pressures and movement. Over the past several thousand years, the chert cliffs have been broken, eroded, and constantly reformed by the unending crash of waves. One roadcut along Conzieman Road, west from the Battery Spencer overlook, has a wonderful example of relatively rare ribbon chert, easily recognized by its thin, ribbon-like strands of twisted and contorted rock.

Conzieman Road, from near the long-abandoned Battery 129, becomes one-way. Continue ahead and the road winds around past batteries Wallace and Mendell, which are also long-abandoned coastal defenses. The road finally leads to the old Fort Berry church, which has been transformed into a visitor center. It's the perfect place to get maps and books about the area's natural and cultural history, along with ranger- and docent-led hike information.

An interesting leftover from the early days of the Cold War is the closed Nike missile site. It's only one of the many visual reminders of the army's long presence on the headlands and the evolution of weapons, from nineteenth century smooth-bore cannons to World War II's 16-inch guns and anti-aircraft weapons and finally to the underground Nike missiles of the Cold War. Each weapon system significantly extended the range that attacking enemy ships or aircraft could be engaged and destroyed.

Today, guided tours of the site are available, including a demonstration alert that rolls and lifts one of the disarmed and unfueled missiles into firing position.

Over many years, ranchers and the army built small dams in headland streambeds, which created lagoons by joining small natural pools and ponds. The lagoons have become important habitat for numerous species of animals. Near the visitor center, Rodeo Lagoon is the largest of the water impoundments. There's a trail around the lagoon, which is mostly fresh water, except when high waves occasionally wash over the sand barrier that separates it from the ocean. Within Rodeo Lagoon's slightly saline waters lives the endangered tidewater goby (*Eucyclogobius newberryi*), which is only about 1 inch long. During spring and summer, most of the ponds are impossible to get close to because of the heavy growth of alders (*Alnus rhombifolia*), arroyo willows (*Salix lasiolepis*), and the ever-present cattails (*Typha latifolia*) and sedges (*Carex* sp.).

Some of the best hiking is along the trails that follow the main waterways, Tennessee Creek and Rodeo Creek. Here, the presence of water in a relatively dry land, especially during California's rainless summers, supports a large variety of plant life. The profusion of vegetation along the creeks and on the surrounding hillsides provides cover and food for dozens of animal and insect species. Butterflies are a bright addition to the spring wildflowers that cover the landscape. Orange sulfers (*Colias eurytheme*) are attracted to yellow mustard, swallowtails favor lupine and fennel, and the endangered mission blue butterfly (*Icaricia icarioides missionensis*) searches for lupine.

Brewer's blackbirds (*Euphaus cyanocephalus*) and sparrows favor the thick creek-side vegetation, while brown towhees (*Pipilo fuscus*) and wrentits (*Chamaea fasciata*) are more likely to be seen in the coastal scrub. Hawks almost always soar overhead or sit on fence or power poles, especially during the fall migration. The always-present and seemingly ominous (but environmentally important) turkey vulture (*Cathartes aura*) uses its 6-foot wingspan to soar effortlessly on the thermals, while depending upon its keen eyesight to locate dead animals on which to feed.

From the visitor center at Fort Barry, pick up Bunker Road to exit the park. The road winds through more of the open country, finally reaching a one-way tunnel controlled by a signal light that allows alternating traffic to pass.

Directions: Marin Headlands lie on the north side of the Golden Gate Bridge, west of US 101. The easiest access is from Conzeiman Road, the first exit after crossing the Golden Gate Bridge, heading north.

Activities: Hiking, camping, picnicking, fishing.

Facilities: Visitor center.

Dates: Fort Berry Visitor Center is open daily.

Fees: None.

Closest town: Sausalito, 2 miles.

For more information: National Park Service, Fort Mason, San Francisco, CA 94123. Phone (415) 331-1540.

TRAILS

There are dozens of miles of trails that lace the Marin Headlands and offer spectacular views of San Francisco Bay, the city beyond, and the Pacific Ocean. They also provide opportunities to explore deep canyons and hidden ponds. It is best to pick up a trail map from any of the visitor centers and dress for quickly changing weather conditions any month of the year.

Miwok Trail: [Fig. 30(2)] Approximately 0.75-mile of trail follows the north shore of Rodeo Lagoon, beginning on the north side of Rodeo Creek, near the Visitor Center at Fort Berry. It connects with another trail that continues around the sand barrier separating the Pacific Ocean from Rodeo Lagoon, passing the old Nike missile site, and finally returning to near the visitor center. The Miwok Trail actually meanders north about 15 miles, ending in Mount Tamalpais State Park and connecting with the Redwood Creek Trail near Muir Woods Road.

Bobcat Trail: [Fig. 30(3)] The trail picks up from the east end of the Miwok trail, about 0.3 mile northeast of the Fort Barry visitor center and continues on the south side of Rodeo Creek approximately 3.2 miles, heading up into the hills. It connects with several other trails, including the Oakwood Trail, S.C.A. Trail, and a 1.5-mile spur trail to the Hawk backpack camping area.

Point Bonita Trail: [Fig. 30(4)] From the parking area just past Battery Wallace, it's just over 1 mile out to the Point Bonita Lighthouse, which is open on weekends during the summer season.

THE PRESIDIO OF SAN FRANCISCO

[Fig. 31] For more than 200 years, the Presidio of San Francisco has stood as a sentry under three national flags, guarding the entrance into San Francisco Bay. The Spanish built the first protective outpost here, a modest adobe-walled compound, in 1776. They added a larger adobe fort in 1779, overlooking the bay's entrance. It had two bronze cannons, which are now exhibited on the grounds of the main compound at Pershing Square. They are among the oldest known cannons in North America, cast in 1679 and 1693.

When Mexico gained its independence from Spain in 1821, Mexico's new government occupied the Presidio, considering it an important defensive point. Mexico abandoned the Presidio, however, when the Russians moved down California's coast and established Fort Ross about 80 miles to the north. The Presidio came under the flag of the United States in 1846, when the U.S. military occupied both San Francisco and the Presidio. The U.S. military officially established a full-time military reservation here in 1850.

What began as barren hillsides in 1883, Major William A. Jones proposed changing to forests that would "crown the ridges…and cover the areas of sand and marsh." Over the next 20 years, the military planted 400,000 tree seedlings of pine, cypress, and eucalyptus, often in orderly, military-like rows. As the army transformed the

The Presidio of San Francisco

The Spanish built the first protective outpost here in 1776.

Ref: Golden Gate National Recreation Area
Presidio of San Francisco NPS Map

1 Fort Point

The Presidio of San Francisco

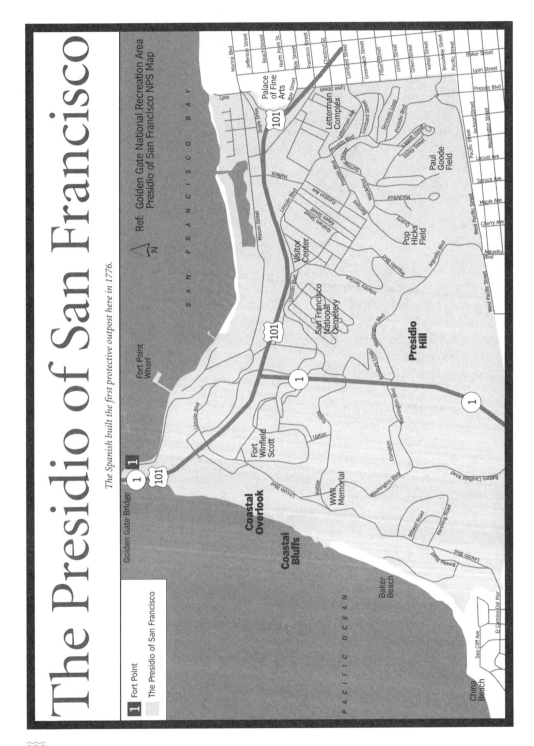

landscape and constructed buildings to meet its ever-increasing needs, it was generally the officers who were the first to benefit from the improvements: "I went to the Presidio... where the soldiers live in barracks and tents. There are beautiful residences where the officers live and a wide cement drive where automobiles and carriages go, with dirt roads for the cavalry," wrote author Laura Ingalls Wilder in 1915.

As the Presidio became more vital to the defense of the West Coast, barracks replaced tents for the enlisted men and comfortable and lavish Victorian homes were soon added for higher-ranking officers. Many other buildings were added, including a hospital and fire station.

Today, the Presidio is a National Park, with tree-lined streets and many of the historic structures restored. There is a 1-mile, self-guided trail that leads past a dozen stops on the main Presidio grounds. The visitor center (Building 201) has guide pamphlets available. It is located on Montgomery Street, across from the main parade ground.

Within the Presidio's 1,480 acres lie many historic buildings and other sites: Crissy Field, the first airfield on the West Coast, Fort Point, the San Francisco National Military Cemetery, and the historic cavalry stables. The Presidio grounds are a favorite place for bicyclists, in-line skaters, walkers, joggers, and sailing enthusiasts.

Directions: The Presidio of San Francisco is located on the northwest tip of San Francisco, near the south end of the Golden Gate Bridge. Lombard Street (going west) turns into Lincoln Boulevard, which weaves through most of the Presidio. Highway 1 (19th Avenue in the city) becomes Park Presidio Boulevard as it passes through the Presidio before connecting with US 101 and reaching the toll entrance to the Golden Gate Bridge.

Activities: Hiking, biking, in-line skating, sight-seeing, fishing.

Facilities: Historic buildings, visitor center.

Dates: Open year-round.

Fees: None.

For more information: Golden Gate National Recreation Area, Presidio, Fort Mason, Building 201, San Francisco, CA 94123. Phone (415) 561-4323.

FORT POINT

[Fig. 31(1)] This underside view of the Golden Gate Bridge is worth seeing, but more intriguing is the brick that went into constructing Fort Point. The U.S. Army Corps of Engineers began blasting the 90-foot cliff at the point in 1853, but work progressed slowly until the threat of the Civil War quickened construction. Finally, in 1861 the first cannon was mounted as Colonel Albert Johnston prepared defenses for the Pacific. His job done, he resigned his commission and joined the Confederate Army. He was later killed at the Battle of Shiloh.

Although the fort never came under attack, the Pacific command saw it as the key to western defenses. But as smooth-bore cannons were replaced by more powerful and accurate breach-loading rifled guns, it became apparent that masonry fortresses could not stand up to modern artillery attacks. Over the next few years, the old guns

San Francisco Bay's Islands

Attorney General Robert Kennedy finally closed Alcatraz on March 21, 1963, ending its 29 years as a federal prison.

N

Ref: USGS 1:24,000
North San Francisco

Belvedere Island

Tiburon Peninsula

Tiburon

Belvedere

RACCOON STRAIT

Point Campbell

Point Simpton

Point Lone

AYALA COVE

SAN FRANCISCO

BAY

Quarry Point

Mount Livermore

Quarry Beach

Point Stuart

RICHARDSON BAY

Sausalito

Sausalito Point

Point Knox

Perle's Beach

Angel Island

Blunt Point

FERRY

FERRY

Marin Peninsula

1

101

Yellow Bluff

FERRY

Alcatraz Island

SAN FRANCISCO

BAY

Lime Point

GOLDEN GATE

Golden Gate Bridge

Fort Point

1

101

FERRY

Alcatraz Ferry
Angel Island Ferry
Tiburon Ferry

Parks

Ferry

Trail

San Francisco

were removed and other uses, from barracks to a World War II anti-submarine net guard unit, were found.

With waves crashing into the granite seawall at its base, the old, three-story brick fort is an architectural delight. Visitors can wander throughout the structure, up dark staircases all the way to the top deck that once held some of the 69 artillery pieces that were placed in the fort. The fort never mounted all of its planned 141 guns, but it did acquire several 10-inch Rodman guns in the lower casemates. They could fire a 128-pound solid steel shot 2 miles.

Today, most of the cannons are gone, but several similar guns are displayed on the ground floor inside the fort. There's a great view of the bay from the top of the fort's walls, properly called the barbette tier, where the old, rusting gun mounts remain. The fort's three spiral stairways are intriguing. They don't have central columns for support. Instead, they rely on the weight of the 1,000 pound, hand-cut granite steps sitting on top of one another to hold the stairway structure in place.

Directions: The fort is located at the south end of the Golden Gate Bridge and there are several different approaches via the web of roads that wind throughout the Presidio of San Francisco. From Crissy Field in the Presidio, take Mason Street west, which essentially parallels US 101 to its south. The road will merge into Lincoln, heading northwest. Following the signs, take Long Street, which is another right turn off Lincoln. Follow it to the end, where there's a small parking lot at the foot of Fort Point.

Activities: Tours, including audio tours.

Facilities: Small visitor center, bookstore, theater.

Dates: Open daily, except Thanksgiving, Christmas, and New Year's. For a recorded schedule, phone (415) 773-1188.

Fees: None.

Closest town: San Francisco

For more information: Fort Point National Historic Site, PO Box 29333, San Francisco, CA 94129. Phone (415) 556-1693.

San Francisco Bay's Islands

[Fig. 32] The changing level of the ocean, strong tidal flows, two great rivers that drain much of the Sierra Nevada, and 300,000 years of shifting tectonic plates created the islands that jut skyward from San Francisco Bay. The advance of the rising ocean through the relatively narrow gorge, now known as the Golden Gate, flooded the lower valleys and hills eastward to the straits of Carquinez, leaving only the tops of the highest eroded hills visible. Two of these remnant hilltops are most prominent, with Alcatraz Island being the most well known, although Angel Island certainly has played a much more important role in California's history. Alcatraz is part of the Golden Gate National Recreation Area, while Angel Island is a California State Park.

San Francisco Bay

In spite of its name and a widespread belief, San Francisco Bay is not a true bay, but rather California's largest estuary. Its waters are very shallow, with 70 percent being less than 18 feet deep at low tide. Sixteen rivers, the two largest being the Sacramento and San Joaquin, drain over 60,000 square miles and run into the estuary to mix and dilute the sea water that is washed in and out by strong tides and winds.

Hydraulic gold mining operations during the late nineteenth century began filling San Francisco Bay's original 720 square miles of open water. Hydraulic mining was outlawed in 1884 because its sediment waste was filling waterways and causing catastrophic flooding of towns and farmlands downstream. Yet developers continued filling the bay well into modern times in order to create new land for development of businesses, airports, and freeways. Adding to the loss of wildlife habitat were the large portions of the shallow south bay that were diked and used as salt ponds. Today, the bay is just 480 square miles of open water and wetlands.

San Francisco Bay attracts 70 percent of the millions of waterfowl and shorebirds that migrate up and down the Pacific Flyway each spring and fall. For millions of other birds, the bay's mud flats, sloughs, and salt marshes serve as homes year-round. Brown pelicans (*Pelecanus occidentalis*), greater scaups (*Aythya marila*), and numerous species of gulls are relatively common during different times of the year. Explore the waters of the tidal sloughs and, besides the ever-present and all-important cordgrass (*Spartina foliosa*), mussels, snails, shrimp, bat rays (*Myliobatis californica*), leopard sharks (*Triakis semifasciata*), mallards (*Anas platyrhynchos*), northern shovelers (*Anas clypeata*), great blue herons (*Ardea herodias*), and harbor seals (*Phoca vitulina*) create a rich and productive milieu. Dig out just two handfuls of mud from the bay's mud flats and 40,000 microscopic organisms, the building blocks of this entire ecosystem, are present.

ALCATRAZ

Native Americans probably first visited Angel Island and Alcatraz as early as 10,000 to 20,000 years ago, but only Angel Island offered any sheltering trees or freshwater. The Ohlone Indians (Ohlone was a Miwok Indian word meaning "western people"), who inhabited much of the area around and to the south of San Francisco Bay, probably gathered bird eggs from the desolate rock, but there was never any attempt to establish a permanent settlement. A few Indians may have been banished to the island as punishment for tribal infractions, and others might have tried to hide on the desolate island in order to escape mission life.

Permanent settlement of the island didn't occur until the U.S. Army began building gun emplacements in the mid-nineteenth century. The U.S. military saw the island as a crucial part of the overall defense of San Francisco Bay and thus, California. The army hauled dirt from Angel Island during the construction of its initial gun emplacements, but their initial attempts to grow simple grass and clover on the island's poor soil failed.

The army continued adding soil, and within a few years better-adapted native plants, such as coyote brush (*Baccharis pilularis*), California poppies (*Eschscholzia californica*), and blackberries (*Rubus ursinus*) finally gained footholds in the soil. During the 1860s, workers blasted pits in the rock and filled them with soil, getting trees and other larger vegetation to grow, with beautiful formal gardens finally being maintained by the 1880s. By the early 1900s, the land around the island's military buildings had been transformed into a multicolored garden.

San Francisco's importance to the Union was aptly illustrated by the platforms for 155 guns that were constructed on the island, including 6- , 8-, and 10-inch Solumbiad cannons mounted on wooden carriages. The army also placed some of the Civil War's largest guns on the island, including the 15-inch Rodman that could fire its 440-pound shot 3 miles. The island's guns fired only one shot during the Civil War and that was at a British ship that had initially failed to identify itself.

The Civil War started what would become Alcatraz's most well-known use—it began serving as a prison for army and navy officers who refused to swear allegiance to the Union. They were followed by Southern sympathizers in California who unwisely spoke too loudly about their loyalties to the Confederate States. Something as simple as a drunken toast to Jefferson Davis, President of the Confederate States of America, landed people in what was quickly gaining a reputation as a harsh prison. Military prisoners broke rock all day while dragging around 24-pound iron balls chained to their legs, meant to discourage escape attempts. Civil War prisoners were followed by Spanish American War prisoners in 1898. Its continued and growing use as a prison prompted additional construction of concrete cellblocks and other facilities.

The military finally abandoned Alcatraz as a prison in 1933, no longer willing to pay the high costs of maintaining and supplying the island. It was then that FBI Director J. Edgar Hoover agreed to take over the prison. It met his need for a "super-prison," capable of handling the most dangerous and infamous criminals that his agents were capturing. The following year it was formally named United States Penitentiary, Alcatraz.

Some of its first "super-prisoners" included Al "Scarface" Capone and "Machine Gun" Kelly, although it was always the prison administration's policy to never an-nounce, confirm, or deny which prisoners were on the "Rock." Such secrecy, coupled with horror stories from released prisoners (one called it the "island of the living dead"), added both mystery and a sense of fear, further enhancing Alcatraz's reputa-tion as the "hardest" prison in the country. Others, including both guards and prisoners, disagreed with that harsh assessment.

Attorney General Robert Kennedy finally closed the prison on March 21, 1963, ending its 29 years as a federal prison. Kennedy closed it for the same reason as the army: the aged and crumbling facility was much too costly to maintain. Plans to transform the abandoned prison into a national park were interrupted by the Native American Indian occupation that began in November 1969 and didn't end until June 1971. While the occupation brought much needed attention to Native American issues, much of the old prison's historic fabric was damaged or destroyed during the occupation.

The National Park Service again assumed control of the island and it became part of the new Golden Gate National Recreation Area. The first public tours began in 1973.

Alcatraz isn't all military and prison history. The island is a refuge for a wide variety of plants and wildlife. Its tidepools are man-made, established on jagged piles of rock, granite, brick, concrete, and other debris that has been dumped on the island's shore for the more than 100 years. Anemones, sea stars, and other common tidepool animals thrive in the waters around the island. On land, animals range from California slender salamanders (*Batrachoseps attenautus*) and deer mice (*Peromyscus maniculatus*) to about two dozen species of birds that are commonly seen. They include brown pelicans (*Pelecanus occidentalis*), peregrine falcons (*Falco peregrinus*), barn swallows (*Hirundo rustica*), black-crowned night herons (*Nycticorax nycticorax*), and red-throated loons (*Gavia stellata*).

Directions: The most popular route to Alcatraz is by ferry from San Francisco's Fisherman's Wharf. The ticket booth is located at Pier 41, near where The Embarcadero merges into Jefferson Street.

Activities: Hiking, tours.

Facilities: Gift shop.

Dates: Open daily. Times and frequency of tours vary seasonally.

Fees: There is a fee for the ferry crossing, which includes entry onto Alcatraz Island. From Apr. through Oct. it is advisable to purchase tickets well in advance. Phone (415) 705-5555.

Closest town: San Francisco.

For more information: Blue & Gold Fleet for ferry times and prices, phone (415) 705-5444. Golden Gate National Recreation Area Headquarters, Fort Mason, Building 201, San Francisco, CA 94123. Phone (415) 705-1042 or (415) 556-0560

ANGEL ISLAND STATE PARK

[Fig. 32] Coast Miwok Indians first used Angel Island, paddling their tule reed boats across the short channel from the Tiburon mainland and establishing villages near today's Ayala Cove, where the West, North, and East garrisons are located. The island's deer, harbor seals, and sea lions, along with ducks, quail, and sea birds provided plenty of food, especially when combined with acorns and various wild roots and bulbs.

In 1775, Spanish lieutenant Juan Manuel de Ayala sailed into San Francisco Bay and mapped its islands and shoreline, naming the island *Isla de Los Angeles.* Little was done with the island, but the Indians were soon pulled off and moved into the nearby missions. In 1837 the governor of Mexican-controlled California granted most of Angel Island to Antonio Maria Osio for a cattle ranch, with a portion retained for a potential coastal defense post. In 1846, with the United States in control of California, Osio lost most of his land.

Often known as the Ellis Island of the West, Angel Island served the United States as a strategic military post for every conflict since the Civil War. In 1864, the army began constructing Camp Reynolds and its defensive cannon emplacements. As the military build-up continued through the end of the nineteenth century, a quarantine station was also established at Ayala Cove. The station fumigated foreign ships entering the port and held immigrants in isolation who were thought to be carrying contagious diseases.

In 1899 the army maintained a detention camp for U.S. veterans who had either contracted or been exposed to contagious diseases. As the war wound down, troops returning from the Philippines during 1901 passed through the island's facilities during their transition from soldier to civilian life.

The Immigration Station in today's North Garrison was in operation in 1910 and handled primarily Asian immigrants. The heartfelt poems and the names of many who passed through the facility can still be seen, written on the inside walls of some of the buildings. This same time period marked the island's beginning as a major army recruit receiving and processing center, primarily in the East Garrison. It included a 600-man barracks and other support facilities. At the beginning of World War I the island added a detention center for "enemy aliens," mostly German citizens who were unfortunate enough to be in U.S. ports when war broke out.

Angel Island was the country's only overseas processing and training facility prior to the beginning of World War II. It served the only U.S. overseas bases at the time, which were located in the Philippines, Hawaii, and in the Panama Canal Zone. During World War II, portions of Angel Island served as prisoner of war camps for Japanese prisoners. It also served as a major defense post, with anti-aircraft guns and searchlights set up on the top of the mountain. The U.S. military ended most of its uses for the island following the processing of returning GIs after Japan's surrender. Then in the mid-1950s the island was seen as an ideal Nike missile site. This was also the same time that efforts were being made to make the island a public park. The missile site was deactivated in 1962.

Today, many of the original military and immigration buildings remain and the island is ringed by a paved trail that provides for a great bike ride. Bikes can either be brought over on the ferries or rented from an island concessionaire. There is also a trail to the top of Mount Livermore. With the summit 750 feet above the bay, the mountaintop views of the Golden Gate and Bay bridges and the City of San Francisco

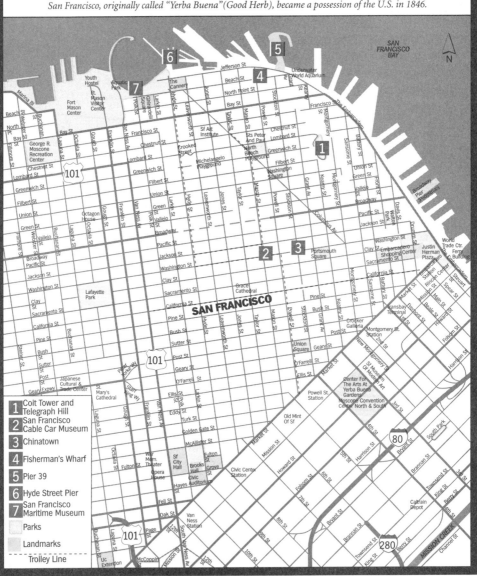

City of San Francisco

San Francisco, originally called "Yerba Buena"(Good Herb), became a possession of the U.S. in 1846.

1 Coit Tower and Telegraph Hill
2 San Francisco Cable Car Museum
3 Chinatown
4 Fisherman's Wharf
5 Pier 39
6 Hyde Street Pier
7 San Francisco Maritime Museum
Parks
Landmarks
Trolley Line

are awe-inspiring on clear, fogless days. Even on days when the fog layers itself across parts of the bay the view is worth the hike.

While ferry service from either San Francisco or Tiburon is the most common way to get to Angel Island, anyone with a boat can use the park's docks and slips. Overnight boat mooring is allowed, but passengers must remain on their boats after the park's day-use hours end.

Directions: Ferry service or private boat is the only way to reach Angel Island. There are numerous daily departures of Blue and Gold Fleet ferries from San Francisco's Pier 39 and Pier 41, located on The Embarcadero, near Fisherman's Wharf. Ferry service is also available from Tiburon.

Facilities: Visitor center, bookstore, bike trail, historic buildings.

Dates: Open daily. For a recorded schedule, phone (415) 773-1188.

Fees: There is a ferry crossing fee, which includes entry onto Angel Island.

Closest town: San Francisco and Tiburon.

For more information: Angel Island State Park, PO Box 318, Tiburon, CA 94920. Phone (415) 435-1915 or (415) 705-5555.

The City of San Francisco

[Fig. 33] San Francisco is one of the few cities in the world that captures the essence of everything a great city should be: sophisticated, beautiful, eclectic, enchanting, and certainly memorable. Five-star restuarants vie with tiny corner cafés featuring a wide variety of ethnic foods, while 100-year-old Victorian bed and breakfast inns compete with elegant suites in the city's finest hotels. Cable cars climbing the steep hills and cars maneuvering Lombard Street, proclaimed the "crookedest street in the world," add to the enchanting hustle and bustle of fishing boats at the wharf and the sounds and smells of freshly boiled crabs being cracked for eager diners.

The United States took possession from Mexico of what were mostly the pastoral hills of San Francisco, then called *Yerba Buena* (good herb), on July 9, 1846. While the U.S. Army saw the strategic importance of the old Spanish and Mexican presidio for protecting the entry to the bay, at the time there was only a trickle of American settlers coming to California. It was the cry of "Gold!" in 1848 that caused San Francisco to burst to life, seemingly overnight, from its most humble beginnings as a primitive western army outpost. Within a year, San Francisco became the primary entry port for tens of thousands of hopeful "49ers," and as gold poured out of the rivers and mines, the city quickly became the center of commerce and banking that supported the gigantic economic boom.

One of many intriguing results of California's gold rush was the deluge of sailing ships that landed in San Francisco Bay to unload supplies, passengers, and far too

Metro San Francisco

The California Academy of Sciences was formed in 1853, had its work destroyed by an earthquake in 1906, and moved to its current location in 1916.

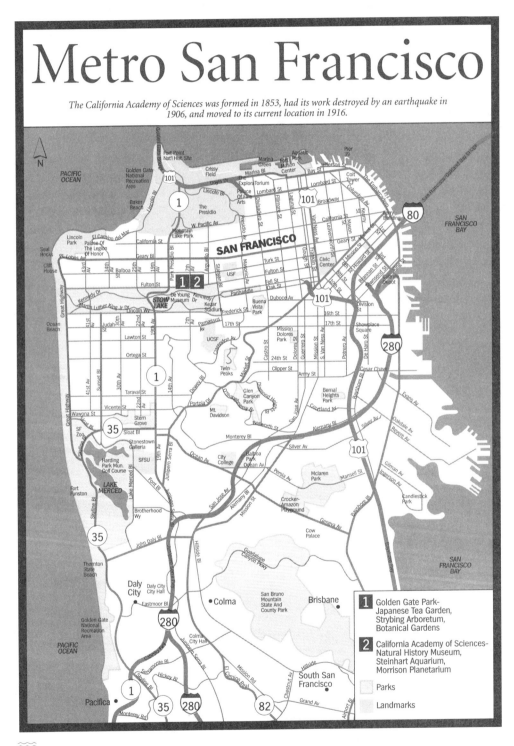

1 Golden Gate Park-
Japanese Tea Garden,
Strybing Arboretum,
Botanical Gardens

2 California Academy of Sciences-
Natural History Museum,
Steinhart Aquarium,
Morrison Planetarium

Parks

Landmarks

often, their entire crews. Unable to lure crews back from the gold fields, many of the ships were turned into floating hotels, offices, warehouses, and one even became a jail. During those early days, ships such as the *Niantic, Euphemia, Bryan, Galen,* and *Thomas Bennet* changed careers from sailing ships to land-locked structures such as docks with soil fill dumped around them, burying their hulls. Fires often raged throughout this floating wooden city during those early years, with the May 4, 1851 fire devastating much of San Francisco and many of the anchored ships. The hulls of some of these maritime relics are occasionally rediscovered during city redevelopment projects.

San Francisco's relatively short history is as interesting as its buried ships. Fort Gunnybags, which was located at 243 Sacramento Street, was more formally known as Fort Vigilance. It served as headquarters for San Francisco's 1856 Vigilance Committee. The committee took the law into their own hands during a time when the city was ravaged by crime and the general public consensus was that too many city officials were on the take. Following the popular lynching of two accused murderers, the city's crime rate decreased significantly.

GOLDEN GATE BRIDGE

[Fig. 32, Fig. 34] Summer fog, strong winds, and unpredictable currents kept Europeans from discovering the narrow entrance into this perfect harbor until 1769, when Spanish explorers first reached it overland. The discovery was actually an accident. Sergeant José de Ortega was looking for the "lost" bay of Monterey to the south. The Spanish called the gateway *La Boca del Puerto de San Francisco.* It was American John C. Frémont who used the name *Chrysopylae,* or Golden Gate for "the form of the entrance into the bay of San Francisco…." Frémont's choice was the name that stuck.

Many naysayers insisted that constructing the Golden Gate Bridge was folly and that such a bridge could never be built, yet it was opened on May 27, 1937, just four years after construction began. The engineering marvel possesses a long list of statistical information: the suspended main span stretches 4,200 feet; the length of one cable is 7,650 feet and is just over 36 inches in diameter; there are 27,572 individual wires in each cable, totaling 80,000 miles and 24,500 tons; and the towers rise 746 feet above the bay and descend 110 feet below the water's surface.

Walking the Golden Gate Bridge is an extremely popular activity for the more adventurous, although most people only go part way across before returning, unwilling to walk the nearly 18,000 feet (3.2 miles) round-trip. Choosing a warm, sunny day helps. When fog or cold winds are present, it's often best to view the bay from inside a car. Parking areas are available on both sides of the bridge. On the San Francisco side of the bay, parking is not far from Fort Point and can be reached either by coming in from Fort Mason on Lincoln Boulevard or by taking the last turn-off (Lincoln Boulevard) before entering the bridge's toll gates. Don't miss the turnoff or you'll have to drive all the way across the bridge and pay the toll to come back south into the city. Dress in warm, layered clothing. On the Marin (south) side of the bridge, the parking lot is just off US 101.

Directions: The Golden Gate Bridge connects US 101 (and Highway 1) between Marin County to the north and San Francisco to the south.

Activities: There is a pedestrian walkway on the east side of the bridge.

Dates: The walkway is open daily.

Fees: There is no fee to use the walkway. There is a vehicle fee collected from all southbound vehicles at tollbooths located on the San Francisco side of the bridge.

Closest town: San Francisco.

For more information: City of San Francisco, phone (415) 666-7200. San Francisco Convention & Visitors Bureau, 201 Third Street, Suite 900, San Francisco, CA 94103. Phone (415) 391-2000.

COIT TOWER AND TELEGRAPH HILL

[Fig. 33(1)] Coit Tower sits atop Telegraph Hill, the hill rising 275 feet above San Francisco Bay. Celebrants, finally getting word on October 29, 1850 that California had been admitted to the Union on September 9, ignited a signal fire on the hilltop, announcing the joyous occasion to the people of San Francisco. Over the years, the steep hillside leading up to the tower has provided homesites for Chileans, Italians, Irish, and in the 1890s, an artist colony. Today, expensive homes cover the hillside, vying for its coveted views of the city and bay. The tower rises an additional 210 feet, its shape designed to resemble a giant fire hose nozzle. The $100,000 used to construct the tower was bequeathed by Lillie Hitchcock Coit, who, as a child in 1851, was made an honorary member of one of the volunteer fire companies. She never forgot the honor. The hill and the tower are located in Pioneer Park and offer breathtaking views of the city and bay.

Directions: Take Lombard Street east past Grant Avenue. The road that winds up to Pioneer Park is on the right. There are directional signs on the roads.

Activities: Viewing the city and bay.

Dates: Open daily.

Fees: None.

For more information: City of San Francisco, phone (415) 666-7200. San Francisco Convention & Visitors Bureau, 201 Third Street, Suite 900, San Francisco, CA 94103. Phone (415) 391-2000.

GOLDEN GATE PARK

[Fig. 34(1)] What was once wind-swept dunes has been transformed into the world's largest ornamental park during the past 140 years. With a dozen small lakes and ponds scattered throughout, there are areas for flycasters to practice, model boat builders to run their newest creations, and romantics to rowboats. A polo field, walking trails, an archery field, and a small golf course add to the opportunities for recreation. Golden Gate Park also features beautiful gardens and some of San Francisco's best art and natural history museums.

The **Japanese Tea Garden** [Fig. 34(1)] began as part of the 1894 Exposition, but has now become a permanent fixture, with paths that wind through Japanese gardens that include groves of bamboo, koi ponds, and beautiful pagodas. There is a small fee. Other gardens within Golden Gate Park, such as the Queen Wilhelmena Tulip Garden on the west end and the Fuchsia Garden on the east end, charge no fees.

Strybing Arboretum & Botanical Gardens [Fig. 34(1)] is 55 acres of gardens within Golden Gate Park featuring plants from around the world. Plants range from those growing in a Mexican cloud forest to the succulents that survive in the world's deserts. Other themed specimen areas include a fragrance garden, a Biblical garden, and a California redwood grove. Strybing is open daily and admission is free, although a donation is requested. The main entrance is at 9th Avenue at Lincoln Way. Phone (415) 661-1316 for more information.

Directions: Golden Gate Park is located in northwest San Francisco, so it's best to obtain a city street map, as there are many possible approaches. From the east, Interstate 80 merges into US 101 near downtown San Francisco. Take the Fell/Laguna Streets Exit and stay on one-way Fell Street for about 2 miles. Fell Street finally splits at the park. Stay to the right into the park on John F. Kennedy Drive. (Portions of John F. Kennedy Drive are closed on Sundays to give pedestrians and bicyclists an auto-free portion of the street.) Two primary roads, John F. Kennedy Drive on the north and Martin Luther King Jr. Drive on the south, run the inside length of the park.

Facilities: Museums, gardens, lakes, boat rentals, snack bars, polo field, tennis courts, walking paths, gardens, and public music venues.

Dates: Golden Gate Park is open daily. Park closes at night.

Fees: The park is free. There are fees for entry into the Japanese Gardens.

For more information: City of San Francisco, phone (415) 666-7200.

CALIFORNIA ACADEMY OF SCIENCES

[Fig. 34(2)] The California Academy of Sciences was formed in 1853 by a group of naturalists concerned about what the gold rush was doing to California's natural resources. They used the academy as a forum for exchanging, documenting, and storing scientific information. They collected, identified, and classified plant and animal specimens. The 1906 earthquake destroyed all of their work, but they immediately started over. The academy moved to its current location in 1916, where they opened the first of several buildings to the public.

Today the academy maintains a natural history museum, the Steinhart Aquarium, and a planetarium in a single large complex, plus eight scientific research departments in the field of natural history. It boasts one of the 10 largest natural history museums in the world. The academy's collections are worldwide in scope, as the nearly 1.5 million visitors each year quickly discover.

The **Natural History Museum's** [Fig. 34(2)] 140 million-year-old, 30-foot dinosaur may dominate many imaginations, but the exhibits that fill the remainder of the museum are equally commanding. Visit an African waterhole and see a mountain gorilla, zebra, and giraffe in re-creations of their natural habitats. In another hall, a 1,350-pound quartz crystal and a 465-pound amethyst-lined geode highlight more than 1,000 gem and mineral specimens. Exhibits on giant bugs, plate tectonics, earthquakes, birds, and butterflies fill other rooms of the museum.

The **Steinhart Aquarium** [Fig. 34(2)] allows visitors to explore the underwater realm of the world's rivers, lakes, and oceans. Nearly 600 species of fish, invertebrates, reptiles, amphibians, and a few penguins fill the exhibits at the aquarium. Learn how fish have adapted to waters as different as San Francisco Bay and an African lake, a Himalayan stream and California's kelp forests. Visitors can stand in the center of a 100,000-gallon circular tank filled with thousands of fast-swimming ocean fish and feel the oddly dizzying effect it causes. And there's a coral reef that showcases the brilliant-colored fish that inhabit tropical ocean waters. There is also a shark tank and a place where blackfooted penguins waddle around, as only penguins can do.

The **Morrison Planetarium** [Fig. 34(2)] features sky shows that realistically simulate the night sky. The shows can re-create views of the different stars and constellations observed from the Northern and Southern hemispheres, giving everyone an opportunity to see planets, stars, and celestial events, such as eclipses, that are not always visible. The shows are changed periodically, often featuring upcoming, popular heavenly events.

Directions: The California Academy of Sciences is located in Golden Gate Park, so it's best to obtain a city street map, as there are many possible approaches. The Academy is located next to the Music Concourse and is accessible from 8th Avenue and Fulton Street and 9th Avenue and Lincoln Way.

Facilities: Gift shop, café, exhibits, public programs.

Dates: Open daily.

Fees: There is a general admission fee, plus an additional fee for the Planetarium's Sky Shows.

For more information: California Academy of Sciences, Golden Gate Park, San Francisco, CA 94118. Phone (415) 750-7145.

SAN FRANCISCO'S CABLE CARS

Riding the cable cars is one thing that everyone who comes to San Francisco must do. It's great fun to watch the operators work and the views from some of the runs are nothing short of breathtaking.

The 125-year-old cable car system underwent a complete overhaul in 1982-84, which is reassuring considering the steep hills the cars are expected to climb and descend. There are three different lines that run from 6:30 a.m. to 12:30 a.m. daily. Passengers can get on at any of the stops and pay either a one-way fare or purchase all-day passes at the main stations.

The Powell-Hyde line runs from Powell and Market streets, over Nob Hill and Russian Hill to Hyde and Beach in Fisherman's Wharf. The Powell-Mason line runs from Powell and Market, over Nob Hill, through North Beach, and down to Fisherman's Wharf. The California Street line leaves California and Market streets in the Financial District, goes through Chinatown, over Nob Hill, and completes its run on Van Ness Avenue.

The **Cable Car Museum** [Fig. 33(2)] is located at Washington and Mason streets. It houses the motors, pulleys, and cables that move the cars through the city. Take either the Powell-Mason or the Powell-Hyde line to get there. Phone (415) 474-1887 for more information.

▨ CHINATOWN

[Fig. 33(3)] San Francisco's Chinatown is one of the most fascinating and colorful areas of the city, and also one of the most popular among visitors. A wonderful and eclectic collection of shops and restaurants sit side-by-side, with merchandise spilling out onto the sidewalks and the aroma of wonderful food wafting through the air. Street-level shops often have narrow interior stairways leading downstairs to cluttered rooms filled with boxes and shelves stocked with everything from fine china to silk neckties. Some of the small restaurants feature street-side windows that allow passers-by to view the food being prepared and roasted, which often includes such things as whole chickens with their heads still intact.

Numerous Chinese communities popped up throughout California as the Chinese began coming here in 1848; 20,000 arrived during the following four years. Most initially headed for the gold fields and, for a variety of reasons, many returned to the cities and towns to set up businesses that often were more profitable than searching for gold. Primarily for protection against the severe discrimination that existed during this time, the Chinese generally lived in small communities that excluded outsiders.

Discrimination was real. California congressmen rallied for passage of an 1882 federal law banning Chinese immigration because the low-paid coolies were seen as a threat to American workers. It was the first time such a law had been passed, and it wasn't repealed until 1943. Similar local laws kept the Chinese out of many of the prime gold-mining areas in California's Mother Lode. Local citizens harassed, beat, and murdered the Chinese, often viewing them as unfair competition. To an observant writer of the time: "The white men have vast advantages in the possession of all the capital, the language, the mechanical skill, the government, and the exclusive right of claiming and preempting farms on the Federal domain. Under these circumstances, if they cannot compete with the Chinaman, then for the welfare of

California, they should give way before the stronger race."

In 1885, about 25,000 people called San Francisco's Chinatown home, but much of the community was destroyed in the 1906 earthquake and the fires that resulted. The area was rebuilt and today is one of San Francisco's great places to wander and explore. The area is easy to spot, with its pagoda-style roofs, lantern-shaped lamp-posts, and the joss houses (Chinese temples).

Directions: The main part of Chinatown is bounded by Stockton Street, Broadway, Kearny and Bush streets, with Grant Avenue serving as its main street.

Activities: Sight-seeing, shopping, eating.

Facilities: Shops, restaurants.

Dates: Open year-round.

For more information: San Francisco Convention & Visitors Bureau, 201 Third Street, Suite 900, San Francisco, CA 94103. Phone (415) 391-2000.

FISHERMAN'S WHARF

[Fig. 33(4)] There is so much to see and do along the City-by-the-Bay's waterfront that a single day will not suffice, especially if eating is on the agenda. The wharf area is actually about seven blocks long, with most of its attractions located near the end of The Embarcadero, on both sides of connecting Jefferson Street, and throughout much of Beach Street, between Powell Street and Van Ness Avenue.

There are several piers that jut into the bay, with **Pier 39** [Fig. 33(5)] being the biggest tourist attraction. It supports dozens of shops and restaurants, as well as the California Welcome Center, which is an area-wide visitor center. There's always something interesting going on at Pier 39. If a painter or juggler isn't amusing passers-by, then there's usually an impromptu theatrical performance or musicians entertaining the ever-changing crowds of people. There's also a great old carousel just waiting for riders.

A few blocks away, the **Hyde Street Pier** [Fig. 33(6)] features ships that are part of one of the largest collections of floating historic ships in the country. The 1886 square-rigger *Balclutha*, the 1895 schooner *C.A. Thayer*, the 1891 scow schooner *Alma*, and the 1890 ferryboat *Eureka* provide a broad-spectrum look at the types of ships that sailed into San Francisco Bay during the nineteenth century. Phone (415) 556-3002 for more details.

The **San Francisco Maritime Museum** [Fig. 33(7)] is located adjacent to the Hyde Street Pier and the cable car turn-around point. The museum houses ship models, paintings, photos, figureheads, and a major permanent exhibit on the history of communications at sea. The museum is free. Phone (415) 556-3002 for more information.

SAN FRANCISCO DINING

Finding places to satisfy your appetite while in San Francisco is an adventure in every sense of the word. There are hundreds of small, out-of-the-way diners and cafés, ethnic restaurants with exotic menu items, and, of course, plenty of places featuring seafood. There are also several fast food restaurants to satisfy the younger set. Prices range from low-budget to astronomical.

John's Grill. 63 Ellis Street near Stockton Street. This was a setting in the *Maltese Falcon* and is one of the oldest dining houses in San Francisco, serving steaks, seafood, and pasta, with live jazz entertainment nightly. *Inexpensive. Phone (415) 986-3274.*

Pompei's Grotto. 340 Jefferson near Leavenworth. This family restaurant is always a delight when down on the wharf. There are fresh seafood specials daily in a casual setting. *Inexpensive to Moderate. Phone (415) 776-9265.*

Maye's Oyster House. 1233 Polk Street, between Sutter and Bush. This is an Italian seafood house with a piano bar. In one form or another, it's been around since 1862. *Inexpensive. Phone (415) 474-7674.*

Aliota's. 8 Fisherman's Wharf. This is another of the many popular restaurants on the wharf. It's been around since 1925, serving fresh seafood and Sicilian specialties. *Inexpensive to Moderate. Phone (415) 673-0183.*

North India Restaurant. 3131 Lombard Street. North Indian, Pakistani Tandoori, and Moghlai lunch and dinner dishes are the specialty. Casual dress. *Inexpensive. Phone (415) 931-1556.*

The Dining Room. Located in the Ritz-Carlton hotel at 600 Stockton Street. Reservations are required and semiformal attire expected. This is one of many fine restaurants offering the finest service. Three- to four-course dinners are served, featuring creative Nouvelle French cuisine. *Expensive. Phone (415) 296-7465.*

Campton Place Restaurant. 340 Stockton Street. Reservations are suggested in order to ensure seating in this fine restaurant serving what it describes as "eclectic dishes with an Asian influence." Serves lunch and dinner. *Inexpensive to moderate.* Phone (415) 955-5555.

Carnelian Room. 555 California Street. Its location on the 52nd floor of the Bank of America Center provides for exceptional views of the city. Semiformal attire is expected. Only dinner is served and reservations are suggested. *Moderate. Phone (415) 433-7500.*

Kan's. 708 Grant Avenue, upstairs. Featuring a Cantonese menu, Kan's is located in Chinatown. Casual dress. Open for lunch and dinner. *Inexpensive.* Phone (415) 982-2388.

Golden Turtle. 2211 Van Ness Avenue. This restaurant serves Vietnamese cuisine for dinner only. Dress casually and make reservations if you wish. *Inexpensive. Phone (415) 441-4419.*

SAN FRANCISCO LODGING

Accommodations in the city range from extravagant to only moderately expensive, with the summer tourist season being the most costly time to visit and the most difficult time to find rooms, especially anything for less than $100 per night. Most of San Francisco's hotel rooms are priced between $100 and $200 per night. It's a good

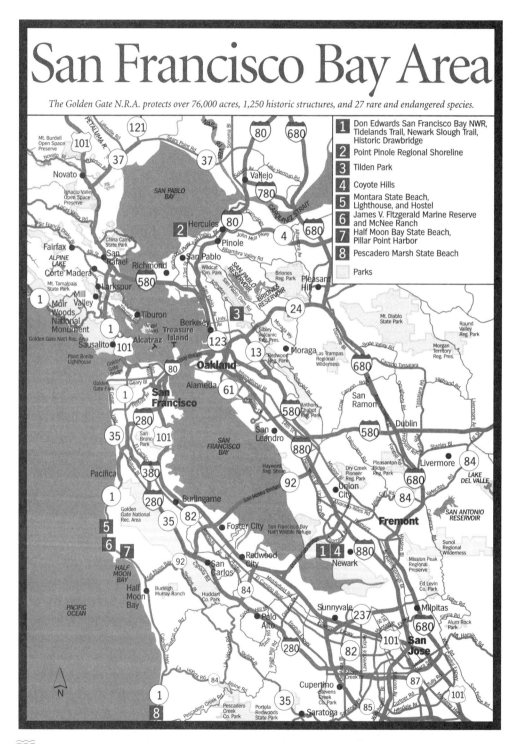

San Francisco Bay Area

The Golden Gate N.R.A. protects over 76,000 acres, 1,250 historic structures, and 27 rare and endangered species.

1 Don Edwards San Francisco Bay NWR, Tidelands Trail, Newark Slough Trail, Historic Drawbridge
2 Point Pinole Regional Shoreline
3 Tilden Park
4 Coyote Hills
5 Montara State Beach, Lighthouse, and Hostel
6 James V. Fitzgerald Marine Reserve and McNee Ranch
7 Half Moon Bay State Beach, Pillar Point Harbor
8 Pescadero Marsh State Beach

Parks

idea to find a hotel in an area where you want to spend most of your time, whether that's down near the wharf, at the clubs at North Beach, or near the convention center. It's easy enough to leave your car parked and take public transportation to most of the city's attractions, since finding parking in some of the more popular areas can always be a problem and gets very expensive.

Archbishop's Mansion. 1000 Fulton Street, San Francisco. The French chateau mansion was built in 1904 for the Archbishop of San Francisco. It is now a bed and breakfast and is located on Alamo Park near many of the city's famous "Painted Lady" Victorians. Period antiques fill the guest rooms, and there are fireplaces and whirlpool baths. *Expensive. Phone (415) 563-7872.*

Chateau Tivoli. 1057 Steiner Street, San Francisco. This Victorian B&B was originally constructed in the late nineteenth century. Gold leaf trim highlights the 22 exterior colors. Inside, the ornamented ceilings, stunning woodwork, and French renaissance furniture make this a great place to fully enjoy San Francisco. *Expensive. Phone (415) 776-5462.*

Inn San Francisco. 943 South Van Ness, San Francisco. Enjoy the elegance of this 1872 Italianate Victorian mansion that has been transformed into a bed and breakfast. Here you can enjoy a feather bed, spas, fireplaces, and an English garden with a hot tub. *Moderate to expensive. Phone (415) 641-0188.*

Royal Pacific Motor Inn. 661 Broadway, San Francisco. Comfortable rooms located in the Chinatown area, between Grant Avenue and Stockton Street. There are plenty of restaurants nearby. *Moderate. Phone (415) 781-6661.*

Mark Hopkins Inter-Continental. 1 Nob Hill, San Francisco. Exquisite comfort and taste with a fine restaurant and gift shop. This is a 17-story tower that is ideal for anyone desirous of pure luxury. *Very expensive. Phone (415) 392-3434.*

Holiday Inn Select. 750 Kearny Street, San Francisco. The 27-story hotel offers rooms with great views of the bay and city. It's located just 1 block from Chinatown and near public transportation. *Expensive. Phone (415) 433-6600.*

The Ritz-Carlton. 600 Stockton Street, San Francisco. This is one of the city's top hotels, with service that is difficult to beat. The neo-classical structure houses an indoor, heated swimming pool. It is located adjacent to the cable car line and Chinatown. *Very expensive. Phone (415) 296-7465.*

Redwood Inn. 1530 Lombard Street, San Francisco. This small, but comfortable inn is one of the less expensive hotels near Fisherman's Wharf. *Moderate to expensive. Phone (415) 776-3800.*

Best Western Tuscan Inn at Fisherman's Wharf. 425 Northpoint Street, San Francisco. It's located just south of the wharf at Mason Street, so there's plenty to do within walking distance. There's an in-house restaurant, but with so many options in the surrounding area, eating where you sleep might be a last resort. *Expensive. Phone (415) 561-1100.*

Best Western Carriage Inn. 364 9th Street, San Francisco. This is one of the smaller hotels, but a few of its large rooms have fireplaces. It is located on the south side of the city, close to the convention center. A free breakfast is included. *Expensive. Phone (415) 552-8600.*

Holiday Inn-Fisherman's Wharf. 1300 Columbus Avenue, San Francisco. This large, 5-story hotel is just a short walk from the bay and from Fisherman's Wharf. It has its own restaurant, coffee shop, and gift shop. *Expensive. Phone (415) 771-9000.*

Travelodge Hotel at Fisherman's Wharf. 250 Beach Street, San Francisco. Another of the hotels near the wharf, the Travelodge is just 1.5 blocks from Pier 39. Some of its rooms have bay views. *Expensive. Phone (415) 392-6700.*

Don Edwards San Francisco Bay National Wildlife Refuge

[Fig. 35(1)] San Francisco Bay was formed only 10,000 years ago, when the rising Pacific Ocean entered through the Golden Gate as the last ice age was ending. The water filled the shallow valley and flooded into the flats that in some areas ran up to the base of the surrounding Coyote Hills. The refuge, which was originally created in 1972 and later expanded to a total of 43,000 acres, includes not only wetlands, but some of the Coyote Hills' dry uplands.

During the Ice Age, the surrounding Coyote Hills were formed as portions of the Pacific and North American plates, shifted, uplifted, and folded the earth's crust. Spend much time around the refuge and you can find sedimentary, igneous, and metamorphic rocks. Red chert and shale make up most of the sedimentary rocks. Greenstone, formed from lava that solidified underwater, is a soft igneous rock. The metamorphic, green-colored serpentine is California's official state rock.

The visitor center is the best place to pick up information and maps to the refuge. The building sits atop of a hill that rises well above the surrounding wetlands. It offers excellent views of the marsh and wetlands that extend nearly as far as you can see to the north and west. Inside the visitor center there are exhibits that help explain the natural history of the area and a good selection of books and other nature-related sales items. Outside the visitor center there's a trail that drops down to the wetland.

Directions: To reach the visitor center, from Highway 84 at the east end of the Dumbarton Bridge exit at Thornton Avenue. Drive south on Thornton Avenue for 0.8 mile to the refuge entrance on the right. Follow this road (Marshlands Road) to the stop sign and turn left into the parking lot.

Activities: Hiking, bird-watching, kayaking, and canoeing.

Facilities: Visitor center, bookstore, trails.

Dates: Trails open year-round. Visitor center closed on Mondays and national holidays.

Fees: None.

For more information: Don Edwards San Francisco Bay National Wildlife Refuge, PO Box 523, Newark, CA 94560-0524. Phone (510) 792-0222.

TRAILS

There are numerous trails within the refuge. Many are on levies that are periodically closed for repairs. It's best to check with the refuge to verify the status of any trails you may be interested in hiking.

Tidelands Trail [Fig. 35(1)] is a 1-mile loop that leaves from the visitor center. It's a raised and level boardwalk that heads out into the wetlands and mud flats. The trail is very popular, especially with school groups and people with younger children not yet ready for more strenuous hiking.

Newark Slough Loop Trail [Fig. 35(1)] is another trail leaving from the visitor center, but it covers 5 miles, all of which is a level walk well out into the refuge. It's a good hike, especially during fall and spring when the refuge is filled with migrating birds.

HISTORIC DRAWBRIDGE

[Fig. 35(1)] Protected within San Francisco Bay National Wildlife Refuge are the remains of the historic town of Drawbridge. It's an intriguing town that was built on a marshy island in the wetlands and, long-since abandoned, is being swallowed by the marshland it was built to exploit.

The town sprang up around the railroad line that San Francisco millionaire Alfred "Hog" Davis and Senator "Slippery" Jim Fair created in 1876 to compete with the Southern Pacific. A drawbridge was required to allow barges to pass through the rail line and the bridge required a tender. The tender built his home near the bridge. A few people soon discovered that this was a great place to hunt waterfowl and fish, and soon others built cabins, with a few support businesses following. The growing community took the name of its nearest identifiable landmark, the drawbridge.

By 1936, Drawbridge began to decline as pollution from sewage outfalls and the creation of salt ponds significantly reduced the numbers of ducks and ended the great fishing. Overpumping of nearby wells caused the community to begin sinking into the marsh. People soon abandoned their cabins and shacks, most of which were used only part time. In subsequent years, many of the original cabins were vandalized and burned. The last resident left in 1979.

Directions: The town is accessible only on tours provided by the San Francisco Bay National Wildlife Refuge.

Activities: Sight-seeing, photography, bird-watching.

Facilities: None, including restrooms.

Dates: Open on periodically scheduled tours only. Call the Refuge Visitor Center for specific dates and reservations.

Fees: None. Children under age 10 or those with walking difficulties are not encouraged to participate.

For more information: Don Edwards San Francisco Bay National Wildlife Refuge, PO Box 524, Newark, CA 94560-0524. Phone (510) 792-0222.

East Bay Regional Parks

On the eastern side of San Francisco and San Pablo bays, and in the nearby inland hills and valleys, lies a regional park district that is comparable in size and diversity to some state park systems. Being so near to the homes of several million people, the regional parks are tremendously popular, yet it is rare to see another person at certain times and places.

Point Pinole Regional Shoreline [Fig. 35(2)] is a 2,147-acre park on the east shore of San Pablo Bay. It boasts numerous trails and a 1,250-foot fishing pier.

To reach Point Pinole's entrance from the town of Pinole off Interstate 80, drive west on San Pablo Avenue to Atlas Road, which turns left and becomes Giant Highway just before the park entrance. There is a weekend and holiday parking fee. Phone 510-562-PARK.

Carquinez Strait features oak woodlands and open grasslands with a wide variety of wildlife, including western bluebirds (*Sialia mexicana*), horned larks (*Eremophila alpestris*), American kestrel (*Falco sparverius*), golden eagles (*Aquila chrysaetos*), gray foxes (*Urocyon cinereoargenteus*), and mule deer (*Odocoileus hemionus*). To reach the

MULE DEER
(*Odocoileus hemionus*)

park from Highway 4 in Martinez, exit at Cummings Skyway. Turn right on Crockett Boulevard, then right again on Ponoma Street in the town of Crockett. Pomona Street becomes Carquinez Scenic Drive. Proceed to the parking area on the left or drive another 1 mile to the next parking area. Phone 510-562-PARK.

Tilden Park [Fig. 35(3)] is just over 2,000 acres and provides, in addition to its wildlands and wildlife, more kinds of experiences than the other East Bay Regional Parks. There are carousel rides, group picnic areas, miniature steam train rides, a golf course, and a regional botanical garden. It also includes several miles of hiking trails. There are many entrances to the park, which is located in the Berkeley Hills, just north of Highway 24. Take the Fish Ranch Road Exit east of the Caldecott Tunnel. Drive up the hill and turn right on Grizzly Peak Boulevard, which passes the park's Lomas Cantadas entrance. Phone 520-562-PARK.

Coyote Hills [Fig. 35(4)] is bordered on its west and south sides by the San Francisco Bay National Wildlife Refuge. Trails lead from Coyote Hills to the adjacent refuge, including the 12-mile Alameda Creek Trail. There's also a marsh boardwalk, paved bike trail, and a visitor center at the 976-acre park. To reach the park from Interstate 880 in Fremont take Highway 84 west, exit at Paseo Padre Parkway and drive north, turning left on Patterson Road. There is a fee. Phone 510-562-PARK.

San Mateo County

▒ SAN MATEO COAST SIDE TRIPS

Drive south on Highway 1 from the always enjoyable and exciting entrapments of San Francisco, and civilization quickly melts away, once again showcasing the power and beauty of nature. San Mateo County stretches for 55 miles down the coast, where it connects with Santa Cruz County. There are numerous public beach access areas along Highway 1. It's a beautiful drive, but beware: summer can bring fog, obscuring many of the vistas and making sunbathing uncomfortably cold. Heavy winter rains can cause mudslides that close the highway for days.

Montara State Beach [Fig. 35(5)] offers 2 miles of public beach popular with anglers, beachcombers, and on sunny days, sunbathers. There are two access points that will get you down from the bluff to the beach. The first is just off Highway 1, about 0.5 mile north of the Chart House restaurant in the community of Montara. The second is located across from Second Street, just south of the Chart House restaurant. Phone 650-726-5213.

Montara Lighthouse & Hostel [Fig. 35(5)] is a historic lighthouse still operated by the U.S. Coast Guard. The surrounding grounds and several of the buildings have been transformed into a very popular hostel. Operated by the American Youth Hostel, there are sleeping facilities, along with a kitchen, laundry, and plenty of bicycle racks for those peddling California's coast. It is located between the small communities of Montara and Moss Beach on Highway 1. Phone 650-728-7177.

James V. Fitzgerald Marine Reserve [Fig. 35(6)] offers 3 miles of coastline with tidepools and sandy beaches. It's a popular scuba diving area, partly because it is illegal to remove or disturb any of the marine life or surrounding habitat. Its shale reefs provide protection for a wide variety of marine life, including giant green anemones (*Anthpleura xanthogrammica*), purple sea urchins (*Strongylocentrotus purpuratus*), and several species of small crabs. There is a hiking trail along the bluff to the south and picnic tables in the sheltered cypress grove. The reserve is part of the Monterey Bay National Marine Sanctuary. Phone 415-728-3584.

McNee Ranch [Fig. 35(6)] has nearly 700 acres available for hikers, mountain bikers, and equestrians. There are great views from the old ranch's hills, now part of the California state park system. Phone 650-726-8819.

HALF MOON BAY STATE BEACH

[Fig. 35(7)] This is one of the more developed coastal access parks along this stretch of the San Mateo County coast. The park, just off Highway 1, actually has several beaches and access points, including Francis Beach at the end of Kelly Avenue in the city of Half Moon Bay, Venice Beach at the end of Venice Boulevard, and Dunes Beach at the end of Young Avenue. Francis beach also has a campground.

There is a nearby private stable where horses can be rented (inquire at the park). They are permitted on some of the trails, such as the trail that runs between Dunes Beach and Francis Beach, but are not allowed on the state beach. The Coastside Trail runs the length of Half Moon Bay State Beach, from Kelly Avenue on the north end to Miranda Avenue on the south side. It gets plenty of use from bicyclists, joggers, and walkers.

Although not affiliated with the state beach, you can join fishing or whale-watching trips out of the **Pillar Point Harbor** [Fig. 35(7)] on the north end of Half Moon Bay. The marina also offers boat berths and launching facilities.

Directions: The park is adjacent to Highway 1, in the town of Half Moon Bay.

Activities: Hiking, biking, horseback riding, sunbathing, surfing, beachcombing.

Facilities: Campgrounds, picnic facilities.

Dates: Open year-round.

Fees: There is a fee for camping and day use.

For more information: Half Moon Bay State Park, c/o Bay Area District State Parks, 250 Executive Park Boulevard, Suite 4900, San Francisco, CA 94134. Phone (415) 330-6300 or (650) 726-8819. Pillar Point Harbor, phone (650) 726-4382.

PESCADERO MARSH STATE BEACH

[Fig. 35(8)] This is a favorite place for school group field trips because the area provides access to both a long, sandy beach and to a marsh and wetlands area. On the east side of Highway 1, Pescadero Creek and Butano Creek join, forming a delta marsh rich with plants and wildlife. Just a few hundred yards away is the North Marsh, another part of the park. There are trails into both areas, none of which take more than 30 minutes to walk. The trail around North Marsh is one of the longest and is only 0.75 mile. On the ocean side of Highway 1 there is a wooden walkway through part of the dunes, allowing disabled access across the sand.

The marsh areas on the east side of Highway 1 are included within the 500-acre Pescadero Marsh Natural Preserve. Autumn brings thousands of waterfowl and other migrating birds into the marsh's brackish waters, while at least 60 species of birds nest in the marsh or on the beach. Great blue herons (*Ardea herodias*), marbled godwits (*Limosa fedoa*), American avocets (*Recurvirostra americana*), sanderlings (*Calidris alba*), brown pelicans (*Pelecanus occidentalis*), surf scoters (*Melanitta perspicillata*), and the endangered snowy plover (*Charadrius alexandrinus*) are common in the area. There are also long-tailed weasels (*Mustela frenata*), red-legged frogs (*Rana aurora*), the endangered salt marsh harvest mouse (*Reithrodontomys raviventris*), and numerous species of waterfowl.

Directions: The park is located on both sides of Highway 1, 17 miles south of Half Moon Bay.

Activities: Hiking, beachcombing, fishing, nature study, bird-watching.

Facilities: None.

Dates: Open year-round.

Fees: There is a day-use fee.

Closest town: Half Moon Bay, 17 miles.

For more information: Bay Area District State Parks, 250 Executive Park Boulevard, Suite 4900, San Francisco, CA 94134. Phone (415) 330-6300 or (650) 879-2170.

AÑO NUEVO STATE RESERVE

[Fig. 38] The sight of a couple of 2.5 ton northern elephant seals (*Mirounga angustirostris*) bellowing, charging, and battling across open dunes only a

GREAT BLUE HERON
(*Ardea herodias*)

few dozen yards away from you is an unforgettable experience. Such is the way winter tours often go at Año Nuevo State Reserve. While the reserve is open all year, it's in late December (when the females begin arriving in large numbers) that visitors also begin flocking to the area. Within a week of their arrival, each of the pregnant females, themselves 10-feet-long and weighing up to 1,600 pounds, give birth to most often a single 75-pound pup.

While all this is happening, the big bulls are battling each other, attempting to establish private harems for mating purposes. The battles can get very bloody at times, but more often the smaller, younger, and less-determined males wisely give up quickly and move away from the alpha bull. While defending their harems, the alpha bulls are also attempting to mate with the females that are nearing the end of the 25 to 28 days they spend nursing their pups. The pups, if they've managed to escape being crushed by charging, fighting bulls, or by the alpha bull attempting to mate with their mothers, grow rapidly on the rich milk, reaching up to 300 pounds during their three- to four-week nursing period.

The adult females and males begin leaving Año Nuevo in March, deserting the young pups that must remain to spend time learning to swim. They finally leave land in late April. The elephant seals generally swim north and feed off the coasts of Washington and British Columbia before returning to land for short periods to molt. The adult females return to Año Nuevo during April and May, the subadult males from May to June, and the adult males during July and August in order shed their old fur.

While northern elephant seals are the primary attraction for most people who visit Año Nuevo State Reserve, the geology, general scenery, and the historic dairy buildings are also big attractions. A walk along Cove Beach reveals cliffs that run parallel with the underlying Año Nuevo thrust fault, part of the larger San Gregorio fault zone. The rock formations that make up most of the coastal range in this area are more than 12 million years old. The Monterey Formation, as it is known, is made up of the silica from skeletons of ancient, one-celled sea animals that were pressed between layers of silt and clay. Before it was uplifted to the surface, high temperatures and tremendous pressures over 12 million years transformed the original materials into light gray-colored mudstone that is very resistant to wind and wave action.

Grizzly bears once roamed the woods and hillsides of Año Nuevo. While grizzlies have been extinct here since the 1880s, many other species of wildlife are common throughout the reserve. On the coastal terrace, just above Cove Beach, a small pond teems with waterfowl such as pintail (*Anas acuta*), America wigeon (*Anas americana*), cinnamon teal (*Anas cyanoptera*), and mallards (*Anas platyrhynchos*). Warblers, thrushes, hummingbirds, vireos, and many more birds migrate through the park each year. Raptors, such as American kestrels (*Falco sparverius*) and northern harriers or marsh hawks (*Circus cyaneus*), are often seen flying just a few feet above the open fields. Along the shoreline marbled godwits (*Limosa fedoa*) and black-bellied plovers (*Pluvialis squatarola*) arrive during the fall migration.

During the mid-December through March birthing and mating season, the reserve is open only for tours led by the park's docents. This policy is designed to protect both the animals and the visitors. It's amazing how quickly a 2-ton elephant seal can move short distances, even across the loose sand. The docents are extremely well-versed in the elephant seal's natural history.

The tours cover about 3 miles, much of it over open sand, and take approximately 2.5 hours. The trail changes daily, depending upon where the mostly immature and non-mating male elephant seals have decided to take their frequent naps. The winter tours are extremely popular, so it's best to make reservations in advance, although unfilled tour slots are available first-come, first-served. They can be made up to 56 days in advance. The tours occur, rain or shine. Dress for rain and wind (umbrellas are not allowed) and hope for a warm, clear winter day. Pets are not allowed anywhere in the reserve, including inside parked vehicles.

AMERICAN KESTREL
(Falco sparverius)

Directions: Año Nuevo State Reserve is located on Highway 1, approximately 19 miles north of Santa Cruz.

Activities: Hiking, bird-watching, elephant seal tours.

Facilities: Visitor center, bookstore.

Dates: Open year-round. During mid-Dec. through Mar., the public must be part of a docent-led tour in order to enter the beach and dunes area where the elephant seals haul out. During other times of the year a permit is required, obtainable at the park entrance.

Fees: There is a vehicle entry fee and a per-person tour fee. Phone (800) 444-7275 for reservations, which are almost always needed for the docent-led tours.

Closest town: Santa Cruz, 19 miles.

For more information: Año Nuevo State Reserve, New Years Creek Road, Pescadero, CA 94060. Phone (650) 879-2025. Recorded information, phone (650) 879-0227.

California's Central Coast

California's Central Coast is over 225 miles long and encompasses Santa Cruz, Monterey, and San Luis Obispo counties.

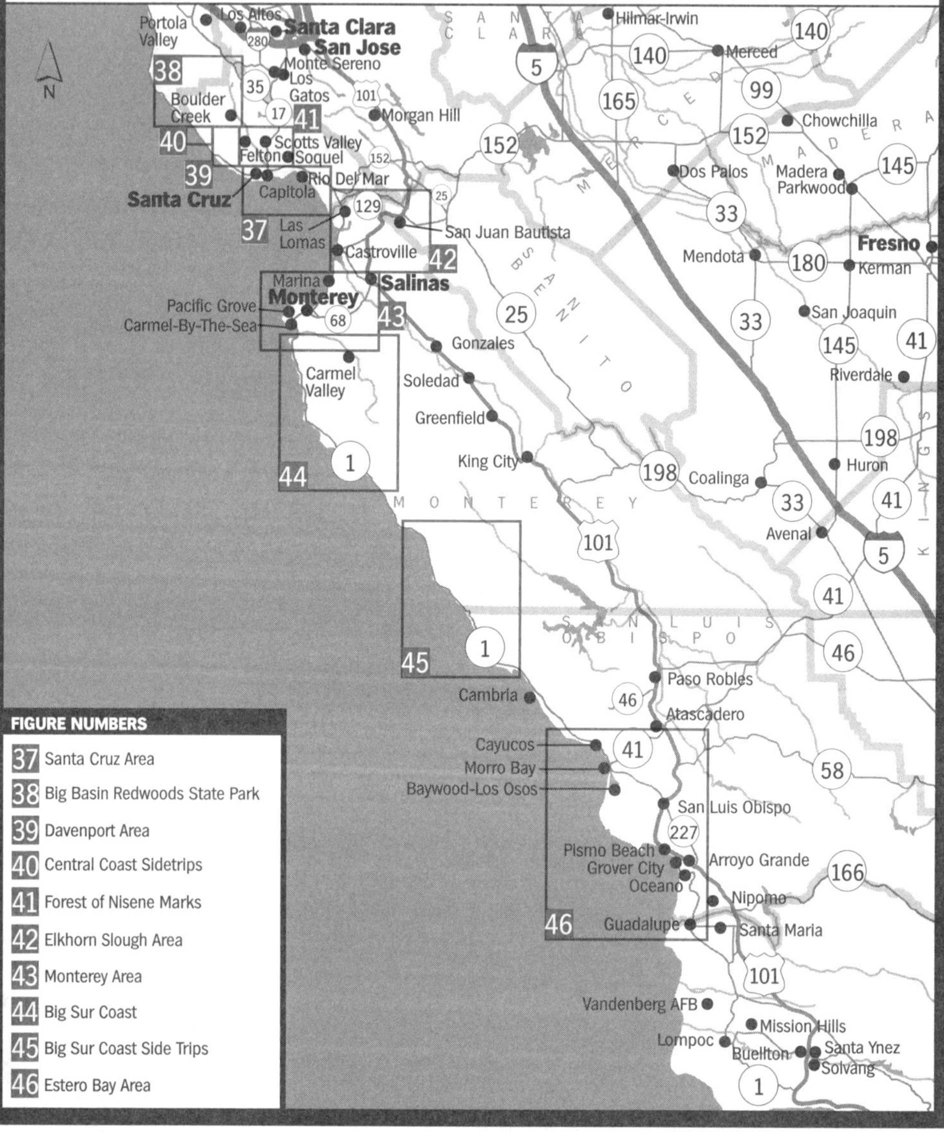

FIGURE NUMBERS

37 Santa Cruz Area

38 Big Basin Redwoods State Park

39 Davenport Area

40 Central Coast Sidetrips

41 Forest of Nisene Marks

42 Elkhorn Slough Area

43 Monterey Area

44 Big Sur Coast

45 Big Sur Coast Side Trips

46 Estero Bay Area

California's Central Coast

The boundaries of California's central coast may vary depending upon who is drawing the lines on a map, but essentially it over 225 miles long, encompassing Santa Cruz, Monterey, and San Luis Obispo counties. With the exception of three moderately sized cities, each taking its name from its respective county, the communities along this portion of the California coast are relatively small or, as in the case of Big Sur, they consist of not much more than a number of isolated homes, a few small tourist-related businesses, and a post office. It's difficult to identify any one section of California's 1,100 mile coast as being more spectacular than another, but the central coast would certainly be high on anyone's list. From towering redwoods to surfing beaches, from spectacular ocean-bluff cliffs to migrating whales, it attracts millions of visitors each year, each searching for his or her own paradise—and generally finding it.

[*Above:* The jagged cliffs of Point Lobos State Reserve]

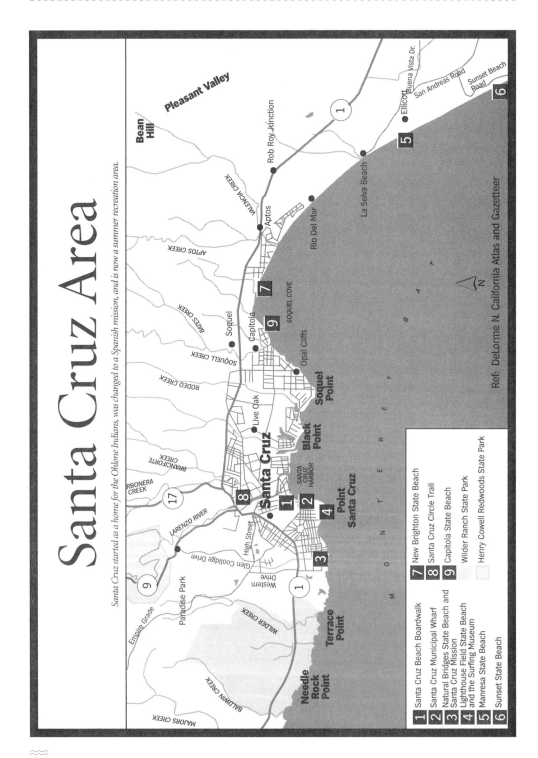

Santa Cruz Area

Santa Cruz started as a home for the Ohlone Indians, was changed to a Spanish mission, and is now a summer recreation area.

Pleasant Valley

Bean Hill

Rob Roy Junction

Ellicott

Buena Vista Dr.

San Andreas Road

Sunset Beach Road

La Selva Beach

Aptos

Rio Del Mar

VALENCIA CREEK

APTOS CREEK

BATES CREEK

SOQUEL CREEK

RODEO CREEK

BRANCIFORTE CREEK

RBONERA CREEK

LARENZO RIVER

Empire Grade

Paradise Park

Glen Coolidge Drive

Western Drive

High Street

WILDER CREEK

BALDWIN CREEK

MAJORS CREEK

Soquel

Capitola

SOQUEL COVE

Opal Cliffs

Live Oak

Soquel Point

Black Point

Santa Cruz

SANTA CRUZ HARBOR

Point Santa Cruz

Terrace Point

Needle Rock Point

M O N T E R E Y   B A Y

N

Ref: DeLorme N. California Atlas and Gazetteer

Legend:

1 Santa Cruz Beach Boardwalk
2 Santa Cruz Municipal Wharf
3 Natural Bridges State Beach and Santa Cruz Mission
4 Lighthouse Field State Beach and the Surfing Museum
5 Manresa State Beach
6 Sunset State Beach
7 New Brighton State Beach
8 Santa Cruz Circle Trail
9 Capitola State Beach
Wilder Ranch State Park
Henry Cowell Redwoods State Park

Santa Cruz County

🦥 BIG BASIN REDWOODS STATE PARK

[Fig. 38, Fig. 39] Deep in the Santa Cruz Mountains, stands of giant coast redwoods (*Sequoia sempervirens*) still survive in great profusion. While the ancient trees are found still farther south in a few protected canyons along the Big Sur coast, Big Basin Redwoods State Park is where extensive stands of 2,000-year-old trees still remain. Efforts to save the trees began in earnest in 1900, when photographer Andrew P. Hill and other early conservationists founded the Sempervirens Club, which led to the creation of Big Basin Redwoods State Park two years later, when 3,900 acres were transferred from private ownership to the State of California. Since its inauguration as California's first state park (if Yosemite's temporary late nineteenth century state ownership is disregarded), Big Basin has grown extensively, now approaching 20,000 acres. Sempervirns Fund, the modern successor to the Sempervirns Club, along with numerous other private individuals and public benefit organizations, have added property over the past 100 years.

What all of these people have seen worthy to protect is the result of the Pacific and North American plates' movement that created a complex assortment of geologic actions. The oldest rocks in Big Basin are found only in the eastern portion of the park. The 70 million- to 90 million-year-old quartz diorite found here originated perhaps a few thousand miles to the south and moved north with the shifting plates. Sandstone, mudstone, siltstone, and shale, all of which range in age from 50 million years old to as young as 8 million years, are the other rock types found within most of the Waddell Creek watershed.

Some 60 million years ago a surge of uplifting began along the Zayante fault that lies within the park. South of the fault, erosion slowly cut the deep gorge that follows Waddell and other creeks, while to the north, eroded sedimentary deposits accumulated behind the rising rock dam. The result was a flat valley floor where park headquarters is now located.

The deep alluvial soils that lie beneath park headquarters, combined with rainfall that averages over 3 feet a year or more in the park, provide an ideal growing medium for coast redwoods. Some of the largest trees in the park are located here, alongside the turbid waters of meandering Opal Creek. But the towering redwoods aren't the only attraction in Big Basin. Wildlife abounds, although many of the animals are more secretive than most visitors would like.

One of the most common creatures is the 6-inch long, slimy banana slug (*Ariolimax columbianus*). These greenish yellow mollusks are common, especially where the ground is wet. Once actively fed by both park employees and visitors, the Columbian black-tailed deer (*Odocoileus hemionus columbianus*) has become less common in the heavy-use areas of the park, but it is still seen. Fortunately for the deer, such harmful

Big Basin Redwoods St. Park

Big Basin Redwoods State Park started in 1902 with 3,900 acres and is now approaching 20,000 acres.

1   Visitor Center and Redwood Trail
2   Skyline to the Sea Trail
3   Sunset-Berry Creek Loop Trail
4   Sequoia Trail
  Portola State Park

Castle Rock St. Park
Big Basin Redwoods State Park
Año Nuevo State Reserve
Trail

Ref: USGS 7.5 minute Franklin Point, Big Basin, Castle Rock Ridge feeding practices have long since ended. Several species of chipmunks (*Tamias* spp.), raccoons (*Procyon lotor*), and chickarees or the Douglas squirrel (*Tamiasciurus douglasii*), are relatively common.

It's not uncommon to see California quail (*Callipepla californica*) running across trails and disappearing into shrubs such as salmon berry (*Rubus spectabilis*) and huckleberry (*Vaccinium* spp.). It's less common, but much more exciting, to see a pileated woodpecker (*Dryocopus pileatus*), whose jackhammer-sounding pecking near the tops of trees echoes through the forest. This largest of the woodpeckers is easily identified by its size, up to 19 inches tall, with a flaming red crest. Then there's the common steller's jay (*Cyanocditta stelleri*), the ever-present camp robber. In fact, anywhere people linger with food, a raucous crowd of squawking steller's jays is likely to appear suddenly. And along the creeks the American dipper or water ouzel (*Cinclus mexicanus*) is a fascinating bird to watch as it dives underwater and swims, searching for small fish or invertebrates.

The Big Basin Redwoods State Park visitor center is located in a 1936-era, Civilian Conservation Corps-constructed log lodge that also serves as the park headquarters and campground registration office. Exhibits tell the story of the area's early history, including the threat of logging that pushed so many people into creating the park and saving the ancient trees. Gunpowder was also made in the Big Basin area. The very hard wood of the madrone (*Arbutus menziesii*), a tree common on the warmer ridges in the park and surrounding mountains and easy to identify by its peeling, reddish-brown bark, made excellent charcoal, required for the manufacture of gunpowder. A large diorama shows the early days of the park when cottages and other structures, such as a barber shop, a post office, tennis courts, and a dance floor were available for visitors' use. It also was a time when campsites cost $.50 per night. Park brochures, hiking maps, and a few nature books are available for sale, and there are chairs set around the old stone fireplace, offering a comfortable place to sit and read or take a break.

A small museum housing a room full of exhibits that tell the natural history story of the park is located across the road from the visitor center, around behind the park store and gift shop. Wander in and take a few minutes to read some of the text on the exhibit panels. Most is fairly short, but each will let you in on the secrets of banana slugs, geology, marbled murrelets (*Brachyramphus marmoratus*), and the redwoods. There's a small back room that's filled with specimens of dozens of the kinds of animals found in the park, all stuffed, except for the snakes that are displayed in long glass tubes filled with a liquid preservative.

Directions: Travel north from Highway 1 at Santa Cruz via Highway 9 to Boulder Creek. At the stop sign, turn left onto Highway 236 and drive about 10 miles to the park.

Activities: Camping, hiking, picnicking.

Facilities: Campground, tent cabins (open-sided cabins with stoves), camp store, gift shop, visitor center, and museum.

Davenport Area

The original town of Davenport was built 1.5 miles farther north but was moved in 1906.

SCOTT CREEK

MILL CREEK

BOYER CREEK

BIG CREEK

Ben Lomond Mountain

SAN VINCENTE CREEK

Alba Road

Empire Grade Road

BOYER CREEK

BIG CREEK

MILL CREEK

Swanton Road

Pine Flat Road

Swanton

LITTLE CREEK

Scott Creek

To
Half Moon Bay

SAN VICENTE CREEK

Ice Cream Grade

1

MOLINO CREEK

Bonny
Doon

MILL CREEK

Pine Flat Road

Swanton Road

SAN VICENTE CREEK

LAGUNA CREEK

Smith Grade Road

PACIFIC OCEAN

Davenport Landing

Bonny Doon Road

EAST BRANCH

YELLOW BANK CREEK

N

1

Davenport

Big Basin Redwoods St. Park

Henry Cowell Redwoods St. Park

Trail

To Santa Cruz

LIDDELL CREEK

Ref: NPS 7.5 minute
Davenport

Dates: Park is open year-round.

Fees: There is a fee for camping and day use.

Closest town: Boulder Creek, 15 miles.

For more information: Big Basin Redwoods State Park, 21600 Big Basin Way, Boulder Creek, CA 95006. Phone (831) 338-8860. For camping reservations phone (800) 444-7275.

TRAILS

There are 80 miles of trails in Big Basin Redwoods State Park, ranging from short, level walks to strenuous, multiday hikes. Many of the trails can be reached from trailheads that begin near park headquarters. Others are accessed from other areas within the park, and a few can be reached from trailheads that begin outside the park. Dozens of combinations of loop and one-way trails are possible, depending upon the time available and the level of adventure desired.

The Redwood Trail [Fig. 38(1)] is a short, 0.5-mile, self-guided nature trail is located across the street from park headquarters and is a great hike for families. Pick up a trail guide at the visitor center before you go. It offers brief explanations about what will be found on the walk. For example, there's a large and very obvious redwood circle at post number one, which is a group of new trees growing from the original roots and in a circle around the slowly decaying stump of its old-growth parent tree. The remainder of the trail holds marked examples of tanbark oak (*Lithocarpus densiflorus*), chimney trees (which are old redwoods hollowed by lightening-caused fires that can smolder inside the trees for months), and other wonders of natural history. This trail also features one of the oldest trees in the park, estimated at 2,000 years, and the tallest tree in the park, the Mother-of-the-Forest, which stands 329 feet.

The **Skyline to the Sea Trail** [Fig. 38(2)] begins in nearby Castle Rock State Park, and the 30-mile trail meanders into Big Basin near China Grade Crossing at the northwest corner of the park. It then heads southwest, and 5 miles later passes just above Opal Creek near Big Basin park headquarters. It continues southwest some 12 miles on a mostly downhill trail, finally reaching the Pacific Ocean at the Rancho del Oso Nature Center. There are several trail camps along the way for those wishing to spend a little more time enjoying the backcountry trails.

The **Sunset-Berry Creek Loop Trail** [Fig. 38(3)] is not for the weak of heart or lungs or legs. This 11.5-mile hike begins on an easy uphill slope from a trailhead located just off the Redwood Trail near park headquarters, reaches the top of a ridge, then plunges about 1,200 feet down a steep canyon trail. At the bottom, the trail passes three wonderful waterfalls, the highest of which, Berry Creek Falls, plunges 60 feet. The tough part is climbing back up the ridge to the top, at Hihn Ahammond Road, before the final short hike back to the beginning of the trail at park headquarters.

While the 4 mile **Sequoia Trail** [Fig. 38(4)] can simply be bypassed and some of its destinations reached more quickly by driving, hiking is a significantly more

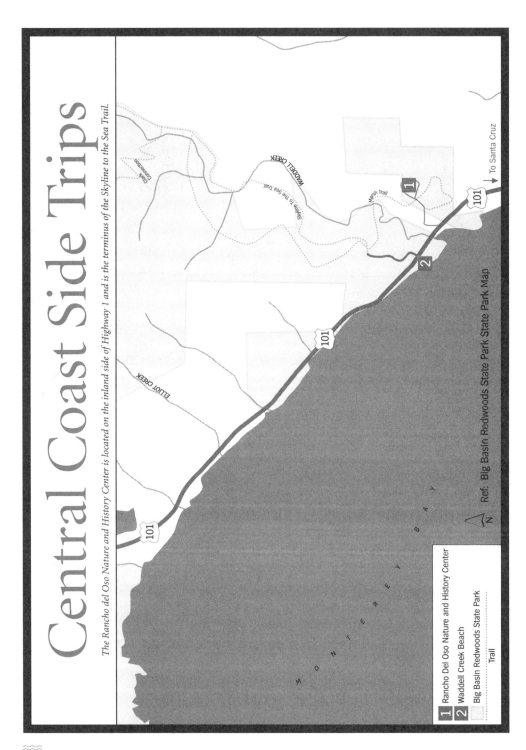

Central Coast Side Trips

The Rancho del Oso Nature and History Center is located on the inland side of Highway 1 and is the terminus of the Skyline to the Sea Trail.

1 Rancho Del Oso Nature and History Center
2 Waddell Creek Beach
   Big Basin Redwoods State Park
   Trail

Ref: Big Basin Redwoods State Park State Park Map

To Santa Cruz

WADDELL CREEK
ELLIOT CREEK
Clark Connection
Skyline to the Sea Trail
Marsh Trail

MONTEREY BAY

N

Monterey Bay National Marine Sanctuary

Established in 1992, the Monterey Bay National Marine Sanctuary encompasses 5,322 square miles of ocean, making it the country's largest marine sanctuary. It also has the distinction of claiming 276 miles of the nation's most beautiful and rugged shoreline. Ocean researchers come from around the world to conduct research on the sanctuary's rich underwater resources, which include not only the plants, geologic features, and the strange creatures found in depths that reach 2 miles, but also the extensive kelp beds that stretch along its entire length.

The sanctuary is operated by the National Oceanic and Atmospheric Administration (NOAA: pronounced Noah). NOAA and numerous research institutes are committed to continuing research and education. Knowing what effects changing water temperatures will have on phytoplankton, the marine food chain's base organism, and what effect those changes can have on the other animals can help scientists make decisions about how to manage marine mammals or what marine resource protections might be added to or reduced.

The sanctuary stretches from Rocky Point, 7 miles north of the Golden Gate to Cambria Rock in San Luis Obispo County. While not prohibiting such things as commercial fishing, the sanctuary's status still provides significant protection for its 26 species of marine mammals, 94 species of seabirds, and 345 fish species. There are also 4 turtle species, 31 phyla of invertebrates, and more than 450 species of marine algae, kelp being one of the most predominant.

For more information: NOAA, 320 Foam Street, Suite D, Monterey, CA 93940. Phone (831) 647-4201.

enjoyable way to go. The trail picks up near park headquarters and loops south and east, then north past the Wastahi Campground, finally reaching Sempervirens Falls. The small, but beautiful waterfall tumbles into a small pool, surrounded by redwoods and a cliff face covered with ferns. Just a couple hundred yards north of the falls is Slippery Rock and the Founders Monument that memorializes the founding of the Sempervirens Club in 1900. The trail continues north and connects with the Skyline to the Sea Trail that then leads south, returning to park headquarters.

CENTRAL COAST SIDE TRIPS

The **Rancho del Oso Nature and History Center** [Fig. 40(1)] is also located on the inland side of Highway 1 and is the terminus of the Skyline to the Sea Trail. It is open weekends and by special arrangement. Phone (831) 427-2288. There is also a wetland on the inland side of Highway 1 that is home to numerous water birds. Nearby **Waddell Creek Beach** [Fig. 40(2)] is about 1 mile south of the San Mateo County line and is part of Big Basin Redwoods State Park.

Forest of Nisene Marks State Park

The Forest of Nisene Marks State Park has 10,000 acres and 30 miles of trails.

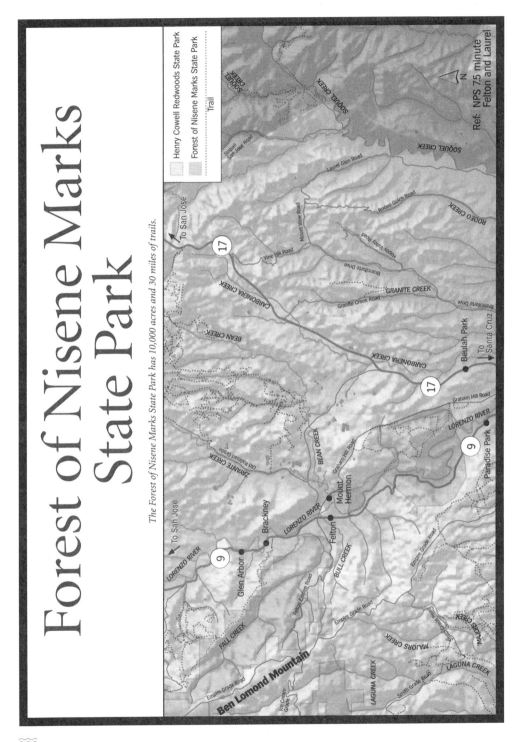

Davenport is about 8 miles south of the San Mateo County line on Highway 1. The small, historic community has its roots in the nineteenth century whaling industry and the early shipping industry. The original town was actually built about 1.5 miles farther north, but it was moved in 1906. A couple of the original buildings remain. There's an overlook on the ocean side of Highway 1. It's a good place to view migrating gray whales in winter.

Henry Cowell Redwoods State Park [Fig. 41] (phone 831-335-4598), an easy place to wander through a magnificent grove of coast redwoods, has a small visitor center, gift shop, camping, and picnicking. There's also a beautiful meadow that fills with wildflowers and butterflies during spring. It's located about 5 miles north of Santa Cruz on Highway 9.

The Forest of Nisene Marks State Park [Fig. 41] (phone 831-763-7062) is located north of Aptos, just off Highway 1. Aptos Creek Road out of Aptos leads into the park. There are 10,000 acres and 30 miles of trails, one of which leads to the epicenter of the Loma Prieta earthquake that did considerable damage to San Francisco and the surrounding cities and towns in 1989.

WILDER RANCH STATE PARK

[Fig. 37] A great fertile crescent, beginning just north of Santa Cruz and wrapping around to the Monterey Peninsula, has served farmers and ranchers quite well since 1791 when the missions began farming here. Even today, the rich soil and mild climate allows such difficult-to-grow crops as artichokes and brussels sprouts to thrive. Although Wilder Ranch is now a state park, brussels sprouts and other crops are still grown on the surrounding lands near the ocean bluffs.

The entrance and parking lot are located just off the ocean side of Highway 1, and then it's a short walk to the old Victorian farmhouse, the barns, and a small visitor center. A group of volunteers helps with the extensive flower and vegetable gardens, and maintains the farm animals that range from chickens to horses. A large shed shelters a wide assortment of antique farm implements and other equipment.

A dirt road through the complex crosses under Highway 1 and leads to a large corral area and an old (reconstructed) cowboy bunkhouse complex. The original bunkhouse was built by the Wilders for their ranch hands, but it served quite often as a gathering place for parties, and practices for the annual rodeos in which many of the area's young cowboys competed. Much of the riding and roping activities stopped following World War II because accidents and their potential for lawsuits brought attorneys into the picture.

Beyond the bunkhouse a maze of dirt roads offers 42 miles of trails for hiking, horseback riding, and mountain biking. Being in shape certainly helps if a mountain bike is your chosen mode of outdoor transportation, because the trails get steep in a hurry. But once on top, the views of the Pacific Ocean on fogless days are spectacular. The mostly grassland hillsides are spotted with hidden ponds and rivers of green

Monarch Butterflies

During winter several areas along California's Central Coast become overwintering grounds for millions of monarch butterflies (*Danaus plexippus*) that often have traveled thousands of miles seeking refuge from harsher climates. These large, showy butterflies, with wingspans that often reach 4 inches, seek the shelter of eucalyptus groves that help to moderate the moderately cold night temperatures. On late winter afternoons as the temperatures begin to drop, the butterflies return to their small section of trees by the thousands and cling to the branches and leaves, creating a shimmering wall of flickering orange and black wings. Each morning, when the ambient temperature rises just enough, the butterflies leave in a swirling mass of color and seeming confusion, abandoning the security of their nighttime perches in search of nectar.

Within California there are several places to view monarchs during winter. They include Natural Bridges State Beach (*see* page 176) in Santa Cruz, the City of Pacific Grove, which dubs itself Butterfly Town U.S.A., and in the eucalyptus grove in the Pismo State Beach's North Beach Campground (*see* page 231), which hosts the largest overwintering monarch butterfly population in California.

As spring approaches, the butterflies leave, with the females laying eggs on milkweed as they head north and west. None, or at least few, make the round trip. It's the offspring from the eggs that are laid by the migrating females that hatch in about four weeks, that actually arrive back at the butterflies' northern summer homes, then head back south again in the fall.

vegetation that meander their way down the gullies toward the ocean below.

Directions: Take Highway 1 north from Santa Cruz, about 1 mile past the traffic light at Western Drive. Signs along the highway are quite visible, but the park entry road, which cuts directly into a high roadcut on the ocean side, is a little more difficult to see until you're nearly on top of it.

Activities: Hiking, mountain biking, picnicking, periodic living history events.

Facilities: Visitor center and a small gift shop, trails, farmhouse, barns, corral area and bunkhouse.

Dates: Open daily.

Fees: There is a day-use fee charged.

Closest town: Santa Cruz, 1 mile.

For more information: Santa Cruz Sector State Parks, 600 Ocean Street, Santa Cruz, CA 93960. Phone (831) 423-9703.

SANTA CRUZ

[Fig. 37] What began as home for the Ohlone Indians and was changed into a mission by the Spanish has been transformed into a summer recreation hot spot, mostly for tens of thousands of San Francisco Bay and Central Valley residents each year. Seems folks living in San Francisco are searching for a slightly less foggy and warmer weekend getaway and those living in the Central Valley are looking for an escape from summer's too often 100-plus degrees Fahrenheit days.

THE SANTA CRUZ BEACH BOARDWALK

[Fig. 37(1)] The colorful and popular boardwalk is one of those places that kids of all ages enjoy. It's loaded with the kinds of fun food that most people probably shouldn't eat more than once or twice a year, and stomach-wrenching roller coaster thrills that can make most people wish that food hadn't been a first priority upon arrival. The boardwalk stretches for nearly 1 mile right at the edge of the city's main beach, itself a vast stretch of sand that attracts thousands of people on warm summer days. The boardwalk itself can be just as crowded as the beach on weekends and lines can be long for some of the more popular rides carrying such ominous names as Tsunami, Crazy Surf, and Whirlwind. For a great overview of what's here, there's a monorail that circles around and above the boardwalk at a leisurely pace. For those interested in nostalgia, the traditional wooden roller coaster that was built in 1924 remains one of the best in the country. The Giant Dipper has been updated over the years, but the views of the bay and the screams that accompany 55-m.p.h. speeds are a must. For those with weaker stomachs, or parents with smaller kids, there is the equally classic Looff Carousel. With its 73 carved horses and its late nineteenth century, 342-pipe band organ, it has thrilled 50 million people since 1911.

Directions: From Highway 1, take the Ocean Street Exit and follow Ocean Street toward the bay to its end at the wharf area. Turn left and drive the four blocks to 400 Beach Street.

Facilities: Rides, games, food.

Dates: Open daily from Memorial Day to Labor Day, then weekends and holidays the remainder of the year; hours also vary by season.

Fees: The boardwalk is free, but there is a fee for the rides.

For more information: Santa Cruz Beach Board-walk, 400 Beach Street, Santa Cruz, CA 95060. Phone (831) 423-5590.

SANTA CRUZ MUNICIPAL WHARF

[Fig. 37(2)] Wharves everywhere seem to attract people. The Santa Cruz Municipal Wharf is no exception, and it has the added attraction of being the longest wharf on the West Coast. It's also a place loaded with shops and restaurants, and fishing can be remark-ably good from the wharf if you'd prefer to catch your own. Halibut, striped bass, jacksmelt, and surf perch

MONARCH BUTTERFLIES
(Danaus plexippus)
This brown to orange-brown butterfly has wings with white-spotted black borders and dark veins.

aren't opposed to taking live bait. The more adventurous can rent wooden skiffs with small outboard motors and head out a bit farther to the offshore rocky reefs where rockfish and larger lincod are occasionally hooked.

Directions: From Highway 1 in Santa Cruz, take the Ocean Street Exit and drive toward the bay where Ocean ends at Beach Street and the wharf.

Activities: Dining, fishing, shopping,

Facilities: Restaurants, bait shop, gift shops, boat and kayak rentals.

Dates: Open daily.

Fees: There is a fee for vehicles. No fee for pedestrians.

For more information: Santa Cruz County Conference & Visitors Council, 701 Front Street, Santa Cruz, CA 95060. Phone (800) 833-3494 or (831) 425-1234.

SANTA CRUZ SIDE TRIPS

Drive the roads (West Cliff Drive and Beach Street) that follow the cliffs along the city of Santa Cruz area and numerous surprises await. **Natural Bridges State Beach** [Fig. 37(3)], (phone 831-423-4609), is north of the main part of town, at the end of West Cliff Drive and has a great beach. It gets its name from the offshore rocks, although the longest wave-carved rockbridge collapsed years ago. The park's eucalyptus grove hosts thousands of wintering monarch butterflies.

The **Santa Cruz Mission's** [Fig. 37(3)] original site is located above the beaches and cliffs at the intersection of High and Emmet streets. The mission was founded in 1791, but an 1857 earthquake destroyed much of the original building. A smaller replica was constructed in 1931 on Emmet Street. The mission chapel is open daily with a donation requested for entrance.

▨ LIGHTHOUSE FIELD STATE BEACH AND THE SANTA CRUZ SURFING MUSEUM

[Fig. 37(4)] Along West Cliff Drive where joggers run and in-line skaters cruise not far from the edge of the bluff, Lighthouse Field State Beach is one of those places that most visitors to Santa Cruz unfortunately miss, especially if their focus is the wilder times to be had at the beach and boardwalk. Here, Point Santa Cruz juts out to mark Monterey Bay's northern boundary.

The original lighthouse was built here in 1869, as an aid to navigation for the constantly increasing numbers of ships that passed by, heading to and from San Francisco. Within 10 years of its construction, the crashing waves had eroded so much of the cliff face that the structure was moved farther inland where it continued in operation until 1941. The lighthouse structure was replaced by an automatic beacon-topped wooden tower and the original wooden lighthouse was sold for scrap.

Today's stone lighthouse that stands near the cliffs was a gift to the people of Santa Cruz. Photographers Chuck and Esther Abbot sponsored the construction of the new lighthouse in memory of their son Mark, who was killed in a surfing accident. Today, the lighthouse houses a small museum dedicated to Santa Cruz's long history of surfing.

Directions: In Santa Cruz, from where Ocean Avenue, Beach Street, and West Cliff Drive intersect near the foot of the wharf, follow West Cliff Drive north along the bluff several blocks to the lighthouse.

Activities: Surfing, fishing, bicycle riding, jogging, bird-watching.

Dates: Lighthouse Point is open daily; the lighthouse surfing museum is open Wednesday through Monday (closed on Tuesdays).

Fees: None.

For more information: Santa Cruz Surfing Museum, West Cliff Drive, Santa Cruz, CA 95062. Phone the museum (831) 420-6289 or the park (831) 429-3429.

SANTA CRUZ CIRCLE TRAIL

[Fig. 37(8)] There are actually two loop trails, parts of which are still being completed. Either can be picked up in any number of places and both trails meander through some of Santa Cruz's most interesting spots, including Natural Bridges State Park, where eucalyptus trees attract thousands of wintering monarch butterflies. Each trail can take three to four hours to walk, longer if any time is spent enjoying such things as Antonelli Pond, the natural history museum, or the wonderful University of California at Santa Cruz Arboretum. Bicycles are allowed on portions of the trail.

The western loop on the west side of the San Lorenzo River is about 12 miles long, and the eastern loop on the east side of the river is 11 miles long. When completed, the trail will pass through the University of California at Santa Cruz campus and total about 27 miles.

Directions: Pick up both trails at the pedestrian bridge that crosses the San Lorenzo River in downtown Santa Cruz in San Lorenzo Park.

Fees: None.

For more information: For a map, contact the Santa Cruz Parks and Recreation Department, phone (831) 420-6160.

SANTA CRUZ LODGING

There are plenty of hotels and motels in this very busy and very popular summer tourist destination. Since the town tends to attract a younger crowd less interested in creature comforts, moderately expensive hotels significantly outnumber their expensive cousins.

Holiday Inn Express. 600 Riverside Avenue, Santa Cruz. Located just 4 blocks from the beach. *Moderate to expensive. Phone (831) 458-9660.*

Comfort Inn Beach Boardwalk. 314 Riverside Avenue, Santa Cruz. It's a short, 1 block walk to the boardwalk and beach. *Moderate. Phone (831) 471-9999.*

Best Western All Suites Inn. 500 Ocean Street, Santa Cruz. The hotel is located on the main street that leads from Highway 1 to the beach boardwalk. It's a little longer walk to the beach, but the accommodations are comfortable. *Moderate to expensive. Phone (831) 458-9898.*

Elkhorn Slough Area

The 3,000 acres of marsh and 7 miles of main water channel of the Elkhorn are sanctuary to more than 400 species of invertebrates and 80 species of fish.

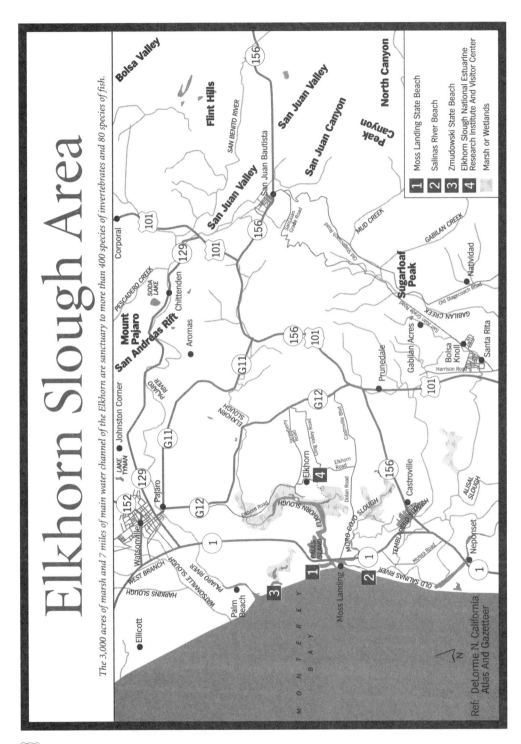

1	Moss Landing State Beach
2	Salinas River Beach
3	Zmudowski State Beach
4	Elkhorn Slough National Estuarine Research Institute And Visitor Center
	Marsh or Wetlands

Ref: DeLorme N. California Atlas And Gazetteer

Ramada Limited. 130 West Cliff Drive, Santa Cruz. Just 2 blocks from the beach and offers a free breakfast. *Moderate to expensive. Phone (831) 423-7737.*

SANTA CRUZ DINING

Blacks Beach Café. 2-1490 East Cliff Drive, Santa Cruz. Located near the beach, the eatery offers a variety of seafood, vegetarian dishes, and sandwiches. Open for breakfast, lunch, and dinner. *Inexpensive. Phone (831) 475-2233.*

Santa Cruz Brewing Company. 516 Front Street, Santa Cruz. Billed as the first legal brewery in California to brew and sell beer on-site, along with food, when the law authorizing such small brewery activities was passed in 1982. It has a large selection of handcrafted beers and a menu of delicious appetizers, sandwiches, and main course meals to keep it all legal. *Inexpensive. Phone (831) 429-8838.*

Stagnaro Bros. Seafood Inc. Located at the end of the Municipal Wharf, Santa Cruz. John and Earnie Stagnaro first opened a small seafood stand at the end of the Municipal Wharf in 1937. They later expanded it to the restaurant and wholesale fish market that is still operated by family members. *Inexpensive. Phone (831) 423-2180.*

Crow's Nest. 2218 East Cliff Drive, Santa Cruz. It's casual dining here with steak and seafood as primary menu items. Reservations are suggested, especially on weekend evenings. *Inexpensive to moderate. Phone (831) 476-4560.*

MONTEREY BAY SIDE TRIPS

As Highway 1 heads southeast from Santa Cruz and begins to circle Monterey Bay, it passes through the town of Capitola, reputed to be the oldest seaside resort on the West Coast. **Capitola City Beach** [Fig. 37(9)] is the first of several nearby beaches. It's located at the mouth of Soquel Creek, east of the wharf.

New Brighton [Fig. 37(7)] (phone 831-464-6330), **Seacliff** (phone 831-685-6442), **Manresa** [Fig. 37(5)] (phone 831-763-7062), and **Sunset** [Fig. 37(6)] **state beaches** (phone 831-763-7062) follow in fairly quick succession traveling south along Highway 1. They have extensive day-use areas. They also have campgrounds, some very near the beach. Campground reservations are nearly always needed. For camping reservations, phone (800) 444-7275.

Elkhorn Slough

[Fig. 42] California's coastal estuaries and marshes are some of the most prolific producers and supporters of wildlife in the world. The 3,000 acres of marsh and tidal flats and the 7 miles of main water channel that comprise much of Elkhorn Slough National Estuarine Research Reserve and the adjacent Moss Landing Wildlife Area are home, either permanently or as a seasonal sanctuary, to more than 400 species of invertebrates and 80 species of fish. There are 267 species of birds on the estuary's bird list. Yet, the unfortunate fact is that during the past century, nearly 90 percent of these same rich wetlands in California have been filled, drained, or in other ways destroyed. Even Elkhorn Slough has seen extensive commercial operations, such as the 200 acres of commercial salt ponds that were in production from the early 1900s until 1974. Today the ponds have been reclaimed and serve a much more valuable role as rich feeding grounds for dozens of bird species and a summer resting ground for the endangered brown pelican.

The salt flats aren't the only areas of the slough that have been restored. Much of the marshland was diked and drained during the earlier part of the century and used as grazing land for the Elkhorn Dairy operation. Two of the old barns remain on the property, and are now home to bats, barn owls, and other wildlife. Most of the dikes are gone, at least those that were able to restrict the ebb and flow of seawater and fresh water. The land that has been reflooded today serves as a valuable research area where the success of such wetland restorations can be studied and new and better techniques developed.

Several trails wind through the estuary, most starting near the visitor center. And the visitor center is a great first stop. The exhibits are both enlightening and entertaining. The gigantic foot of a great blue heron, stepping down through the center's ceiling onto an equally oversized model of an underwater mud flat, its beak grasping a fish, is quite fascinating. The model also provides a great look at the creatures that thrive in the water and under the mud flats of the estuary. For wildflower enthusiasts, another exhibit displays a sampling of the flowers and plants that are most likely to be seen near the trails. The plants and wildflowers found here during any season are as varied and rich as the bird life. Sticky monkey flower (*Mimulus aurantiacus*) and wild buckwheat (*Eriogonum nudum*) are found in the drier areas, along with fennel (*Foeniculum vulgare*) and Socrates' last drink, poison hemlock (*Conium maculatum*). Closer to the edges of the marsh are mugwort (*Artemisia douglasiana*), pickleweed (*Salicornia virginica*), and salt marsh dodder (*Cuscuta salina* var. *major*). About 90 percent of the vegetation covering the salt marsh is pickleweed, one of several plants that have adapted to the high concentrations of salt water. Leaves, which store the excess salt absorbed during the growing season, are dropped during winter. Along the upper trails, dark green swathes of oak woodland, with their coast live oak (*Quercus agrifolia*), contrast with patches of open grasslands. And to reinforce the need to remain on the trails some areas are bordered by thick hedges of poison oak (*Toxicodendron diversilobum*).

The visitor center also provides free bird lists that include the seasons when the different birds are most likely to be seen. Summer brings large numbers of brown pelicans (*Pelecanus occidentalis*) to the mud flats, along with numerous species of shorebirds searching the wet mud for food. The prominent white, great egrets (*Casmerodius albus*) are here year-round, as are the great blue herons (*Ardea herodias*). As an important winter stopover along the Pacific Flyway, Elkhorn Slough provides refuge for Canada geese (*Branta canadensis*), green-winged teal (*Anas crecca*), pintails (*Anas acuta*), gadwalls (*Anas strepera*), American widgeon (*Anas americana*), common goldeneyes (*Bucephala clangula*), and ruddy ducks (*Oxyura jamaicensis*). Jaegers (*Stercorarius pomarinus*), gulls (*Larus* sp.), terns (*Sterna* sp.), and a plethora of more terrestrial birds are commonly seen by bird watchers.

Directions: From Highway 1 at Moss Landing, turn onto Dolan Road and drive approximately 4.6 miles to Elkhorn Road. Turn left and drive another 2 miles to the visitor center entrance on the left.

Activities: Hiking, bird-watching.

Facilities: Visitor center with a small gift shop, trails.

Dates: Open Wednesday through Sunday.

Fees: None for anyone with a valid California hunting or fishing license, otherwise a small fee for those age 16 and over.

Closest town: Moss Landing, 6.5 miles.

For more information: Elkhorn Slough Office, 1700 Elkhorn Road, Watsonville, CA 95076. Phone (831) 728-2822.

TRAILS

The **Long Valley Loop Trail** is a short (0.8 mile) loop that leaves from the visitor center, passes through an area of oak woodland, then drops down a short hill and follows along one of the fingers of a waterway known appropriately as Five Fingers.

Most of the **Five Fingers Loop Trail** stays on the hillside for great views looking toward Monterey Bay in the distance. The trail can be picked up from the Long Valley Loop or directly via the short, paved trail that connects with the visitor center. While anywhere within the estuary is great for bird-watching, there is a wonderful blind that has been constructed in the treeline at about the halfway point in the loop. It overlooks the old salt mining area and provides cover for photographers and their equipment. It's also large enough to handle several people. The entire loop is about 1.2 miles.

The South Marsh Loop is a great trail (about 2.2 miles) that quickly drops down from the visitor center, passes the old Elkhorn Farm barns, and meanders around the south marsh area. Most of the walking is relatively level.

The **Wheelchair Trail** is a paved trail that heads west for maybe 100 yards from the visitor center (the same trail that connects with all the other dirt trails), and ends in a paved circular area with two spotting scopes that overlook the majority of the estuary waters.

KAYAKING THE ESTUARY

For a different view of the waterways and their wildlife, kayaking the estuary is extremely popular. Most of the estuary's channels are accessible, as are many of the small side channels, at least at high tide. It's always important to be aware of the tides. Being caught on the wrong side of a shallow area that quickly becomes a mud flat as the tide races out is not only embarrassing, but a major pain when trying to tow a kayak out across deep mud that feels like it's trying to suck your feet off your ankles. You might want to time your trip so that the afternoon winds will be at your back. It's equally important to remember that tidal flows around the harbor can create problems when trying to negotiate under the Highway 1 bridge, in addition to difficulty maneuvering around the commercial and private boat traffic that moves in and out of the Moss Landing Marina.

There are only two places to launch kayaks in the estuary. Kirby Park has a small launch ramp and is located north of the Elkhorn Slough Visitor Center on Elkhorn Road. The second launching facility is the Moss Landing Harbor District launch ramp. While kayaking is a great way to experience the wildlife, it's also important to stay back at least 200 feet from the harbor seals, California sea lions, and otters that are common in the slough. If the animals you see begin to appear nervous, then you're getting too close.

MOSS LANDING

[Fig. 42] About halfway around Monterey Bay, at the mouth of Elkhorn Slough, is the small fishing village of Moss Landing. The harbor is home to dozens of boats, both pleasure and commercial fishing vessels. The small, quaint community is mostly an interesting collection of antique shops that are always fun to wander through and explore. But what most people, especially Monterey Peninsula locals, come here for is the food. Two restaurants stand out as great places to eat, not only for the good food, but also for their reasonable prices. The first, **The Whole Enchilada** (phone 831-633-3038, inexpensive), is an interesting pink building right off Highway 1 at the intersection of Moss Landing Road. As the name implies, great Mexican food is its specialty and the prices are remarkably reasonable.

For a very different kind of eating experience, continue on Moss Landing Road a very short block, and turn right onto Sand Holdt Road. The narrow two-lane road crosses an even narrower one-lane bridge, which can be a bit of a challenge to get over, although hundreds of cars make the trip daily. Generally, rather than alternating one car at a time when crossing, the several cars that may be backed up go across, while those on the opposite side simply wait until there's a break and they can go in a group. The bridge is scheduled for widening in the future, so you may not experience the minor delay getting across.

Once across, it's even more obvious that this is a working, commercial fishing harbor. Drying nets and other fishing-related equipment line the narrow roadway. The new building on the left is the home of the Monterey Bay Aquarium Research Institute (MBARI). While inquiring minds can wander into MBARI's headquarters and get an overview of the institute's mission and goals, the old run-down-looking building next door is a must-see.

Phil's Fish Market (phone 831-633-8611, inexpensive) from the outside, appears to be an old fish-processing warehouse and not much more. Park wherever you can find a spot, along the road or behind the market, then wander inside. Senses can be overwhelmed, so just enjoy the sights and sounds. In the center of the small room with its old wood walls and wet concrete floor, there is a large, open table of crushed ice, covered with whole fresh fish—salmon, halibut, rock cod, or whatever's been caught—along with a variety of shellfish, including clams, oysters, and mussels. Some employees clean fish in the open, while others are behind counters cooking. There's also a refrigerated glass case filled with fish filets and steaks. A small side room, nearly always crowded, is where the line forms to place lunch or dinner food orders. There's an extensive menu, featuring mostly fish, including the day's specials scribbled on the erasable menu wallboards. Find a seat at one of the inside or outside tables, sometimes a challenge on summer weekends, and your food will soon be delivered. Afterward, take a walk on the beach, which is just behind Phil's.

Directions: From Highway 1 at Moss Landing, turn onto Moss Landing Road.

Activities: Dining, fishing, beachcombing.

Facilities: Boat rental, restaurants.

Dates: Open daily.

For more information: Fishing charters are available through Tom's Sport Fishing on a 50-foot boat. Phone (831) 633-2564.

MOSS LANDING SIDE TRIPS

At the north end of this small fishing community is **Moss Landing State Beach**. Moss Landing State Beach [Fig. 42(1)] also has an overnight parking area where self-contained recreation vehicles may camp. **Salinas River State Beach** [Fig. 42(2)] is located at the southern end of the community of Moss Landing and less than 1 mile off Highway 1. It offers a long stretch of open beach sand that is popular with anglers and beach explorers. There's usually a great deal of driftwood along the beaches. All of these waters are dangerous for swimmers. **Zmudowski State Beach** [Fig. 42(3)] is another few miles south and couple of miles west through the open farm fields often planted with strawberries. Its long and wide beach is similar to its nearby neighbors, Salinas River and Moss Landing state beaches.

Directions: Signs along Highway 1 identify the turnoffs to all three beaches.

For more information: For all three beaches call Marina State Beach, phone (831) 384-7695.

MONTEREY BAY SIDE TRIPS

[Fig. 43(9)] Closer to Monterey, **Marina State Beach** (phone 831-384-7695), at the Highway 1 exit at Reservation Road, is a fun place to stop. In addition to having a public beach similar to others around Monterey Bay, Marina has a concessionaire that provides hang-gliding supplies and lessons. It's a popular place for such

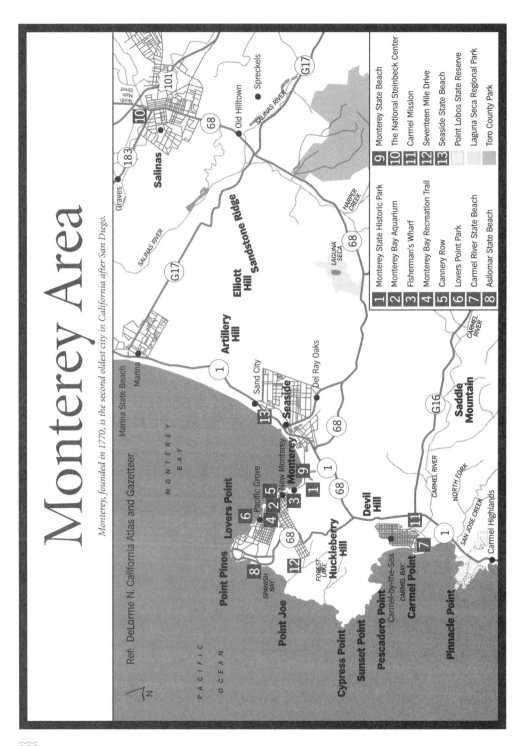

Monterey Area

Monterey, founded in 1770, is the second oldest city in California after San Diego.

Ref: DeLorme N. California Atlas and Gazetteer

1	Monterey State Historic Park
2	Monterey Bay Aquarium
3	Fisherman's Wharf
4	Monterey Bay Recreation Trail
5	Cannery Row
6	Lovers Point Park
7	Carmel River State Beach
8	Asilomar State Beach
9	Monterey State Beach
10	The National Steinbeck Center
11	Carmel Mission
12	Seventeen Mile Drive
13	Seaside State Beach
	Point Lobos State Reserve
	Laguna Seca Regional Park
	Toro County Park

activities, and even if hanging about in midair doesn't sound fun, watching the graceful flyers can be quite enjoyable. There's also a boardwalk into the dunes that passes by numerous threatened and endangered dune plants that are doing very well in the rehabilitated dune habitat. This is a great place to sit in the evening and look across at the lights of Monterey and Pacific Grove. Marina State Beach is also an active nesting area for the endangered snowy plover.

Approaching the city of Monterey on Highway 1, **Seaside State Beach** is just off the freeway at the Del Ray Oaks/Seaside Exit. There are several parking areas along the couple miles of beach. This beach often attracts large numbers of kite flyers, especially on weekends. Phone (831) 384-7695 or (831) 649-2836.

Monterey Peninsula

While the younger, wilder, college set tends to favor Santa Cruz, just across the bay, the Monterey Peninsula brings the more mellow and slightly older generation who can better afford more expensive hotels, restaurants, and golf courses. Of course, there are many reasonably priced places to stay and eat, but you have to look. Daytime temperatures are generally a few degrees cooler on the Monterey side of the bay. The Monterey Peninsula includes the cities of Monterey, Pacific Grove, Carmel, and the gated community of Pebble Beach with its famous golf courses and Seventeen Mile Drive. Most people include Seaside and Marina in the list of Monterey Peninsula cities.

The Monterey Peninsula is known for many things, not the least of which are long sandy beaches and incredible tidepools. Beaches circle around from the mouth of the Salinas River, across land that once was part of the U.S. Army's Fort Ord, now mostly abandoned. The beach portions will soon become a state park. Sand continues until the granite outcroppings begin to appear near Fisherman's Wharf and continue around past the peninsula's protruding point at Pacific Grove's Point Pinos.

The waters of the bay are much too cold for swimming, although a few hardier souls, mostly youngsters, like to chase waves in a few of the more protected coves during summer and get wetter then they had originally planned. Surfers, clad in wet suits, have several favorite spots, depending on the direction and size of the waves. Lovers Point and Asilomar State Beach are two favorite surfing locations, especially during winter when the waves are big. For those less inclined to brave the cold waters, exploring the many rock-bound tidepools is a popular past-time. The entire area is part of either the National Marine Sanctuary, state parks, or marine preserve, so everything in the tidepools needs to be left where it is. Look at the sea stars and urchins, the sculpins and crabs, but don't take them home. They won't live, and they smell very bad when dead.

If you have a bicycle, bring it. There's a great bicycle trail that runs from Lovers Point in Pacific Grove to Monterey's Fisherman's Wharf and is very level and very kid-accessible. Actually, the bike trail continues northeast around the bay another 10 miles or so to the town of Marina. It's a nice ride, although there are several short, steep portions, as the trail must climb over several freeway overpasses.

MONTEREY STATE HISTORIC PARK

[Fig. 43(1)] Monterey is the second oldest city in California, founded in 1770. San Diego is just a year older, but it was Monterey that served as Spain's and then Mexico's center of government for their respective California empires. Monterey was also the center for trade, and for many years the only customhouse was located here on the shore of the bay. The Custom House, like most of Monterey's eighteenth and nineteenth century buildings, was constructed of adobe bricks, molded from a combination of clay and straw, dried, then stacked into walls, and finally covered with plaster to protect them from the rain.

Unlike most parks with obvious entrances, Monterey State Historic Park is a collection of adobe buildings spread throughout several blocks of old Monterey. There are two good places to begin tours of the historic park, and both are on Custom House Plaza, adjacent to the historic old Custom House and Fisherman's Wharf. The first is at the **Stanton Center,** which houses the Maritime Museum of Monterey, the Monterey Peninsula Visitor Center, and the Monterey State Historic Park visitor center. A free orientation film in the Stanton Center Theater provides a quick overview of Monterey's history and is the starting point for both guided and self-guided walking tours of the old city and its Path of History. Across Custom House Plaza from the Stanton Center is the historic **Pacific House**. Originally a government storage building during the 1800s, it now serves as a museum and orientation center for the state historic park.

Within Monterey State Historic Park there are several intriguing buildings that are musts to see. In 1879, Robert Louis Stevenson moved to Monterey, mostly living off the good graces of friends, since he had not yet become the famous writer that he would in the years that followed. The rooming house where he stayed has been restored, and many of his later possessions have been donated and are exhibited in what has become known as the **Stevenson House**. Nearby, the **Cooper-Molera Adobe** complex offers a look at a fully furnished adobe home with a beautiful gardens. Many of the historic homes in Monterey have beautiful gardens, and during summer docents lead special garden tours. Many of the historic adobes are featured on the different tours, as are city-owned historic buildings such as **Colton Hall** where California's Constitution was written (in both English and Spanish) and signed in 1849.

Directions: Follow the signs on Highway 1, taking either the Del Monte Avenue or the Munras Avenue exits through town to the Fisherman's Wharf parking lot. Custom House Plaza is the large, brick open area to the left on the short walk between the parking lot and the wharf. The Stanton Center and Pacific House face one another on opposite sides of the plaza.

Activities: House and walking tours, periodic living history events, many weekend ethnic celebrations on the plaza during summer.

Facilities: In the area: bike trail, restaurants, museums, bookstores, historic houses.

Dates: Historic buildings and the Stanton Center are open daily except Thanksgiving, Christmas and New Year's Day. Tour hours vary. The Pacific House is open daily from 9 to 5.

Fees: There's a moderate fee for guided walking tours and house tours. Visitors may go on a free, self-guided walking tour by following the gold tiles in the walkways.

For more information: Contact the Monterey State Historic Park office at 20 Custom House Plaza, Monterey, CA 93940. Phone (831) 649-7118, or the Monterey Visitor and Convention Bureau, 380 Alvarado Street, Monterey, CA 93940, phone (831) 649-1770.

MONTEREY BAY AQUARIUM

[Fig. 43(2)] Concealed inside the reconstructed facade of an old cannery on historic Cannery Row, the Monterey Bay Aquarium features one spectacular live exhibit after another. The first features full-sized models of orcas, gray whales, dolphins, and sharks suspended from the ceiling of the foyer. A left turn and a short walk leads to the first of the aquarium's huge tanks. An entire kelp forest undulates to the rhythm of artificially produced waves, as dozens of species of fish take their positions as they do in the bay just a few dozen yards away. Within the forest of giant kelp (*Macrocystis pyrifera*) swim dozens of species of fish. Leopard sharks (*Triakis semifasciata*) and schools of Pacific sardines (*Sardinops sagix*) swim within a few feet of each other. Blue rockfish (*Sebastes mystinus*), generally looking for a meal of jellyfish or crustaceans, bob in the water behind the 7-inch-thick acrylic windows. One of the most curious fish in the kelp forest is the sheephead (*Semicossyphus pulcher*). All begin life as females. Once they grow to a foot or more in length, one or several of them will change colors, developing broad stripes of red, white, and black, and more interestingly, change sex, becoming males. Several benches are situated in front of the windows where many people sit mesmerized by this scuba diver's perspective of the underwater world.

Nearby, numerous smaller live exhibits provide up-close looks at many species of octopi. A curious looking cousin, the cuttlefish (*Sepia officinalio*) lies on the sandy bottom of its tank. It watches for prey, and when dinner happens by, the cuttlefish shoots out two tentacles that captures its meal. When something bigger comes looking to make a meal of the cuttlefish, it changes color to better match its surroundings, then disappears in a cloud of ink.

Around the corner, sharks greet the shredded fish their feeders drop in the tank, displaying the damage their teeth can inflict on flesh. Check the feeding times that are posted. Within this large tank, with its remarkably realistic shale reef reproduction, swim many more fish. Jack mackerel (*Trachurus symmetricus*), a beautiful seven gill shark (*Notorynchus cepedianus*), chinook or king salmon (*Onochynchus tshawytscha*) that will have any angler's mouth watering, striped bass (*Morone saxatilis*), and vermillion rockfish (*Sebaste miuiatus*), which are sometimes mistakenly called rockcod or red snapper. Anemones and sea stars, some incredibly large, live on the bottom of the pool adding to its realistic appearance.

Not everything in the aquarium is devoted to just creatures that live underwater. The aviary is a wonderful refuge for examples of many of the shorebirds found outside. In a reproduced wetland and beach area, with waves slapping gently on its sandy shoreline, are avocets (*Recurvirostra americana*), western sandpipers (*Calidris mauri*), sanderlings (*Calidris alba*), and willits (*Catoptrophorus semipalmatus*). And for anyone interested in seeing the endangered snowy plover (*Charadrius alexandrinus*) up close, there's usually one bobbing its way over the sand.

Just outside the aviary, for kids of all ages, are the touch tanks where a large assortment of live sea creatures spend time in saltwater pools. Aquarium volunteers make the creatures available for the public to handle. Equally exciting and fun is the large pool that houses a number of harmless bat rays (*Myliobatis californica*), some 2 feet or more across. Dozens of hands reach into the pool, and with patience, successfully pet these amazing and harmless creatures.

A newer section of the aquarium is upstairs. Entering this part of the aquarium can be a dizzying experience. Swimming above the entrance hall in a huge circular tank are thousands of anchovies. Passing through the anchovies, the lights dim, reminiscent of the deeper waters found farther offshore in Monterey Bay. This is the jellyfish exhibit. Windows illuminated by dramatic colored lights offer a look at some of the most extraordinarily delicate and beautiful creatures in the ocean. Visitors see jellyfish ranging in size from basketballs to thimbles. Anyone who has swum into the floating stream of the orange-brown sea nettle's (*Chrysaura fuscescens*) tentacles might not agree that it is delicate and beautiful creature. The sea nettle paralyzes its prey before eating it. It also causes severe stinging pain to swimmers who inadvertently cross its drifting path.

The largest aquarium window in the world is in the Monterey Bay Aquarium's Outer Bay. Inside what again represents the deeper waters of Monterey Bay and the Pacific Ocean, are many larger sea creatures. Yellowfin tuna (*Thunnus albacares*), skipjack tuna (*Katsuwonus pelamis*), and Pacific bonito (*Sarda chiliensis*) swim in large numbers throughout the tank. A large and strange looking ocean sunfish (*Mola mola*), a huge fish that looks like something ate its back two-thirds, moves slowly, while the sea turtle (*Chelonia* sp.) occasionally swims from the bottom to float closer to the surface for awhile.

Plan to spend at least two hours in the aquarium and much longer if you are especially fascinated by the ocean. Also, check the feeding times for the otters in the otter tank, one of the most popular of the attractions. Additional programs are shown in the outside viewing areas and in the aquarium's theaters.

Directions: From Monterey's wharf area take Del Monte Avenue west through the tunnel. Here, Del Monte turns into Lighthouse Avenue. Take the first right turn onto Foam Street and follow it several blocks until it ends. Turn right at the traffic light. The aquarium is very visible a block down the hill at 886 Cannery Row.

Activities: Special talks and movies. Periodic special evening events for members.

Facilities: Gift shops, restaurant and snack bar, outside seating and viewing areas.

Dates: Open daily 10 to 5. Extended hours during summer.

Fees: There is a moderate entrance fee charged for adults and a lesser fee for children. During summer weekends the line to enter can stretch up the street quite a distance.

For more information: Monterey Bay Aquarium, 886 Cannery Row, Monterey, CA 93940. Phone (831) 648-4800.

FISHERMAN'S WHARF

[Fig. 43(3)] Monterey actually enjoys two wharves. The Fisherman's Wharf that draws most people's attention juts into the bay from near the front of the historic Custom House and the adjacent Custom House Plaza. It's a sensual jumble of sights, smells, and sounds that draws thousands of people each day, especially during summer. Food is one of the real attractions here. In front of many of the small stands, proprietors offer free samples of their delicious clam chowders, while fresh fish and

CALIFORNIA SEA LION
(Zalophus californicus)
The trained "seals" of zoos, circuses, and aquariums are usually California sea lions.

crab lie atop mounds of ice, and slabs of salmon smoke slowly on open smoke pits. There are a half dozen restaurants, all offering good food, along with great views of the harbor. Many people who wander onto the wharf simply pick and choose samplings of shrimp and crab cocktails, fried calamari, or the plethora of other seafood that tempts the palate. And there's always the gift shops filled with T-shirts and postcards and stores selling taffy, ice cream, and chocolate-covered frozen bananas.

The wharf is also the place to catch fish. Not from the wharf itself, but from any one of several fishing boats that leave early each morning, weather permitting, and seek halibut, cod, salmon, sea bass, or other species of game fish, either in the bay or in the open waters of the Pacific Ocean. It's always enjoyable to watch the gulls and brown pelicans (*Pelecanus occidentalis*) that swoop in, looking for free handouts around the fish cleaning dock. They're often joined by one or more California sea lions (*Zalophus californicus*) also willing to fight for chunks of discarded fish entrails. For those not inclined to catch fish, boats also head out several times each day on whale-watching trips. During January and February the most sighted subjects are gray whales (*Eschrichtius robustus*), which are heading south to their birthing grounds. Summer brings the giant blue whales (*Balanenoptera musculus*) into they bay, along with huge schools of dolphins (*Delphinus delphis*) and occasional pods of orcas or killer whales (*Orcinus orca*). Whale-watching boats, often for reasons of time, seldom venture out beyond the relatively sheltered waters of the bay, but even here, anyone prone to motion sickness should take appropriate precautions.

For a little closer look at the commercial fishing boats unloading their catches, the commercial wharf and marina, located a few hundred yards east of Fisherman's Wharf, is the place to go. Gulls, pelicans, and sea lions shadow the fishing boats as they motor into the wharf and tie-off. Their fish cargoes are sorted and packed with ice into large transport containers. Unknown to most people, this is also the best place for the public to purchase whole fish by the pound. The prices are the lowest you'll find anywhere around, and the fish come really fresh, sometimes still wriggling. The sellers will clean and fillet the fish for you for a small additional fee. Or, if you have a fishing pole and tackle, you can try your luck from the commercial wharf, as many people do. It's not a bad way to spend a couple of hours.

Directions: Both wharves and the marina are located near the Custom House Plaza in Monterey, paralleling Del Monte Avenue in Monterey. There are two well-marked entrances.

Activities: Fishing, shopping, eating, whale watching.

Facilities: Restaurants, gift shops, fresh fish sales, fishing and whale-watching trips.

Dates: Open daily.

Fees: Both wharves are free. The commercial fishing wharf has metered parking. The adjacent Monterey Fisherman's Wharf does not allow vehicles, but there's an adjacent parking lot.

For more information: Monterey Peninsula Visitor and Convention Bureau inside the Stanton Center/Maritime Museum of Monterey on Custom House Plaza. Phone (831) 649-1770.

FISHING AND WHALE WATCHING

Monterey's Fisherman's Wharf, features numerous shops filled with the typical tourist souvenir stuff: sweatshirts that unprepared visitors may need, several good restaurants, and vendors with their crab pots boiling and fresh fish on ice. There are also four companies offering fishing and whale-watching boat tours. Fishing can be very good nearly any month, but many people show up during July when the salmon move into the bay. Either bring your own poles, tackle, and bait, or rent supplies at the wharf. January through March are the best months to see the most whales because this is when the gray whales are heading south to their birthing waters near Baja. During summer the larger blue whales, along with orcas and dolphins, are seen pretty regularly, but in fewer numbers than the grays. The competing whale-watching boats actually work together, using radios to communicate sightings, and their prices are pretty much the same.

Directions: Fisherman's Wharf and the commercial wharf are located just off Del Monte Avenue, near the Custom House Plaza in Monterey. There are two well-marked entrances.

Dates: Trips are available daily, weather permitting. Call for reservations and departure times.

Fees: Whale-watching trips cost between $15 and $20. Fishing trips, especially if fishing poles and tackle are provided by the boat operator, can be moderately expensive, but generally will run upward from about $50. The price for fishing often depends on the type of fish sought, which determines how far out the boat may have to go and how long it will be out.

For more information: Each of the following companies offer both whale-watching and fishing trips: Chris' Fishing Trips, phone (831) 375-5951; Monterey Sport Fishing Cruises, phone (831) 372-3501; Randy's Fishing Trips, phone (831) 372-7440; and Sam's Fishing Fleet, phone (831) 372-0577.

MONTEREY BAY RECREATION TRAIL

[Fig. 43(4)] Beginning at Pacific Grove's Lovers Point, a paved and relatively level recreation trail meanders with the give-and-take of the shoreline. Following a historic and abandoned railroad right-of-way, it passes the Monterey Bay Aquarium and through the middle of the Cannery Row area. If you happen to be around Cannery Row without a bike, there are several rental shops along the trail, which goes on to San Carlos Park, which is next to the Coast Guard pier and is also a favorite gathering and preparation area for scuba divers. The trail next swings in around the harbor and passes between Fisherman's Wharf and the historic Custom House, and around behind the Maritime Museum of Monterey. It parallels Monterey State Beach and Seaside State Beach and soon takes a weird twist over the freeway, behind a shopping center, then back to the beach in Sand City and Seaside. Following between the railroad tracks and Highway 1 (freeway) it heads on to the town of Marina, in all more than 12 miles. Through Pacific Grove and Monterey the trail is very level. After passing Seaside State Beach it begins a series of ups and downs as it passes over and down freeway overpasses, or beside them.

This is a very popular trail, overseen by several governmental jurisdictions. If speed is what you're looking for, then staying away from the Pacific Grove/Cannery Row/Fisherman's Wharf area should a priority during summer, unless you are biking or running very early in the morning in the fog. By the time the afternoon sun comes out, the trail is much too crowded for fast-peddling bicyclists. The trail is open to pedestrians and in-line skaters, although in some areas pedestrians are directed by signs to walk on the dirt walkway adjacent to the paved trail, while bicyclists and in-line skaters use the paved trail. Pedestrians don't always do so. The trail is not lighted for night use.

Directions: The best place to park and unload bicycles is either at Lover's Point Park parking lot in Pacific Grove or in the parking lot just off Del Monte Avenue, just east of Sloat Avenue and across the street from the gate into the Naval Post Graduate School. The Fisherman's Wharf parking lot off Del Monte Avenue also offers easy access to the recreation trail.

Activities: The bike trail is open to walkers, runners, bicyclists, and in-line skaters. Skateboards are prohibited.

Facilities: Except at Lovers Point and Fisherman's Wharf, there are no stand-alone restrooms along the trail.

Dates: The trail is open daily.

For more information: Monterey Peninsula Visitor and Convention Bureau inside the Stanton Center/Maritime Museum of Monterey on Custom House Plaza. Phone (831) 649-1770.

CANNERY ROW

[Fig. 43(5)] The stench of sardines that permeated the heart and soul of this corner of Monterey and extended into neighboring Pacific Grove 50 years ago has long since disappeared, although a quick read of John Steinbeck's *Cannery Row* can quickly bring it back to life, at least in one's imagination. Also gone are the canneries that first began appearing here in 1902. Those first canneries processed salmon and abalone for the San Francisco market. As that market faded, the sardine fishery slowly began to take its place. Within a few years, improved technology and work practices allowed fishing boats to unload their holds more efficiently and quickly, and factories to significantly increase the speed and efficiency of their canning processes.

As World War II raged, sardines became the mainstay of the Monterey fishing industry. Following a night of fishing, the boats, most large purse seiners, would return to unload as much as 70 tons of sardines into the factories, which processed most of the fish into fishmeal and fertilizer. On the first night of the sardine fishing season in 1949, some 52 purse seiners and 16 smaller boats returned to Monterey's canneries with over 2,500 tons of sardines.

By the early 1950s, the sardine industry was in serious trouble. An entire season would see no more than what had been a slow night's catch in 1940. Over-fishing, water temperature changes, pollution, and any number of other contributing factors brought the sardine industry to its knees and sent its owners into bankruptcy. The years that followed were not any kinder to the Cannery Row waterfront. The abandoned canneries fell into disrepair, and the entire area became a blight on the edge of Monterey Bay. Urban redevelopment and an increasing tourist industry finally started bringing the Row back to life. Some of the remaining canneries were transformed into shops, restaurants, and amusement centers. The opening of Monterey Bay Aquarium in 1984 brought a huge increase in tourism to the area. It also spurred further enhancements to the surrounding areas.

MOSQUITO
(Anopheles communis)
Female mosquitoes have stiletto-like mouthparts that are usually down when the insect is at rest.

Just wandering around Cannery Row's several blocks can be an adventure in itself. Many of the old structures are a maze of corridors and walkways, stairs, and passages that lead from one unique shop to another and from myriad restaurants to wine tasting rooms. There are carousels and jewelry stores, kayak rentals and bicycle rentals.

At the east end of Cannery Row, adjacent to the U.S. Coast Guard pier entrance, scuba divers have discovered **San Carlos Beach**. Actually the city of Monterey developed the park, including plenty of parking (metered), and added a restroom and outside showers specifically to accommodate the large number of scuba divers who come here. It's a very popular place for beginning divers. The large grassy area offers plenty of space for picnics and for just relaxing after a day of diving.

Directions: From Del Monte Avenue near Fisherman's Wharf, stay in the right lanes and continue west through the tunnel. Take the first right turn, which is Foam Street. Drive to the first traffic light and turn right, go the two blocks to the bottom of the hill. The road swings left and becomes Cannery Row. San Carlos Park is on the right.

Activities: Walking, dining, scuba diving, shopping.

For more information: Monterey Peninsula Visitor and Convention Bureau inside the Stanton Center/Maritime Museum of Monterey on Custom House Plaza. Phone (831) 649-1770.

KAYAKING MONTEREY BAY

There's nothing more relaxing than paddling silently, almost effortlessly, across the calm waters of Monterey Bay, watching the sea otters watch you. The kelp beds offer sanctuary to many animals, and sitting in a kayak is the best way to experience the edge of the bay. Mornings are the best time to go, before the afternoon winds have managed to kick up the waves a bit more than beginning kayakers might find comfortable. For renters, there are two basic types of kayaks available in the rental shops in Monterey. Many people choose the sit-on-top kayaks, which are great if it happens to be a warm day and you don't mind getting a little wetter than you would paddling in a sit-inside kayak. But both are great fun. Lessons are available and a short session with a qualified instructor from any of the shops will make the day much safer and more enjoyable for beginners. For anyone with his or her own kayak, **Monterey State Beach**, across Del Monte Avenue from Lake El Estero, has a long, gentle, sandy beach that offers easy kayak launching. There's free parking along Del Monte Avenue and it's just a short carry across the grass to the beach.

Directions: Easiest launching is just off Del Monte Avenue, across from Lake El Estero at Monterey State Beach.

Fees: Parking along the street is free. There is a small, metered parking lot at the end of the grassy area, adjacent to the Monterey Bay Kayaks shop.

For more information: Several companies rent kayaks including Adventures by the Sea, 299 Cannery Row in Monterey, phone (831) 372-1807; Monterey Bay Kayaks, 693 Del Monte Avenue, Monterey, phone (831) 373-5357.

MONTEREY PENINSULA BEACHES

Central coast beach waters are generally too cold for swimming, except for younger children who seem immune to such things, at least for short periods of time. It's amazing how children can completely ignore their own shivering when visions of sandcastles and the slap of ocean waves are so inviting. While there are several miles of sandy beaches and an equal number of rocky tidepool areas along the Monterey Peninsula, one of the most popular swimming areas, especially for parents with children, is the protected cove at **Lovers Point Park** (phone 831-648-3130) in Pacific Grove. The slope is gentle, the waves small, and the area is reasonably well protected from the afternoon breezes. Outside the cove, surfers often catch some pretty good-sized waves off the point. The park has a kayak and bike rental shop and snack bar open during the summer.

Asilomar State Beach [Fig. 43(8)] (phone 831-372-4076) (*see* also page 195) also in Pacific Grove and adjacent to the very popular Sunset Drive, is another sandy beach, not just for wetsuit-clad surfers, but for those hardy enough to chase waves without spending too much time in the water. It faces the generally cold onshore ocean winds, and the open-ocean waves that wash ashore are much larger than those found in the cove at Lovers' Point.

Carmel City Beach (phone 831-624-3543), located at the end of Ocean Street and managed by the city of Carmel, is another open, sandy beach, which is especially popular with dog owners. It's one of the few public beaches where dogs can run free without such hindrances as leashes.

An important few words of warning: All of these waters can be dangerous, especially during winter when even colder waters and higher waves can and do sweep unsuspecting beach-goers and tidepool explorers off shore. Sleeper waves, a single wave or set of waves much larger than those that may have washed ashore for quite some time, strike suddenly and without warning. They sweep people to their deaths every year.

PACIFIC GROVE

The self-proclaimed "Last Hometown" is a quaint and beautiful small town that sits on the point of land that separates Monterey Bay from the open waters of the Pacific Ocean. Generally draped in fog during summer, while its neighbor Monterey enjoys afternoon sunshine, Pacific Grove's main street, Lighthouse Avenue, provides a short few blocks of wonderful antique shops, restaurants, the Scottish Bakery (which is a local favorite), a bookstore, and more. During the Christmas season, the trees and buildings are brilliantly illuminated in white and multicolored lights.

From where it begins near the Monterey Bay Aquarium, Pacific Grove's Ocean View Boulevard meanders along the coast, adjacent to the Monterey Bay Recreation Trail, to Lovers Point. Continue on Ocean View Boulevard where several parking areas on the low, coastal bluff offer great opportunities to explore the rocky tidepools that the town is so well known for. Near Point Pinos the same road turns into Sunset Avenue and continues around the point.

Look closely at many of Pacific Grove's older Victorian and smaller, more quaint homes, and notice many have small wood plaques near their doors indicating the late nineteenth and early twentieth century dates of their construction. Pacific Grove was founded as a Christian retreat. And indeed, Pacific Grove's **Asilomar State Beach and Conference Grounds** was constructed in 1914 as a Young Women's Christian Association (YWCA) summer camp. Many of its original buildings were designed by Julia Morgan, the renowned California architect who designed Hearst Castle. Today, Asilomar is a world-renowned conference center owned by California State Parks. Asilomar also accepts non-conference guests in its moderately priced accommodations.

Asilomar State Beach easily is the peninsula's most popular spot for sunset watching. While summer's fog often obscures the sun behind a thick gray curtain, during the rest of the year cars begin parking along the road an hour or more before sunset in order to guarantee the perfect viewing spot. Here, the open ocean's crashing waves, especially during winter, offer ample opportunities for great memories and beautiful photographs.

Sunset Avenue circles around Pacific Grove crossing Seventeen Mile Drive (*see* page 199), which offers access to one of several gates into Pebble Beach. Actually, Seventeen Mile Drive begins (or ends) in Pacific Grove, crossing Lighthouse Avenue a few blocks west of the town's business district.

One of the favorite trips for bicyclists in Pacific Grove is the Sunset Drive to Ocean View Avenue coastal route. While Ocean View is reasonably level with gentle hills, Sunset Drive has a fairly long and steep descent from well above its beginning at Highway 68, just above Seventeen Mile Drive. There is also lots of traffic, most of which travels slowly, which is good; but be aware that most drivers are looking at the ocean and not for bicyclists.

Directions: From Highway 1 heading south from Monterey to Carmel, take the Highway 68 Exit to Pacific Grove, Pebble Beach and Asilomar. Turn right onto Highway 68 at the freeway overpass traffic light and continue on to Pacific Grove. Continue on Highway 68 through the commercial part of the town's two traffic lights. Highway 68 turns left and becomes Sunset Drive. Drive about 1 mile more to Asilomar State Beach and Conference Grounds at the bottom of the hill, along the coast.

For more information: Asilomar State Beach and Conference Grounds, 800 Asilomar Avenue, Pacific Grove, CA 93950. Phone (831) 372-8016 or (831) 372-4076. For additional information contact the Monterey Peninsula Visitor and Convention Bureau, phone (831) 648-5358.

PACIFIC GROVE MUSEUM OF NATURAL HISTORY

This is one of those hidden treasures that will remain undiscovered, unless you happen to be traveling slightly off the main tourist route of popular Lighthouse Avenue. Outside the museum is a concrete replica of a gray whale, which kids can't help but climb on. Sometimes the tough part is getting them inside. But once inside, anyone interested in the Central Coast natural history is in for a surprise. All those birds, from avocets and western sandpipers, to willits and brown pelicans, that inhabit the coastal shore and are difficult to identify using a bird book, are waiting inside a large glass exhibit case. Unfortunately they've been stuffed, but at least they don't move and their names are printed neatly next to them.

Additional exhibits on geology, mammals, insects, and more fill the small museum. And for those who drop in occasionally, there is always a major exhibit in the museum's large exhibit hall. Special guest lectures are also a feature. It's a good place to spend time becoming oriented to the area's diverse natural history.

Directions: From Pacific Grove's Lighthouse Avenue in the central business district, drive down toward the Bay 1 block to Central Avenue, which parallels Lighthouse Avenue. The museum is at the corner of Forest and Central avenues.

Activities: Lectures, occasional children's programs.

Facilities: Natural history exhibits, small gift shop.

Dates: Open daily except Mondays. Closed Thanksgiving, Christmas, and New Year's Day.

Fees: None.

For more information: Pacific Grove Museum of Natural History, 165 Forest Avenue, Pacific Grove, CA 93950. Phone (831) 648-3116.

MONTEREY PENINSULA LODGING

There are well over a hundred hotels, motels, and bed and breakfasts in the Monterey area. There's no magic for choosing the right place to stay; the decision is going to be based primarily on where you want to be and what you want to see.

Monterey Plaza Hotel & Spa. 400 Cannery Row, Monterey. If it's an up-close and personal ocean view that you want, then this is the hotel to stay in. It sits right on the beach, on historic Cannery Row. *Expensive. Phone (831) 646-1700.*

Seven Gables Inn and Grand View Inn. 555 and 557 Ocean View Boulevard, Pacific Grove. If you're looking for something really special, such as ocean views and Victorian or Edwardian elegance, then either of these grand bed and breakfasts inns will be perfect and should easily meet your needs. These magnificent nineteenth century mansions have been transformed into elegant and comfortable bed and breakfast inns that are perched on the hillside, on Ocean View Boulevard, overlooking the rocky coast of Pacific Grove. *Expensive. Phone (831) 372-4341.*

Green Gables Inn. 104 5th Street, Pacific Grove. On Ocean View Boulevard and the corner of 5th Street in Pacific Grove, is a Victorian built in 1888. It too, has spectacular views of Monterey Bay and is also just across the street from the Monterey Bay Recreation Trail. Bring your bicycles and it takes a few minutes to ride to the Monterey Bay Aquarium. *Expensive. Phone (831) 375-2095.*

The Centrella Inn. 612 Central Avenue, Pacific Grove, CA 93950. Located near the center of Pacific Grove and it shops and restaurants, this nineteenth century Victorian hotel is just a few short blocks up the hill from Monterey Bay and the recreation trail. *Expensive. Phone (831) 373-3372.*

Borg's Ocean Front Motel. 635 Ocean View Boulevard, Pacific Grove, CA 93950. If you're not looking for luxury, but would like to stay in a great location at a reasonable price, this is it. Many of the rooms offer spectacular views of the bay and Lovers Point, both of which are located just across the street. *Moderate to expensive. Phone (831) 375-2406.*

Best Western Monarch Resort. 1111 Lighthouse Avenue, Pacific Grove, CA 93950. The hotel is located in a quiet section of Pacific Grove that is surrounded by a residential area. There are often deer wandering the streets and munching in the gardens in this part of Pacific Grove. *Expensive. Phone (831) 646-8885.*

Casa Munrus Garden Hotel. 700 Munrus Avenue, Monterey, CA 93940. Located just a couple blocks from old Monterey, it's an easy walk to numerous historic adobes and with a little more effort, also to Fisherman's Wharf. *Expensive. Phone (831) 375-2411.*

Merritt House. 386 Pacific Street, Monterey, CA 93940. Set in the middle of old Monterey, historic adobes, the wharf, and the shops and restaurants of Alvarado Street are just a couple of blocks away. *Expensive. Phone (831) 646-9686.*

Travelodge-Monterey/Carmel. 2030 North Fremont Street, Monterey, CA 93940. If you don't need anything fancy, and don't mind being a mile or so away from old Monterey, the wharf and other attractions this is a good and one of the less expensive places to stay on the Monterey Peninsula. *Moderate. Phone* (831) 373-3381.

For more information: For overnight accommodations contact the Monterey Peninsula Visitors and Convention Bureau. Phone (831) 648-5358.

▓ MONTEREY PENINSULA DINING

Finding a restaurant on the Monterey Peninsula isn't a problem. Trying to decide where to go is always the dilemma. There are too many dozens of choices to try to count, from small Mexican eateries to restaurants that feature some of the finest food anywhere.

Old Monterey Café. 489 Alvarado Street, Monterey. This is a small café in historic downtown that serves one of the best breakfasts on the peninsula. It's always busy in the morning, so expect to wait a short while, but it's worth it. Also serves lunch. Very casual and very popular with locals. *Inexpensive. Phone (831) 646-1021.*

First Awakenings. 125 Ocean View Avenue, Pacific Grove. Located at the east end of the American Tin Cannery Premium Outlets just a half block from the Monterey Bay Aquarium, this is another very popular breakfast place with locals. The food is great and they serve plenty. *Inexpensive. Phone (831) 372-1125.*

Monterey's Fish House. 2114 Del Monte Boulevard, Monterey. What appears from the outside as an old, tan-colored house (which it is) is actually a restaurant that serves some of Monterey's best lunches and dinners, if it's fresh fish you're looking for. Here, the menu is only a guide. You're encouraged to order what you want and how you would like it cooked. They also serve great steaks for those who do not care for fish. *Inexpensive to moderate. Phone (831) 373-4647.*

Stokes Adobe. 500 Hartnell Street, Monterey. Located in the nineteenth century Stokes adobe in old Monterey, the menu features innovative country Mediterranean cuisine that includes delicious fish, pork, beef. Reservations are suggested. *Inexpensive to moderate. Phone (831) 373-1110.*

Fandango. 223 17th Street Pacific Grove. This is another special place for locals. It offers fabulous food that includes mesquite-grilled seafood and steaks, pastas, couscous, and heavenly desserts. *Inexpensive to moderate. Phone (831) 372-3456.*

GOLF ON THE MONTEREY PENINSULA

For thousands of people each year, there is one primary activity that the Monterey Peninsula is known for, and it's not sailing on blue water or watching beautiful sunsets. It's playing golf. The annual AT&T ProAm, with its combination of top professional players and Hollywood and other celebrities, has certainly helped spur public awareness of some of the peninsula's most spectacular courses. The ProAm is played on three of the most famous courses—**Pebble Beach, Poppy Hills, and Spyglass Hill**. Unfortunately, these particular golf courses are generally out of the range of most golfers, not in terms of difficulty (although they are extremely challenging), but in terms of price, with green fees for 18 holes hovering near the three century mark for anyone not staying in the resort's hotel. But even with money in hand, be sure to make reservations well in advance because drop-ins don't have much luck getting tee times. But it remains the dream of most golfers to someday play Pebble Beach, (phone 831-624-3811). Just plan ahead.

If playing golf while enjoying views of the Pacific Ocean is a personal dream, but so is coming up with the green fees to play Pebble Beach, then the best golf bargain on the Monterey Peninsula has to be **Pacific Grove's Municipal Golf Links** (phone 831-648-3177). Operated by the City of Pacific Grove, the course is challenging and well-maintained, and several holes parallel the coast so that golfers get to enjoy ocean views similar to those at Pebble Beach, and contend with the sometimes challenging winds. The biggest difference is that this golf course's green fees give you change from a fifty-dollar bill.

Other courses that are very popular include the **Del Monte Golf Course** (phone 831-373-2700) in Monterey, established in 1897, making it the oldest course on the peninsula, and **Rancho Cañada** (phone 831-624-0111) located just off Carmel Valley Road, with its two reasonably priced championship courses. In the general vicinity of Monterey there are a couple of dozen other quality courses with varying green fees. During summer advance reservations are always a good idea.

For more information: There's no centralized center for golfing information. It is best to contact the Monterey Peninsula Visitors and Convention Bureau, phone (831) 648-5358.

PEBBLE BEACH AND SEVENTEEN MILE DRIVE

[Fig. 43(12)] A must-do tour while on the Monterey Peninsula is the famous Seventeen Mile Drive that meanders through Pebble Beach. The original Seventeen Mile Drive began in Monterey, from the Victorian-style Hotel Del Monte, which, when constructed in 1880, was the "Queen of American Watering Places" and considered the most elegant seaside resort in the world. Fire destroyed the original hotel, but another was rebuilt. The replacement structure may be seen on the original hotel's site at today's Naval Post Graduate School headquarters in Monterey. The original tours from the hotel used horse-drawn wagons; today's tours begin at the private gates into Pebble Beach, with visitors using their own cars or bicycles.

Pebble Beach evolved from properties, including the coastline and the Del Monte Forest, originally consolidated into Del Monte Properties by railroad magnate Charles Crocker. Crocker began developing portions of the property, including a beach bathhouse and a racetrack, but the economics of the time took a downturn. Subsequently a young Samuel F. B. Morse, a very, very distant relative of Samuel F. B. Morse, best known for his invention of the telegraph, and a group of investors purchased the property in 1915. Soon afterward, Morse began developing Pebble Beach into what it is today.

While today's tours may not total the full 17 miles, the views remain as memorable as those seen by visitors a century ago. From the Pacific Grove gate into Pebble Beach, Seventeen Mile Drive leads past the Inn at Spanish Bay and down to Spanish Bay where many people come for the long, sandy beach. The tour road continues weaving between the Spanish Bay golf links. There almost always is a large population of feeding deer on the fairways. There are several popular stops along this stretch of Seventeen Mile Drive, including Point Joe, where the ocean's currents cross paths with currents from Monterey Bay, creating constantly crashing waves and ocean mist just offshore. The sounds of barking sea lions coming from Bird Rock, also favorite resting place for seabirds, can easily be heard over the ocean waves. China Rock memorializes the Chinese who established fishing villages, not only here, but in other areas between Monterey and Point Lobos. Wind your way up to Cypress Point Lookout, and on clear days Point Sur lighthouse, located 20 miles down the Big Sur coast, is visible.

Why has Seventeen Mile Drive remained so popular for so long? It certainly has something to do with the spectacular views of the coast. There are also the incredible homes tucked into the coastal cliffs and partially hidden in the Del Monte Forest, homes with prices that generally fall into the seven- and eight-figure range. If traffic and crowds are any gauge, the most popular site along Seventeen Mile Drive is the famed Lone Cypress that is perched rather precariously near the end of a rocky point surrounded by the swirling surf. The Lone Cypress is estimated to be somewhere between 200 and 300 years old, which is remarkable considering its extremely inhospitable home, surrounded by sea, wind, and non-fertile rock.

Traffic, especially on summer weekends, can become a bit snarled, so an alternative to fighting it is to make your way to the vicinity of the Lodge at Pebble Beach and drop into the **Tap Room Bar & Grill**. It's always a fun place to be, the food's great, and the food is moderately priced. It's also a place where many of golfing and Hollywood stars drop in during the AT&T ProAm. Reservations are always a good idea. Phone (831) 625-8535.

Seventeen Mile Drive is a popular place for bicycle touring, but this is not a place for beginning or infrequent riders. There are several steep hills, and often there isn't much space between passing cars and bicyclists. Also, some parts of Pebble Beach are off limits to bicyclists. But, otherwise, a good place to enter is through the Pacific

Grove gate. Bicyclists must sign in. Actually, cyclists sign a waiver of liability form that includes a map of the bicycle route along with permitted routes of travel.

Directions: There are actually several entry gates to Pebble Beach and Seventeen Mile Drive. The two most popular are the Pacific Grove Gate near the intersection of Highway 68 (Sunset Drive) and Seventeen Mile Drive. This entrance is closest to Spanish Bay and farthest from the Lodge at Pebble Beach. The other popular entrance is just off Highway 1 at the Highway 68 Exit, between Monterey and Carmel. From this entrance, the **Lodge at Pebble Beach** (*expensive*) is a short, five-minute drive away.

Activities: Scenic driving with numerous stops, golf, beach walking, horseback riding, picnicking, fine dining.

Facilities: Hotels, restaurants, golf courses.

Dates: Open daily.

Fees: There is a small fee for nonresident vehicles to enter Pebble Beach and Seventeen Mile Drive. Bicyclists must sign the release form located near the entry gate and enter at no cost. Hotels, most restaurants, and golf courses are expensive.

Closest town: Carmel and Pacific Grove are adjacent to Pebble Beach.

For more information: The Lodge at Pebble Beach, PO Box 1128, Pebble Beach, CA 93953. Phone (831) 624-3811.

THE NATIONAL STEINBECK CENTER

[Fig. 43(10)] Salinas, about 20 minutes from Monterey, was the birthplace of John Steinbeck, whose many novels and short stories have entertained millions of people. His Pulitzer Prize-winning novel, *The Grapes of Wrath*, also angered many of those who lived and worked in the Salinas Valley. Apparently Steinbeck hit a little too close to home with his descriptions of the lives of farm workers and how the farm owners treated them. Some of Steinbeck's other books, such as *Cannery Row* and *Tortilla Flat*, brought to life some of the more colorful characters who lived and worked in 1930s Monterey.

Today, Salinas is home to the National Steinbeck Center, a multimedia experience of the famous author's life. Themed galleries feature exhibits related to his many novels and theaters show clips of the many films that were based on his writings. One of the center's prized possessions is "Rocinante." It's the GMC pick-up truck with a custom camper that Steinbeck drove across the country while doing research for *Travels with Charley*. For the more academically inclined, the center houses over 30,000 pieces of oral histories, photographs, original manuscripts, and first edition books.

Directions: From the US 101 freeway as it passes through Salinas, take the Business US 101 Exit, which is also North Main Street and State Highway 183. The Center is about 0.25 mile south of US 101 freeway. From Monterey, take Highway 68 (Monterey-Salinas Highway) north to Salinas. Highway 68 becomes Main Street once in Salinas, then turns to North Main. The center is located at 1 Main Street.

Facilities: Galleries, theater, gift shop.

Dates: Open daily. Closed Thanksgiving, Christmas, and New Year's Day.

Fees: There is a moderate entrance fee with discounts for children and seniors.

For more information: The National Steinbeck Center, 1 Main Street, Salinas, CA 93901. Phone (831) 796-3833.

CARMEL MISSION

[Fig. 43(11)] One of California's better-known missions is San Carlos Borromeo, better known as the Carmel Mission. As Padre Presidentes of California's missions, it became Father Serra's headquarters for most of his last years. On June 3, 1770, Father Serra arrived in Monterey and founded his second mission, the first having been San Diego the previous year. Feeling that he had located his Monterey mission too close to the newly established Monterey Presidio (fort), the following year Serra moved it to where it remains today in Carmel. The mission's primary goal was to convert local Indians to Christianity and, ultimately, into Spanish citizens. Unfortunately, Spain's plans were implemented at the expense of the Indians' native cultures.

There is a certain charm that attracts people from all over the world to the Carmel Mission. Its place in California's history certainly plays a part in that attraction, but there is much more. Wander through the restored, yet remarkably old-appearing complex, and enjoy its beautiful gardens, the awe-inspiring church, and the rooms filled with the history of this two century-old house of worship. Artists often try to capture its physical beauty on canvas, and photographers, amateur and professional alike, have taken untold millions of photographs.

Maybe part of the attraction is the fact that Father Serra died here in 1784, and was buried with his friend and fellow padre, Father Crespi, before the main altar. Perhaps part of the attraction is the memory of the 4,000 neophytes, as the Indians were called, who were baptized during the mission's most active years, between 1770 and 1836. Maybe it's that so many of those same Indians died here of European diseases to which they had no natural immunities.

It was more than a decade after Serra's death that one of his predecessors began construction of the present stone church, but it fell into disrepair following Mexico's secularization of the missions in 1834. With the church's lands divided and gone, the buildings disintegrated, many into nothing more than partial walls. Finally, in 1931, local residents began a major effort to restore the mission to what it is today.

Directions: From Highway 1 in Carmel turn west on Rio Road and drive approximately 0.5 mile. The mission is on the left at Lasuen Drive.

Facilities: Gardens, courtyard, church, small gift shop.

Dates: Open daily, with extended hours into the early evening during summer.

Fees: A small donation is requested.

For more information: Carmel Mission Gift Shop, 3880 Rio Road, Carmel, CA 93921. Phone (831) 624-3600.

Central Coast Winery Tour

Monterey County has dubbed itself "the other wine country," and its wineries, many of them small and family owned, produce excellent wines that rival the best in the world. A **Taste of Monterey** is the county's wine tasting visitor center that offers a good introduction to the area's wineries. Located at popular Cannery Row near the Monterey Bay Aquarium, the visitor center offers an opportunity to taste many local wines and provides maps, directions, and other details about Monterey's wineries.

Several of the wineries require advance notice, but most allow drop-ins and offer free tastings or minimally priced samplings. The nearest winery to downtown Monterey is **Ventana Vineyards'** tasting room (phone 831-372-7415) located just south of Highway 1, off Highway 68 in the Old Stone House.

Driving up Carmel Valley Road, beginning at Highway 1 in Carmel, the **Chateau Julien Wine Estate** (phone 831-624-2600) offers wine tasting, as does **Durney Vineyards** (phone 831-659-6220), **River Ranch Vineyards** (phone 831-659-1525), **Galante Vineyards** (phone 800-GALANTE), and **Bernardus** (phone 800-223-2533). Many more wineries and vineyards are found in the hills surrounding US 101 between Chualar and Greenfield, the farthest of which is only about an hour's drive south from Monterey. **Cloninger Cellars** (phone 831- 675-9463) and **The Monterey Vineyard** (phone 831-675-4060), both not far from Gonzales, offer tastings, as does **Smith & Hook** (phone 831-678-2132), **Chalone Vineyard** (phone 831-678-1717), and **Paraiso Springs Vineyards** (phone 831-678-0300) and **Cobblestone** (phone 831-678-0300), located near Soledad. Closer to the town of Greenfield, two wineries, **Jekel Vineyards** (phone 831-674-5522), and **Scheid Vineyards** (phone 831-386-0316), are open to the public on a drop-in basis. Since many of the tasting rooms' days and times of operation change, especially from season to season, it's always a good practice to call ahead.

While most of the vineyards have tasting rooms, most of the tasting rooms are far removed from their respective wine-making operations. Because of this, only a few of the wineries offer tours of their operations, including **Chalone**, **Smith and Hook**, and **Galante**. Call ahead, as tours are often offered only on weekends or by reservation.

Directions: The Taste of Monterey Visitor Center and Tasting Room is located at 700 Cannery Row in Monterey. From Del Monte Avenue near the wharf, drive west through the tunnel (where Del Monte turns into Lighthouse Avenue). Take the first right turn (Foam Street) and drive to the end, then turn right and drive two blocks down the hill to Cannery Row. The Visitor Center is about a block from the Monterey Bay Aquarium.

Activities: Wine tasting, tours at only a few wineries.

Facilities: Most tasting rooms and wineries have gift shops. Some have food services.

Dates: Most are open year-round.

Fees: Some wineries charge a small fee for sampling their wines.

For more information: Taste of Monterey Visitor Center and Tasting Room, phone (831) 646-5446; or the Monterey Peninsula Visitor and Convention Bureau, phone (831) 649-1770.

Carmel River State Beach

[Fig. 43(7)] Carmel River State Beach, with its lagoon and wetland, is located about 1 mile south of Carmel on Highway 1. There's a small beach with pull-out parking along the highway, and it's only a short walk to the water. Carmel River State Beach, or at least the small section closest to Highway 1, is better known locally as Monastery Beach. Scuba divers frequently use this beach. It's also a dangerous beach, with sleeper waves, cold water, and a fairly steep drop-off. Stay back, and don't allow children to play close to the water.

There are two additional accesses to the long stretch of beach area that is much larger than it appears when speeding down Highway 1. There is access to a wonderful wetlands area and much more beach if you hike for about 15 minutes along the beach from the highway. An alternative access to the wetland area is located off Highway 1, just south of the Carmel River bridge. Turn onto Ribera Road into a small, hilltop residential neighborhood. There is a trail to the wetland area and to the beach where the street dead-ends into a cul-de-sac. There's also a hill promontory that provides a nice view of the area. Be sure not to block anyone's driveway when parking.

A third alternative is to drive into the town of Carmel and meander around the twisting streets down to Scenic Avenue, which parallels the coast and passes homes that rival many of those in Pebble Beach. There's a parking lot off Scenic Avenue at the mouth of the Carmel River. Depending upon whether or not the river is flowing all the way to the ocean or is blocked by the seasonally forming sand dam, you can explore many more miles of beach.

Directions: Carmel River State Beach is located adjacent to Highway 1, about 1 mile south of Carmel.

Activities: Beach exploring, scuba diving, hiking, bird-watching.

Dates: Open daily.

Fees: None.

Closest town: Carmel, about 1 mile north.

For more information: Point Lobos State Reserve, about 2 miles south of Carmel, phone (831) 624-4909.

Point Lobos State Reserve

[Fig. 43] Point Lobos is one of those jewels that has attracted people since the earliest of times. Although permanent Native American villages were never possible because fresh water was not available year around, Indians did live along San Jose Creek, just a 0.5 mile or so to the northeast. Point Lobos has seen many changes during the past 150 years. It was used as a whaling processing site, an abalone processing and canning plant, and a shipping point for coal that was mined from the nearby mountains. At the end of the nineteenth century, the land was even subdivided by a developer who envisioned making a fortune selling homesites. Fortunately, with a combination of private donations and funds from Save-the-Redwoods League, the property became a state park in 1933.

While the surface lands of Point Lobos may have been changed, at least superficially, by those wanting to exploit its natural resources, what hasn't changed much in millions of years is the underlying geology. The relatively coarse-grained Santa Lucia Granite that formed deep below the surface some 110 million years ago was uplifted to form the jagged headlands along the reserve's northern shore. Near the center of the reserve, from near Sea Lion Point, the Carmelo Formation, a sedimentary conglomerate, is most prevalent. Only 60 million years old, the more easily erodable conglomerate is composed of smaller stones in what appears as a yellowish-colored concrete. Throughout the reserve, the conglomerate has eroded to form jagged cliffs and graceful arches. Yet scattered in a few protected coves, several sandy beaches await exploration, while others remain inaccessible.

Besides the obvious terrestrial beauty, 750 underwater acres are also part of the reserve. Point Lobos is an incredibly popular scuba-diving spot, generally requiring reservations weeks in advance. One of the reasons it remains such a treasure for divers is that the number of divers is limited each day and everything is protected. Any spearfishing has to be done outside the reserve's boundaries.

Many people first

Point Lobos Scuba-Diving

Much of Point Lobos State Reserve can only be enjoyed by those willing to don a mask and scuba gear. More than half of the park is located where an incredibly rich marine environment has created one of California's most diverse and beautiful underwater areas. Because both warm and cold ocean waters meet here, species that thrive in both habitats live in the reserve. Like the terrestrial portion of Point Lobos, the underwater portion of the park is protected, so the taking of any plant or animal is not allowed. In order to protect the underwater park, a limited number of divers is allowed each day. While reservations aren't required, it's likely most divers will be disappointed if they arrive without them. Dive reservations are best made on the Point Lobos State Reserve Web site: http://pointlobos.parks.state.ca.us.

coming to the reserve are surprised by the numbers and varieties of wildlife that live in the reserve. The seemingly ubiquitous sea otters frolic in the cold waters and during spring and early summer they can be seen caring for their young offspring. The most vocally boisterous animals are the sea lions. Aptly named, Sea Lion Rock offers a small sanctuary from the crashing waves for large numbers of California sea lions (*Zalophus californianus*) at almost any time of the year. The adult males, which can weigh up to 800 pounds, leave the local waters during the first months of summer and swim to rookeries farther south. During the time of year when they are at Point Lobos in greater numbers, it is impossible to miss their loud, incessant barking or their antics on the offshore rocks. Their loud and persistent barking is what caused the early Spanish explorers to name the area *Punta de los Lobos Marino*: Point of the Sea Wolves.

Birds are another major attraction of Point Lobos. On almost any day, dozens of different species can be seen in the reserve. For Brandt's cormorants (*Phalacrocorax penicillatus*) and black oystercatchers (*Haematopus bachmani*), western gulls (*Larus occidentalis*) and great blue herons (*Ardea herodias*), the sea, and the lands around it, provide rich feeding grounds. It's not at all unusual, especially late in the afternoon, for deer to wander out into the open forest or meadows amidst grasses and wildflowers to graze, while coyotes and even more rarely, a mountain lion, cross the reserve's several miles of trails.

In wind-protected Whalers' Cove, there is a small wood cottage that has been around since the 1850s when Chinese fishermen and their families moved to Point Lobos. The museum houses numerous exhibits and whaling-era artifacts such as harpoons. A short walk down the road from the museum is where scuba divers park and enter the cove. There's also a restroom and a picnic table or two. Over its history, the area occupied by today's parking lot, has served as a whale rendering area, held an abalone cannery, and been home to a quarry that supposedly provided stone for part of the San Francisco Mint.

Directions: Point Lobos is 2 miles south of Carmel on Highway 1.

Activities: Hiking, bird-watching, whale watching, scuba diving, wildlife watching, museum touring, picnics in designated picnic areas only.

Facilities: Museum, trails, a small outdoor gift "cart."

Dates: Opens daily at 9 to 7 during Pacific daylight time and closes at 5 during Pacific standard time.

Fees: There is a fee for vehicles entering the reserve. Walk-ins are free.

Closest town: Carmel, 2 miles.

For more information: Point Lobos State Reserve, phone (831) 624-4909.

▨ TRAILS

There are many trails that meander throughout the reserve, reaching headland promontories and secluded beaches. There are several coastal areas where scrambling among the rocks and cliffs, which can't be harmed by the hundreds of thousands of people who visit Point Lobos each year, is allowed. But generally, because of the extra level of protection afforded the reserve, hikers are restricted to the trails where they wind through the forests and grasslands. In many areas it's also in the best interest of hikers, because poison oak thrives throughout the Central Coast, including at Point Lobos.

The **North Shore Trail** [Fig. 44(1)] begins at Whalers' Cove and immediately heads uphill. Spring and summer wildflowers highlight the trail and deer are not uncommon sights. The jagged cliffs of the shoreline and the small, nearshore islands are homes to numerous nesting birds, including cormorants (*Phalacrocorax* spp.), western gulls (*Larus occidentalis*), and pigeon guillemots (*Cepphus columba*). The trail winds for 1.4 miles through the forest and ends at the Information Station at the Sea Lion Point parking lot.

The **Sea Lion Point Trail** [Fig. 44(2)] begins at the Sea Lion Point parking lot and is just over 0.5 mile long. It ends in an open bluff area that offers a great look at a part of the park's geology. The pounding waves and rain have sculpted the 60-million-year-old Carmelo Formation conglomerate into wonderful shapes. Harbor seals (*Phoca vitulina*) often lie balanced and sleeping on some of the smaller rocks just offshore, while barking California sea lions generally cover the large rock known as Sea Lion Rock, farther offshore. Between shore and Sea Lion Rock, an area called Devil's Cauldron turns the approaching ocean waves into crashing, churning, spectacular white geysers of water.

Bird Island Trail [Fig. 44(3)] begins at the far southern parking lot and passes through the coastal scrub, finally ending on a bluff that overlooks Bird Island. On the way, the trail passes two sandy beaches that can be reached by staircases. While birds abound and otters play in the kelp just offshore, it is the hundreds of Brandt's cormorants (*Phalacrocorax penicillatus*) that cover Bird Island during spring and summer that make this short hike unforgettable.

Big Sur Coast

[Fig. 44] Highway 1, where it meanders along the Big Sur coast, is designated as both a National Scenic Highway and an All-American Highway. Heading south from Carmel, it is about 26 miles to Big Sur, yet when visitors ask the Big Sur locals just exactly where Big Sur is, they are generally answered with a shrug. Big Sur is thought of more as a state of mind than a specific place. It's the sheer rugged terrain and the fog-shrouded cliffs that tower above the highway. It's the waves that crash into the rocky shore and the wildflowers that cast their colorful hues on the mosaic of mountainside vegetation. It's the remoteness, the quiet, the night skies, bright with stars, and the daytime skies even more blue than the Pacific's vast waters. It is a state of

Big Sur Coast

Highway 1 along the Big Sur coast is designated as both a National Scenic Highway and an All American Highway.

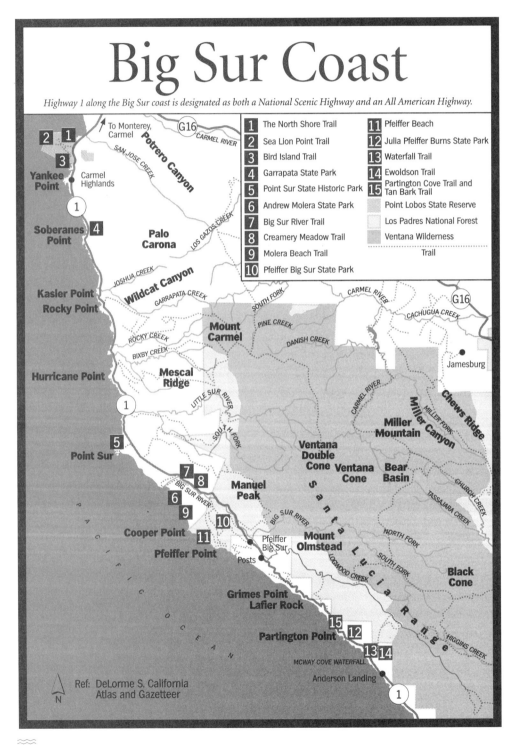

1. The North Shore Trail
2. Sea Lion Point Trail
3. Bird Island Trail
4. Garrapata State Park
5. Point Sur State Historic Park
6. Andrew Molera State Park
7. Big Sur River Trail
8. Creamery Meadow Trail
9. Molera Beach Trail
10. Pfeiffer Big Sur State Park
11. Pfeiffer Beach
12. Julia Pfeiffer Burns State Park
13. Waterfall Trail
14. Ewoldson Trail
15. Partington Cove Trail and Tan Bark Trail

Point Lobos State Reserve
Los Padres National Forest
Ventana Wilderness
Trail

Ref: DeLorme S. California Atlas and Gazetteer

mind. But, the Big Sur coast does not end at the community of Big Sur. It continues south, unofficially ending somewhere near San Simeon.

🦠 GARRAPATA STATE PARK

[Fig. 44(4)] The park possesses absolutely nothing in the way of human creature comforts, but it does offer several public access points to miles of rugged Big Sur coast and several more miles of trails that climb the steep mountains that immediately rise to the east. In Spanish, *garrapata* means "tick." And ticks abound in the area, especially during spring and early summer. But in spring, the sight of entire mountainsides carpeted with the rich yellows and reds and purples of wildflowers is worth taking a few simple precautions, such as applying repellent, to protect yourself from ticks. There's a fence that parallels much of the park along the west side of Highway 1, with several numbered gates located at the trailheads that lead to trails or stairways that offer relatively safe access from the ocean terrace down the steep cliff face to the beaches. Generally, just look for other cars parked along the highway to find the most popular access points.

The ocean here can be extremely hazardous, especially during summer. Sleeper waves are relatively common, sweeping people off beaches and rocks every year. Never turn your back on the ocean.

Directions: Take Highway 1, about 4 miles south of Carmel.

Activities: Hiking, fishing, beach exploring.

Facilities: There are a couple of chemical toilets.

Dates: Open daily.

Fees: None.

For more information: Point Lobos State Reserve, 2 miles south of Carmel, phone (831) 624-4909; or Monterey District State Parks, 2211 Garden Road, Monterey, CA 93940. Phone (831) 649-2836.

🦠 POINT SUR STATE HISTORIC PARK

[Fig. 44(5)] California's coast was a dilemma for the maritime traders who followed in the footsteps of the early European explorers. Fog, jagged offshore rocks, jutting headlands, unpredictable winds, surging tides, and storm-driven waves caused many captains to lose their ships, their cargoes, and their lives. As maritime shipping became more common along California's coast, the number of lighthouses slowly increased. The Point Sur lighthouse was first lit in the summer of 1889. The light actually sits lower than the top of the Rock, as its rock promontory is referred to, placed so that it would shine below where the fog most often settled.

For most Big Sur coast travelers, Point Sur is easily one of the most prominent landmarks they pass. The Rock juts up nearly 400 feet above the long, shoreline beach. The light was originally a first order Fresnel lens that could be seen from 23 miles out to sea. While the lens certainly aided navigation safety, it didn't insure that

Ticks and Lyme Disease

Ticks are a fact of life throughout much of the country, including most of California. While there are several species, it's only the western black-legged tick (*Ixodes pacificus*) that transmits the infectious Lyme disease. The disease was first recognized in Old Lyme, Connecticut in 1975, and in California just three years later. While the disease can be both serious and difficult to diagnose, it is also relatively easy to avoid.

Adult female ticks climb to the ends of branches and grasses and wait to attach themselves to any passing mammal, including humans. Once attached, ticks crawl to bare skin where their harpoon-like mouthparts are used to penetrate the skin. Wearing light-colored clothing makes seeing ticks easier, and a good insect repellent sprayed on clothing generally helps convince them not to stick around. Check yourself, your kids, and pets often, especially if hiking along brushy trails.

Removing ticks is relatively easy. Simply grasp the tick, preferably with tweezers or a tissue and gently pull it straight out. If all of the mouthpart comes out, wash the affected area with soap and water and apply an antiseptic. If a portion remains, drop the tick into a small container for later identification and seek medical care.

If, from 3 days to 30 days following time spent in tick county, especially if you know you've been bitten, a red, blotchy, circular rash develops anywhere on the body, possibly accompanied by flu-like symptoms, seek medical attention. Also be aware that the symptoms may appear and reappear intermittently for several weeks.

ships and rocks still wouldn't meet. The *Los Angeles* was lost in 1894, the *Majestic* in 1909, and several more vessels, including the *Howard Olson* in 1956, went down near Point Sur. Each time a ship broke apart, its cargo was scattered along the coast bringing out the locals who were quite happy to help clean up the beaches.

Perhaps the most famous shipwreck near the Rock was the crash of the USS *Macon*, a helium-filled rigid airship that went down on February 12, 1935. The 785-foot-long, lighter-than-air ship served as a flying aircraft carrier, able to launch and retrieve small, single-engine airplanes. The *Macon* crashed into the Pacific with its 83 crew members, all of whom survived but two. The small visitor center at the top of the Rock includes exhibits on the *Macon*.

Today, while the Coast Guard still maintains an automated light at Point Sur, the remainder of the Rock is part of Point Sur State Historic Park. Several buildings are part of the light station, including a barn, blacksmith shop, two-story head keeper's house, and the triplex where three assistant keepers and their families lived. There is an ongoing restoration program.

Directions: Point Sur State Historic Park is located about 19 miles south of Carmel on Highway 1. The entrance is at a farm gate adjacent to Highway 1, about 0.25 mile north of the abandoned Point Sur Naval Facility, a casualty of the Cold

War's end. There are plans to use the Naval Facility as a visitor center in the future.

Activities: Tours of the lighthouse, headkeeper's house, the small museum, and other buildings as they are restored. This is a great winter whale-watching site during winter tours.

Facilities: Visitor center and small gift shop.

Dates: Tours are held on a first-come first-served basis and take about two hours. They require participants to walk to the top of the Rock as parking is limited and private vehicles are not allowed to drive up the narrow road to the top. Docents lead tours on weekends and during midweek. Tour times and days may change, so call ahead. A warning: Occasionally there are warm, sunny, beautiful days on the "Rock." But most often it is cold and extremely windy, not to mention foggy. Wear, or at least bring, several layers of clothing, even during summer.

Fees: There is small tour fee.

Closest town: Carmel, 19 miles north.

For more information: The park is not staffed. Call the park's automated information phone at (831) 667-0528. During winter it's always a good idea to call because tours will be canceled if rain is likely. Additional information can be obtained during normal business hours by contacting the Monterey District State Park Office, 2211 Garden Road, Monterey, CA 92940. Phone (831) 649-2836.

ANDREW MOLERA STATE PARK

[Fig. 44(6)] The Esselen Indians were the first to live in this area of Big Sur, although their home was first invaded by the Spanish, then taken over by the Mexicans, who were then soon overwhelmed by the Americans. The pioneers who settled the Big Sur area during the Mexican and the early American eras were a hardy and independent bunch. Andrew Molera State Park originally was part of a nearly 9,000 acre Mexican land grant known as Rancho El Sur, much of which remains intact today.

Captain John Rogers Cooper, born in England but living in America, sailed around the Horn, landing in California where his skills as a seafaring captain

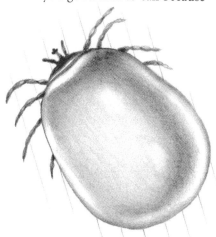

WESTERN BLACK-
LEGGED TICK
(Ixodes pacificus)
Tick hatchlings climb vegetation and latch onto a passing host. After a meal, they drop off, molt, and climb onto another host, repeating the process until they are full-grown.

provided the money to purchase property. In 1840, he traded his Salinas Valley property for Rancho El Sur, which passed to his children following his death. Over the years the property transferred down the line of heirs, finally ending in the hands of Frances Molera. The Coopers, and later through marriage, the Moleras, operated their land as a cattle and dairy ranch. Andrew Molera became well known locally for the wagonloads of Monterey Jack cheese he regularly hauled to Monterey. In 1968, Frances Molera sold what was to become Andrew Molera State Park to The Nature Conservancy with the provision that it not be developed. The park was named for her gracious and well-liked brother, Andrew.

Today, Andrew Molera State Park provides public access to hills and meadows and to the Big Sur River where it meanders through Creamery Meadow and empties into the Pacific Ocean. The park offers a number of recreation opportunities, including rental horses during summer and a hike-in campground, access to over 2 miles of beach, and many miles of trails that allow exploration of coastal chaparral, oaks, and redwoods. There are exceptional views from the park's bluff and ridge trails.

The old Molera ranch house, located a short walk from the park's entrance kiosk, has been restored and turned into a visitor center and museum. The volunteers who operate the facility can answer questions about trails and the park's history. Some of the ranch house rooms contain exhibits from the Ventana Wilderness Society, which works nearby in the park doing avian research and rehabilitation and release of California condors.

The campground is unique in state parks. There are no specific campsites; simply find a spot in the large meadow that is designated for camping. It's all first-come first-served and it's a short walk of about 0.25 mile from the parking lot to the campground. It's not unusual to see people hauling camping equipment in backpacks or in little red wagons. It's also very important to remember that some of the wiliest raccoons around thrive in the campground, sometimes shredding tents and opening ice chests to get to food. Keep all food well secured and remember that food inside a tent or in a backpack is not secure.

As soon as the trails dry from winter's rain, the horseback riding concessionaire in the park opens for business. It provides an opportunity to ride many of the trails, including out to the beach. It's a great way to introduce the younger set to trail riding.

Directions: The park is about 20 miles south of Carmel on Highway 1, and about 2 miles south of Point Sur State Historic Park.

Activities: Hiking, bird-watching, fishing, beachcombing, horseback riding, camping, bicycling.

Facilities: Visitor center and horse rentals during summer, campground.

Dates: Park is open daily. The visitor center open hours and days vary.

Fees: There are small fees for day-use vehicle entry and for the hike-in campground. The visitor center is included in the day-use fee.

Closest town: Carmel, about 20 miles north is the closest to offer full services. Limited public services are available about 6 miles south in the community of Big Sur.

For more information: Big Sur Station, 0.25 mile south of the Pfeiffer Big Sur State Park entrance. Phone (831) 667-2315.

TRAILS

The **Big Sur River Trail** [Fig. 44(7)] is easily the most traveled because it leads from the parking lot on the northwest side of the river, through the hike-in campground, and ends at the mouth of the Big Sur River. The trail passes the old Cooper cabin, which is nestled in a grove of eucalyptus trees. The trees, in turn, attract thousands of monarch butterflies during winter. Hike up a short spur trail from near the mouth of the Big Sur River to the promontory at the head of Molera Point, which is a great place to sit and contemplate life or watch for whales. During summer there's usually a seasonal bridge in place near the mouth of the river, but if not, most people simply wade across, although the water can be nearly waist deep. It's best to ask at the entrance gate about the river's level, or simply watch where some of those who visit the park on a more regular basis safely cross.

Also leaving from the parking lot, the **Creamery Meadow Trail** parallels the river on the southeast side, loops through the meadow, and after about 0.75 mile meets several other trailheads as it nears the beach. It's quite level and many people like to ride bicycles. The only problem with this trail is that the seasonal bridge that crosses the Big Sur River at the parking lot is removed in the fall and isn't reinstalled until late spring or early summer, when the river's water level drops.

While the **Molera Beach Trail** [Fig. 44(9)] is not an actual trail, the beach stretches to the south of the Big Sur River mouth more than 2 miles. While there are a couple of rocky outcroppings that block passage at high tides, during very low tides there is access to some very lonely and very beautiful stretches of beach. Just don't forget to pay attention to the tide tables or getting back will be impossible, at least until the next low tide. The bluff above the beach is difficult, if not impossible to scale in most places.

PFEIFFER BIG SUR STATE PARK

[Fig. 44(10)] If you spend much time wandering along the Big Sur River, through the redwood groves, or along the trails to the park's mountain promontories, it becomes immediately apparent why the early settlers fell in love with this land. Michael Pfeiffer and his wife Mary became the first European settlers in the area when they built their home in nearby Sycamore Canyon in 1869. To make a living, they cut redwood trees for lumber, farmed the land, and kept bees that feasted on the flower-covered hillsides, making plenty of honey. Their son John homesteaded a 160-acre parcel near the Big Sur River and moved to where the historic Homestead Cabin is located today.

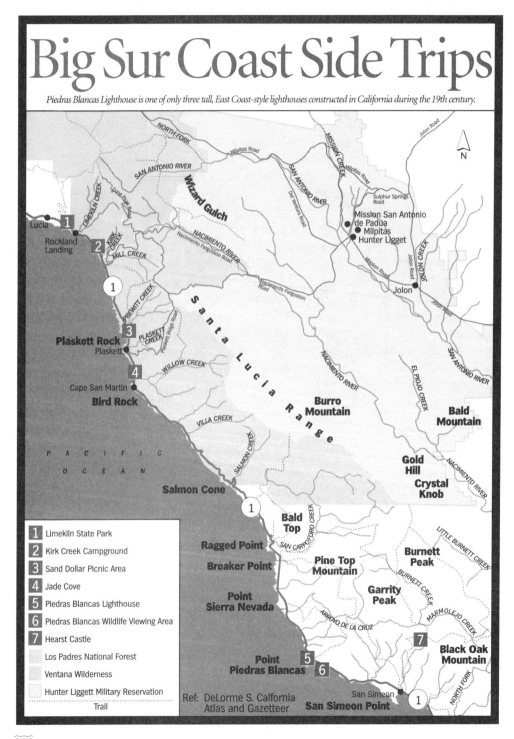

Big Sur Coast Side Trips

Piedras Blancas Lighthouse is one of only three tall, East Coast-style lighthouses constructed in California during the 19th century.

N

NORTH FORK

Milpitas Road

SAN ANTONIO RIVER

Jolon Road

MISSION CREEK

SAN ANTONIO RIVER

Wizard Gulch

Milpitas Road

Del Venturo Road

Sulphur Springs Road

Mission San Antonio de Padua

Milpitas

Hunter Ligget

Lyons Peak Road

LIMEKILN CREEK

Lucia

1

Rockland Landing

2

KIRK CREEK

MILL CREEK

NACIMIENTO RIVER

Nacimiento Fergusson Road

Nacimiento Fergusson Road

Mission Road

Jolon Road

JOLON CREEK

Jolon

Jolon Road

1

PREWITT CREEK

S a n t a   L u c i a   R a n g e

NACIMIENTO RIVER

3

PLASKETT CREEK

Plaskett Ridge Road

Plaskett Rock
Plaskett

WILLOW CREEK

EL PIOJO CREEK

SAN ANTONIO RIVER

4

Cape San Martin

Bird Rock

VILLA CREEK

Burro Mountain

Bald Mountain

P A C I F I C
O C E A N

SALMON CREEK

Gold Hill

NACIMIENTO RIVER

Crystal Knob

Salmon Cone

1

SAN CARPOFORO CREEK

Bald Top

LITTLE BURNETT CREEK

Ragged Point

Pine Top Mountain

Burnett Peak

Breaker Point

BURNETT CREEK

Garrity Peak

Point Sierra Nevada

ARROYO DE LA CRUZ

MARMOLEJO CREEK

7

Black Oak Mountain

Point Piedras Blancas

5

6

San Simeon

1

NORTH FORK

San Simeon Point

1	Limekiln State Park
2	Kirk Creek Campground
3	Sand Dollar Picnic Area
4	Jade Cove
5	Piedras Blancas Lighthouse
6	Piedras Blancas Wildlife Viewing Area
7	Hearst Castle
	Los Padres National Forest
	Ventana Wilderness
	Hunter Liggett Military Reservation
	Trail

Ref: DeLorme S. Calfornia Atlas and Gazetteer

By the turn of the century, Big Sur's redwoods and its rugged coast were drawing the more adventurous hunters and fishermen who were willing to travel the rugged coastal trail from Monterey. Seeing an opportunity for additional income, John Pfeiffer's wife Florence started Pfeiffer's Ranch Resort, built where today's Big Sur Lodge is located. During those early years, the Pfeiffers operated a small lumber mill in addition to several private guest cabins. In 1933, John Pfeiffer sold 680 acres to the California State Park System. That original acreage, plus another 300-plus acres that have been acquired over the years, is now Pfeiffer Big Sur State Park.

Even though the park lies near the southernmost limit of the coast redwoods range, and most of its old-growth trees were cut during the Pfeiffers' ownership, the groves that remain are quite impressive. The park's largest tree is located near the group picnic area. Named the "Colonial Tree," it measures 27 feet in circumference. Not far from the lodge a grove of 800- to 1,200-year-old redwoods make up the "Proboscis Grove."

Most of the redwoods grow on the flat that follows the Big Sur River as it runs the length of the park. Sycamores (*Platanus racemosa*), willows (*Salix* spp.), black cotton-woods (*Populus trichocarpa*), and alders (*Alnus* spp.) create a thick forest of riparian growth, which in turn provides food and homes for dozens of animal species. Hiking up one of the trails, the moist riparian vegetation quickly changes to species better adapted to handle the hot, dry summers on the mountainsides, especially along the south-facing slopes. In many places the chaparral plants grow so densely that going off trail is nearly impossible. Chamise (*Adenostoma fasciculatum*), toyon (*Heteromeles arbutifolia*), manzanita (*Arctostaphylos* spp.), California coffeeberry (*Rhamnus californica*), and ceanothus (*Ceanothus* spp.) are some of the most common chaparral shrubs.

Pfeiffer Big Sur State Park is easily the most popular park in the Big Sur area. Its large campground is full all summer, mostly with families and the sounds of kids having fun. The Big Sur River is the main attraction, with people swimming or wading, especially during the warmest days. There's a trail that meanders up the north side of the river, officially ending perhaps 0.25 mile upriver from the Whalen bridge. From there, most people continue, sometimes scrambling over the rocks, sometimes wading in the river or swimming across the small, deeper pools, exploring an area called the "Narrows."

Directions: The park entrance is located about 26 miles south of Carmel on the east side of Highway 1.

Activities: Camping, hiking, picnicking, softball, nature study.

Facilities: The park has two group camps, each with a 35 person capacity and 215 developed campsites, but none with RV hook-ups. Since riding the coast on bicycles is such a popular way to experience Big Sur there are 10 bicycle environmental campsites. Camping reservations are almost always required during summer and spring holiday weekends. Phone (800) 444-7275. The Big Sur Lodge offers cabins, some with kitchens. There's also a swimming pool for lodge guests. Phone (831) 667-2171 for lodge information and reservations.

Dates: The park is open daily.

Fees: Both day-use and camping fees are collected in the park

Closest town: The local Big Sur community has minimal services. The nearest major community is Carmel, 26 miles north on Highway 1.

For more information: Contact the Big Sur Station, 0.25 mile south of Pfeiffer Big Sur State Park. Phone (831) 667-2315.

▓ LOS PADRES NATIONAL FOREST

[Fig. 44] Stretching for over 200 miles, the Los Padres National Forest covers nearly 2 million acres of California's Central Coast. It's a rugged and beautiful country, much of it accessible only on foot. Within the forest lands, there is a 19.5-mile stretch of the Big Sur River and 33 miles of Sisquoc Creek that have been designated as Wild Rivers under the Wild and Scenic Rivers Act.

Hiking for any distance within either Los Padres National Forest or the contiguous Ventana Wilderness provides ample opportunities to experience the real Big Sur, the portion that motorists who focus primarily on the ocean and coastal cliffs never experience: the rugged, steep-sided mountains that seem always to climb higher and offer still more spectacular views, the cascading rivers and creeks that fight their way through narrow, rocky gorges, and unimaginable views of spring wildflowers that stretch to the distant ocean. The only things missing are the discordant sounds of modern civilization, which quickly become only a distant memory.

Many plants grow in their own little niches. Small, isolated groves of redwoods thrive in narrow, protected river canyons, while Ponderosa pine (*Pinus ponderosa*) and bristlecone fir, also known as the Santa Lucia fir (*Abies bracata*), grow on the drier slopes. Valley oaks (*Quercus lobata*) replace the shorter coast live oaks (*Quercus agrifolia*), and cottonwoods (*Populus* spp.) join willows (*Salix* spp.) in the riparian areas. Coastal wildflowers cover the open fields, with the purple hues of lupine (*Lupinus* sp.) and the golden yellow of California poppies (*Eschscholtzia californica*) being prominent.

The **Ventana Wilderness,** along with nine other designated wilderness areas, lies within the Los Padres National Forest, its 167,000 acres adding a higher level of protection and another reason to explore this part of the Santa Lucia Mountain Range.

While there are many popular trailheads popular with both day-hikers and backpackers, the **Pine Ridge Trail** entrance at the Big Sur Station, located just 0.25 mile north of Pfeiffer Big Sur State Park, is one of the most frequently used accesses. Wilderness permits and maps are available, as is parking in a lot that is patrolled. One of the real reasons this is such a popular jumping-off point is that it's about an 11 mile hike from here to the hot spring near Sykes Campground. The hot spring is about 0.25 mile downriver from the campground area, on the south side of the Big Sur River. Its waters hover around 100 degrees Fahrenheit, but the area can occasionally become a bit overused because it is so popular.

Directions: A primary trailhead is located at the far end of the Big Sur Station parking lot, 0.25 mile south of the entrance to Pfeiffer Big Sur State Park, just off Highway 1. Trail maps and information are available daily at the visitor center.

Activities: Camping, hiking.

Facilities: None inside the forest or wilderness area.

Dates: The National Forest and Wilderness are open daily.

Fees: There is a small, daily parking fee for leaving vehicles in the Big Sur Station parking lot.

Closest town: Carmel, 26 miles north.

For more information: For general information contact the U.S. Forest Service's Goleta office (phone 831-683-6711); the King City office (phone 831-385-5434); or the Big Sur Station (phone 831-667-2315).

PFEIFFER BEACH

[Fig. 44(11)] Most of Los Padres National Forest is located on the inland side of Highway 1, but there are several areas within its boundaries where access to the Pacific Ocean is possible. About 0.25 mile south of the Big Sur Station, a narrow, barely marked road turns off Highway 1 and leads through Sycamore Canyon to Pfeiffer Beach. It's easy to miss the turn-off and once on the road to the beach, meeting a motorhome creates problems on the mostly one-lane road. During summer weekends, the parking lot will generally fill and if all goes well, someone will place the "full" sign at Highway 1 as a warning not to attempt the drive.

Directions: The access road is located about 0.5 mile south of the entrance to Pfeiffer Big Sur State Park, on the ocean side off Highway 1.

Activities: Picnicking, beachcombing, fishing.

Facilities: None.

Dates: Open daily, however, on summer weekends the parking lot can fill early, so access could be limited.

Fees: There is a small day-use fee.

For more information: U.S. Forest Service Office in Goleta, phone (831) 683-6711, the King City office, phone (831) 385-5434, or the Big Sur Station, phone (831) 667-2315.

JULIA PFEIFFER BURNS STATE PARK

[Fig. 44(12)] The steep canyon walls that rise from the parking lot make this appear to be a small park, yet it covers 3,600 acres, with 1,680 of its acres offshore and underwater. Most visitors seldom get beyond the short trail that leads to an overlook above McWay Falls, which drops 80 feet, at one time directly into the ocean, but now onto an inaccessible stretch of beach. There's a small stand of redwoods up the McWay Creek, beginning at the parking lot. The few picnic tables in the area get substantial use. A short distance up a dirt road at the end of the parking lot turn-around, the McWay barn is slowly deteriorating, although work has begun on restoring it. Spring and early summer are the best times to visit. The creek is running full and the hillsides are covered with wildflowers.

The park's underwater reserve is open to very experienced divers only. Diving permits are required. The inland portion of the park extends from the rocky shore to nearly 3,000 feet in elevation in the mountains immediately to the east. McWay Creek canyon supports small groves of coast redwoods. Scattered among the redwoods, tanoak (*Lithocarpus densiflorus*), madrone (*Arbutus menziesii*), and California laurel (*Umbellularia californica*) are the dominant trees, with redwood sorrel (*Oxalis oregana*), trillium (*Trillium ovatum*), and columbine (*Aquilegia formosa*) thriving beneath their shading branches. Farther up the hillsides, the Central Coast's common chaparral species dominate. Sticky monkey-flower (*Mimulus aurantiacus*) and morning glory (*Ipomoea purpurea*) are joined by shrubs such as the ubiquitous poison oak (*Toxicodendron diversilobum*).

Christopher McWay and his son Christopher Jr. originally settled this area of the Big Sur coast in 1874, when they began their ranching operation. Over the next two decades they filed land claims for what became known as Saddle Rock Ranch. Today many of the area's landmarks still retain the McWay name.

In 1921, former New York State Congressman Lathrop Brown and his wife, Helen Hooper of Boston, following 10 years of active social, political, and business activity, began traveling extensively throughout the world. They fell in love with Big Sur, and within a few years had acquired much of the original McWay property. The house they built, although not extravagant by the standards set by William Randolph Hearst's home farther south, had a much more spectacular view. Their "Waterfall House," was perched on the cliff overlooking McWay Cove and the 80-foot-high waterfall that tumbled directly into the ocean. They also had electricity in their home long before powerlines stretched along the Big Sur coast, the power created by a small Pelton wheel generator set on nearby McWay Creek.

Their remote home allowed for few neighbors, but Mrs. Brown became especially good friends with Julia Pfeiffer Burns, the daughter of Michael Pfeiffer, head of Big Sur's best known pioneer family. The Browns did enjoy entertaining, and following the completion of Highway 1, access to the retreat became much easier. While a list of their guests isn't known, Lathrop Brown, in his college years, roomed with Franklin Delano Roosevelt at Harvard and was also best man at Roosevelt's wedding. It's likely the Brown's guests included many well-known socialites of the day.

Mrs. Brown insisted that their house be demolished when she gave Saddle Back Ranch to the California State Park System in 1962. She also required that the new state park be named after a "true pioneer" and her good friend, Julia Pfeiffer Burns, who had died 35 years earlier. Today, all that remains of the Brown's home is a stone terrace and some of the surviving exotic plants that the Brown's had imported for their gardens. During January through March the terrace is a great place to watch migrating gray whales.

Directions: Drive south on Highway 1, about 12 miles south of Big Sur. The main entrance and parking lot are on the inland side of Highway 1.

Activities: Hiking, whale-watching, camping, and picnicking.

Facilities: There are picnic tables at the parking lot and two environmental campsites on the ocean bluff.

Dates: Open daily.

Fees: There are day-use and camping fees.

Closest town: Big Sur, about 12 miles north.

For more information: Contact the Big Sur Station, phone (831) 667-2315.

TRAILS

From the parking lot that is located just off the east side of Highway 1, the **Waterfall Trail** [Fig. 44(13)] is a short walk through a tunnel that passes under Highway 1 and then continues along the bluff overlooking McWay Falls. While the waterfall that cascades over the cliff once splashed directly into swirling ocean waves, during the El Niño winter of 1983-84, a massive landslide from the steep cliffs above raised the beach several feet. The waterfall now crashes onto the beach very near the waves that wash across the shore. The trail continues on another 100 yards or so offering ever-changing views of the falls. The short trail ends at a promontory that was the site of the Brown's house.

The **Ewoldson Trail** [Fig. 44(14)] begins at the eastern end of the parking lot at McWay Canyon and meanders up the canyon and out across the mountainside. It's about 4.5 miles roundtrip and offers spectacular views back into the mountains and of the ocean.

GRAY WHALE
(Eschrichtius robustus)
Gray whales often swim only a few hundred yards offshore as they migrate along California's coast on their way to their sheltered breeding lagoons in Baja California.

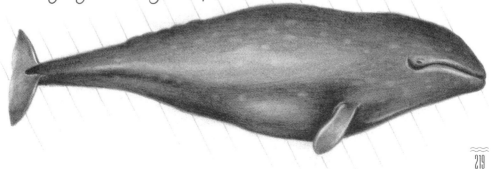

The **Partington Cove Trail** [Fig. 44(15)] is located near the north boundary of the Julia Pfeiffer Burns State Park, along Highway 1. On the Ocean side of the highway there's a wide, dirt pull-off at Partington Cove, but unfortunately, no road sign to identify the cove. Often there are other cars parked here. There are two trails, one on each side of the highway. On the ocean side, it's a quick 0.4 mile walk down to a small, rocky cove where Partington Creek runs into the ocean.

At the same Partington Cove parking area, but on the inland side of the highway, the **Tan Bark Trail** [Fig. 44(15)] picks up and meanders up the canyon and into the mountains for about 3 miles. There's an optional route back, but unfortunately it returns to Highway 1 about 1.5 miles south of Partington Cove, so it's a bit of a hike back to the parking area.

BIG SUR COAST SIDE TRIPS

Limekiln State Park, [Fig. 45(1)] in addition to having a small campground, provides one of the few easy accesses to the ocean and beach along this section of the Big Sur coast. An easy 15-minute hike up the canyon to a break in the second-growth redwoods reveals the remnants of the old kilns used for cooking limestone into lime. In the 1870s there was a landing at the beach that was used to haul barrels of lime to waiting ships and on to San Francisco. Camping reservations (phone 800-444-7275) should be made during summer. The park located is about 2 miles south of Lucia, just off Highway 1.

Kirk Creek Campground [Fig. 45(2)] (phone 831-385-5434) is part of Los Padres National Forest and is about 2 miles south of Limekiln State Park on Highway 1. The campground is filled with an introduced weed, pampas grass, along with eucalyptus trees. There's a major effort to eliminate pampas grass along the Big Sur coast because native plants can't compete with it. There's a bluff along the campground with a steep trail leading anglers, surfers, and coastal explorers to the narrow beach.

Pass through Mill Creek and continue south for 4 miles on Highway 1 to reach **Sand Dollar Picnic Area and Beach** [Fig. 45(3)]. A trail leads from the picnic area to the bluff overlooking the small bay. A steep trail leads to the beach.

Jade Cove, [Fig. 45(2)] located about 3 miles south of Plaskett Creek on Highway 1, is a place where people can pick up small pieces of jade from the beach, as long as the stones are found below the mean high tide line. The idea is to keep people from digging in the serpentine cliff. Divers offshore have found huge pieces of jade.

Piedras Blancas Lighthouse [Fig. 45(5)] is one of only three tall, East Coast-style lighthouses constructed in California during the nineteenth century. Along much of California, the coastal cliffs stood high enough above the ocean that exceptionally tall towers did not have to be constructed in order to raise navigational aids to heights visible to ships 15 or more miles offshore. Much of the East Coast lacked California's high coastal terraces, forcing the Lighthouse Service to construct exceptionally tall towers so that the signal light's height needs could be met, significantly increasing their usefulness.

A first-order Fresnel lens, its prisms significantly magnifying the light of the lamp's wicks, originally graced the top of the tower that rises 115-feet above the sea, providing a reassuring point of reference for passing ships. As with all the original lighthouses on California's coast, technology has long since replaced the Fresnel lenses. Piedras Blancas is one of many California lighthouses that had its original lens removed. The nearby town of Cambria now has the lens on exhibit.

Today, the U.S. Fish and Wildlife Service uses the light station as a research station. It is closed to the public, but it can be viewed from Highway 1.

About 1 mile south of Piedras Blancas is an identified **wildlife viewing area** [Fig. 45(6)], and what an area it is. During summer there may only be a 100 northern elephant seals (*Mirounga augustirostris*) snoozing along the beaches, but come winter, several thousand cover the surrounding beaches, occasionally moving out onto Highway 1, sleeping, fighting, mating, and giving birth to their young. Bull elephant seals can weigh 2 tons and often appear slow and lethargic. But they can move very quickly over short distances, so stay at least 50 feet away. They are also protected by law, so getting any closer could bring legal problems.

Little remains of the small town of **San Simeon**, [Fig. 45] located about 4 miles south of Piedras Blancas light station. The town was founded as a whaling station in the 1860s. It later became part of George Hearst's extensive ranch holdings that included a wharf where Hearst shipped hides and tallow from his ranching operations and quicksilver from his cinnabar mine. Today, a beautiful beach, the wharf, and picnic area await visitors. Fishing trips can also be arranged and kayaks rented.

🏵 BIG SUR COAST LODGING

For anyone not willing to camp, finding lodging along the Big Sur coast can be difficult. There are a few small motels and significantly fewer larger, more luxurious accommodations.

Post Ranch Inn. Highway 1, Big Sur. This is arguably the most exclusive place to stay on the entire Big Sur coast. It is consistently at the top of the major travel magazines' places to stay. While the Post Ranch goes back to the nineteenth century, the facilities here today are absolutely world class, and so are the views from the rooms' forested, mountainside perches. *Very expensive. Phone (831) 667-2200.*

Glen Oaks Motel. Highway 1, Big Sur. The motel is more a series of cabins that are cute, clean, and near the center of what could best be described as the community of Big Sur, since it has no really defined boundaries. During summer its rooms fill quickly, so call ahead for reservations. *Moderate. Phone (831) 667-2105.*

🏵 BIG SUR COAST DINING

Restaurants on the Big Sur Coast aren't any more plentiful than overnight accommodations. For many travelers, packing a lunch is perhaps the best way to go. It's very easy to find spectacular viewpoints and sit and enjoy a good bottle of wine, slices of cheese, and some good crackers.

Cielo. Ventana Inn, Highway 1, Big Sur. Fine dining in a warm and casual setting in one of Big Sur's finest Inns. The menu ranges from steamed artichokes and sandwiches to osetra caviar and fresh seafood. Reservations are suggested. *Moderate. Phone (831) 624-4812.*

Big Sur Lodge Restaurant. Located in Pfeiffer Big Sur State Park, Highway 1, Big Sur. It's usually easy to get a seat for the casual dining in this restaurant located on the Big Sur River inside Pfeiffer Big Sur State Park. *Inexpensive. Phone (831) 667-3100.*

Nepenthe. Highway 1, Big Sur. Its Greek name means "Isle of No Care." Such is the feeling while sipping wine or eating one of their specialty Ambrosia Burgers on the outside dining area that sits high on a forested bluff. Below and as far as the eye can see is the Pacific Ocean. Nepenthe is located about 2 miles south of Pfeiffer Big Sur State Park. *Inexpensive to moderate. Phone (831) 667-2345.*

Hearst Castle

[Fig. 45(7)] As William Randolph Hearst's publishing fortune accumulated to levels most people could only dream about, his growing collection of primarily European art and art treasures also grew. While creating a repository for his art collection was certainly one of the reasons for beginning construction of what was to become commonly known as Hearst Castle, he also wanted to upgrade "camp hill" where his father had brought his family and friends on outings. After William Randolph Hearst's mother died in 1919, he apparently began the complete transformation of "camp hill" with a simple message to his San Francisco architect: "...Miss Morgan, we are tired of camping out in the open at the ranch in San Simeon and I would like to build a little something...." What followed was 30 years of almost continuous construction and improvements to "camp hill," which Hearst renamed *La Cuesta Encantada*, The Enchanted Hill.

The castle's isolation and its grand elegance required a huge army of very skilled craftsmen and workers. Ocean steamers delivered the tons of necessary construction materials, including concrete, steel, and lumber, to the pier at San Simeon where strong backs and the underpowered trucks of the day hauled everything to the top of the 1,600-foot-high construction site, 5 miles away.

Spectacular views of the ocean and the surrounding mountains greeted Hearst's guests as they enjoyed the 137-foot-tall, 130-room Hispano-Moresque main mansion he named Casa Grande and the guests' houses, Casa del Mar, Casa del Monte, and Casa del Sol. Hearst's guests were nearly always the rich and famous, especially

Hollywood stars. They weren't restricted to the hilltop. Hearst encouraged horseback riding excursions to the distant parts of the 75,000 acres of his ranch, just a portion of the 250,000 acres that his father, George Hearst, originally owned.

Some of what Hearst used to decorate his 137-acre hilltop home—the paintings and tapestries, the furniture, the vases and lamps—are originals purchased over a lifetime of collecting from around the world. Others, such as many of the sculptures, are pieces that he recruited the best sculptors of the day to create for him.

Hearst Castle is one of those places that is impossible to adequately describe in a few paragraphs. Its elaborately tiled outdoor and indoor swimming pools, the multilevel gardens filled with thousands of flowers, the eclectic collection of art pieces such as the beautiful French Gothic mantel, Spanish choir stalls, Flemish tapestries, bronze, gold, and silver sculptures, and fantasy beds require more than words. They must be seen.

Directions: Hearst San Simeon State Historical Monument is located about 30 miles north of Morro Bay, just off Highway 1, in the small village of San Simeon.

Activities: The only way to see Hearst Castle is to join a guided tour, which includes a bus ride to the top of the hill where the home is located.

Facilities: The tour staging area has food service, a large gift shop, a theater, and a visitor center. The visitor center provides a glimpse into the history of Hearst Castle and the man who built it. It also provides a close-up look at many of the artifacts, the research that went into developing the exhibits, and some of the work required to restore many of Hearst's treasures.

Dates: The castle is open daily, except Thanksgiving, Christmas, and New Year's Day.

Fees: There is a moderate fee for each of the four tours.

Closest town: Cambria, 8 miles south.

For more information: Reservations are almost always required. For tour reservations, phone (800) 444-4445.

▦ HEARST CASTLE AREA LODGING

There are numerous choices for lodging near the town of San Simeon and nearby Hearst Castle. Most are adjacent to Highway 1, which is very near the coastline here.

California Seacoast Lodge. 9215 Hearst Drive, San Simeon. The lodge's accommodations are a combination of French elegance and English country, with some rooms having the added bonus of fireplaces. *Moderate to expensive. Phone (805) 927-3878.*

El Rey Garden Inn. Highway 1, PO Box 200, San Simeon. It is near the beach and Hearst Castle, and many of the rooms have ocean views. *Moderate to Expensive. Phone (805) 927-3998.*

Quality Inn. 9280 Castillo Drive, San Simeon. Comfortable and not far from either the beach or Hearst Castle. *Moderate. Phone (805) 927-8659.*

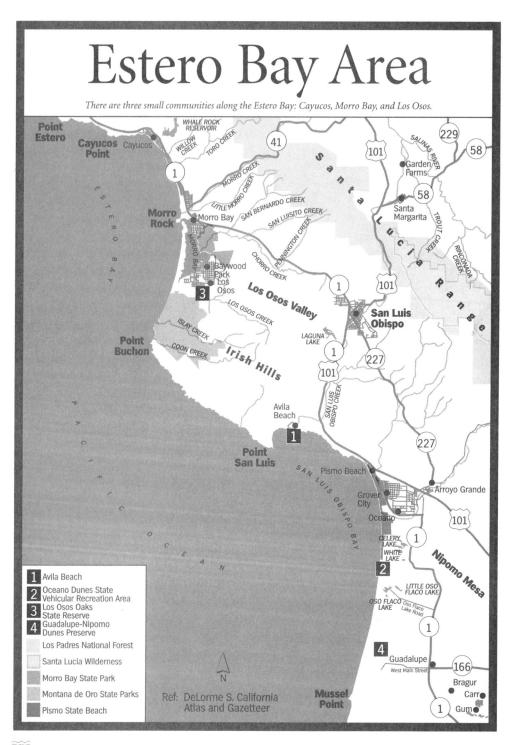

Estero Bay Area

There are three small communities along the Estero Bay: Cayucos, Morro Bay, and Los Osos.

Legend:

1. Avila Beach
2. Oceano Dunes State Vehicular Recreation Area
3. Los Osos Oaks State Reserve
4. Guadalupe-Nipomo Dunes Preserve

- Los Padres National Forest
- Santa Lucia Wilderness
- Morro Bay State Park
- Montana de Oro State Parks
- Pismo State Beach

Ref: DeLorme S. California Atlas and Gazetteer

Blue Whale Inn Bed & Breakfast. 6736 Moonstone Beach Drive, Cambria. In addition to the normal B&B fare of a full breakfast, its six mini-suites have fireplaces, canopy beds, and ocean views. *Expensive. Phone (805) 927-4647.*

Olallieberry Inn. 2476 Main Street, Cambria. Historic nineteenth century Greek Revival home restored as a B&B. *Expensive. Phone (805) 927-3222.*

For more information: The Cambria Chamber of Commerce, phone (805) 927-3624, or the San Luis Obispo Countywide Lodging Information Line, phone (800) 634-1414.

HEARST CASTLE AREA DINING

Most of the restaurants near Hearst Castle are either part of the larger hotels in the area or are found in nearby Cambria. Cambria's main street parallels Highway 1 and is filled with unique shops and small restaurants.

The Brambles Dinner House. 4005 Burton Drive, Cambria, 2 blocks south of Main Street. An English cottage that serves steak, chicken, seafood, and pasta. *Inexpensive. Phone (805) 9274716.*

Mustache Pete's Italian Eatery. 4090 Burton Drive, Cambria, south of Main Street. Its name describes its menu. *Inexpensive. Phone (805) 927-8589.*

The Sow's Ear Café. 2248 Main Street, Cambria. Diverse menu featuring chicken, beef, and seafood, along with its own homemade breads. *Inexpensive. Phone (805) 927-4865.*

Estero Bay

[Fig. 46] Estero Bay is one of those indentations in the California coast that offers little or no protection from ocean storms, but still it is called a bay. There are three small communities along the Estero Bay: Cayucos, Morro Bay, and Los Osos. Cayucos lies at the northern end of the bay, adjacent to Highway 1. Turn off Highway 1, which actually runs east and west here, and head south to the **Cayucos Pier,** for what is generally very good ocean fishing. Like anywhere, the fish bite when they're ready to bite, but here, there's a better-than-even chance of hooking something besides kelp. It also helps to check one of the nearby bait shops or ask another fisherman on the pier about what's being caught and what everyone is using for bait.

In close, near the breaking surf, anglers regularly catch barred surfperch (*Amphistichus argenteus*). Out a bit farther, brocaccio (*Sebastes pancispinis*) and walleye surfperch (*Hyperprosopon argenteum*) are commonly landed, and the deeper water at the end of the pier produces catches of small (8-inch) shiner perch (*Cymatogaster aggregata*), which are then used as bait for much larger and tastier Pacific halibut (*Hippoglossus stenolepis*).

Morro Stand State Beach (phone 805-772-7434) is not far off the Highway 1, and is also in the town of Cayucos. There's a 3-mile stretch of sandy beach that is popular for fishing, beachcombing, and picnicking.

Directions: From Morro Bay, drive 6 miles north on Highway 1 to Cayucos and take either Ocean Boulevard or Cayucos Drive and continue south to the pier.

Activities: Fishing, beachcombing.

Facilities: The surrounding town of Cayucos offers complete services.

Dates: Open daily.

Fees: None for use of the pier.

For more information: Cayucos Chamber of Commerce, 241 South Ocean Avenue, Cayucos, CA, 93430. Phone (800) 563-1878 or (805) 995-1200.

MORRO BAY STATE PARK

[Fig. 46] Besides being the largest town on Estero Bay, Morro Bay (the water portion) has the distinction of being a bay that lies within a bay. Morro Bay lies within Estero Bay and is nearly landlocked by a long sandspit that ends near Morro Rock. Morro Rock, the area's most prominent landmark, is one of several ancient, volcanic hills that rise in a southeastward line beginning inland and extending into the ocean. These andesitic plugs, of which Morro Rock is the most spectacular, are composed of primarily dacite porphyry with crystallized quartz, black hexagonal plates of biotite, and white orthoclase.

Even on clear days, a shroud of fog can cling to the top of Morro Rock. Since its discovery in 1542 by Juan Cabrillo, the 23-million-year-old Morro Rock has been a maritime milepost. Cabrillo named the 580-foot-tall andesite outcropping "Morro" because he thought it resembled a Moorish turban. Today, Morro Rock is a protected State Historic Landmark, but such reverence for this special geologic landmark has not always been popular. Beginning in about 1880, tons of rock were blasted away from Morro Rock and transported by boat to nearby Avila Bay for construction of its breakwater. The quarry operation continued until 1963, when conservationists, concerned for Morro Rock's protection, finally helped get the operation shut down.

Morro Rock is off limits to people, partly as a result of too many overly adventurous folks getting in trouble while climbing on its steep ledges, but primarily because it serves as a nesting site for a pair of peregrine falcons. While sighting the sleek hunters is always possible, it is generally much easier to see some of the other nesting birds around Morro Bay.

But it takes a walk back about 140 million years in time to know how Morro Rock was created and to understand why such a large variety of minerals is common in the area, including the iron-stained dunes, volcanic rhyolite tuff, and the sedimentary chert. From 100 to 140 million years ago, the area now occupied by Morro Bay was a shallow depression that subsequently filled with seawater, which was followed by rocks, sand, and other detritus. With the nearly constant moving of California's tectonic plates, the pressures created deep beneath the surface formed cracks in the overlying rock that lay beneath the sea. Ultimately, molten rock was forced upward as the faulting and folding continued and the sea retreated. Then, 20 million years ago (middle Miocene) the subsurface pressures became so great that volcanoes erupted, again pushing molten rock to the surface.

From 1 million to 4 million years ago, strong compressive forces folded and elevated all of the older rock formations during what became the Central Coast's most intensive mountain-building period. The seas that had flooded the area once again withdrew, and many of the southern coastal ranges were formed.

As much as the changing geology, the fluctuating sea level has had significant impacts on the Morro Bay region. Beginning 20,000 years ago, melting ice caps and glaciers began to cause the ocean to rise. At that time the beach was about 4 miles farther offshore. Twelve thousand years later, about 8,000 years ago, the ocean water was only about 5 feet to 10 feet shallower than it is in today's estuary.

Morro Bay's estuary covers 2,300 acres of mud flats, tidal wetlands, and open water, all of which serves as a repository and mixing bowl for the fresh water that flows from the nearly 50,000 acres of surrounding watershed. It also holds one of the least human-disturbed saltwater marshes in California, providing a rich mix of habitats that support one of the most diverse collections of bird species in the country. Because of its key position within the Pacific Flyway and its habitat offerings, some 250 species of birds have been observed here. They include birds that make the area their permanent home and many more that migrate through, often including threatened and endangered bird species such as the peregrine falcon (*Falco peregrinus*), black brant (*Branta bernicla*), brown pelican (*Pelecanus occidentalis*), and snowy plover (*Charadruis alexandrinus*).

Morro Bay State Park, in addition to having a very popular campground and one of the very few golf courses owned by California State Parks, is home to a wonderful museum that sits at the edge of an uplifted segment of sedimentary chert overlooking the bay's shoreline. It also offers a view across the tidal flats that reach the harbor, its boats, and beyond to Morro Rock. Inside the museum is a wonderful collection of both natural and cultural history exhibits that provide a thorough introduction to the area. There are numerous birds and fish (all stuffed), along with a small gift shop featuring primarily nature-related publications. Docents at the museum also lead tours and offer other interpretive programs.

Just a short walk from Morro Bay State Park's natural history museum is a grove of eucalyptus trees that has been adopted by great blue herons as their primary nesting site in the area. Some of the nests are 4 feet across, added to each year by the returning herons. While great blue herons are year-round residents at Morro Bay, the best time to see them in their treetop nests is beginning in February when their courtship rituals begin, through spring and summer when the surviving broods finally leave their nests.

Directions: The town of Morro Bay is adjacent to Highway 1, also known as the

Cabrillo Highway along this stretch, and is located about 13 miles north of San Luis Obispo. Morro Bay State Park and its adjoining estuary can most easily be reached by following the signs and driving just past Morro Bay on Highway 1 and turning south onto South Bay Boulevard. Then go right onto State Park Road into the park.

Activities: Bird-watching, golf, boating, fishing, camping, picnicking.

Facilities: Museum, golf course, campground, picnic area, marina, and golf course.

Dates: The park is open daily; the museum is open daily, except Thanksgiving, Christmas, and New Year's Day.

Fees: There's a small fee at the museum and moderate camping fees. Reservations are generally required during summer. Phone (800) 444-7275. There is no fee for day use in the remainder of the park.

Closest town: Morro Bay.

For more information: Contact Morro Bay State Park, State Park Road, Morro Bay, CA 93442. Phone (805) 772-2560 or (805) 772-2694.

MORRO BAY LODGING

The Inn at Morro Bay. 60 State Park Road, Morro Bay. It features views of the bay, feather beds, and nearby golf. *Expensive. Phone (800) 321-9566.*

Embarcadero Inn. 456 Embarcadero, Morro Bay. The inn offers harbor views from most of its rooms' balconies. *Expensive. Phone (805) 772-2700.*

Best Western Tradewinds Motel. 225 Beach Street, Morro Bay. Located about 1 block from downtown Morro Bay and the same distance from the waterfront. *Moderate to Expensive. Phone (805) 772-7376.*

MONTAÑA DE ORO STATE PARK

[Fig. 46] It takes a bit of out-of-the-way driving to get here, but the rewards are worth the effort. It's also quickly evident that those people who would like to eliminate the tall and aromatic eucalyptus trees that some enterprising souls introduced into California from Australia in the nineteenth century have far to go. The narrow road passes through several groves of the trees, which emit a toxin from their leaves that pretty much eliminates most understory plants that might provide any competition. Unfortunately, with all the native plants go all the native animals that depend on them for food and shelter. What results is a relatively open forest filled with a single plant species.

As you emerge from the eucalyptus groves, the park opens onto a marine terrace rich with native coastal scrub. During spring, wildflowers, such as sticky monkey flower and California poppies, splash the hillsides with gold, helping the park live up to its translated name: Mountain of Gold. To the west, often not more than a few hundred yards from the entry road, waves crash against the rocky cliffs and wash across the intermittent sandy beaches tucked between the extended fingers of land.

While the road that leads into the park winds about 7 miles and finally dead-ends near the south boundary, there's an intricate system of trails, many of which are open to equestrians, that pass along the cliff tops, across the coastal dunes, and to the tops of the nearby peaks, such as 1,649-foot-high Alan Peak.

Like much of coastal California, at least the southern half of the state, Spain's intrusion into this new land marked the end for the Native Americans. In 1769, Don Gaspar de Portolá's expedition to establish Spain's missions and presidios marked the end for the Chumash. It is estimated that as many as 30,000 Chumash lived in small villages spread from Morro Bay to as far south as Malibu. They had the ability to survive nature for thousands of years, but European diseases decimated their numbers.

By the late nineteenth century, dairy operations were the economic mainstay for the Americans who now controlled the land. One of those owners, Alexander Hazard, in a failed experiment to meet the lumber needs of the nearby growing communities, planted eucalyptus trees. His dairy operations proved much more successful. Most of the early dairy buildings were destroyed in 1947, when a grass fire swept up the coast from Diablo Canyon.

Exploring the park offers an opportunity to see firsthand the power of nature. Following millions of years of uplifting, tilting, and periodic seawater inundation, much of the park's geology is quite visible. The popular beach at Spooner's Cove is surrounded by rocky cliffs that show the power and stresses created by two great tectonic plates moving against one another. Tremendous pressures raised the area's predominant rock, Monterey shale, from its more humble beginnings as mudstone from the ancient sea floor to the surface. The mudstone, a mixture of mud and sand, combined with the leftovers of dead ocean organisms, solidified into thick layers of diatomite, clay porcellanite, dolomite, and chert. The cliffs both north and south of Spooner's Cover offer excellent examples of Monterey shale. The evidence of the receding ocean and the uplifted landmass can be seen along the trail to the top of Valencia Peak (1,347 feet). From points along the trail, the marine terraces to the south that once served as ancient beaches also become visible.

The park also includes **Morro Dunes Natural Preserve**, the prominent sandspit that rises as much as 85 feet and extends from the south end of the Morro Bay tidal flats, northward toward Morro Rock and separates the bay from the ocean.

When the park's 8,000 acres and its 7 miles of shore became a state park in 1965, the name that its last private owner gave to it, stayed, Montaña de Oro. One of the few remaining structures, the Spooner Ranch house (another early owner), is now a visitor center that's operated primarily by volunteers. It's located about 4 miles into the park.

Directions: Montaña de Oro State Park is located just southwest of the town of Los Osos on Pecho Valley Road, which dead-ends in the park.

Activities: Hiking, horseback riding, mountain biking, fishing, beachcombing, camping, picnicking.

Facilities: There are 50 primitive campsites plus the equestrian camp area, which has two group sites and three individual sites. There is also a small visitor center.

Dates: The park is open daily, the visitor center periodically.

Fees: There is a small camping fee.

Closest town: Los Osos, 7 miles.

For more information: Montana de Oro State Park, Pecho Valley Road, Los Osos, CA 93402, or California Department of Parks and Recreation, San Luis Obispo Coast District Office, 3220 South Higuera Street, Suite 311, San Luis Obispo, CA 93401. Phone (805) 549-3312, (805) 528-0513 or (805) 772-7434.

San Luis Obispo Bay

AVILA BEACH

[Fig. 46(1)] Choosing to depart the main highways and cities for a little side road exploration can generally reveal wonderful surprises. Such is the case with Avila Beach, tucked into the hills along the coast at the end of Avila Beach Drive, not far from Highway 1. This small coastal town, situated at the tip of the upside down fishhook-shaped San Luis Obispo Bay, provides a sheltered cove for a popular pier and swimming beach. The wide sand beach is a very busy place, as is Port San Luis, which is located at the end of the road. The pier, in addition to having a restaurant, offers an opportunity to board a sport fishing boat and see whales from December through March, or during summer, lets fishing enthusiasts regularly catch rock cod, halibut, and albacore. For those not willing to fish for their fish, either live or freshly caught fish can be purchased at the pier. There are a few restaurants, a bait shop, and a boat launch.

For more information: There is no central contact point for Avila Beach. Contact the San Luis Obispo Countywide Lodging Information Line, phone (800) 634-1414.

PISMO STATE BEACH

[Fig. 46] Besides the hustle and bustle of people moving in and out of restaurants, surf shops, motels, and tourist gift shops in the city of Pismo Beach, the adjacent Pismo State Beach offers a unique experience for California's millions of beach-goers. The long stretch of beach has sand firm enough to support motor vehicles, so thousands of people each year drive their street-legal cars on the beach. On nearly any given day there are hundreds of passenger cars, motorcycles, truck-towed mobile homes, and motorhomes driving up and down the beach, all 8 miles of it. The experience can be a little disconcerting at first, especially when driving in something other than a four-wheel drive vehicle past the park entrance kiosk and then down the ramp and onto the beach sand.

It's always wise to drive on the wet sand just above the breaking waves, especially during high tide when vehicles are forced higher up the beach toward what is generally the looser sand. Get too high up the beach and two-wheel drive vehicles are more likely to get stuck. The speed limit is 15 m.p.h. along the beach, and there's at least one place where a small stream runs down the beach and empties into the ocean. But the stream, Arroyo Grande Creek, at least during summer when it's not particularly high, is easy enough to cross. Winter storms can create a much different scenario.

The beach provides great surf fishing, always a popular sport, and good sand castle-building opportunities for kids, but digging for the famed Pismo clam has been a favorite pastime for generations of beachgoers. The only problem is that today, the clam population is nowhere near what it was in past decades. Check the current fishing regulations for the open season and license needs. There's a minimum size limit of 4.5 inches, and it can often be challenging to find clams large enough to keep. For those not interested in digging in the sand searching for dinner, it's only a short drive off the beach and back into town where a plethora of restaurants awaits.

Directions: Pismo State Beach is located on Highway 1 and US 101, 12 miles south of San Luis Obispo and about 2 miles south of the town of Pismo Beach.

Activities: Fishing, surfing, swimming, beachcombing, camping, digging for clams.

Facilities: Besides the open camping on Pismo State Beach, two other nearby state park campgrounds away from the beach offer less primitive campsites. **Oceano Campground**, located at 555 Pier Avenue in nearby Oceano offers 80 campsites, while **North Beach Campground** (a primary monarch butterfly overwintering site), just off Highway 1 in Pismo Beach has just over 100 campsites. Reservations are generally required at Oceano and North Beach campgrounds during summer. Phone (800) 444-7275 for reservations.

Fees: There is a small day-use and a moderate camping fee per vehicle.

Closest town: Pismo Beach and Grover City.

For more information: Pismo State Beach, Ranger Staton, 555 Pier Avenue, Oceano, CA 93445. Phone (805) 489-1869 or (805) 489-2684.

OCEANO DUNES STATE VEHICULAR RECREATION AREA

[Fig. 46(2)] Oceano Dunes sits near the center of a stretch of dunes that begins near the town of Pismo Beach, includes Pismo State Beach, and continues south to near Point Sal. The sand, originally washed down from the mountains by the nearby Santa Maria River and other smaller creeks and waterways, is pushed ashore by wave action, then blown inland into the high dunes by the often-strong prevailing winds. But these particular dunes are a wide-open playground for off-road enthusiasts. Here, dune buggies, quadrunners, and a few vehicles that don't look like anything that would ever be seen on a city street, blast their way over the high dunes and across the open beach sands.

This is also the place to come for cheap beach camping. Summer weekends can bring several hundred tents, motorhomes, and trailers set up just above the expected high tide line. The owners of the trailers and motorhomes set up cardboard and push sand up to the bottoms of their vehicles to keep the wind from blowing through. Barbecues and beach fires are everywhere. The only problem is expecting that the quiet slap of waves and the occasional squawks of birds will be the only nighttime sounds. The sound of revving engines is often more noticeable.

Like dunes along several other areas of California's coast, the dunes here also serve as nesting areas for the threatened snowy plover and the endangered California least tern. Surprisingly, their nesting success has been extremely good in the off-highway vehicle area. During the March-through-September breeding and fledging season, their nesting sites are fenced for protection from beach goers and sand-thrashing off-highway vehicle tires.

Other areas of Oceano Dunes are set aside as preserves where native dune plants such as arroyo willow (*Salix lasiolepis*) and California sagebrush (*Artemisia californica*) thrive in the seemingly hostile dune environment. A couple of rare dune plants, surf thistle (*Cirsium rhothophilum*) and giant coreopsis (*Coreopsis gigantea*) also grow in portions of the dunes.

Directions: Oceano Dunes State Vehicular Recreation Area can be reached via either Grand Avenue or Pier Avenue in the City of Grover Beach.

Activities: Off-highway vehicle use, fishing, camping, picnicking, swimming.

Facilities: Seasonal quadrunner rental in the park. In town, full facilities.

Dates: Open daily.

Fees: Small vehicle fee for day-use and camping.

Closest town: Pismo Beach and City of Grover Beach

For more information: Oceano Dunes SVRA, 576 Camino Mercado, Arroyo Grande, CA 93420. For recorded information, phone (805) 473-7223 or (805) 489-2684.

Los Osos Oaks State Reserve

[Fig. 46(3)] If a single tree had to be identified with California's central coast, the coast live oak (*Quercus agrifolia*) would be at the top of any list. It lacks the grand size and graceful symmetry of some of its cousins, such as the valley oak (*Quercus lobata*). Instead, as if serving as inspiration to the many artists and other creative minds who have settled California's coast, the multi-trunked coast live oaks appear to grow in conformance to the whims and wishes of the coastal winds and the contours of the rolling hills they inhabit. Let the fog blow through this oak woodland, and walking the trails of this small but important reserve can become a surreal adventure. But even on clear days, it's an extraordinary experience.

There is a figure-eight-shaped trail in the preserve that begins at the small parking lot. From the grasslands near the parking lot, the trail crosses a bridge over a small stream and leads directly into a grove of coast live oaks. Going left quickly leads to the riparian habitat along perennial Los Osos Creek. Since this 85-acre site sees few people and offers several different biotic communities, wildlife is almost always present. Whether or not it will allow itself to be seen is another matter. Fortunately, western rattlesnakes (*Crotalus viridis*) tend to shy away from people, and southern alligator lizards (*Gerrhonotus multicarinatus*) also prefer to escape from humans. The seemingly ever-present western fence lizard (*Sceloporous occidentalis*), with its blue sides and belly, will likely be the most visible reptile.

The most obvious residents here are birds. Nuttall's woodpeckers (*Picoides nuttallii*) and California thrashers (*Toxostoma redivivum*) are generally around, with many smaller birds keeping to the underbrush. The occasional tall pile of sticks is home to the 12- to 18-inch-long dusky-footed woodrat (*Neotoma fuscipes*). Gray foxes (*Urocyon cinereoargenteus*) and bobcats (*Felis rufus*) occasionally slip-up and get caught in plain view near the trail.

The trail passes through 30-foot-tall oaks, many contorted by the salt air and winds that kill new buds, creating the limbs' stubby, twisted shapes. Continue up a small hill and the trees are still as old as those first encountered, but now they are only from 6 feet to perhaps 10 feet tall. These dwarf trees simply occupy an environment that offers poorer soil with fewer nutrients, less water, and more wind, all of which combine to significantly stunt their growth.

Continue beyond the oaks whose acidic leaves create soil conditions that most understory plants cannot endure and the woodland is replaced by the drier chaparral. Here is where black sage (*Salvia mellifera*) and bush monkey flower (*Mimulus* sp.) are joined by splashes of spring wildflowers such as mock heather and western peony (*Paeonia brownii*).

Directions: Take Los Osos Valley Road for about 1 mile southwest of the town of Los Osos, south of Morro Bay.

Activities: Hiking, bird-watching.

Facilities: None.

Dates: Open daily.

Fees: None.

Closest town: Los Osos.

For more information: California Department of Parks and Recreation, San Luis Obispo Coast District Office, 3220 South Higuera Street, Suite 311, San Luis Obispo, CA 93401. Phone (805) 528-0513.

BOBCAT
(*Felis rufus*)

Oso Flaco Lake

[Fig. 46] Don Gaspar de Portola was traveling south with his Spanish land expedition in 1769 when his soldiers killed what he described as *un oso flaco* or a lean bear. Why they referred to a 10-foot-tall, 375-pound grizzly bear as lean is somewhat curious. Today, California's grizzlies have been extinct since 1922, and Oso Flaco Lake is home to herons, rails, grebes, and a wide range of other birds, especially during winter migrations.

From the entrance parking lot, it's about a five-minute walk to the lake where a boardwalk leads out across the shallow waters. The boardwalk is an excellent place for parents to take their kids fishing. Small bass and other fish can be caught. But it can be just as much fun to watch the fog drift in over the tules and the flat, reflective lake waters.

Oso Flaco Lake is near the beach, and sand from the constantly moving dunes has reached right to the edge of the lake. Work has been done to try and keep them from moving into the lake, and some of it has succeeded. What helps keep everything intact is the fact that only foot traffic is allowed in the park.

Directions: From Highway 1, about 3 miles north of Guadalupe, drive 3 miles west on Oso Flaco Road. It dead-ends at the park entrance.

Activities: Hiking, fishing.

Facilities: None.

Dates: Open daily for day use only.

Fees: There is a small fee for each vehicle to enter and park. Walk-ins are free.

Closest town: Arroyo Grande, about 10 miles.

For more information: There is no office in the park, so contact Oceano Dunes SVRA, 576 Camino Mercado, Arroyo Grande, CA 93420. For recorded information, phone (805) 473-7223 or (805) 489-2684.

Guadalupe-Nipomo Dunes Preserve

[Fig. 46(4)] There's an 18-mile stretch of coastal dunes that is a fascinating home to both fact and fiction. The facts include that the middens filled with shells indicate that Chumash Indians used the dunes for perhaps 8,000 years prior to the arrival of Juan Cabrillo in 1542 and Gaspar de Portolá's expedition in 1769. It's also a fact that famed director Cecil B. DeMille created a huge set here for his 1923 silent film, *The Ten Commandments*. It's fiction that the set still exists buried beneath the sand, although some remnants of the bulldozed structure remain visible.

It's also true that during World War II this portion of California's coast, like many others, was in need of constant observation to be sure that a Japanese invasion was not imminent. But not all was as it appeared. The bunkers sported long poles designed to imitate the cannons that didn't exist.

This stretch of sand has the highest beach dunes in the western United States. Wind began forming the dunes here 18,000 years ago, resulting in huge accumulations of sand such as found at Mussel Rock Dune, which rises 500 feet above the nearby ocean. The oldest dunes are actually farther inland, atop the Nipomo and Orcutt mesas east of the preserve. They have been stabilized by vegetation, leaving only the newer beach dunes created since the end of the Pleistocene Epoch to blow and move with the ocean winds.

Few plants can survive the sharp, cutting edges of blowing grains of sand and the overall hostile growing environment that sand provides. With the reduced number of dunes along California's coast, many of these plants have also become rare or endangered. La Graciosa thistle (*Cirsium longcholepis*), beach spectacle pod (*Dithyrea maritima*), crisp dune mint (*Mondardella crispa*), and surf thistle (*Cirsium rhothophilum*) have managed to develop the ability to slow the blowing sand enough to create stable deposits that in turn allow other plants to become established. Within the bare dunes and the more stable coastal dune scrub more than 200 species of birds live, either as residents or migrants. Brown pelicans (*Pelecanus occidentalis*), least terns (*Sterna antillarum*), and snowy plovers (*Charadrius alexandrinus*) are relatively easy to see, even considering their status as threatened species.

Directions: There are two entrances to Guadalupe-Nipomo Dunes Preserve. From Highway 1 drive to Oso Flaco Road about 4 miles north of the town of Guadalupe. Turn west and follow the Oso Flaco Road to the park entrance and the parking area. It's a short walk to the lake and to the dunes just beyond. The second entrance allows visitors to drive through the dunes and park at the beach. From Highway 1 turn west onto West Main Street (Highway 166) just south of the town of Guadalupe and drive about 3 miles down a road that passes through farm fields to the entrance. It's another 2 miles to the beach parking lot.

Activities: Hiking, fishing, beachcombing.

Facilities: None.

Dates: Open daily.

Fees: The first access (Oso Flaco Lake) is through state park property, so there is a small day-use fee. The second entrance is through The Nature Conservancy gate. A small donation is requested to enter.

Closest town: Guadalupe, 5 miles or Arroyo Grande, about 18 miles.

For more information: The Nature Conservancy, Public Use Manager, Guadalupe-Nipomo Dunes Preserve, PO Box 1004, San Luis Obispo, CA 93406. Phone (805) 544-1767.

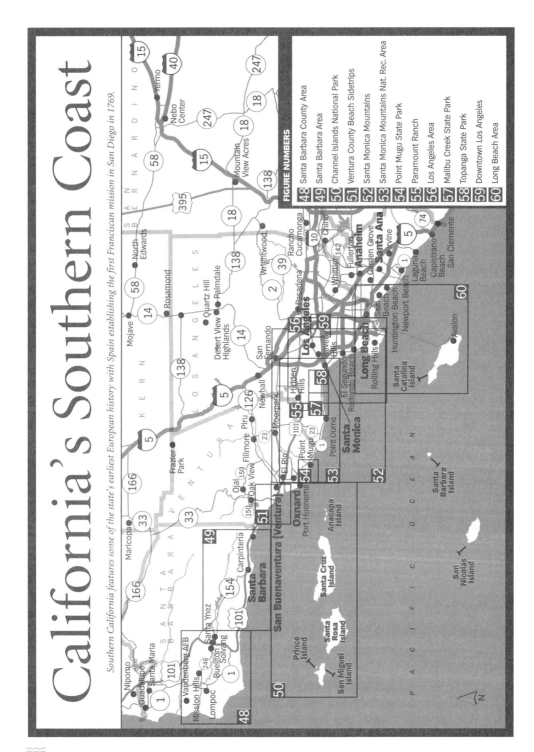

California's Southern Coast

Southern California features some of the state's earliest European history with Spain establishing the first Franciscan mission in San Diego in 1769.

FIGURE NUMBERS

48	Santa Barbara County Area
49	Santa Barbara Area
50	Channel Islands National Park
51	Ventura County Beach Sidetrips
52	Santa Monica Mountains
53	Santa Monica Mountains Nat. Rec. Area
54	Point Mugu State Park
55	Paramount Ranch
56	Los Angeles Area
57	Malibu Creek State Park
58	Topanga State Park
59	Downtown Los Angeles
60	Long Beach Area

California's Southern Coast

Trace California's coastline from north to south, and there is a very obvious eastward shift in its orientation that begins at Point Conception, near the Santa Barbara County line. This shift in coastal orientation has many consequences, at least regarding weather. With a few exceptions, storms are less violent and the beaches tend to retain more of their sand than beaches farther north. The climate is generally warmer as high-pressure ridges hold back all but the strongest cold, wet storms that regularly swirl down from the Arctic and crash into Washington, Oregon, and Northern California.

The idyllic combination of warm sun, white sand beaches, and the blue Pacific Ocean is the most prevalent image that comes to mind when most people are asked to describe California. From young, live-on-the-fly surfers, to established, well-to-do movie stars, California's southern beaches offer excitement, relaxation, and, more

[*Above:* Riparian beauty along Malibu Creek in Malibu Creek State Park]

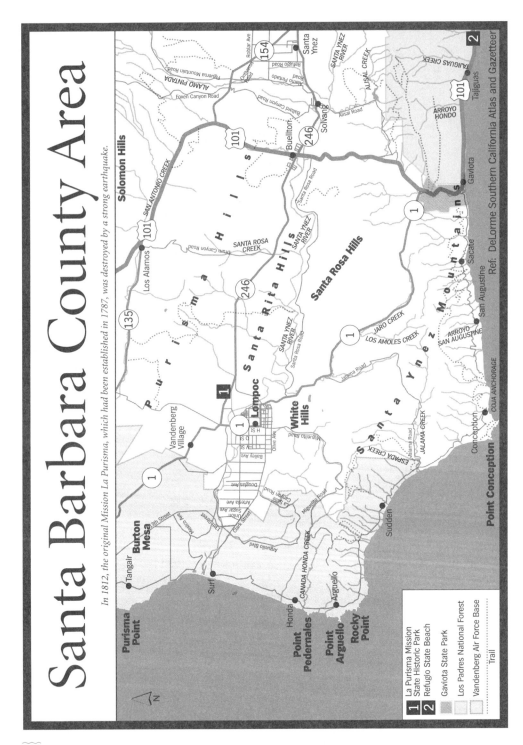

Santa Barbara County Area

In 1812, the original Mission La Purisma, which had been established in 1787, was destroyed by a strong earthquake.

Ref: DeLorme Southern California Atlas and Gazetteer

	La Purisma Mission State Historic Park
1	
2	Refugio State Beach
	Gaviota State Park
	Los Padres National Forest
	Vandenberg Air Force Base
	Trail

than anything, a retreat from often-hectic life in a very fast-paced world.

The Hollywood film industry has done more than any direct advertising campaign to promote the Southern California image. Frolicking beach movies of the 1950s and '60s, such as *Beach Blanket Bingo* and continuing with television shows like *Bay Watch*, have encouraged the pursuit, or at least imitation, of the idealistic Southern California lifestyle throughout the country and around much of the world.

Beyond the surfboards, sunscreens, and microbathing suits, there is a world of nature that still exists and flourishes along the beaches and in the mountains that rise, in some areas, straight up from the waves pounding the shoreline. In many areas, coyotes, bobcats, and deer live only a few hundred feet away from shopping centers and crowded freeways. Miles of hiking, biking, and equestrian trails draw millions of recreationists each year to these wildlife islands.

Southern California also saw some of the state's earliest history, with Spain establishing the first Franciscan mission in San Diego in 1769, several years before the original 13 states had formed their union on the opposite side of the continent. From the earliest years, and especially from the nineteenth century onward, land speculation, job opportunities, and mild weather have drawn millions of people to Southern California. This constant influx of new arrivals has created vibrant cities, incredible wealth, and a unique cultural blend that continues to lead the nation in popular trends. The growth and wealth has also resulted in the creation of some of the world's finest museums, restaurants, hotels, and other indicators of sophistication and refinement.

Santa Barbara County

▓ LA PURISIMA MISSION STATE HISTORIC PARK

[Fig. 48(1)] Unbeknownst to the Spanish missionaries, they chose some of California's most geologically active real estate on which to build their adobe missions. As a result, earthquakes took their toll on many of the early missions, including *Misión la Purísima Concepción de María Santísima*. In 1812, the original mission, which had been established in 1787, was destroyed by a strong quake. The mission's leaders decided to rebuild, but they moved the mission from its original location near today's town of Lompoc to its present location in *La Cañada de los Berros*, the "Canyon of the Watercress."

Following the U.S. takeover of California in 1846, many of the missions were abandoned and began falling into disrepair. La Purisima was no different. By the early 1900s little remained except a few adobe walls and foundations. During the 1930s, under President Roosevelt's WPA and CCC programs, restoration work began on the mission. The result is the most completely and authentically restored mission in California.

California's Coastal Crops

The mild weather and moderate rainfall along California's central and southern coasts provides the ideal climatic conditions for growing several specialty crops. Originally introduced from New Zealand, the fuzzy, brown-skinned kiwi is about the size and shape of an egg. Its green fruit has the sweet taste that some people compare with a strawberry. About one-third of the crop is exported to the Europe and Japan.

Among the thistle family of plants there is a strange-looking species that some people laugh at, while others savor its somewhat bland flavor. The artichoke grows well along the central coast, the large heads producing a strange food that is mostly inedible. After people boil or steam it, they eat only the fleshy inside base of each leaf by scraping it off between their teeth. The heart, located at the base of the flower near the stem, is also edible once the white and purple thistle hairs are removed.

San Mateo and Santa Cruz counties produce most of the country's brussels sprouts, a member of the mostly weed-producing mustard plant family. The sprouts look like miniature cabbages and grow on tall stalks.

While strawberries are grown along much of the central and southern coast, oranges, grapefruit, and avocados are generally found only in the more southerly parts of California where winter frost is a very rare visitor. There are numerous small stands where fresh fruits and produce are sold, especially off the main highways, often adjacent to the fields and groves.

There is a self-guided trail that begins near the parking lot at a small visitor center and museum. It will take about two hours to walk the 0.75-mile pathway that winds through and around all of the restored buildings. The first area the trail passes is a large corral with its sheep and cattle. Then the trail leads across the historic *El Camino Real*, a stretch of dirt road that once was part of the King's Highway that connected all 21 missions. Ahead are the main buildings, including the church and cemetery. During the mission's reconstruction, archeologists discovered that hundreds of Indians and numerous Spaniards were buried here. It's likely that some of the Spanish soldiers were killed during a major Indian uprising in 1824.

The pathway continues, and you are free to wander inside the church, the shops, and the soldiers' quarters and residences. There is also the pottery shop, gristmill, blacksmith shop, and the site of the original Indian barracks. The Chumash Indians were coerced into abandoning their traditional cone-shaped thatched huts for two long adobe buildings that were divided into two-room apartments. There is also a mission garden that includes pomegranate, fig, and pear trees, grape vines, and other plants that were taken as cuttings from original plants still growing at other missions.

Directions: From Lompoc take Highway 246, 3 miles west to Purísima Road. The mission is on the right.

Activities: Walking tours, living histories.
Facilities: Visitor center, museum, exhibits.
Dates: Open daily.
Fees: There is a day-use fee.
Closest town: Lompoc, 3 miles.
For more information: La Purisima Sector Headquarters, 2295 Purisima Road, Lompoc, CA 93436. Phone (805) 733-3713.

▦ SOLVANG

[Fig. 48] Solvang is a small, quaint town that has transformed itself from its original roots as a Danish farming community into a favorite stop for people traveling north and south along US 101 through Santa Barbara County. It is tucked into a small valley between the Santa Ynez and San Rafael mountain ranges. There are about 12 blocks of gift shops, restaurants, bakeries, and antique shops, nearly all sporting a Danish theme. This is a great walking town, so park the car and enjoy a half-day or more wandering through the shops and sampling the many fine foods.

Danish educators looking for the perfect site for a Danish-style folk school founded Solvang, meaning "sunny field," in 1911. The school was successful for many years, but when attendance declined the school was closed and the structure demolished in 1970. While the school was the original reason for the settlers coming here, they also took up farming the rich land as a way to earn money.

Just as the land around Solvang remains primarily undeveloped and used for agriculture and ranching, the many Danish-Americans who live in the small community still practice Danish customs. One of the customs is *refsefilde*, which is a celebration held at the raising of the highest rafter on a new building. Many in the community also are members of the Royal Order of Dannebrog, an organization that recognizes the efforts of the town's citizens to strengthen linkages between Denmark and the United States.

Directions: From US 101 at Buellton, drive east on Highway 246 for 5 miles.
Activities: Shopping, dining.
Facilities: Shops, restaurants.
Closest town: Buellton, 5 miles.
For more information: Solvang Visitor Center, 1511 5th Street (corner of 5th Street and Highway 246), Solvang, CA 93463. Phone (805) 658-6144 ext. 519.

▦ SOLVANG DINING

Bit 'O Denmark Restaurant. 473 Alisal Road, Solvang. Serves a smorgasbord lunch and dinner of American and Danish foods. Dress is casual and reservations aren't required. *Inexpensive. Phone (805) 688-5426.*

Birkholm's Bakery. 1555 Mission Drive, Solvang. This is a family-owned bakery that specializes in pastries, cookies, petit fours, and breads. Either purchase to take

Grunion Runs

These strange little fish, which don't grow to much more than 6 inches in length during their three or four years of life, flop their way on shore to lay their eggs on Southern California's sandy beaches. They are quite predictable, coming ashore en masse in what are commonly called "grunion runs." On those nights with the highest tides following full and new moons, the fish head toward shore. They time their spawning assaults so that when the females lay their 1,000 to 3,000 eggs each, the incoming high tide has just begun to ebb so the eggs won't be washed back out to sea. The females use their tails to drill into the wet sand up to their pectoral fins. Temporarily anchored in place, they lay their eggs as the males curl themselves around the females and release milt, which fertilizes the eggs.

The baby grunion develop inside a protective membrane and are ready to hatch within about nine days. A few days later the next series of high tides arrives and the wave action triggers an enzyme that causes the eggs to hatch. The waves carry the newly hatched grunion out to sea where they grow for about a year before becoming mature enough to begin their own spawning cycles.

Grunion runs occur from March through August and each one usually lasts about three hours. The fish may be caught, generally during March, June, July, and August, but only with bare hands. For anyone age 16 and older, a valid California fishing license is required. Always check current fishing regulations for possible changes in open seasons.

home or sit and enjoy with expresso, cappuccino, or a specialty coffee. Kids enjoy fresh juice and smoothies. *Inexpensive. Phone (805) 688-3872.*

SOLVANG LODGING
Svendsgaard's Danish Lodge & Suites. 1711 Mission Drive, Solvang. This is a delightful stone-accentuated, very Danish-looking lodge located just a block from the center of the community's main downtown area. *Moderate to expensive. Phone (800) 733-8757 or (800) 341-8000.*

The Petersen Village and Inn. 1576 Mission Drive, Solvang. The Old World village includes the inn, shops, sidewalk cafes, and a Danish bakery. *Expensive. Phone (805) 688-3121.*

The Chimney Sweep Inn. 1564 Copenhagen Drive, Solvang. The enchanted, picture-book cottages and suites should appeal to anyone. *Moderate to expensive. Phone (805) 688-2111.*

GAVIOTA STATE PARK

[Fig. 48] Gaviota State Park has nearly 3,000 acres of coastal mountains and 5.5 miles of ocean beaches and cliffs. During Spanish explorer Gaspar de Portolá's expedition in 1769 his soldiers named this part of California *gaviota*, which means "seagull." And while there are still plenty of gulls, there's much more here to see and do.

The park is a popular place for boaters and fishing enthusiasts. The short pier has a boat launch and plenty of room for fishing. With railroad tracks running much of the length of Southern California's coast, railroad trestles pass through many coastal parks, requiring cars or pedestrians to cross under them to reach the beaches. In addition to the old wooden trestle there's also a small campground, a seasonally operated beach store, and several miles of trails.

Besides the beach, which during summer is always popular for swimming, fishing, and beachcombing, there's a marsh at the east end of the main parking lot. It's a good place to see great blue herons (*Ardea herodias*) and perhaps a red-tailed hawk (*Buteo jamaicensis*) swooping down low, hoping to grab a wayward pocket gopher (*Thomomys* sp.) or western harvest mouse (*Reithrodontomys megalotus*). Jaumea (*Jaumea carnosa*) and pickleweed (*Salicornia* sp.) are two of the important plants found in the marsh.

Directions: The park is located 33 miles west of Santa Barbara on US 101.

Activities: Swimming, fishing, surfing, beachcombing, hiking, camping.

Facilities: Campground, pier, seasonal store.

Dates: Open daily.

Fees: There are camping and day-use fees.

Closest town: Buellton, 10 miles.

For more information: Gaviota Sector State Parks, #10 Refugio Beach Road, Goleta, CA 93117. Phone (805) 968-3294 or (805) 968-1033.

REFUGIO STATE BEACH

[Fig. 48(2)] As with all the beaches along this stretch of California's coast, Refugio runs east to west, which means it faces south, where it is warmed by the sun and protected from northerly ocean swells. Here, where the Santa Ynez Mountains mark the westernmost end of the east-west orientation of the Transverse Range, ancient marine terraces stand against crashing ocean waves. At the cliff bases are sandy beaches and rocky tidepools, with a scattering of streams and canyons that cut through the cliffs to reach the sea.

This land was originally inhabited by the Chumash Indians who lived on the

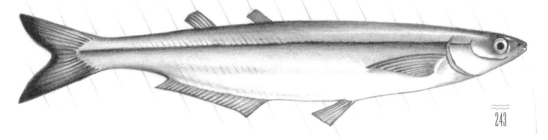

GRUNION

Grunion are noted for the regularity with which they come inshore to spawn at the time of a nearly full moon.

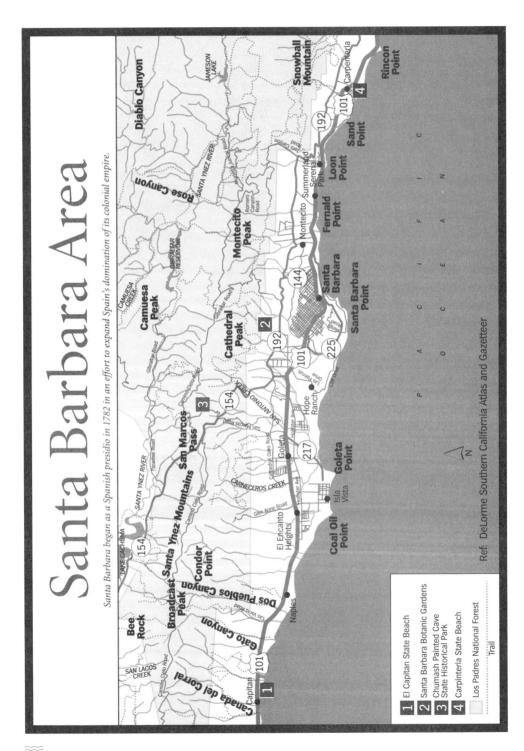

Santa Barbara Area

Santa Barbara began as a Spanish presidio in 1782 in an effort to expand Spain's domination of its colonial empire.

Ref: DeLorme Southern California Atlas and Gazetteer

1 El Capitan State Beach
2 Santa Barbara Botanic Gardens
3 Chumash Painted Cave State Historical Park
4 Carpinteria State Beach

Los Padres National Forest

Trail

mainland and on the Channel Islands offshore. Their culture depended on the sea for survival, with their villages situated close to the ocean where food was gathered. Using crude stone tools they were able to split wood planks from trees, then lash them together with milkweed fiber to build their boats. They sealed the cracks with asphaltum, the naturally occurring tar found along this part of the coast.

The beach park also is a good place to see a large number of animals. Great horned owls (*Bubo virginianus*), barn owls (*Tyto alba*), red-tailed hawks (*Buteo jamaicensis*), red-shouldered hawks (*Buteo lineatus*), and black shouldered kites can all be seen here. There are also the shoreline birds that constantly follow the beach waves probing the sands for insects and small animals. Found here are curlews (*Numenius americanus*), sandpipers (*Calidris minutilla*), short-billed dowitchers (*Limnodroumus griseus*), and the ever-present gulls.

A bike trail runs along the beach bluff connecting with El Capitán State Beach 2.5 miles east. The park has a campground that will accommodate tents and campers, and there's a seasonal snack shop and a large grass picnic area near the beach. In the park are also a lot of non-native palm trees in the park, which Southern Californians seem to enjoy growing.

Directions: The park is located just off US 101, approximately 23 miles northwest of Santa Barbara.

Activities: Swimming, fishing, camping, beachcombing, bike riding, hiking.

Facilities: Picnic tables, campground, snack bar.

Dates: Open daily.

Fees: Camping and day-use fees are charged.

Closest town: Santa Barbara, 23 miles.

For more information: Gaviota Sector State Parks, #10 Refugio Beach Road, Goleta, CA 93117. Phone (805) 968-3294 or (805) 968-1033.

▒ EL CAPITÁN STATE BEACH

[Fig. 49(1)] While this is a very popular summer swimming beach, it's equally popular year-round with the surfing crowd and fishermen, especially off El Capitán Point. Anglers catch kelp bass (*Paralabrax clathratus*) and Pacific halibut (*Hippoglossus stenolepis*) from the beach and rocky outcroppings.

This is a relatively small park of only 168 acres, made up of the sandy beach, a picnic area, and the popular campground. The park's name came from El Capitán Jose Franciso de Ortega, who first owned *Rancho Nuestro Senora del Refugio*, "Our Lady of Refuge Ranch." The ranch was much larger than the beach park, extending up to 4 miles inland and west to Cojo Canyon near Point Conception.

In addition to the sandy beach and rocky tidepools, El Capitán State Beach features stands of sycamores and oaks along El Capitán Creek. A paved ramp leads from the bluff parking lot to the beach, and a bike trail connects the park with Refugio State Beach, 2.5 miles away.

Amtrak Coast Starlight

A train always attracts attention, especially if it's crossing a high trestle with the blue Pacific for a backdrop. Traveling by train, at least on the West Coast, is an adventure that, unfortunately, relatively few people pursue today. But the Coast Starlight offers travelers an opportunity to experience parts of California's coast that can't be seen from the freeways or back roads. The Coast Starlight runs daily between Seattle and Los Angeles, making numerous short stops along the way.

After staying inland throughout Northern and much of Central California, the Starlight finally reaches the coast just south of San Luis Obispo at Pismo Beach. As it darts across Vandenberg Airforce Base, still about an hour north of Santa Barbara, passengers are treated to views of rocket launch pad towers scattered about the 35-mile-long base. Vandenberg is the West Coast launch facility for many military satellites and for the space shuttle.

As the train continues south toward Los Angeles it comes close enough along some sections of the ocean that during strong storms large waves may even spray the sides of cars. If you happen to be staying in one of the coastal campgrounds or using one of the beaches, be assured that either the Coast Starlight or a freight train will pass by. Wave and chances are good that the Starlight's passengers will wave back. For Amtrak schedule information phone (800) 872-7245.

Directions: The park is adjacent to US 101, 17 miles west of Santa Barbara.
Activities: Swimming, surfing, beachcombing, fishing, bike riding, camping.
Facilities: Campground, picnic grounds, seasonal snack bar.
Dates: Open daily.
Fees: There are camping and day-use fees.
Closest town: Santa Barbara, 17 miles.
For more information: Gaviota Sector State Parks, #10 Refugio Beach Road, Goleta, CA 93117. Phone (805) 968-3294 or (805) 968-1033.

SANTA BARBARA

[Fig. 49] The city of Santa Barbara's near-perfect weather, combined with its beach, wharf, and historic district create a special ambiance that makes this a favorite vacation spot for thousands of people each year. Santa Barbara began as a Spanish presidio that was built in 1782 in an effort to stop Russia's threat of continued southerly expansion down the California coast. Within another 100 years the growing town had already gained a reputation as a wonderful coastal resort, a reputation it retains today.

El Presidio de Santa Barbara State Historic Park, 123 East Canon Perdido Street, (805) 965-0093, houses the only two original presidio adobe structures that have survived in the town. One of those original structures is El Cuartel, which is the oldest building in Santa Barbara and the second oldest in California. What today is a museum and gift shop originally was built to house 42 Spanish soldiers and their wives and children soon after they arrived here in 1782. The presidio fell into disuse following the American takeover of California in 1846. Earthquakes and the frenzied development that followed as Santa Barbara's popularity increased resulted in many buildings being either destroyed or razed. The Santa Barbara Trust for Historic Preservation has been heading a restoration and reconstruction program since 1964. The chapel, padre's and comandante's quarters, and soldiers' quarters across Santa Barbara Street are well worth a visit. The presidio's other surviving building is the Canedo adobe, which houses museum exhibits.

Downtown Santa Barbara has managed to retain much of its Old World feeling, with its combination of Mediterranean, Spanish Colonial, early Californian, Mexican, Moorish, and Islamic architecture. From restaurants to the city's court and government buildings, here you'll find no steel and glass highrises, but attractive buildings with white plaster walls and arched windows, doorways, and facades, all complemented by their low-pitched tile roofs and decorative wrought iron work. Hidden patios and gardens are part of the overall design of many of Santa Barbara's buildings.

It wasn't always this way. A population boom in the late nineteenth century brought an eclectic assortment of architecture, much of it Victorian. Of the many Victorian structures built during that time, the Upham Hotel still remains, making it the oldest continually operating hotel in Southern California. In the 1880s many prominent citizens of the growing city called for controls on the styles of architecture that could be added. Even today ordinances help define architectural styles in downtown Santa Barbara, allowing it to retain its Spanish-Mediterranean style.

The **Red Tile Walking Tour** is an easy, 12-block stroll through the historic district of Santa Barbara where many of the most important historic buildings and landmarks are located. El Presidio de Santa Barbara State Historic Park, located at the corner of Canon Peridido and Santa Barbara streets, is a good place to begin. The tour heads north on Santa Barbara Street (away from the ocean) for 2.5 blocks, then west on Anapamu Street for 2 blocks, south on State Street for another 4 blocks, then east for 2 blocks on De la Guerra Street. El Presidio State Park, the beginning point, is then just 1 block north. From here there's also a quick 1 block jog to the south along Santa Barbara Street, which will take you to the Presidio Gardens, the beautiful county courthouse, the Presidio Chapel, and several historic adobe buildings.

Stearns Wharf, (805) 564-5518, extends from the end of State Street into the blue waters of the Santa Barbara Channel. John Peck Stearns built the wharf in 1872. It's been in continual operation since then, although it has changed owners over the years. During the 1940s, actor Jimmy Cagney and his brothers were part owners. There's a fanciful dolphin fountain near the foot of the wharf, a favorite spot for photographs. The wharf offers the typical seafood market, a bait and tackle store, several restaurants, wine-tasting spots, gift shops, and The Nature Conservancy's visitor center (805-962-9111).

Chase Palm Park, located along Cabrillo Boulevard and the beach west of Stearns Wharf is a 10-acre play land designed for kids and their parents. It has a beautifully restored antique carousel and a shipwreck playground, complete with a turn-of-the-century schooner and meandering faux riverbeds. The park also has a 3-mile paved bike trail that parallels the waterfront.

Santa Barbara Historical Museum, 136 East De la Guerra Street, (805) 966-1601, is a historic adobe home that now exhibits a regional history collection that includes fine art, saddles, costumes, and antique toys. The museum also houses the Gledhill Library with its extensive holdings of books, photographs, maps, and manuscripts, making it a rich resource of information for history buffs. Two other nineteenth century adobes are adjacent to the museum and surround a tree-shaded courtyard. The museum is closed Mondays. Admission is free, but donations are appreciated.

The **Santa Barbara Museum of Natural History**, 2559 Puesta del Sol Road, (805) 682-4711, is nationally renowned for its California and North American West Coast natural history. Highlights include a diorama of prehistoric Chumash Indian life in the Santa Barbara area and the skeleton of a giant blue whale. The museum also has a planetarium. The museum is open daily except Thanksgiving, Christmas, and New Year's Day. There is an admission fee.

Mission Santa Barbara, 2201 Laguna Street, (805) 682-4713, is the 10th of California's 21 missions. It was founded on December 4, 1786, and soon became known as the Queen of the Missions because of its striking architecture, which included twin bell towers and an extraordinarily beautiful setting. Local Chumash Indians supplied the construction labor for the mission, as well as the work force for the mission's cattle and agricultural efforts. Many of the thousands of Chumash who succumbed to European diseases are buried on the church grounds. Most California missions, including this one, had their original buildings damaged by earthquakes, the first one striking here in 1812. The replacement stone church that sits on today's park-like setting was begun in 1815 and completed in 1833, but it had to undergo additional repairs following a 1925 earthquake.

The mission continues as a Catholic parish church with the main chapel, historic cemetery, gardens, and a small museum open to the public for self-guided tours. The mission is open daily except Easter, Thanksgiving, Christmas, and New Year's Day. There is a small admission fee.

Directions: US 101 bisects Santa Barbara, 27 miles north of Ventura.

Activities: Shopping, walking tours, sight-seeing, fishing, swimming, boating.

For more information: The Santa Barbara Tourist Information Center, 1 Garden Street, Santa Barbara, CA 93101. Phone (805) 965-3021. Santa Barbara Hot Spots, 36 State Street, Santa Barbara, CA. 93101. Phone (800) 793-7666.

SANTA BARBARA DINING

Original Enterprise Fish Company. 225 State Street, Santa Barbara. Features mesquite broiled seafood, but with many other selections, including a kid's menu. Serves beer and wine and expects casual dress. Reservations are suggested. *Inexpensive. Phone (805) 962-3313.*

Eladio's. 28 West Cabrillo Boulevard, Santa Barbara. With its ocean view comes a good selection of steak, seafood, and pasta. Causal dress. Reservations can be helpful on weekends. *Inexpensive. Phone (805) 963-4466.*

Citronelle Restaurant. 901 Cabrillo Boulevard, Santa Barbara, in the Santa Barbara Inn. Panoramic ocean views with fine dining on French and California cuisine. Casual dress and reservations are suggested. *Inexpensive to moderate. Phone (805) 963-0111.*

SANTA BARBARA LODGING

Santa Barbara Inn. 901 East Cabrillo Boulevard, Santa Barbara. Located across the street from the beach, many of its rooms have beautiful ocean views. *Expensive. Phone (805) 966-2285 or (800) 966-2285.*

Ramada Limited. 4770 Calle Real, Santa Barbara. Each room features a private balcony with many overlooking a lush freshwater lagoon. *Moderate to expensive. Phone (805) 964-3511.*

Simpson House Inn. 121 East Arrellaga Street, Santa Barbara. The city's only Historic Landmark Inn, it features quality furnishings and service good enough to rate five stars. Stay in the Italianate Victorian home, the cottage, or the barn suites. This bed and breakfast is surrounded by an acre of English gardens and offers its guests a gourmet breakfast. *Very expensive. Phone (800) 676-1280.*

Marina Beach Motel. 21 Bath Street, Santa Barbara. There is a meal plan available and a required two-day stay on weekends during much of the year. It's located just a half-block from the beach and near the wharf. *Moderate to expensive. Phone (805) 564-4102.*

SANTA BARBARA BOTANIC GARDEN

[Fig. 49(2)] The Santa Barbara Botanic Garden is tucked into the hills above Santa Barbara and is California's oldest botanic garden dedicated to showcasing the state's native plants. The garden's 5.5 miles of trails wander through 65 acres with over 1,000 indigenous and rare plants growing in organized plant communities. Here's an opportunity to walk through a redwood grove, mountain meadows, and canyons and see 66 taxa (species, subspecies, and varieties) of manzanita (*Arctostaphylos*), 40 taxa of California lilac (*Ceanothus*), 26 taxa of buckwheat (*Eriogonum*), and the list goes on.

The botanic garden also offers excellent views of the Pacific Ocean and of several of the Channel Islands. If you're interested in obtaining native plants, the garden's nursery grows specimens that are made available for sale.

Directions: From downtown Santa Barbara take Los Olivos northeast past the Santa Barbara Mission toward the mountains. At Foothill Road (Highway 192) turn right and then take the first left onto Mission Canyon Road. Stay right at the fork. The garden is 0.5 mile down on the left.

Activities: Docent-led walks, self-guided walks.

Facilities: Gift shop, nursery.

Dates: Open daily with extended seasonal hours.

Fees: There is a small entry fee.

For more information: Santa Barbara Botanic Garden, 1212 Mission Canyon Road, Santa Barbara, CA 93105-2126. Phone (805) 682-4726.

CHUMASH PAINTED CAVE STATE HISTORIC PARK

[Fig. 49(3)] Middens, essentially buried garbage dumps filled with long-discarded shells and occasional stone tools, are often the only evidence that Chumash Indians lived along this portion of California's coast for thousands of years. There is a wonderful exception. The walls of a sandstone cave located high in the mountains above Santa Barbara are covered with exquisite examples of Chumash art. The colorful religious paintings depict the lives of the Indians, including images of coastal Native American fishermen.

The cave is located up a short path from the road. Its wide entrance to the relatively shallow cave is closed by a cage to protect its walls, whose brilliant-colored paintings are easily seen or photographed from outside.

Directions: From Santa Barbara and US 101, take Highway 154 east approximately 5.9 miles and turn right on Painted Cave Road, which is easily missed. Follow the very narrow, twisting, and steep Painted Cave Road about 1.9 miles. A sign on the left side of the road marks the site. There is parking space for only a couple of vehicles and a short trail to the cave. Trailers and motorhomes must not attempt to drive up Painted Cave Road.

Activities: Viewing the cave.

Facilities: None.

Dates: Open daily.

Fees: None.

Closest town: Santa Barbara, 8 miles.

For more information: Channel Coast District Office, Gaviota Sector, #10 Refugio Beach Road, Goleta, CA 93117. Phone (805) 968-1711.

CARPINTERIA STATE BEACH

[Fig. 49(4)] This 1-mile beach is the primary attraction in the small town of Carpinteria. The beach has a reef offshore that softens the ocean's movement, essentially eliminating the rip currents that are found along most other southern California beaches. As far back as 1602 the Spanish who first arrived here recognized the natural beach conditions and described this as *cosa segura de buen gente*, or "the safest beach on the coast." Near Carpinteria State Beach's popular sandy shore, which is favored by sunbathers, there are also tidepools containing their share of anemones, sea stars, crabs, snails, and sea urchins.

While wading at the edge of the surf or walking on the beach, it's not at all unusual to step on small blobs of gooey tar. The tar isn't the result of a major offshore oil tanker spill. The tar is continually washed ashore from naturally occurring seeps in the Santa Barbara Channel's sea floor. Geologically induced pressures beneath the surface force the thick oil through the porous sediment floor where it then floats to the surface, often attaching itself to kelp or simply washing ashore. Marine biologists have discovered that some species of shrimp, sand dabs, and bacteria have evolved so they can thrive near the seeps. Bacteria of the genus *Beggiatoa* are able to consume the oil's hydrogen sulfide and convert it into sugar.

The ample supply of tar is the reason the native Chumash Indians chose this spot to build their large seagoing canoes. They used the tar to seal the seams of the plank boats. The Spanish discovered the Indians' manufacturing endeavor and named the site *Carpenteria* or "carpentry shop." Archeological investigations have discovered the remains of prehistoric animals, similar to those found in the more famous La Brea Tar Pits in Los Angeles, also died in some of Carpinteria's tar pits. Tar from the Carpinteria pits also was used by the early settlers in the construction of piers and wharves, and some was even collected and shipped to San Francisco.

Carpinteria State Beach has a large campground, which is a good choice for anyone wanting to stay near the beach overnight. There are only a few hotels in

Black Gold

Native Americans used the thick tar that oozed naturally to the land's surface or washed ashore from undersea seeps along Southern California's coast to seal their boats and baskets. Today, both onshore and offshore wells pump this "black gold" from thousands of feet below the surface. Offshore wells produce only about 15 percent of California's oil, about 60 million barrels each year.

The first offshore wells were constructed in 1896 on wooden piers and were able to drill only about 600 feet down. Beginning in the mid-1950s, oil companies, under state and federal leases, built artificial islands well offshore, which were used as drilling platforms. Today, oil wells are located in water deeper than the 600 feet the original wells could reach, then drilled as much as 9,000 feet below the ocean floor.

While test or exploratory wells are often sunk, work doesn't begin without a significant amount research to first determine where to drill. The oil is hidden in ancient faults and folds or in salt plugs or domes. Geologists use magnetic, electrical, and seismic research, in conjunction with their test drilling, to determine where best to sink new oil wells.

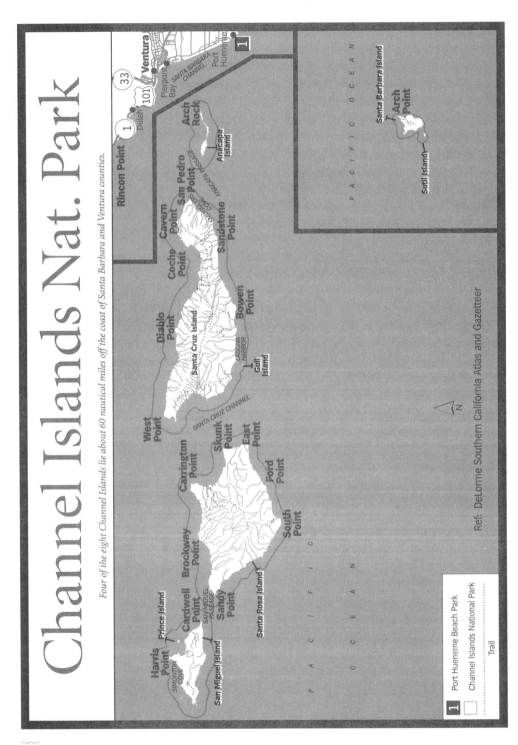

Channel Islands Nat. Park

Four of the eight Channel Islands lie about 60 nautical miles off the coast of Santa Barbara and Ventura counties.

Ref: DeLorme Southern California Atlas and Gazetteer

Legend:

1	Port Hueneme Beach Park
	Channel Islands National Park
	Trail

Carpinteria, and they aren't located along the beach.

Directions: Carpinteria State Beach is 12 miles south of Santa Barbara. From US 101, turn west onto Highway 224, which leads into town and the beach.

Activities: Swimming, sunbathing, beachcombing, fishing.

Facilities: Campground with RV hookups.

Dates: Open daily.

Fees: There are camping and day-use fees. Summer reservations are suggested, phone (800) 444-7275.

Closest town: Carpinteria.

For more information: Channel Coast District State Parks, 1933 Cliff Drive, Suite 27, Santa Barbara, CA 93109. Phone (805) 684-2811 or (805) 899-1400.

Ventura County

CHANNEL ISLANDS NATIONAL PARK

[Fig. 50] Four of the eight Channel Islands lie from 14 to 55 miles off the coast of Santa Barbara and Ventura counties. The islands provide an effective barrier, deflecting winter storm-produced waves from the mainland, which at Point Conception makes a very obvious turn east. The islands are part of the Transverse Range and were once a single large island that geologists call Santarosea. Most of that island now lies beneath the Pacific Ocean. At one time the islands were also connected with the mainland. Rising oceans and moving landmasses separated the Channel Islands from their mainland mountain cousins thousands of years ago. That separation has resulted in many plant and animal species that once were identical to those on the mainland to change in size, color, and shape. The Santa Cruz Island scrub jay; six separate subspecies of the island fox, which are found on six different islands and thought to be related to the mainland gray fox; and a subspecies of the spotted skunk, but with broader face and shorter tail than its mainland cousins, are found only on the Channel Islands. The threatened island night lizard lives on Santa Barbara Island and on San Nicolas and San Clemente islands outside the national park is another endemic species. While the Torrey pine, which is found on Santa Rosa Island, is also found only at Torrey Pines State Park on the mainland, the Santa Cruz Island pine is found nowhere else but its Channel Island home.

The weather on the islands can be harsh, ranging from cold and very windy to hot and dry. There are many miles of trails on the islands and numerous beaches and tidepools available for exploration. Please remember that most of the islands and their surrounding waters are protected. That includes the animals in the tidepools, the plants on the islands, and even the remnants of shipwrecks that are accessible to scuba divers.

San Miguel Island is the westernmost of the islands, lying directly south of Point Conception. Only 8 miles long and 4 miles across at its widest point, its 14,000 acres provide a resting ground for California sea lions (*Zalophus californicus*), stellar sea lions (*Eumetopias jubatus*), northern elephant seals (*Mirounga angustirostris*), harbor seals (*Phoca vitulina*), Guadalupe fur seals (*Arctocephalus townsendi*), and northern fur seals (*Callorhinus ursinus*). Point Bennett is the largest pinniped rookery on California's coast.

As with several of the Channel Islands, much smaller islands, which in some cases are not much more than barren, rocky outcroppings, are included as part of the primary island. Another unique aspect of the island is the caliche forest. The "ghost forest" was created thousands of years ago when calcium carbonate sand, composed primarily of powdered lime skeletons of dead shellfish, blew inland and covered the vegetation. Organic chemicals from within the plants reacted with the sand and cemented it together. As the plants died and decayed, they left behind the eerie gray castings of their original forms. Winds continue to erode and bury some of the brittle castings while uncovering new ones. There is also a memorial at Cuyler Harbor that commemorates Juan Rodriquez Cabrillo, the first European to see the islands. Year-round landing is allowed only at Cuyler Harbor Beach with no permit. All other beaches and coastline are closed year-round.

Santa Rosa Island is the next in the east-west line of ancient mountaintops. It's the second largest of the island chain with its 84 square miles covered mostly by non-native grass introduced over more than a century of cattle and sheep grazing. There are about 15 rare or endangered species, along with three endemic species, the tree poppy (*Dendromecon harfordii*), island manzanita (*Artostaphylos tomentosa insulicola*), island oaks (*Quercus tomentella*). There is also a remnant Torrey pine (*Pinus torreyana*) forest that has been here since the Pleistocene Era. In 1994 archeologists here discovered the fossilized skeleton of a pygmy mammoth, which is on display at the National Park Service visitor center in Ventura. As on some of the other islands, there are numerous scattered Chumash burial and midden sites on Santa Rosa.

There is a campground at Bechers Bay with windbreaks and pit toilets. Boat landings are permitted on most of the beaches year-round, although there are exceptions. Contact the park office (phone 805-658-5730) for specific closures and for required camping reservations.

Santa Cruz Island's 62,000 acres make it the largest of the Channel chain, and with its highest peak at 2,400 feet, it also possesses the tallest of the islands' mountains. The western 90 percent of the island is owned by The Nature Conservancy, which allows public day use access. The remaining 10 percent that lies east of a line between Chinese Harbor on the north and Sandborne Point on the south, remains in private hands and access is generally not allowed. The 24-mile-long by 10-mile-wide island has some 650 species of plants and trees within its 10 different plant communities. Eight of the plants are endemic, found nowhere else in the world. Such varied habitat helps account for the more than 140 terrestrial bird species that have been recorded here.

In 1988 The Nature Conservancy (phone (805) 969-9111) acquired 90 percent of Santa Cruz Island. A permit is required to land on the conservancy's portion of the island, and the conservancy also offers organized day trips to the island. Contact The Nature Conservancy for more specific information about permits and organized trips (The Nature Conservancy, Santa Cruz Island Project, 213 Stearns Wharf, Santa Barbara, CA 93101).

TORREY PINE
(Pinus torreyana)
This rare, protected tree grows 20 to 60 feet tall and has a dense, round-topped cone.

Anacapa Island is actually three small islands covering only 700 acres, making it the smallest of the northern Channel Islands. The 5-mile-long island chain was once used to graze sheep, but the National Park Service removed the animals when the island became a national monument in 1938. Anacapa is the West Coast's primary nesting site for brown pelicans (*Pelecanus occidentalis*). To protect the pelican rookery West Anacapa is closed to the public.

Anacapa Island's steep cliffs are punctuated by sea caves, and on the east end Arch Rock is a natural 40-foot bridge. You can wander among the old U.S. Coast Guard station buildings and hike the hills where the grasses are highlighted by yellow sunflower trees. Camping is allowed on East Anacapa and landing access is allowed at Landing Cove. Although there is no camping fee, reservations and a permit are required. Contact park headquarters (phone 805-658-5730) for information.

Santa Barbara Island is the smallest of the Channel Islands and lies off the coast of Ventura. Most of its 640 acres are comprised of an ancient marine terrace with two peaks, the highest being 635-foot Signal Peak. The National Park Service rangers use a World War II Navy Quonset hut as an office, visitor center, and museum. There are several trails that wind through a much-changed environment. Goats were introduced to the island in 1846, followed by heavy farm use, grazing, and intentional burning of the land. The introduction of rabbits completed the near total destruction of the native habitat, but the National Park Service has removed the non-native wildlife and has a very successful ongoing restoration program. Stands of giant coreopsis (*Coreopsis gigantea*), a sunflower that can reach 10 feet high, thrive on parts of the island, and western gulls (*Larus occidentalis*) use the island as a nesting area.

A campground is located near Landing Cove. No fee is charged, but a permit is required. There also is no water, so it must be packed in. Contact park headquarters (phone 805-658-5730) for information and permits. Boat landings may be made at anytime without a permit in Landing Cove.

Directions: The islands are located from 14 to 55 miles off the coast of Santa

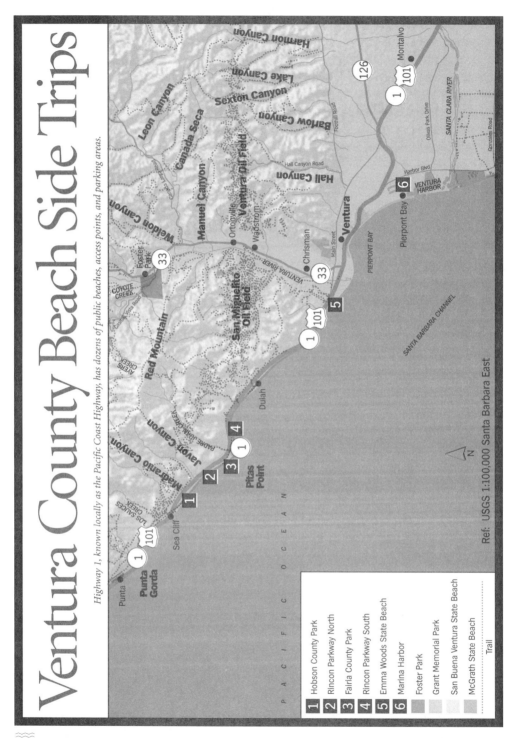

Ventura County Beach Side Trips

Highway 1, known locally as the Pacific Coast Highway, has dozens of public beaches, access points, and parking areas.

Ref: USGS 1:100,000 Santa Barbara East

1. Hobson County Park
2. Rincon Parkway North
3. Faria County Park
4. Rincon Parkway South
5. Emma Woods State Beach
6. Marina Harbor
   Foster Park
   Grant Memorial Park
   San Buena Ventura State Beach
   McGrath State Beach
   Trail

Barbara and Ventura counties and can only be reached by boat, although there is some very limited private air service available. Some areas of some islands are off-limits to the public or require a ranger guide. Pets and open fires are not allowed on any of the islands.

Activities: Hiking, scuba diving, camping, bird-watching, picnicking.

Facilities: There are few amenities on the islands, with some having no visitor services or facilities.

Dates: Open daily, but there are numerous restrictions at landing areas and access points. Permits are required to visit most of the islands and may be obtained from the National Park Service.

Fees: Charter boat fees vary. There is a camping reservation fee. Phone (800) 365-2267.

For more information: National Park Service, Channel Islands Visitor Center, 1901 Spinnaker Drive, Ventura, CA 93001-4354. Phone (805) 658-5730, (805) 644-8262 or 644-8157. Island Packers Nature Discovery Tours is the official National Park Service concessionaire providing access to the islands. Contact them at 3600 South Harbor Boulevard, Oxnard (at the Channel Islands Harbor). Phone (805) 382-1779. They also depart from 1867 Spinnaker Drive, Ventura, CA 93001-4353. Phone (805) 642-1393. For flight information contact Channel Islands Aviation, 305 Durley Avenue, Camarillo, California 93010. Phone (805) 987-1301. The following two companies offer fishing trips to the islands or to the Santa Barbara Channel: Wave-Walker at the Marina 3 Gate, Santa Barbara Harbor, telephone (805) 964-2046 or cell phone (805) 895-3273, or Sea Landing, 301 West Cabrillo Boulevard, Santa Barbara, CA 93101. Phone (805) 963-3564.

RINCON POINT

[Fig. 50] Besides being one of the most popular surfing spots in southern California, Rincon Point also marks the boundary between Santa Barbara and Ventura counties. Rincon Beach County Park encompasses the jutting point of land. From the parking lot bluff there are great ocean views and a stairway that leads down to the beach. Park officials have designated a swimming-only beach north of the stairway in an attempt to keep a reasonable distance between the conflicting needs of surfers and swimmers.

Directions: Take Bates Road off US 101, 2 miles south of Carpinteria.

Activities: Swimming, surfing, picnicking, fishing.

Facilities: Picnic area, restrooms.

Dates: Open daily.

Fees: None.

Closest town: Carpinteria, 2 miles.

For more information: Santa Barbara County Department of Parks and Recreation, 105 Anapamu Street, Santa Barbara, CA 93101. Phone (805) 568-2460.

Santa Monica Mountains

The Santa Monica Mountains range from sea level to 3,000 feet in elevation.

San Gabriel Mountains

Verdugo Mts

Cahuenga Peak

Los Angeles Basin

Franklin Canyon

Palos Verdes

Santa Susana Mountains

San Fernando Valley

O A K R i d g e

Simi Valley

Simi Hills

Simi Peak

● National Park Service Headquarters

S A N T A   M O N I C A   M O U N T A I N S

M a l i b u

Saddle Peak

Topanga Canyon

Malibu Canyon

Point Dume

Zuma Canyon

P A C I F I C   O C E A N

Sandstone Peak

Big Sycamore Canyon

Laguna Peak

Oxnard Plain

Point Mugu

N

Ref: Santa Monica Mountains NPS Map

▓ VENTURA COUNTY BEACH SIDE TRIPS

[Fig. 51] Drive along Highway 1, better known locally as the Pacific Coast Highway or PCH, and in between the growing number of beachside houses and businesses you can find dozens of public beaches. The best and safest way to reach the beaches is by using the well-marked public beach access points and parking areas. But for the more adventurous there are unmarked beach access points all along the southern coast that can usually be identified by several vehicles parked in wide pullouts along the road. Long ago, surfers identified where the best waves broke and either found, or created through constant use, trails to reach these beaches. Listed here are only those beaches with officially recognized and signed public beach access points.

Hobson County Park [Fig. 51(1)] is a small day-use beach, campground, and concession stand. The park may be closed during strong storms. The park is adjacent to Highway 1, just south of Sea Cliff and about 7 miles north of Ventura. Phone (805) 654-3951.

Rincon Parkway North [Fig. 51(2)] is a roadside parking area along the Pacific Coast Highway seawall, between Hobson County Park to the north and the Faria County Park to the south. There are 112 designated campsites available for self-contained RVs on a first-come, first-served basis. Phone (805) 654-3951.

Faria County Park [Fig. 51(3)] lies south of Rincon Parkway North and has stairs that allow access to its combination rocky shoreline and sandy beach. The park offers both tent and RV campsites next to the ocean. As with nearby Hobson County Park, Faria County Park may be closed during times of heavy surf. It's located just off the old Pacific Coast Highway, which parallels Highway 1 on the ocean side at Pitas Point. Phone (805) 654-3951.

Rincon Parkway South [Fig. 51(4)] is another of the series of Ventura County parks located along the old Pacific Coast Highway. There are designated campsites for RVs and plenty of beach access. The park is located about 6 miles north of Ventura.

Emma Wood State Beach [Fig. 51(5)] is a great place to spend a day swimming, surfing, or fishing. Anglers regularly catch sea or shiner perch (*Cymatogaster aggregata*) and cabezon (*Scorpaenichthys marmoratus*). There's a freshwater marsh near the southwest end of the beach where resident and migrating songbirds can be seen, while red-tailed hawks soar high overhead as they search for food. The ruins of a World War II coastal artillery site can also be seen. The small campground is for hikers and bikers. The beach is located about 2 miles northwest of Ventura on US 101.

San Buena Ventura State Beach [Fig. 51] is long and wide with a 1,700-foot pier at its northwest end. The pier has a restaurant, bait shop, and snack bar. On the beach there are volleyball courts, picnic sites, beach equipment rentals, and dressing rooms. The main beach entrance is off San Pedro Street from Pierpont Boulevard in Ventura. Phone (805) 654-4744 or (805) 654-4610.

Marina Harbor [Fig. 51(6)] is a well-developed facility with two marinas, boat charters, a free launch ramp, sailboat rentals, and other facilities. Nearby there are

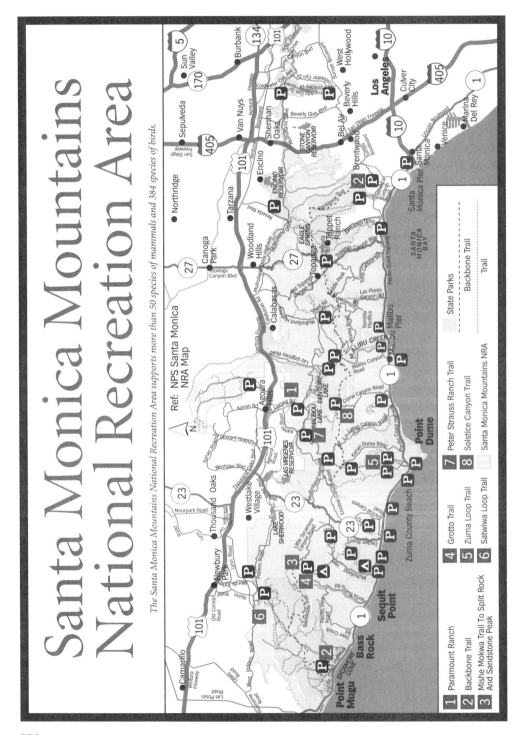

Santa Monica Mountains National Recreation Area

The Santa Monica Mountains National Recreation Area supports more than 50 species of mammals and 384 species of birds.

Ref: NPS Santa Monica NRA Map

two public golf courses. Phone (805) 642-4303 or (805) 642-2231. For harbor information, phone (805) 642-8538.

McGrath State Beach [Fig. 51] is located in Oxnard, off Harbor Boulevard. In addition to the park's nearly 300 acres, its rolling dunes, and 2 miles of beach, there's a marsh at the mouth of the Santa Clara River, which is protected within the Santa Clara Estuary Natural Preserve and is well worth exploring. The beach park also has a popular campground. While swimming and surfing are popular here, there are strong rip currents along the shore, so extreme caution is advised. Phone (800) 444-7275 for camping reservations. For beach information, phone (805) 654-4744 or (805) 654-4610.

Port Hueneme Beach Park [Fig. 50(1)] offers a wide sandy beach, day-use facilities, including playground equipment, and a snack bar. There's a T-shaped pier that extends out into the ocean 1,240 feet. It has a bait shop and lights, and is open 24 hours. Phone (805) 986-6555.

SANTA MONICA MOUNTAINS NATIONAL RECREATION AREA

[Fig. 53] This is an island paradise that exists in the middle of a vast sea of humanity. It amazes most newcomers to the Los Angeles area that in the middle of 15 million people and their businesses, freeways, and homes is a vast mountain wilderness where the sounds and sights of civilization completely vanish. The park lies within the Santa Monica Mountains, a rugged stretch of terrain, much of which is accessible only on trails or the few roads that manage to navigate the steep, narrow, and winding canyons. The national recreation area is actually a cooperative effort among the National Park Service, state parks, various conservancies, and private landowners who are working together to protect the land's resources while allowing and encouraging public access.

This part of Southern California enjoys a true Mediterranean climate. Summers are hot and dry, ranging from 80 to 100 degrees Fahrenheit, with cool, comfortable nights. Winters are relatively wet and cool, ranging from 40 to 70 degrees Fahrenheit, although freezing nighttime temperatures in protected mountain valleys are not uncommon. The maritime influence generally keeps the ocean side of the mountains 10 to 15 degrees cooler than the inland side. During winter the pattern is reversed with warmer temperatures more common along the coast.

The Chumash and Gabrielino Indians originally inhabited the land. The Spanish arrival in the 1500s marked the beginning of the end for the Native Americans' way of life. While real colonization efforts didn't begin for 200 more years, European diseases and the mission system soon decimated native populations and ended their cultural ways. Following Spanish, Mexican, and finally in 1846, American control of California, much of what is now the national recreation area ended up in the hands of Frederick and May Rindge, who purchased the property for about $10 an acre. They called their acquisition *El Rancho Topanga Malibu Sequit*. If not for their efforts at keeping development and roads out of these mountains during those early years, it's unlikely there would be much public open space existing here today.

This is a land of sandy beaches and dry chaparral, lush streams and open meadows, all of which work together to support more than 50 species of mammals and 384 species of birds. From deer, mountain lions, coyotes, and bobcats to golden eagles, snowy plovers, scrub jays, and great horned owls, the chain of life is alive and doing reasonably well here.

While much of the national recreation area use is centered on the popular beaches, there are ever-increasing demands for new trails. Most summer weekends bring steady streams of people using the more popular trails. Equestrians, mountain bikers, and hikers share some of these trails, but many are only available to hikers.

Anyone using the trails, no matter their chosen mode of transportation, should carry a map, plenty of water, sunscreen, and a couple of light layers of clothing, even on warm summer days, because the fog can roll in quickly. A good first place to visit for maps, trail guides, and general information about the Santa Mountains National Recreation Area is the National Park Service Visitor Center located in Thousand Oaks.

For those who would like a slightly different experience in the Santa Monica National Recreation Area than the beaches and mountain hiking, visit the **Paramount Ranch**. [Fig. 55, Fig. 53(1)] This is a great place to spend a few hours and see a little bit of Hollywood's history, and perhaps a bit of current Hollywood action. The ranch originally consisted of 2,400 acres that Paramount Pictures purchased in 1927 to use as a movie making area. It was an extremely active filming location with directors such as Cecil B. Demille and famous actors of the day like Gary Cooper and Claudette Colbert on the ranch regularly.

The varied terrain allowed movie directors the ability to recreate locales such as ancient China (*The Adventures of Marco Polo*), the South Seas (*Ebb Tide*), and San Francisco (*Wells Fargo*). Paramount finally sold the property in 1953 to film fan William Hertz, who created a permanent western townsite using old sets and prop storage sheds. The result was a resurgence of filming interest as television came on the scene. Westerns became the focus with the producers of *The Cisco Kid* and *Dick Powell's Zane Grey Theater* becoming regulars at the ranch. Hertz sold the ranch in 1955 and filming continued until finally the National Park Service purchased the area in 1980.

Today, film crews still use the old sets; *Dr. Quinn, Medicine Woman* was filmed here from 1991 to 1998. Visitors always have a good chance of running across a film crew working here.

Directions: There are dozens of access points throughout the Santa Monica Mountains National Recreation Area, which in general is located west of Griffith Park in Los Angeles County and to the east of the Oxnard Plain in Ventura County. US 101 (Ventura Freeway) borders the mountains on the north, and Highway 1 (Pacific Coast Highway or PCH) and the Pacific Ocean form the southern boundary.

Access to most park areas is available via the several roads that cross the mountains linking US 101 and Highway 1. The national recreation area's primary interior access roads are Kanan Dume Road, Las Virgines Road, and Topanga Canyon Boulevard, each of which runs north-south through the national recreation area connecting US 101 with Highway 1.

The National Park Service Visitor Center is located at 401 West Hillcrest Drive in Thousand Oaks, California. From Ventura Freeway (U S 101) take the Lynn Road Exit and drive north on Lynn Road for one block. Turn east (right) on Hillcrest Drive and drive about 0.3 mile and turn left onto McCloud Avenue. Take the first driveway on the right (Civic Center Drive) and continue up the hill to the end of the road. The parking lot sits above and behind the visitor center. There's a stairway and an elevator down to the main visitor center level.

Chaparral Fire Ecology

Southern California's chaparral has evolved over millions of years, making it a hardy survivor of this dry land's periodic wildfires. Lightning strikes most often start the devastating fires, which burn through the low, resinous chaparral plants, often sending flames more than 100 feet in the air and creating temperatures of 2,000 degrees Fahrenheit.

When the fire has cooled, all that remains is a layer of ash and the few charred skeletal remains of the bushy chaparral plants. Most animals escape unharmed, either by running or flying away, or by remaining deep in their burrows. But within weeks, even during summer when rain is still months away, green sprouts begin showing. The "dead" plants "stump sprout," sending new shoots out from near their bases. The first late autumn rain provides life-giving moisture so that grasses, wildflowers, and other broad-leafed plants quickly begin to sprout, covering hillsides with their differing hues of green. And the wildlife returns, often in greater numbers, now that a tender, nutritious new food source is growing so profusely.

Today, many state and national parklands, primarily in backcountry areas, either allow wildfires to burn naturally, or they start what are termed "prescription burns." When temperature, wind, humidity, and fuel moisture content are all at acceptable levels, fires are purposely started in control areas and closely monitored. Allowing fires to burn and starting controlled fires reduce dangerously high fuel levels, so that when wildfires do occur, they tend to burn cooler, causing less damage to plants and animals, while giving firefighters a better chance to protect human life and nearby developed properties.

Activities: Hiking, camping, swimming, surfing, horseback riding, fishing, mountain biking, nature walks, picnicking, historic house tours.

Facilities: Campgrounds, picnic areas, museums, visitor centers, gift shops.

Dates: The public lands are open daily. There may be winter closures of some trails due to mudslides. Open hours at the museums and visitor centers vary widely.

Fees: There are day-use and camping fees at the state parks (Point Mugu, Malibu Creek, Topanga), which are within boundaries of the national recreation area. With the exception of vehicle parking fees in some areas, there are no fees for using the beaches and trails.

Closest town: Malibu on the south (Highway 1) and Calabasas, Agoura Hills, and Thousand Oaks on the north along US 101.

For more information: National Park Service, 401 West Hillcrest Drive, Thousand Oaks, CA 91360. Phone (805) 370-2301. California State Parks, 1925 Las Virgenes Road, Calabasas, CA 91302. Phone (818) 880-0350.

TRAILS

The **Backbone Trail** [Fig. 53(2)] covers 60 miles across the rugged and beautiful Santa Monica Mountains, running through much of the Santa Monica Mountains National Recreation Area and several state parks. This is not a trail for the weak-of-heart. It's a sometimes torturous pathway that begins and ends near sea level, but it encompasses several major gains and losses, with elevations ranging from less than 200 feet to nearly 3,000 feet above sea level. It can be hot, dry, wet, foggy, muddy, dusty, and steep, sometimes during the same day. The views, the rock formations, and the spring wildflower shows can take your breath away in a much more pleasant way than the steep climbs.

What most people do is to catch short portions of the Backbone Trail on day hikes that begin from any number of starting points along the trail. But for anyone wishing to do the entire trail, there are designated camping sites available. A short section of the western end of the trail at the Ventura/Los Angeles county line remains unfinished, but public roadways (primarily Little Sycamore Canyon Road) allow hikers to reconnect with the trail.

The northwestern end of the trail is in Point Mugu State Park. In the south, the trailhead is in Will Rogers State Historic Park. In between, the trail passes through the Circle X Ranch, crosses from Ventura County into Los Angeles County, meanders through Malibu Creek State Park, Trippet Ranch, and Topanga State Park, and finally ends in Will Rogers State Historic Park at its farthest point southeast.

Before attempting the trail, be sure to pick up a good map, take plenty of water, and dress in layers. Sunscreen, insect repellant, and a hat are also helpful.

Mishe Mokwa Trail to Split Rock [Fig. 53(3)] is a 3.5-mile round trip that winds through riparian, coastal sage scrub, and chaparral plant communities. There are great views of Balanced Rock and a wonderful oak grove picnic site at Split Rock. Begin at the Backbone trailhead approximately 6 miles up Yerba Buena Road, which intersects with Highway 1 about 1.7 miles west of Leo Carrillo State Park.

Mishe Mokwa Trail to Sandstone Peak [Fig. 53(3)] is a strenuous 6-mile round trip that follows a portion of the Backbone Trail, beginning at a trailhead off Yerba Buena Road. After reaching Split Rock (1.75 miles), the trail loops about another 3 miles to Sandstone Peak at an elevation of 3,111 feet. The trail connects with and follows a portion of the much longer and more heavily used Backbone Trail. Along the Backbone Trail portion of this 6-mile trip, hikers are likely to encounter mountain bikers and equestrians who are not allowed on most of the narrower connecting trails.

The **Grotto Trail** [Fig. 53(4)] is a moderate to strenuous 3.5-mile round-trip hike that begins at the Circle X Ranch ranger station and the Happy Hollow Campground. The Grotto Trail begins here and heads downhill on some pretty rough terrain. The trail follows the hillside and the West Fork of the Arroyo Sequit. Obviously, it's uphill on the way back, so be prepared. Circle X Ranch, a former Boy Scout camp, is located on Yerba Buena Road, about 5 miles north of Highway 1. On Highway 1, the Yerba Buena Road turn-off is located about 1.7 miles west of Leo Carrillo State Park.

Paramount Ranch offers three short (less than 1 mile each), round-trip hikes. **Coyote Canyon Trail** offers hikers an easy stroll through a chaparral-covered canyon. **Medea Creek Trail** is open to hikers and equestrians and loops through streamside riparian and oak woodland areas. The **Overlook Trail**, also open to hikers and equestrians, heads up from Coyote Canyon (leaving from the western town) to a viewpoint of the western mountains. From US 101 in Calabasas, take the Las Virgenes Road Exit and drive south about 3 miles, turning right (west) on Mulholland Highway. Paramount Ranch is located just off Mulholland Highway, about 3 miles west of Las Virgenes Road.

Zuma Loop Trail [Fig. 53(5)] is an easy, 2.5-mile trail that wanders through a rare (for California) riparian hardwood forest of oak, sycamore, willow, and black walnut trees. Zuma, a word derived from the Chumash language that means "abundance," aptly describes the diversity of habitat and the wildlife that lives here. The trail begins at a parking area at the end of Bonsall Drive, which is about 1.5 miles north on Kanan-Dume Road. Kanan-Dume Road intersects Highway 1 about 6.5 miles west of Malibu.

Satwiwa Loop Trail [Fig. 53(6)] is another easy, 1.5-mile trail that leads through the grasslands and chaparral of the Satwiwa Native American Indian Natural Area. The area has been set aside to preserve and celebrate Native American cultures. To reach the Satwiwa Native American Culture Center, from US 101 in Thousand Oaks, take the Lynn Road Exit and drive south to Via Goleta and turn left into the park.

Peter Strauss Ranch Trail [Fig. 53(7)] is a short, 0.6-mile loop through chaparral and oak woodlands. The old ranch, through which the trail meanders, was named after actor Peter Strauss who purchased the property after falling in love with it while filming *Rich Man, Poor Man* here in 1976. During the 1930s the owners created "Shoson," a fairyland attraction for children and parents. It was later renamed "Lake Enchanto." There are still remnants of the amusement park here, including the terazzo dance floor and the swimming pool, which in 1940 was the largest on the West Coast, able to accommodate 3,000 people. Take the Las Virgenes Road Exit from US 101 (Ventura Freeway) in Calabasas and drive south about 3 miles, turning right (west) on Mulholland Highway. The parking entrance is located near the intersection of Troutdale Drive and Mulholland Highway, about 5.1 miles west of Las Virgenes Road.

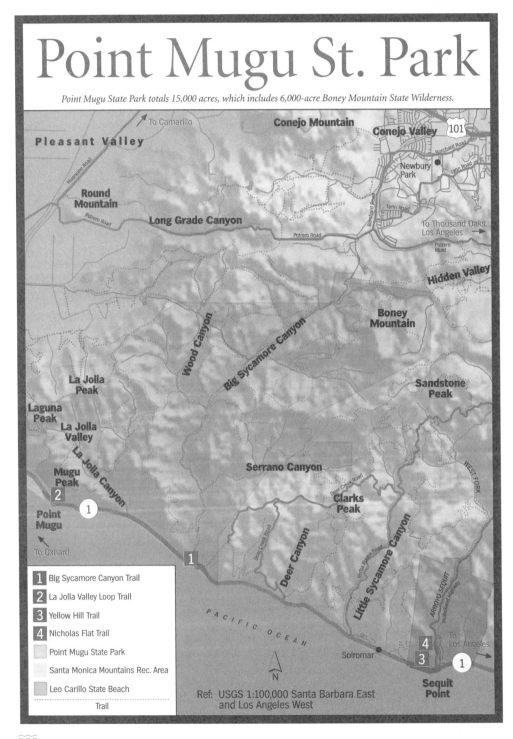

Point Mugu St. Park

Point Mugu State Park totals 15,000 acres, which includes 6,000-acre Boney Mountain State Wilderness.

To Camarillo

Conejo Mountain

Conejo Valley

101

Pleasant Valley

Huaneme Road

Borchard Road

Newbury
Park

Lynn Road

Round
Mountain

Potrero Road

Long Grade Canyon

Borchard Road

Lynn Road

Potrero Road

To Thousand Oaks,
Los Angeles

Potrero
Road

Hidden Valley

Wood Canyon

Big Sycamore Canyon

Boney
Mountain

La Jolla
Peak

Sandstone
Peak

Laguna
Peak

La Jolla
Valley

La Jolla Canyon

Serrano Canyon

WEST FORK

Mugu
Peak

2

1

Point
Mugu

To Oxnard

Deer Creek Road

Clarks
Peak

Deer Creek Road

Deer Canyon

Verna Buena Road

Little Sycamore Canyon

ARROYO SEQUIT

Mulholland Highway

1

1	Big Sycamore Canyon Trail
2	La Jolla Valley Loop Trail
3	Yellow Hill Trail
4	Nicholas Flat Trail

Point Mugu State Park

Santa Monica Mountains Rec. Area

Leo Carillo State Beach

Trail

PACIFIC OCEAN

Solromar

4

3

To
Los Angeles

1

N

Sequit
Point

Ref: USGS 1:100,000 Santa Barbara East
and Los Angeles West

Solstice Canyon Trail [Fig. 53(8)] is only 2.1 miles long, but it traverses a relatively level canyon floor that was the site of several fascinating structures, including the Keller House, built about 1865 and thought to be the oldest stone building in Malibu. In 1952 the Roberts family built their home here. Only remnants remain of the landmark house's foundation, a fishpond, and the concrete bomb shelter, a sign of the times. The Roberts also leased part of their property to Space Technology Laboratories, Inc. as a testing site for satellite equipment, including *Pioneer 12*. The trail begins at the parking area located off Corral Canyon Road, which intersects with Highway 1, about 6 miles west of Malibu.

POINT MUGU STATE PARK

[Fig. 53] The Chumash Indians called this area Muwu, or "beach." Today, the area remains a popular ocean beach, but the vast majority of the park lies inland encompassing the Santa Monica Mountains. The state park extends about 7 miles inland from the beach and includes the 6,000-acre Boney Mountain State Wilderness. Within the park's total 15,000 acres, its highest point rises 3,010 feet above sea level.

Most of the visitation is focused along the beach and in Big Sycamore Canyon that runs northwest through the length of the park. From the campground near the coast there is a wide trail that leads east across the park. It ends near the Satwiwa Cultural Center, a visitor center that is part of the Santa Monica Mountains National Recreation Area and is operated by the National Park Service. Big Sycamore Canyon is home to the largest groves of sycamores (*Platanus racemosa*) protected within California State Parks. Both sycamores and coast live oaks (*Quercus agrifolia*) dominate the lower canyons, while chaparral covers the sides of the upper mountains. Blue elderberry, wild rose (*Rosa* sp.), California bay (*Umbelluria californica*), and the ubiquitous poison oak (*Toxicodendron diversilobum*) are very common. A side trail, the La Jolla Valley Loop, travels through a native tallgrass prairie, something very rare to see in California anymore.

With such a diversity of habits, from grasslands and oak woodlands, to chaparral and the bedrock outcroppings of the Boney Mountains, wildlife within the

CALIFORNIA BAY
(Umbellularia californica)
Also known as California-laurel and Oregon-myrtle, this low-growing shrub is found in southern California, where it is flattened by wind and salt spray.

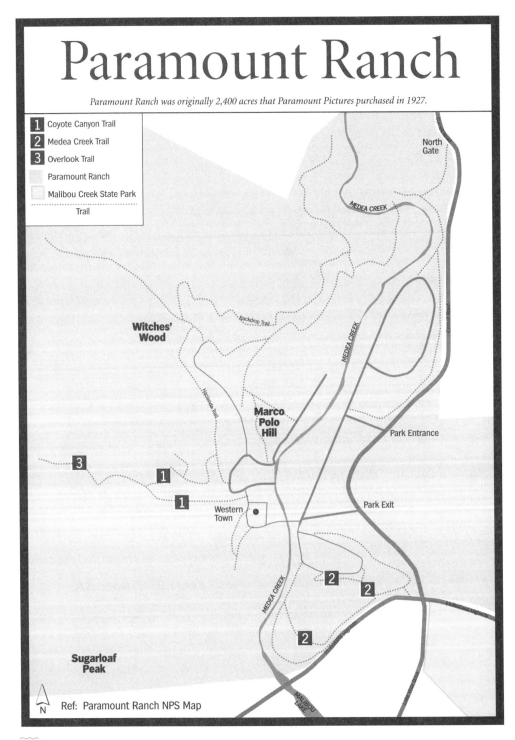

Paramount Ranch

Paramount Ranch was originally 2,400 acres that Paramount Pictures purchased in 1927.

1 Coyote Canyon Trail
2 Medea Creek Trail
3 Overlook Trail

Paramount Ranch
Malibou Creek State Park
Trail

North Gate

MEDEA CREEK

Witches' Wood

Backdrop Trail

MEDEA CREEK

Hacienda Trail

Marco Polo Hill

Park Entrance

Park Exit

Western Town

MEDEA CREEK

Sugarloaf Peak

N

Ref: Paramount Ranch NPS Map

park is equally diverse. Southern mule deer (*Odocoileus hemionus*), gray foxes (*Urocyon cinereoargenteus*), striped skunks (*Mephitis mephitis*) and spotted skunks (*Spilogale gracilis*), badgers (*Taxidea taxus*), bobcats (*Felis rufus*), and mountain lions (*Felis concolor*) live here, just a few miles from several million people. Along the coast, California sea lions (*Zalophus californicus*) and harbor seals (*Phoca vitulina*) can often be seen playing along the surf line, while gray whales (*Eschrichtius robustus*) and large schools of dolphins often pass near to shore during their migrations. The monarch butterfly (*Danaus plexippus*) is a common and welcomed winter visitor.

Directions: Highway 1 separates the beach portion of the park from the inland mountains part of the park. The main entrance and beach are 15 miles south of Oxnard.

Activities: Camping, fishing, swimming, mountain biking, hiking, horseback riding, picnicking, beachcombing.

Facilities: Campground, picnic facilities.

Dates: Open daily.

Fees: Camping and day-use fees are charged.

Closest town: Oxnard, 15 miles.

For more information: Point Mugu State Park, 9000 W. Pacific Coast Highway, Malibu, CA 90265. Phone (310) 457-8143.

TRAILS

Point Mugu State Park has about 70 miles of trails, many of which meander on relatively flat terrain, but others climb to peaks that rise to 1,600 feet above sea level. It is best to stop at the park's campground or one of the visitor centers and pick up a park trail map. Without a map, becoming confused and lost on the many different trails and loops can be relatively easy for those unfamiliar with the area.

This is a very popular hiking, equestrian, and mountain biking park. Mountain bikes are restricted to the wider, designated fire roads and are not allowed on narrow, single-track trails or within the Boney Mountain State Wilderness. Be aware that summer temperatures can climb into the 90s in these mountains and within a few minutes fog can sweep in and drop temperatures to the 60s. Be sure to carry plenty of water and dress in layers in anticipation of weather changes.

The **Big Sycamore Canyon Trail** [Fig. 54(1)] begins at Point Mugu State Park's Sycamore Canyon Campground just off Highway 1 and passes through some of California's best remaining examples of sycamores. The trail is relatively level, ending at Ranco Sierra Vista, off Potrero Road in the town of Newbury Park. Near Potrero Road the trail (a paved road at this point) passes the National Park Service's Satwiwa Cultural Center, about 8 miles from the Highway 1 starting point. There is also a walk-in campground about 5 miles up the canyon trail from Highway 1.

La Jolla Valley Loop Trail [Fig. 54(2)] begins at the Ray Miller trailhead located about 2 miles north of the Point Mugu State Park headquarters' entrance along Highway 1. While the trail passes near the top of 1,266-foot Mugu Peak, most of the

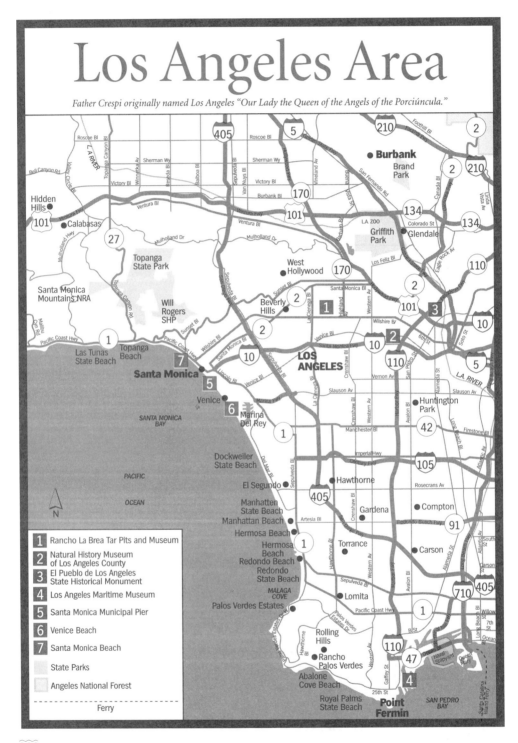

Los Angeles Area

Father Crespi originally named Los Angeles "Our Lady the Queen of the Angels of the Porciúncula."

1 Rancho La Brea Tar Pits and Museum

2 Natural History Museum of Los Angeles County

3 El Pueblo de Los Angeles State Historical Monument

4 Los Angeles Maritime Museum

5 Santa Monica Municipal Pier

6 Venice Beach

7 Santa Monica Beach

State Parks

Angeles National Forest

Ferry

approximately 5-mile loop is not uncomfortably steep. Part of the trail passes through a native tallgrass prairie. It's not too unusual to see a fox, bobcat, and coyote out hunting, even during the daytime here. The trail also leads to the La Jolla Valley walk-in campground, which is about 2 miles from the Highway 1 parking area.

Los Angeles County

▓ LEO CARRILLO STATE BEACH

[Fig. 54] This beach, like several of Southern California's beaches and parks, has taken the name of a film celebrity. Although most people today may not recognize the name Leo Carrillo, as an actor he had a very successful film, Broadway, and television career. Perhaps his best-known part was that of Pancho, the Cisco Kid's sidekick in the 1950s television series. Leo Carrillo, the great grandson of one of California's last governors during Mexico's rule, was instrumental in the acquisition of several key state parks, including the one carrying his name.

Leo Carrillo State Beach's 2,000 acres include not only more than 1 mile of beach, but also a large area of inland acres that rise into the mountains east of the Pacific Coast Highway. It also connects with over 1,000 acres of Santa Monica Mountains National Recreation Area lands, providing access to additional opportunities for hiking. All of this contiguous, diverse, and undeveloped land provides excellent wildlife habitat. Among the California bay (*Umbellularia californica*), black walnut (*Juglans californica*), and sycamore (*Platanus racemosa*) trees, scrub jays (*Aphelocoma coerulescens*), great horned owls (*Bubo virginianus*), and acorn woodpeckers (*Melanerpes formicivorus*) either rest, feed, or nest. California quail (*Lophortyx californicus*) and warblers hide in the chamise (*Adenostoma fasciculatum*), mountain mahogany (*Cercocarpus* sp.), and manzanita (*Arctostaphylos* sp.) that form the low, dense chaparral. Coyotes (*Canis latrans*), bobcats (*Felis rufus*), and gray foxes (*Urocyon cinereoargenteus*) spend their days and nights hunting small mammals, while Pacific rattlesnakes (*Crotalus viridis*), gopher snakes (*Pituophis melanoleucus catenifer*), and common king snakes (*Lampropeltis getulus californiae*) search for many of the same small mammals, birds' eggs, and other small food sources.

Along the beach there is plenty of sand for beachcombing and swimming. Arroyo Sequit, a small, seasonal creek that runs through the middle of the park, forms a low, rocky, intertidal area where it empties into the ocean, not far from the park's entrance. It's a great place to explore during low tides. Sea slugs, tube worms, turban snails, mussels, and sea urchins live on and among the rocks.

While most of the animals in the tidepools are protected, ocean fishing beyond the tidepools is allowed and is a popular activity. Below lifeguard towers numbers 2 and 3 are favorite fishing spots. Anyone with the equipment and a little luck can

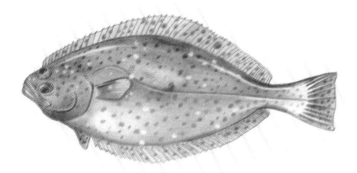

PACIFIC HALIBUT
(Hippoglossus stenolepis)
This halibut supports one of the oldest and most valuable fisheries on the Pacific coast.

catch kelp bass (*Parala-brax clathratus*), surf or shiner perch (*Cymato-gaster aggregata*), an occasional Pacific halibut (*Hippoglossus stenolepis*), and surf perch fishing from the beach. A little more exciting are the thresher sharks, shovel-nose guitar fish, and California corbina that anglers also pull from the surf.

Scuba divers also like the beach at Leo Carrillo. Easy access to nearby kelp beds, the clear water, and the bounty of underwater plant and animal life gives divers great opportunities for exploration. Just remember not to dive alone.

The park has three campgrounds, one of which is for groups only. The others will handle tents, with some sites accommodating trailers and motorhomes. There are no hookups. The campground on the ocean side of Highway 1 does not allow RVs because the access tunnel that goes beneath Highway 1 allows only vehicles under 8 feet in height.

Directions: The park is on Highway 1 (Pacific Coast Highway), at the intersection of Mulholland Highway, about 26 miles north of Santa Monica.

Activities: Swimming, diving, beachcombing, hiking, camping, fishing, picnicking.

Facilities: Campgrounds, visitor center.

Dates: Open daily.

Fees: Camping and day-use fees are charged.

Closest town: Santa Monica, 26 miles.

For more information: Malibu Sector State Parks, 39996 Pacific Coast Highway, Malibu, CA 90265. Phone (310) 457-8143 or (818) 880-0350.

TRAILS

Yellow Hill Trail: This is a fire road that is relatively easy to hike, even for younger children. It heads into the park's backcountry hills, offering panoramic views of the Pacific Ocean. On clear days Anacapa and Santa Cruz islands, two of the closest of the Channel Island group, are visible offshore. The trail starts near the park entrance and winds for about 3.5 miles one way.

Nicholas Flat Trail: This trail is steeper than the Yellow Hill Trail, rising much more quickly into the inland mountains. Besides spring wildflowers and great views, there's a pond at Nicholas Flat, about 3 miles from the trailhead near the park entrance.

🏖 LOS ANGELES COUNTY BEACHES SIDE TRIP

Santa Monica Beach, [Fig. 56(7)] operated by the city of Santa Monica, is where the majority of the Los Angeles beach-going population comes to escape during their day-long summer respites. Their cars squirt out of the Los Angeles Basin from the end of Interstate 10, then spread both north and south, their numbers diminishing with distance. Santa Monica sees perhaps a quarter of the 15 million people who visit this stretch of California's southern coast each year.

The city of Santa Monica is in the midst of change as urban renewal replaces many of the old downtown buildings with new. Along the beaches, new and expansive hotels have been built that offer great views of the ocean, quick access to the sand and surf, and plenty of isolation within their gardens and pools should escaping the beach crowds be one's preference.

Study a map of Los Angeles County, which includes all of the Santa Monica Bay shoreline, and it's evident that probably 80 percent of the thin strand of beach is held in the public domain, either by national, state, county, or city parks.

Beginning at the northern end of Los Angeles County, the long series of public beaches offers swimming (with lifeguard service during summer and busy non-summer weekends), surfing, fishing, and beachcombing. Some feature concessions that rent bikes and skates for use along their paved bike trails, and several have piers for fishing and sitting. Most offer off-street parking for a small fee, but many people prefer to park along Highway 1 and pay nothing. Busy summer days can put the free roadside parking at a premium, and crossing busy Highway 1 can be quite dangerous.

This stretch of blue water along **Malibu's** sandy beaches and rugged cliffs is where the rich and famous love to build their homes. Malibu is well known for its enclave of Hollywood actors, producers, and directors, many of whom own beachfront homes suspended on spindly piers and jutting out into the bay. Many more prefer the bluffs and rugged mountains on the east side of the Pacific Coast Highway, which runs around the edge of the bay.

Along some parts of the coast the line of businesses and homes sometimes crowds against one another forming an impenetrable wall between highway and beach. But there are plenty of public access points to the miles of beaches and rocky tidepools. The beaches here are also popular Hollywood filming locations. It's not unusual to see a film production company's gaggle of trucks, trailers, and other support vehicles parked along the highway.

Zuma County Beach (310-305-9545 or 310-305-9546), located at the north end of Los Angeles County, is a very popular summer swimming, surfing, and sunbathing destination. An "arroyo" or ravine tumbles down through Trancas Canyon from the Santa Monica Mountains to the beach here. Canyons like Trancas bring much of the sediment down to the edge of the ocean where littoral or nearshore currents transport and deposit it helping to replenish sand on the beaches during summer. During winter increased wave action tends to wash some of the sand away, reducing the width of the beaches. While the difference between summer and winter beach width often isn't dramatic, that's not always the case. A storm in the late 1950s removed 50 feet of Zuma Beach in a single 24-hour period.

There are two marine terraces near **Point Dume** and Point Dume itself rises 215 feet above the ocean. Some geologists believe that this erosion-resistant volcanic rock was once an island that was connected to the mainland by a tombolo. A tombolo formation is created when waves are diffracted around a rock or small island, which reduces their energy and causes them to drop out the sediments they are carrying. As the sediments continue piling up behind the island they ultimately create a link to other islands, or as here, with the mainland.

Santa Monica Municipal Pier [Fig. 56(5)] (310-393-7593) has a wide assortment of restaurants, snack bars, boat rentals, and an amusement park with a restored antique carousel and its hand-carved wooden horses. Constructed in 1920, the pier and surrounding beach attract thousands of people on warm sunny days, so arriving early can make finding nearby parking easier. The area was seriously considered as a major new harbor in 1889 when the U.S. Senate Committee of Commerce planned to develop a port either here or at San Pedro. San Pedro got the nod, and in 1899 construction began on the San Pedro Breakwater, which marked the beginning of the Los Angeles/Long Beach Harbor Complex. The Santa Monica pier is located at the foot of Colorado Avenue.

Venice Beach (310-581-1690) is probably best known for its oceanfront walkway where on any given summer day hundreds of uninhibited youth show their physical wares, most often just barely tucked inside scanty bathing suits, as they skate, bike, jog, lift weights, and walk along its length. There are numerous tourist shops, specialty boutiques, and artists' booths along the street. The town of Venice was founded in 1905 and originally had several miles of interconnected canals. Some of the canals have been lost to development, but a few remain. This is another good place to find movie crews working.

Directions: The Los Angeles County beaches are located along Highway 1 (Pacific Coast Highway).

Activities: Swimming, sunbathing, surfing, fishing, beachcombing, volleyball, biking, skating.

Facilities: Some have concessions with bike, boat, and skate rentals, showers, restrooms, fire rings, volleyball courts, piers.

Dates: Open daily.

Fees: Most of the beaches have off-street parking with fees charged. Limited free parking is generally available along Highway 1.

Closest town: Malibu, Santa Monica, El Segundo, Redondo Beach, San Pedro.

For more information: Los Angeles County Division of Beaches and Harbors, Visitors Information Center, 13837 Fiji Way, Marina del Rey, CA 90292. Phone (310) 305-9545 or (310) 305-9546.

MALIBU AND SANTA MONICA DINING

Beau Rivage. 26025 Pacific Coast Highway, Malibu. Located in trendy Malibu, Beau Rivage emphasizes Italian and French cuisine in a casual dress atmosphere. It serves cocktails and entertainment is offered. This is a dinner-only restaurant, except for its Sunday brunch. Reservations are required. *Moderate to expensive. Phone (310) 456-5733.*

Geoffrey's. 27400 Pacific Coast Highway, Malibu. When weather permits, which is most of the time, patio dining overlooking the Pacific is offered. This favorite restaurant features California and Continental cuisine, occasionally with an Italian flair. They serve lunch and dinner in a casual dress setting. Reservations are suggested. *Moderate to expensive. Phone (310) 457-1519.*

Duke's Malibu. 21150 Pacific Coast Highway, Malibu. The oceanfront restaurant serves seafood, prime rib, and steaks, but specializes in Hawaiian cuisine. Enjoy the view while sipping wine or cocktails. Casual dress and reservations are suggested. *Moderate to expensive. Phone (310) 317-0777.*

Chinois On Main. 2709 Main Street, Santa Monica. Serves wonderfully prepared Chinese and American cuisine. There's a cocktail lounge. Dress casual and reservations are required. *Expensive. Phone (310) 392-9025.*

Lavande. 1700 Ocean Avenue, Santa Monica. Located in Loews Santa Monica Beach Hotel, the restaurant offers excellent French cuisine along with beautiful ocean views. Casual dress with reservations suggested. *Expensive. Phone (310) 576-3180.*

MALIBU AND SANTA MONICA LODGING

Malibu Beach Inn. 22878 Pacific Coast Highway, Malibu. The inn is located near the Malibu Pier and several miles of beautiful beaches popular with surfers, sunbathers, and the movie industry. There are fireplaces in most of the rooms and balconies with ocean views. Be sure to check about required advance cancellation policies. *Expensive. Phone (310) 456-6444.*

Malibu Country Inn. 6506 Westward Beach Road, Malibu. The motor inn is located at the corner of Highway 1, so it is an easy walk to the beach. For those not inclined to brave the Pacific Ocean waters, there are two pools, and to warm up, some of the rooms have fireplaces. *Expensive. Phone (310) 457-9622.*

Bayside Hotel. 2001 Oceanside Avenue, Santa Monica. The location is great with rooms overlooking the nearby sandy beach. Pacific Park and Third Street Promenade are within easy walking distance. *Moderate to expensive. Phone (310) 396-6000 or (800) 525-4447.*

DoubleTree Guest Suites. 1707 4th Street, Santa Monica. Located in downtown

Santa Monica just minutes from the Pacific Coast Highway and beaches. Restaurants and shopping are within easy walking distance. The hotel is designed around the business person's needs, with a business center, in-room faxes, two-line phones with data ports, and work stations. *Expensive. Phone (800) 222-TREE or (310) 395-3332.*

Best Western Ocean View Hotel. 1447 Ocean View, Santa Monica. There are ocean views from many of its rooms and the beach and restaurants are within easy walking distance. *Moderate to expensive. Phone (310) 458-4888.*

Channel Road Inn Bed & Breakfast. 219 West Channel Road, Santa Monica. This 1910 colonial revival house has just 14 rooms, some with ocean views. The three-story inn is just a block from the beach. *Expensive. Phone (310) 459-1920.*

Shangri-La Hotel. 1301 Ocean Avenue, Santa Monica. The 1939 art deco design hotel offers views of the ocean and directly fronts Palisades Park, Santa Monica Beach, and the Pacific Ocean. Serves complimentary continental breakfast and afternoon tea. *Expensive. Phone (310) 394-2791.*

Loews Santa Monica Beach Hotel. 1700 Ocean Avenue, Santa Monica. This is a large eight-story, beachfront hotel with accommodations ranging from single rooms to several thousand dollars per night suites. It's a short walk to the Santa Monica Pier. *Expensive. Phone (310) 458-6700.*

Travelodge Santa Monica. 3102 Pico Boulevard, Santa Monica. A less expensive alternative to the beachfront hotels is the Travelodge, about four blocks from the beach. It's quite comfortable and some of the rooms have kitchens. *Moderate. Phone (800) 231-7679 or (310) 450-5766.*

MALIBU LAGOON STATE BEACH

This is a relatively small park covering only 22 acres, but most of the land is beach property. The most notable exception is where Malibu Creek passes into the park and opens into a large lagoon before finally emptying into the Pacific Ocean. The park's **Surfrider Beach** is very popular with surfers and sunbathers.

Frederick Rindge, the recipient of a $2 million inheritance, originally acquired the park's land in 1892. He purchased the 13,000-acre Rancho Malibu from Henry Keller and moved west from his Cambridge, Massachusetts home. He planned to create a farm or ranch in what he described as the "American Riviera." Initially, Rindge constructed a home in Malibu Canyon, but fire destroyed it in 1903. The following year, the ever-expanding Southern Pacific Railroad was attempting to extend its transportation empire by building track along the coast from Santa Barbara through the still roadless Malibu coast. To keep Southern Pacific out, Rindge built his own Hueneme, Malibu, and Port Los Angeles Railroad, designed to bring in supplies and to ship out his cowhides and grain.

When Frederick Rindge died in 1905, his wife Rhoda May continued working the ranch. She also continued her husband's opposition to allowing other avenues of public transportation to intrude on their private domain. But, the county and state acquired a right-of-way and finally constructed a coastal highway in 1928.

In 1915 Rhoda Agatha Rindge, daughter of Frederick and Rhoda May married the ranch's superintendent Merritt Adamson. Besides being an attorney, Adamson was also an expert in farming; his family owned a sheep farm in Arizona. He began the *Adohr* (Rhoda spelled backwards) *Stock Farms*, one of the world's largest producing dairies. Merritt Adamson died in 1949.

What sets Malibu Creek State Beach apart from the many other similar Southern California beaches is the **Adamson House**. Twenty years before his death, Merritt Adamson and his wife hired well-known architect Stiles Clements to design a new house. It had a spectacular location on a low hill above the beach, and Clements designed the two-story home to include large amounts of a special tile being manufactured about 0.5 mile down the coast from the nearby Malibu Pier.

Malibu Tile is considered historically significant because of the secret formulas that were incorporated into the company's hundreds of design motifs that included Spanish, Mayan, Persian, neo-classical, and modern. The Malibu Tile plant went out of business in 1932, but not before seeing its tiles incorporated into numerous private residences in Los Angeles, the Los Angeles City Hall, the Hollywood Roosevelt Hotel, and the Mayan Theatre, among many others.

Good soil from nearby mountain canyons was trucked in and used to cover the sand surrounding the house. Gardeners then planted mature olive trees, roses, Chinese magnolias, and many other shrubs, trees, and flowers around the grounds in the new soil that was from 5 to 10 feet deep.

The home's original seven-car garage has been transformed into a museum that features exhibits on the original Native Americans who inhabited this part of California. The museum is also a good place to see rare artifacts, photographs, and documents relating to the early history of Malibu, including the Malibu Railroad, the Malibu movie colony, and the Malibu Dam.

Directions: Malibu Lagoon State Beach is located about 1 mile east of Malibu on the south side of Highway 1 (Pacific Coast Highway).

Activities: Swimming, surfing, picnicking, fishing, beachcombing, house tours.

Facilities: Museum, gift shop, picnic area. There is no parking on the Adamson House grounds. Parking is available along Highway 1 or in the adjacent county lot, which does charge a fee.

Dates: Beach open daily. The Adamson House is open for tours, but tour times vary, so call in advance. Museum open daily, except major holidays.

Fees: There are no fees for using the beach unless you park in one of the county pay lots. There is a small tour fee for the Adamson House.

Closest town: Malibu, 1 mile.

For more information: Malibu Lagoon State Beach, 23200 Pacific Coast Highway, Malibu, CA 90265. For Adamson House tour information, phone (310) 456-8432 or (310) 456-1770. For lagoon nature tour information, phone (818) 880-0363.

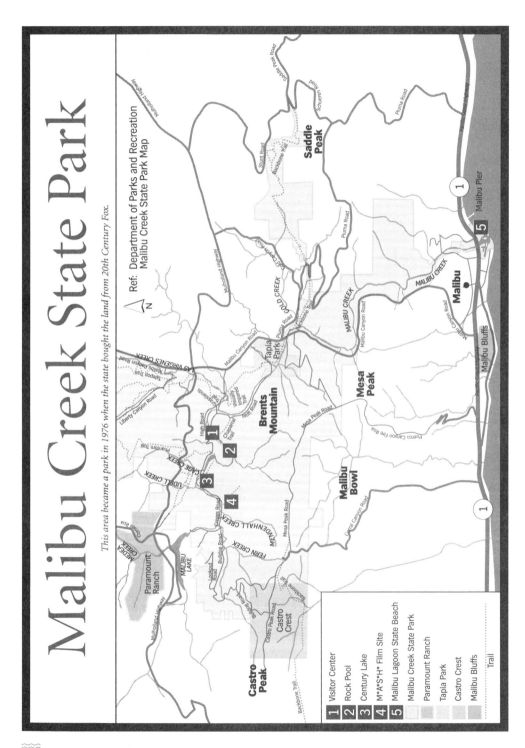

Malibu Creek State Park

This area became a park in 1976 when the state bought the land from 20th Century Fox.

Ref: Department of Parks and Recreation
Malibu Creek State Park Map

N

1. Visitor Center
2. Rock Pool
3. Century Lake
4. M*A*S*H* Film Site
5. Malibu Lagoon State Beach
   Malibu Creek State Park
   Paramount Ranch
   Tapia Park
   Castro Crest
   Malibu Bluffs
   Trail

MALIBU CREEK STATE PARK

[Fig. 57] This park is for walkers, mountain bicyclists, and horseback riders. The trails are relatively level and surprises await you around every corner. There is a small campground not far from the entrance road parking lot, but nearly everything else, from the visitor center and creek, to Century Lake and the old *M*A*S*H** filming site, takes walking or riding to reach.

Local businessmen acquired much of the original property during the early 1900s and formed the Crags Country Club. After the club folded in 1936, 20th Century Fox entered the picture, filming *How Green Was My Valley* in 1941. The company purchased the property in 1946 and made hundreds of movies in the surrounding hills, including such diverse films as *M*A*S*H** and *Planet of the Apes*.

The area became a park in 1976 following the state's purchase of the studio's property, along with the adjacent Hope and Reagan ranches. Today, there are 8,200 acres to explore. Within the park lie three natural preserves, which protect a rare and beautiful stand of valley oaks (*Quercus lobata*), a nesting area for golden eagles (*Aquila chrysaetos*), and beautiful volcanic formations, along with rare plants. Riparian plant communities abound within the park as sycamore (*Platanus racemosa*), cottonwood, willow (*Salix* sp.), and bay trees (*Umbellularia californica*) grow in profusion along Malibu Creek and some of the smaller feeder streams. California sagebrush, black sage (*Salvia mellifera*), purple sage (*Salvia leucophylla*), and wild buckwheat (*Eriogonum* sp.) cover many of the drier hillsides.

With such a variety of plant communities comes an equally wide range of wildlife. Red-tailed hawks (*Buteo jamaicensis*) and golden eagles are relatively common in the skies, with the bizarre-looking regal horned lizard occasionally seen with more common lizards sunning themselves on the rocks. Buffleheads and mallards are frequent visitors along the creek, with rattlesnakes, gopher snakes, king snakes, bobcats, coyotes, and mule deer occasionally seen throughout the park.

Directions: From US 101 (Ventura Freeway) in Calabasas, take the Las Virgenes Road Exit and drive west for about 3 miles to the park entrance.

Activities: Hiking, camping, mountain biking, horseback riding, fishing, picnicking.

Facilities: Campground, picnic area, visitor center with small gift shop.

Dates: Open daily.

Fees: There are day-use and camping fees.

Closest town: Calabasas, 3 miles.

For more information: Malibu Sector State Parks, 1925 Las Virgenes Road, Calabasas, CA 91302. Phone (818) 880-0350.

TRAILS

The **visitor center** is reached by way of a trail that begins at the Malibu Creek State Park parking lot. The trail then follows a service road for about 1 mile (a little less if the Malibu Creek ford can be crossed), where it crosses a bridge that leads to the visitor center, an old country club home.

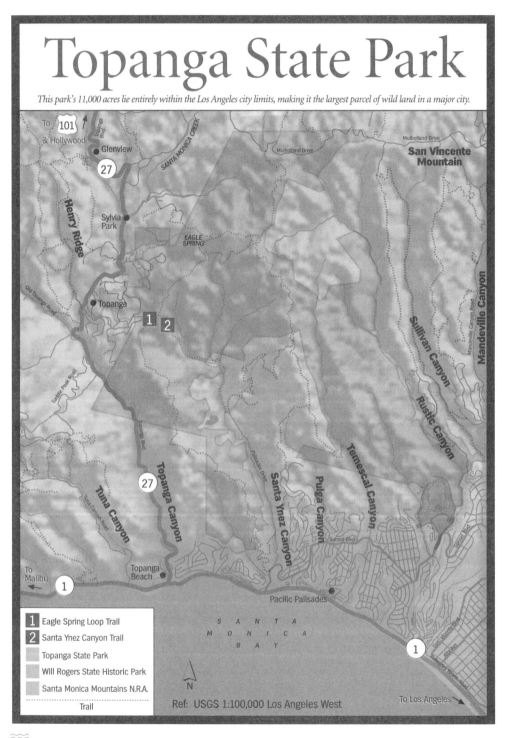

Topanga State Park

This park's 11,000 acres lie entirely within the Los Angeles city limits, making it the largest parcel of wild land in a major city.

To 101 & Hollywood

Topanga Blvd

Glenview

27

SANTA MONICA CREEK

Mulholland Drive

Mulholland Drive

San Vincente Mountain

Henry Ridge

Sylvia Park

EAGLE SPRING

Old Topanga Road

Topanga

1 2

Saddle Peak Road

Topanga Blvd

Mandeville Canyon Road

Mandeville Canyon

Sullivan Canyon

Rustic Canyon

27

Topanga Canyon

Tuna Canyon

Tuna Canyon Road

Palisades Drive

Santa Ynez Canyon

Pulga Canyon

Temescal Canyon

Sunset Blvd

Sunset Blvd

To Malibu

1

Topanga Beach

Pacific Palisades

1

San Vicente Blvd

Alta Ave

Palisades Beach Road

1 Eagle Spring Loop Trail

2 Santa Ynez Canyon Trail

Topanga State Park

Will Rogers State Historic Park

Santa Monica Mountains N.R.A.

Trail

S A N T A
M O N I C A
B A Y

N

To Los Angeles

Ref: USGS 1:100,000 Los Angeles West

Hollywood on Location

During the early twentieth century, Southern California, which typically experiences nine months or more of dry weather, quickly became the fledgling film industry's favorite place to make movies. Legendary filmmakers Cecil B. Demille, Samuel Goldwyn, and Jesse Lasky Sr. made Hollywood's first film, *The Squaw Man*, in 1912-14. They shot their movie in a makeshift studio built inside a barn at the corner of Selma Avenue and Vine Street. The historic building was subsequently moved to the 2100 block of Highland Avenue and now serves as the Hollywood Studio Museum.

While Universal Studios is a great place to see how movies are made and some of the sets that have been used, many more movies, or at least parts of them, are shot on location, rather than inside soundstages. It's not at all unusual to run across movie sets while driving nearly anywhere in the greater Los Angeles area. Beaches, such as Leo Carrillo, Malibu, and Dan Blocker, are always popular shooting locations. Movies ranging from *Planet of the Apes* to *M*A*S*H** have been filmed in Malibu Creek State Park, which sometimes hosts dozens of film companies each year.

One thing that first-time observers quickly discover about filming a movie is that there is much more downtime, as lights, reflectors, and cameras are moved and reset, than there is action. But it's still fun to see the real thing.

The **Rock Pool** [Fig. 57(2)] is just a couple of hundred yards from the visitor center [Fig. 57(1)]. Cross back over the bridge and turn left down a short trail that passes through a small oak grove to the wide pool in Malibu Creek. During late summer there may not be much of the pool remaining; spring and winter are the best times to visit. There are some beautiful rock formations here. Although the pool looks inviting, especially on a hot summer day, diving or jumping into the water is prohibited.

The 20-acre **Century Lake** [Fig. 57(3)] lies about 0.5 mile north of the visitor center. The lake, formed behind a dam built in 1901, is a popular fishing spot, although, after a century of siltation, it's mostly a tule- and willow-filled marsh now.

The **M*A*S*H* Film Site** [Fig. 57(4)] is one of the more popular hiking and biking destinations in the park. There are a couple of the old military vehicles used in the television series left on the site. It's located about 0.75 mile from Century Lake.

TOPANGA STATE PARK

[Fig. 58] In the Santa Monica Mountains surprises await anyone willing to spend a little time looking. Topanga State Park is one of those surprises. The park's 11,000 acres lie entirely within the Los Angeles city limits and it is therefore considered the largest parcel of wild land located in a major city. Within the park's variety of habitats, ranging from oak woodlands to chaparral-covered mountains, its streams and ponds serve as water sources for the abundance of wildlife that lives here.

Like much of the Santa Monica Mountains, the steep mountains and weather-worn rock formations found in the park have evolved over the past 18 million years. The area began as mostly submerged sedimentary rocks with areas of intrusive volcanic basalt. About 3 million years ago the Santa Monica Mountains began to rise, and as they did, streams carved narrow canyons through the soft sandstone and shale. More earthquakes and ongoing upward thrusting continued the geologic molding process, and with two fault lines within the park, the shaping continues even today.

The first European to see these mountains was Juan Rodriguez Cabrillo who sailed along the California coast in 1542. But humans had occupied this area for at least 7,000 years before he passed by. The Gabrieleno Indians lived in the mountains here and also the San Fernando Valley to the east. The Chumash lived along the coast, just a few miles away. It appears that for the most part they lived peacefully along an indistinguishable boundary. Topanga, or in early documents, "Topango," is a Gabrieleno word that is believed to mean something similar to "the place where the mountains meet the sea." It is the most westerly known landmark possessing a Gabrieleno name. Once the Spanish arrived in the late eighteenth century, the lives of the Indians changed quickly. Most either died of European diseases or were absorbed into the mission system as workers. Afterward much of the land was given as grants. Topanga State Park is part of what was once *Rancho San Vicente y Santa Monica*.

Trippet Ranch, [Fig. 53] named after federal court judge Oscar Trippet who owned a 60-acre ranch during Woodrow Wilson's presidency, is a good place to start a visit to the park. When spring wildflowers begin to bloom, the grasslands, intermittent streams, and scattered oaks around the ranch house support some the best viewing opportunities. Blue-eyed grass (*Sisyrinchium bellum*), goldenstars (*Bloomeria humilis*), wild onion (*Allium* sp.), and mariposa lilies (*Calochortus* sp.) paint patches of bright colors in the grasses. The park maintains a wildflower hotline (818-768-3533), which provides weekly updates about wildflower blooms throughout much of Southern California's mountains and deserts. In the cooler canyons where streams tend to run throughout the year, or at least much longer than they do on the open hillsides, coast live oak, willows, and western sycamores provide a canopy over maidenhair ferns and miner's lettuce.

Wildlife is abundant throughout the park with each species finding its own special niche and a few, such as bobcats, mule deer, and mountain lions, able to range over dozens of miles of mountains and valleys. Wrentits (*Chamaea fasciata*), scrub jays (*Aphelocoma coerulescens*), and California thrashers (*Toxostoma redivivum*) create their own cacophony in the trees and bushes. Red-tailed hawks and golden eagles fly overhead searching for a good meal of ground squirrel (*Spermophilus beecheyi*) or cottontail rabbit.

There is only a trail camp available in the park. It is located about 1 mile from Trippet Ranch. It's available for hikers, mountain bikers, and equestrians.

Directions: From US 101 east of Calabasas, take the Topanga Boulevard Exit and drive south for 7 miles, over the pass and into the community of Topanga. Continue another 3 miles and turn left on Entrada Road. From Highway 1 (Pacific Coast Highway), 7 miles south of Malibu turn north onto Topanga Boulevard and drive about 3 miles. Turn right on Entrada Road. Once on Entrada Road it's about 1 mile to the parking lot at Trippet Ranch.

Activities: Hiking, camping, picnicking, mountain biking, horseback riding.

Facilities: Campgrounds, picnic sites.

Dates: The park is open daily.

Fees: There are camping and day-use fees.

Closest town: Santa Monica, 11 miles.

For more information: Topanga State Park, 20825 Entrada Road, Topanga, CA 90290. Phone (310) 455-2465 or (310) 454-8212 or (818) 880-0350.

TRAILS

Topanga State Park has 36 miles of trails. While all of the trails are open to hikers, only the fire roads are open for mountain bikes. Trippet Ranch is a good place to park and access several trailheads.

Eagle Spring Loop Trail can be reached from Trippet Ranch by first hiking about 2 miles to Eagle Junction. From Eagle Junction there is a 2.6-mile loop that passes by Eagle Rock, a 1,957-foot promontory made up of ancient volcanic rock. There are spectacular views from the boulder outcroppings.

Santa Ynez Canyon Trail begins from Trippet Ranch as a 1.5 mile hike that descends into the canyon. There is wonderful weather-formed sandstone along the way where eroded pockets collect enough moisture that small plants grow, creating cliff gardens. At a fork in the trail near the bottom of the canyon head left (north) for 0.8 mile to where a beautiful waterfall cascades down over the rock formations. Continue heading south at the trail fork for about 0.5 mile to reach the park boundary at Vereda Montura (paved road) that leads into the community of Palisades Highlands.

WILL ROGERS STATE HISTORIC PARK

[Fig. 58] Will Rogers, best known for his "cracker barrel" humor, made his Hollywood debut in 1919. He saw only moderate success in silent films under Samuel Goldwyn until the "talkies" made him a star. Most often seen spinning his rope, he added a trademark drawl to make his point, a point which often was aimed directly at lethargic, uncaring, and self-important politicians.

At the top of his show business career in 1935 Rogers died tragically in an Alaska plane crash, along with his good friend, Wiley Post. He had developed not only fame as a film star but also as a radio commentator and newspaper columnist. Some of his best known comments said a lot about the man: "I never met a man I didn't like," and "You must judge a man's greatness by how much he will be missed."

Several years before his death, Rogers moved his wife Betty and their three children to a 183-acre ranch in Pacific Palisades. His wife continued living in the 31-room ranch house until her death in 1944. Following her death the ranch became a state park. Today, the park boasts a polo field where Hollywood stars such as Sylvester

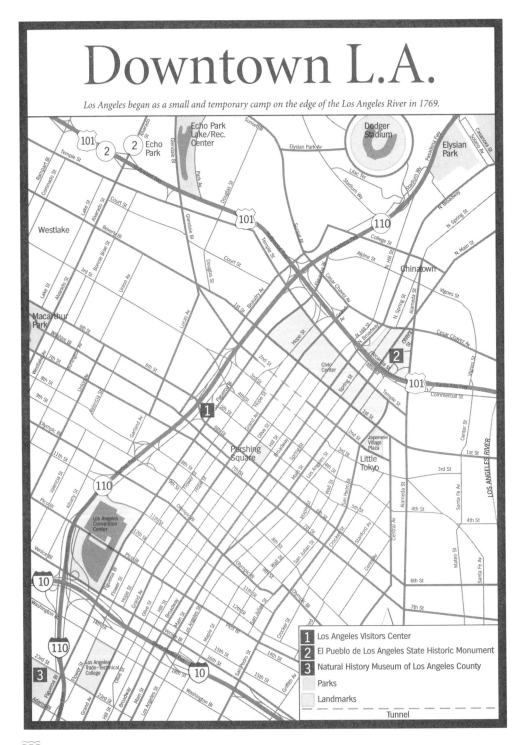

Downtown L.A.

Los Angeles began as a small and temporary camp on the edge of the Los Angeles River in 1769.

1 Los Angeles Visitors Center

2 El Pueblo de Los Angeles State Historic Monument

3 Natural History Museum of Los Angeles County

Parks

Landmarks

Tunnel

Stallone occasionally play on weekends. There are also several miles of trails that loop through the hills behind the ranch house or connect with longer trails into the Santa Monica Mountains National Recreation Area

Directions: From Highway 1 (Pacific Coast Highway) in Santa Monica, turn east onto Sunset Boulevard. Drive 4.5 miles and turn left onto Will Rogers State Park Road. The entrance kiosk is just ahead.

Activities: Hiking, horseback riding, historic house tours, picnicking.

Facilities: Visitor center, polo field, equestrian stables, picnic area.

Fees: There is a day-use fee.

Closest town: Pacific Palisades.

For more information: Will Rogers State Historic Park, 1501 Will Rogers State Park Road, Pacific Palisades, CA 90272. Phone (310) 454-8212.

Los Angeles

The City of the Angels began as a small and temporary camp on the edge of the Los Angeles River in 1769. Traveling with Spanish explorer Gaspar de Portolá, Father Crespi named the campsite *Nuestra Señora la Reina de los Angeles de la Porciúncula,* "Our Lady the Queen of the Angels of the Porciúncula." *Porciúncula* referred to a parcel of land near a church in Assisi, Italy where St. Francis received a revelation in 1206. In Los Angeles it was also the site of an Indian village.

During their exploration, Portolá's party passed the La Brea tar pits and camped near today's La Cienega Boulevard, between Gregory Way and Olympic Boulevard in Beverly Hills. Over the next several months they visited numerous other sites in and around present-day Los Angeles, including the Santa Monica Mountains and the San Fernando Valley. The Spanish, and later the successor Mexican government, expanded their settlements into the area, dividing the land into great ranchos and giving it as land grants to various deserving individuals. *Rancho Los Alamitos* later became the city of Long Beach, *Rancho Santa Gertrudes* is now Downey, *Rancho El Encino* is Encino, *Rancho El Escopión* is Calabasas, and *Rancho Rincón de San Pasqual* now includes Pasadena and Altadena. The only remnants of the original ranchos are a few adobe buildings, for the most part maintained in state and local parks.

Directions: The city of Los Angeles and its outlying communities can be reached via several highways including Interstate 5, Interstate 10, Interstate 110, and US 101.

For more information: Downtown Los Angeles Visitor Information Center, 685 Figueroa Street (between Wilshire Boulevard. and 7th Street), Los Angeles, CA 90017. Phone (213) 689-8822.

🔲 EL PUEBLO DE LOS ANGELES STATE HISTORICAL MONUMENT
[Fig. 59(2)] The color, sounds, and smells are what make this historic center of Los

Driving in Los Angeles

For the uninitiated, driving the streets and freeways of Los Angeles can seem like a nightmare. With millions of cars vying for space on the freeways and surface streets, timing is often critical. Try to avoid the morning and evening commute times, which can typically last for several hours. Often you can reach your destination much more quickly on surface streets rather than on the freeways. Find a radio station and listen for traffic updates. Always plan ahead.

Navigating across the greater Los Angeles area is not difficult if you remember a few things. Understand the freeway system. While all the major highways and freeways have numerical designations, the common names they have been given locally are often more prominent on the overhead directional signs. These names can change, depending on where in the greater Los Angeles area you may be traveling. So be aware of both names and numbers when planning your trips.

Freeways with odd number designators (I-5, US 101, etc.) run generally north-south. Those with even numbers (I-10, I-210, etc.) travel east-west. Know which way you're heading and be aware of the direction of major cities. Periodically signs will provide the freeway's name, number, and a distant city (Sacramento or San Diego for example) as an indicator of what direction you are, or will be, heading.

Here is a list of the major freeways and highways in the Los Angeles area:

I-5	Golden State and Santa Ana Freeway
I-10	Santa Monica and San Bernardino Freeway
Highway 60	Pomona Freeway
Highway 91	Artesia and Redondo Freeway
US 101	Hollywood Freeway
I-105	Century Freeway
I-110	Harbor and Pasadena Freeway
Highway 134	Ventura Freeway
I-210	Foothill Freeway
I-405	San Diego Freeway
I-605	San Gabriel River Freeway
I-710	Long Beach Freeway

Angeles a special place to spend an afternoon. During festivals, colorfully dressed dancers whirl to the sound of Mexican music, and excellent, flavorful food is always in abundance. The hustle and bustle of shoppers and shopkeepers as they deal for Mexican crafts and clothes adds to the wonderful feeling of being in Old Mexican California.

The Spanish officially founded *El Pueblo de Nuestra Señora la Reina de los Angeles*, the pueblo or town's full name, on September 4, 1781, making it the third of their Alta or upper California settlements. The current location of the historic pueblo is actually the last of three sites the Spanish attempted to build on. The first two were washed away when nearby dry streambeds swelled suddenly with seasonal rains.

Around the historic plaza that is here today, the **Church of Nuestra Señora la Reina de los Angeles**, which was completed and dedicated in 1822, remains the oldest building. It is located in the plaza at 535 North Main Street. Just south of the church is Los Angeles's first cemetery. The oldest house in Los Angeles is also here in the park. It was originally completed in about 1818 with additions in later years, and then removal of some portions, probably before 1920. Commodore Robert Stockton made his headquarters in this adobe for several days in 1847, following the U.S. takeover of California from Mexico.

Olivera Street is the central focus of the park. Many shops and restaurants have been built in and around the old adobes. There's also a small museum with exhibits that include the story of water in the Los Angeles area, an often hotly contested issue historically and even today. The park is on the National Register of Historic Places, and 16 of its 27 historic buildings are listed separately.

Directions: The park is bounded by the US 101 freeway on the south, Alameda Street on the east, Spring Street on the west, and Macy Street on the north. Main Street runs through the middle of the historic monument.

Activities: Shopping, dining, special cultural events.

Facilities: Shops, booths, restaurants, museum, historic buildings.

Dates: Most facilities are open daily, some closed Thanksgiving and Christmas.

Fees: Free self-guided walking tours.

For more information: El Pueblo de Los Angeles State Historical Monument, (Los Angeles City Parks), 125 Paseo de la Plaza, Suite 400, Los Angeles, CA 90012. Phone (213) 628-1274.

RANCHO LA BREA TAR PITS AND MUSEUM

[Fig. 56(1)] For a look at the plant and animals that inhabited this portion of California from 40,000 to about 10,000 years ago, the tar pits, located in what is now downtown Los Angeles, provide the perfect window. Long-extinct dire wolves and the more famous saber-toothed cats are the most common animal bones found in the ancient tar. Less common, yet equally extinct, are native horses, camels, mammoths, and the long-horned bison.

As it has for thousands of years, crude oil oozes to the surface in this part of southern California, and as the lighter oil evaporates, the remaining sticky asphalt accumulates in pools. Smaller mammals and birds—rabbits, mice, ducks, and hawks—still step or fly into the tar and become stuck. But prior to the development of the surrounding city, local carnivores descended on the free meals. Occasionally, bigger animals also became stuck and ultimately died, so many that more than 1 million individual specimens, representing 59 mammals species and 135 species of birds, have been recovered from the tar pits. Only one human skeleton has ever been found in the pits, a 9,000-year-old Indian woman.

The tar served many useful purposes for the area's primitive peoples. The ancient Chumash used it to waterproof their canoes and to seal baskets. The early Spanish smeared tar on the roofs of their houses to keep out the seasonal rains.

Located in a park that is open and free to the public, the tar pits are fenced for safety reasons. There are 23 acres of observation pits, with replicas of some of the mammals that once roamed this area. The George C. Page Museum of La Brea Discoveries is located within the park's boundaries and displays hundreds of examples of the animals recovered from their sticky burial grounds. The Page Museum is part of the Natural History Museum of Los Angeles County. The museum offers numerous exhibits, including hundreds of recovered dire wolf skulls mounted inside a dramatically lighted wall display. Visitors can also watch scientists working inside the "fishbowl" as they clean, identify, and label newly recovered animal bones.

Directions: From Interstate 10 (Santa Monica Freeway) take the La Brea Avenue Exit and drive north on La Brea Avenue and turn right (west) on Wilshire Boulevard. The park is about nine blocks down, on the right. There is street parking and a pay parking lot behind the museum. If you use the parking lot, show the ticket when paying the museum admission fee for a discount.

Activities: Tours.

Facilities: Exhibits, gift shop.

Fees: There is an entry fee.

Dates: Pit 91 is open to the public daily. The museum is open daily, but call to verify hours on holidays such as Thanksgiving, Christmas, and New Year's Day.

For more information: The Page Museum at the La Brea Tar Pits, 5801 Wilshire Boulevard, Los Angeles, CA 90036. Phone (323) 936-2230.

NATURAL HISTORY MUSEUM OF LOS ANGELES COUNTY

[Fig. 59(3)] This is a wonderful museum filled with many truly rare treasures. It is also the third largest natural science and cultural history museum in the United States, holding more than 35 million artifacts and specimens. Walking inside can take your breath away as the sculptured skeletons of a *Triceratops* and a *Tyrannosaurus rex* face each other in battle in the museum's main foyer.

One of the rarest specimens to be seen anywhere is Megamouth (*Megachasma pelagios*), a strange-looking and extremely rare shark with a huge bathtub-shaped mouth. Preserved in a large case, the shark is nearly 15 feet long and weighs 1,550 pounds. Megamouth was first discovered in 1976 off the coast of Hawaii, and only the second specimen ever to be caught (off Catalina Island), is now displayed here.

It can take several hours to see everything in the museum's several floors of exhibits. On the main floor in several galleries there are life-zone dioramas filled with appropriate mammals, from grizzlies and wolves to bison and deer. For anyone interested in geology, or simply fascinated by rare and valuable gems, the mineral collection is superb. In addition to samples of hundreds of minerals and precious and

Palos Verdes Peninsula Marine Terraces

Although most people admire the incredible cliff-edge views of the ocean to the west, instead, turn around and study the land that rises behind you. It's very easy to identify the prominent ancient marine terraces as they rise steeply, then level off on their way up to the top of the hill. Here, 10 million years of geologic and ocean actions have joined forces, as they have along all of California's 1,100-mile coast, to create a series of ancient marine terraces. The wider, more prominent terraces are where the roads that circle the peninsula have been constructed.

There are several observation points and coves along Paseo del Mar, the road that circles around the peninsula. Bluff Cove and Lunada Bay can be reached by way of steep trails or stairways. Near the northern end of Paseo del Mar the pavement becomes very rough. Here is where the continually moving earth is pushing the roadway on its inevitable journey to the sea.

semiprecious gems, there are exhibits that explain the geologic forces that create these wonders of nature. For example, it takes 50 kilobars of pressure, the equivalent of 150 adult elephants all standing on 1 square inch, to produce a diamond. And while all other gems are formed within 6 miles of the earth's surface, diamonds are formed from 90 to 200 miles down.

For anyone hiking Southern California's chaparral hillsides, the chaparral fire cycle exhibit demonstrates how these fire-adapted plants continue to survive. The exhibit features the stages of chaparral regrowth: first mature stands, then burned hillsides, followed by revegetation by annuals within six months, and finally the regrowth and spread of the perennial shrubs after about three years.

A rather interesting area is the hall of birds. It includes not only specimens in glass cases and in natural habitat exhibits, but also a few strange mechanical birds that move. There's a rain forest where visitors can view the plants and animals at ground level, and a walkway that leads to the canopy of the same jungle where completely different animals live.

There is much more to see here, from models of extinct dinosaurs to marine habitats featuring common, endangered, and extinct mollusks. There are also exhibits on historic Americana.

Directions: The museum is located in central Los Angeles, across the street from the University of Southern California, at 900 Exposition Boulevard.

Activities: Self-guided and docent tours, lectures.

Facilities: Gift shop, restaurant.

Dates: The museum is open daily, but call to verify hours on holidays such as Thanksgiving, Christmas, and New Year's Day.

Fees: There is an entry fee.

For more information: Natural History Museum of Los Angeles, 900 Exposition Boulevard, Los Angeles, CA 90007. Phone (213) 763-DINO.

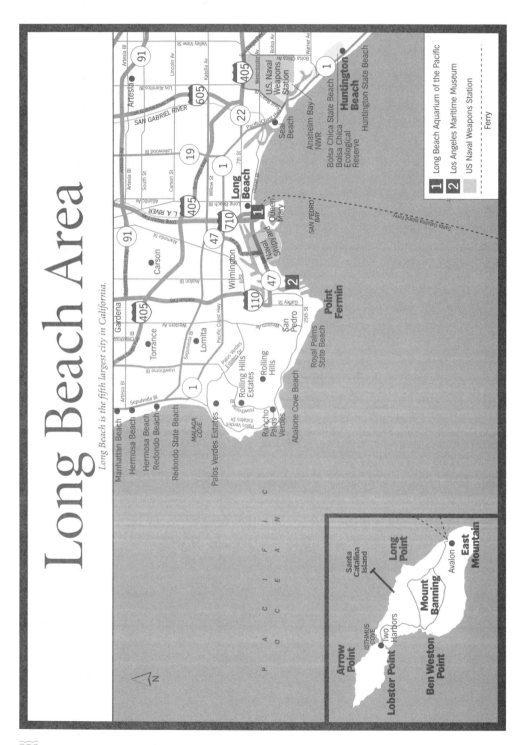

Long Beach Area

Long Beach is the fifth largest city in California.

1 Long Beach Aquarium of the Pacific
2 Los Angeles Maritime Museum
US Naval Weapons Station
Ferry

🌊 LOS ANGELES MARITIME MUSEUM

[Fig. 60(2)] This is truly a maritime historian's paradise with some of the best exhibits and artifact collections of any maritime museum in the country. Visitors have the opportunity not only to see the large and beautiful models of historic ships, something found in nearly all maritime museums, but also to stand on the deck of the real thing.

The tug *Angels Gate* was originally built in Alabama for the military in 1944 as the ST (small tug) *695*. It found its way to the Los Angeles Port of Embarkation where it continued its duties until after World War II. The military transferred title to the Los Angeles Harbor Department in 1947, where it continued to work until 1992 when it was given to the Los Angeles Maritime Museum. What is remarkable is that after more than a half-century of use most of the original equipment is still onboard the old tug.

Inside the museum is the 22-foot-long, movie studio-built SS *Poseidon* constructed in great detail for the 1972 film *The Poseidon Adventure*. Another model, the HMAV *Bounty*, is a replica of the ship used in the Clark Gable and Charles Laughton movie *Mutiny on the Bounty*, which was filmed here in San Pedro. And not to forget the more recent epic sea film *Titanic*, the museum features a very detailed 18-foot scaled model of the HMS *Titanic*.

Exhibits and artifacts cover the wide range of maritime history ranging from the early tallships, the grand sailing vessels engaged in the nineteenth-century trade and whaling industries, to recreational sailing and the merchant marine. Naval history is also a theme, along with the commercial shipping industry, which is especially appropriate because the Los Angeles-San Pedro Port is the busiest in the world.

Directions: In San Pedro, take Interstate 110 (Harbor Freeway) south until it ends. Turn left at the freeway exit onto Gaffey Street and continue to 6th Street. Turn left on 6th Street, going past Miner Street to Berth 84 and the maritime museum.

Activities: Tours, seminars, maritime festivals, and visits by tallships.

Facilities: Gift shop.

Dates: The museum is open Tuesdays through Sundays, closed on Mondays.

Fees: A donation is requested.

Closest town: San Pedro.

For more information: Los Angeles Maritime Museum, Berth 84, Foot of 6th Street, San Pedro, CA 90731. Phone (310) 548-7618.

Long Beach

[Fig. 60] A vibrant waterfront city, Long Beach often disappears in the shadow of Los Angeles, which is unfortunate because it has so much to offer. Long Beach is the fifth largest city in California, and its harbor and neighboring Port of Los Angeles together form one of the busiest shipping centers in the world.

Unlike its larger cousin city to the north, Long Beach's business district lies at the water's edge where there is plenty of nearby shopping, sailing, bicycling, fishing, and beachcombing, along with a plethora of museums to explore. There's a great beach with a bike trail along the business district's entire 5.5-mile length, which then connects with another bike trail that heads still farther south.

Long Beach has made getting around the downtown area easy. The bright red **Passport Shuttle** is a complimentary bus service that can take you nearly anywhere tourists are likely to want to go. For a very small fee the Passport will even take you up to Belmont Shore and Naples Island, seaside communities filled with shops and restaurants where Italian-style gondoliers cruise along the canals. The shuttles stop along most of Long Beach's main streets and in front of the city's main attractions.

The ***Queen Mary*** (562-435-3511), located in the harbor not far from downtown Long Beach, offers a unique dining and shopping experience. The retired cruise ship, originally built in 1937, is now a floating museum of art deco luxury from an earlier era. Located just across Queensway bridge, which crosses narrow Queensway Bay, the ship is open for tours.

Within easy walking distance of the Long Beach Convention Center is **Shoreline Village**, an intriguing little cluster of waterfront businesses that includes restaurants and shops.

On the campus of California State University, Long Beach, the **Earl Burns Miller Japanese Garden** (562-985-8885) is a great example of a true Japanese traditional garden with a lake filled with koi, Buddhist statues, a pagoda, and a teahouse. A path winds among Japanese pines, willows, golden bamboo, and flowers, and past a waterfall. The **El Dorado Nature Center** (562-570-1745) is a wildlife sanctuary with trails that meander through native California plants. The 102-acre center features a museum with exhibits and interactive children activities and programs.

COYOTE
(Canis latrans)

Nearby is the tallship ***Californian*** (800-432-2201), a great sailing ship that looks very impressive sitting in port and even more impressive in a brisk wind under full sail. The ship offers wanna-be old time sailors an opportunity to go sailing for a day or longer.

Directions: Long Beach is located on Highway 1 and Interstate 710, about 14 miles south of Los Angeles.

Activities: Shopping, dining, fishing, sailing, swimming, beachcombing.

For more information: Long Beach Area Convention and Visitors Bureau, One World Trade Center, Suite 300, Long Beach, CA 90831. Phone (562) 436-3645.

LONG BEACH AQUARIUM OF THE PACIFIC

[Fig. 60(1)] The beautifully designed aquarium sits near the water's edge in downtown Long Beach and features 10,000 fish and other sea creatures from waters around the world. The aquarium is divided into several different maritime regions, from the cold waters of the north Pacific to the coral lagoons of the tropical Pacific.

The rocky intertidal exhibit contains strange-looking animals such as giant keyhole limpets (*Megathura crenulata*), warty sea cucumbers (*Parastichopus parvimensis*), and aggregating anemones (*Anthopleura elegantissima*). For tropical fish fanatics, black and white Moorish idols (*Zanclus cornutus*), yellow and green scralled filefish (*Aluterus scriptus*), and the brilliant blue, yellow, and green king angelfish (*Holacanthus passer*) swim among nearly a dozen other species in the Sea of Cortez tank.

Other tropical fish galleries include species such as the harlequin tuskfish (*Choerodon fasciatus*), which is a yellow-and-turquoise-striped fish, the strange-looking humphead wrasse (*Chelinus undulatus*), and the zebra shark (*Stegastoma fasciatum*). Within the same series of tanks are blue-spotted stingrays (*Taeniura lymma*), porcupine fish (*Diodon hystirx*), and clown triggerfish (*Balistoides conspicillum*).

In addition to the 500 species of fish, there are harbor seals (*Phoca vitulina*) and California sea lions (*Zalophus californianus*). There's also a diving bird exhibit with tufted puffins (*Fratercula cirrhata*), crested auklets (*Aethia cristatella*), and rhinoceros auklets (*Cerorhinca monocerata*).

Directions: The aquarium is near the Long Beach downtown waterfront. From Interstate 710 drive south until the freeway turns into Shoreline Drive. Follow the signs, turning right on Aquarium Way. There's a parking garage adjacent to the aquarium.

Activities: Self-guided tours, special programs.

Facilities: Café, kids' area, child care station, gift shop.

Dates: Open daily, except Christmas day.

Fees: There is an entrance fee.

Nearest town: Long Beach.

For more information: Long Beach Aquarium of the Pacific, 100 Aquarium Way, Long Beach, CA 90802. Phone (562) 590-3100.

☷ LONG BEACH DINING

Belmont Brewing Company. 25 39ᵗʰ Place, Long Beach. Here's a microbrewery with a great ocean view. In addition to the freshly brewed beers, a full menu of California cuisine is available. Open for lunch and dinner. Dress is casual and reservations generally aren't required. *Inexpensive to moderate. Phone (562) 443-3891.*

Parker's Lighthouse. Shoreline Village, 435 Shoreline Drive, Long Beach. This is a very popular waterfront restaurant with incredible views of the bay and of the *Queen Mary.* The best time to be here is just as the sun is setting and the lights of the ship, the harbor, and the city are all coming on. The steaks, prime rib, pasta, lobster, and other fresh seafood are delicious. There's also a bar upstairs. Dress is casual and reservations are suggested. *Inexpensive to moderate. Phone (562) 432-6500.*

Simon & Seafort's Steak, Chop & Oyster House. 340 Golden Shore, Long Beach. The restaurant's name says it all as far as the menu goes. The food and atmosphere are both quite pleasant. Casual dress and reservations are suggested. *Inexpensive. Phone (562) 435-2333.*

Tequila Jack's. Shoreline Village, 407 Shoreline Drive, Long Beach. For tequila lovers this is the place to be, with a taxi waiting to take you back to your hotel. This restaurant/bar offers great margaritas and well over 100 kinds of tequila to wash down the full menu of Mexican food. It sits on the waterfront and is an easy walk from the Long Beach business center. Dress is casual and reservations aren't required, but are suggested on weekends and holidays. *Inexpensive. Phone (562) 628-0454.*

☷ LONG BEACH LODGING

Guesthouse Hotel. 5325 East Pacific Coast Highway, Long Beach. Although not near the waterfront, it's only a few minutes drive away. Some of the rooms have whirlpools and there's a heated pool. *Moderate. Phone (800) 214-8378.*

Hilton Long Beach. Two World Trade Center, Long Beach. Just off the I-710 freeway and near the Trade Center, the hotel has a pool and restaurant. *Expensive. Phone (562) 983-3400.*

Hyatt Regency Long Beach. 200 South Pine, Long Beach. The 16-story hotel is adjacent to the Long Beach Convention and Entertainment Center. The waterfront is just a short walk away. It has a heated pool and restaurant. *Expensive. Phone (562) 491-1234.*

Renaissance Long Beach Hotel. 111 East Ocean Boulevard, Long Beach. There are ocean views from many of the 12-story hotel's rooms. Suites are available. The hotel has a pool, sauna, and gift shop. *Expensive. Phone (562) 437-5900.*

Santa Catalina Island

[Fig. 60] Today nearly 90 percent of Santa Catalina island is owned by the Santa Catalina Island Conservancy, which is trying to restore the island to a more natural state, while providing for recreational opportunities. Catalina is the most popular tourist island off the Southern California coast. Hundreds and sometimes thousands of people each day take boat trips across the open waters that separate Catalina from harbors at either San Pedro, Long Beach, Newport Beach, or Dana Point. The trip of just over 20 miles takes one to two hours depending on the departure port and the type of passenger boat booked. Others visitors skip the boat trip and fly into the island's small airport.

What attracts most of these people are opportunities to tour the island, scuba dive, fish, hike, bicycle, or simply wander the quiet streets of Avalon and its quaint shops and restaurants. For anyone who has never seen bison, what most people refer to as buffalo, several hundred of the shaggy creatures now wander the island. The non-native beasts were originally brought here in 1924 for the film, *The Vanishing American.* When the filming was completed the original 14 buffalo were allowed to remain. Over the years their numbers have been augmented by births and by additional bulls introduced in order to strengthen the genetic line. Today they number about 400, and they are actively managed to maintain their numbers and health.

Easily the most famous and the most prominent building on the island is the **Catalina Casino**, which was built in 1929. The tall, white, circular structure is home to Avalon's movie theater, a local museum, an art gallery, and the world's largest circular ballroom, which in another era was famous for its Big Band dances. Famous theater and art deco artist John Gabriel designed and oversaw the painting of the marine-themed murals on the concrete walls. Other lavish and beautiful artwork is found throughout the building.

When the Spanish first discovered Santa Catalina Island the people living here called themselves Pimungans and their island home Pimu. For perhaps 7,000 years they were traders who paddled their plank canoes across the channel to trade with other Indians. The Spanish diseases and mission system soon ended the Pimungans' ability to survive on the island, which by the 1800s also had been invaded by American, Russian, and Aleut sea otter hunters. The American era brought squatters, along with silver miners, and even the U.S. Army for awhile. In the 1920s William Wrigley Jr., the chewing gum magnate whose favorite motto was "Nothing great was ever achieved without enthusiasm," began to acquire the island, which by this time was owned by a corporation.

Wrigley introduced controlled development, actually building and selling homes to residents at very reasonable prices. He also established various businesses to help the island's inhabitants support themselves. Following his death in 1932, his son took over and continued his father's legacy, although with much less money available for investment. The interruption of World War II completely shut the island down to tourism. The post-war period soon brought a dramatic increase in tourism to the island. But, by the 1970s taxes forced SCICo, the company that Wrigley purchased and which still controlled the island, to deed to the newly formed Santa Catalina Island Conservancy in perpetuity the 88 percent of the property that was planned to be retained as open space.

The geologic history of Catalina is as fascinating and dynamic as the cultural history. Near Big Fisherman's Cove on the leeward side of the isthmus, where the University of Southern California's Marine Science Center operates, diatomaceous earth cliffs are readily visible. They were formed mostly from the ancient "microfossils" of planktonic organisms. The cliffs also contain fossils of shellfish such as scallops.

On the opposite side of the island, Ribbon Rock provides an excellent example of metamorphosed sedimentary rocks. Its name comes from the alternating horizontal layers of light and dark rock. The light ribbons were originally sand that heat and pressure transformed into quartz feldspar, while the dark layers were originally mud and other fine sediments that were laid down. Closer to the center of the main part of the island Kennedy Rock, an ancient volcanic plug, is evidence of the lava flows that periodically covered portions of Southern California millions of years ago.

One of the better things about the island is the obvious small number of cars. Visitors can't bring their own and must depend on what's already on the island. But there's plenty of transportation available, and for those not venturing too far, everything in the small community of Avalon is within easy walking distance. There are literally dozens of clothing, jewelry, and general gift shops within a few blocks of the wharf area.

While you can pay a little extra to bring a bicycle over on one of the ferries, bikes can also be rented on the island from **Catalina Auto & Bike Rentals** (Crescent Avenue and Metropole Avenue, Avalon, phone 310-510-0111), or **Brown's Bikes** (107 Pebbly Beach Road, Avalon, phone 310-510-0986).

Catalina Island Conservancy leads a wide variety of tours of Avalon and sight-seeing tours across the island. It also leads visitors in activities including biking, boating, diving, fishing, and hiking. For tour information contact Catalina Island Conservancy Tours, PO Box 2739, Avalon. Phone (310) 510-2595 ext. 105.

Directions: There are several ferry companies that depart the harbors at San Pedro, Long Beach, Newport Beach, and Dana Point. The Catalina Express (800-464-4228) leaves from San Pedro, Long Beach, and Dana Point. The Catalina Flyer (800-830-7744) departs from Newport Beach.

Activities: Shopping, scuba diving, fishing, hiking, dining, camping, sight-seeing.

Facilities: Hotels, shops, restaurants, harbor.

Fees: Cost of transportation to the island varies considerably, but ferry service is available for about $40 or less, round-trip for adults.

For more information: Catalina Island Visitors Bureau and Chamber of Commerce, PO Box 217, Avalon 90704. Phone (310) 510-1520.

SANTA CATALINA ISLAND DINING

There are many dining possibilities on the island, but on weekends there may be longer than normal waits to get a table. Many of the restaurants are closed on major holidays such as Thanksgiving and Christmas. Generally, plan early and make reservations whenever possible.

The Blue Parrot. 205 Crescent Avenue, Avalon. Just the name makes you want to dine here, but the view of the harbor adds to its popularity. This restaurant serves a popular American menu in a casual dress atmosphere. Reservations suggested. *Inexpensive. Phone (310) 510-2465.*

Café Prego. 605 Crescent Avenue, Avalon. As the name indicates, Italian food is the specialty here. There are early bird specials and cocktails are available. Reservations are suggested and the dress is casual. *Inexpensive. Phone (310) 510-1218.*

El Galleon. 411 Crescent Avenue, Avalon. The nautical-themed restaurant features seafood and steak, and casual dress is expected. *Inexpensive to moderate. Phone (310) 510-1188.*

SANTA CATALINA ISLAND LODGING

Making overnight reservations well in advance is the only way to come here with any expectation of staying longer than the day. While it's possible to get a room at the last minute for some non-holiday weekday periods, especially in winter, spring through autumn any such spur-of-the-moment success is only an accident. Room prices also vary widely, with summer rates sometimes twice that of winter rates. There can also be minimum stays required, especially over weekends, and several day advance cancellations may be required in order to escape cancellation penalties.

Catalina Canyon Resort & Spa (Best Western). 888 Country Club Drive, Avalon. The three-story structure sits on the hillside and features a pool, sauna, and full-service spa. *Moderate during winter, expensive in summer. Phone (310) 510-0325.*

El Terado Terrace. 230 Marilla Avenue, Avalon. Sits on the hill providing an ocean view from some rooms. A few rooms have full kitchens. It's located just 1.5 blocks from the harbor. *Moderate to expensive. Phone (310) 510-0831.*

The Old Turner Inn. 232 Catalina Avenue, Avalon. This is a two-story bed and breakfast inn that is located in residential Avalon. There is a meal plan available. *Expensive. Phone (310) 510-2236.*

Snug Harbor Inn. 108 Sumner, Avalon. Some of these nautically themed rooms, and there are only six in the complex, offer bay views. There is a meal plan available. *Expensive. Phone (310) 510- 8400.*

Orange and San Diego Counties

California's two southernmost counties are known for their sandy beaches and warm climates.

FIGURE NUMBERS

62 Orange County Area

63 Mission San Juan Capistrano Area

64 San Diego County Area

65 San Diego Area

66 Downtown San Diego

Orange and San Diego Counties

California's two most southern coastal counties are well known for their sandy beaches and warm climate. The mild climate is able to support an incredible variety of plants, from annual wildflowers to cacti. With such a dry climate, fresh water is at a premium, not only for the millions of people who have settled these areas, but also for the plants that have adapted to the near-desert weather patterns. The rugged hillsides are covered with chaparral and seldom by trees, unless they have been planted by residents who also are willing to irrigate. San Diego's many parks are testaments to what a mild climate, adequate water, and 150 years or more of dedicated planting can bring to a land that sees only a few inches of rain each year.

[*Above:* Torrey Pines State Reserve and Beach protects the rarest pine tree in the United States]

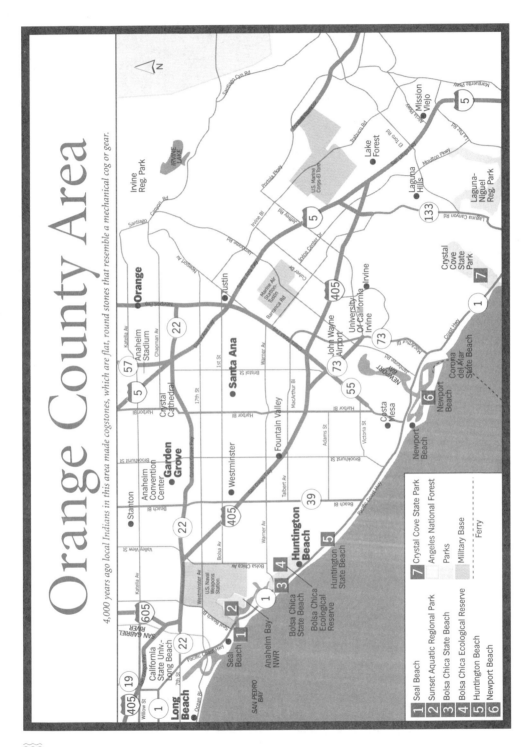

Orange County Area

4,000 years ago local Indians in this area made cogstones, which are flat, round stones that resemble a mechanical cog or gear.

Key:

1 Seal Beach
2 Sunset Aquatic Regional Park
3 Bolsa Chica State Beach
4 Bolsa Chica Ecological Reserve
5 Huntington Beach
6 Newport Beach
7 Crystal Cove State Park

Angeles National Forest
Parks
Military Base
Ferry

Orange County

🏵 ORANGE COUNTY COAST SIDE TRIPS

While most of the county's namesake orange trees that were first planted here in the late nineteenth century have been swallowed by development, what remains are the cliffs, the beaches, and the warm climate that continue to attract people to this part of California. While surfers can be found riding the coastal waves at any time of the year, most of the beach use comes during summer, and usually later in the day after the rising sun has burned off the morning fog.

With miles of beautiful sandy beaches and thousands of people flocking here, there is lifeguard service in most areas during the beach-going season. While use of the beaches is free, parking seldom is. In most of the beach areas there is a parking fee, which is sometimes collected at an entry gate, such as at Huntington and Bolsa Chica state beaches, or via parking meters in most of the city parking spaces.

Rip currents are prevalent along many of the beaches, so caution is always advised. Remember, anytime you find yourself being pulled out to sea by an outgoing current, don't fight it. Instead, swim parallel to the shore until you break free from the generally narrow currents, then swim back to shore.

Seal Beach [Fig. 62(1)] (213-430-2613) is a long and sandy beach that stretches south beginning near the mouth of the San Gabriel River in the town of Seal Beach along Highway 1. A paved bike trail starts near the beach on the south side of the river and heads inland for several miles. There's grassy area above much of the beach, along with restrooms, a pier, and a jetty.

Sunset Aquatic Regional Park [Fig. 62(2)] (714-846-0179) is a small boat harbor at the end of Edinger Avenue on the north side of Huntington Harbor. Ocean access is available through its connection with Anaheim Bay, which is located about 0.5 mile north. There are picnic tables and a boat launch facility. The park is adjacent to Seal Beach National Wildlife Refuge, but unfortunately the refuge's 1,200 acres of salt marshes lie within the boundaries of the U.S. Naval Weapons Station and are off-limits to the public.

Bolsa Chica State Beach [Fig. 62(3)] (714-846-3460 or 714-848-1566) is 6 miles of sand along the west side of Highway 1, starting at Warner Avenue in Huntington Beach. In addition to the sand and surf, a portion of the beach's

*A California gull (*Larus californicus*).*

parking lot is reserved on a first-come, first-served basis for "enroute" camping, which allows those with self-contained motorhomes, campers, and trailers to spend one night for a fee. There is also a paved bike trail that runs the length of the beach.

BOLSA CHICA ECOLOGICAL RESERVE

[Fig. 62(4)] The reserve is one of an increasing number of successful wetland restoration efforts occurring along the length of California's 1,100 miles of coast. This area was originally a wetland that covered several thousand acres. For thousands of years Native Americans found its waters and mud flats to be rich and dependable sources of food. In 1900 hunters hoping to improve their duck hunting prospects closed the tidal opening that fed the wetlands. Their attempts for improved waterfowl hunting failed, and the wetlands and surrounding upland areas were subsequently used for agriculture, cattle grazing, and World War II shore artillery defense. Following the sinking of the first successful oil well here in 1920, it also became California's richest oil production area. Land developers have always eyed this valuable coastal land, but fortunately, most of their efforts have been thwarted.

Today, most of the remaining 1,300 acres of surrounding wetlands are in public ownership controlled by the California Department of Fish and Game. The Bolsa Chica Conservancy is very involved in the restoration and interpretation of the wetlands. Its members also continue raising funds to purchase the remaining undeveloped land that surrounds the current holdings.

There is a 1.5 mile trail that circles Inner Bolsa Bay and offers numerous opportunities to view many of the 200 bird species that have been seen here. Along the trail, evidence of the efforts to restore the wetland is prevalent. Numerous culverts, levees, and water control gates have been added, determining where and when both salt water and fresh water flows. From the parking lot there is a boardwalk that crosses the waterway, allowing views of some of the creatures that serve as food for the thousands of birds that live here year-round or migrate through annually. California horn snails (*Cerithidea californica*) are extremely abundant, as evidenced by their trails on the mud flats; the numerous shells of dead jackknife clams (*Tagelus californianus*) testify to their successful return to this restored wetland.

The wetland serves as a spawning area and nursery for many species of animals, including the translucent common jellyfish (*Aurelia aurita*), round stingrays (*Urolophus halleri*), several species of sharks, and anchovies (*Engraulis mordax*). During the summer nesting season, endangered California least terns (*Sterna antillarum*) and threatened snowy plovers (*Charadrius alexandrinus*) nest on South Island. During April and May several species of terns begin their aerial courtship displays before nesting on North Island.

There is a curious archaeological aspect to the wetlands, or at least on the bluff where the spur trail leads. About 4,000 years ago the local Indians made cogstones here. Cogstones are flat, round stones ranging in diameter from 3 to 5 inches and are about 1 inch thick. They have notches around their edges and many have holes in their centers, making them appear to be some type of ancient mechanical cog or gear. The only problem with this theory is that none of the cogstones found show any indication of wear and there is no apparent pattern of matching "teeth" among the cogs. Archaeologists assume they served as ceremonial or religious objects.

Directions: Bolsa Chica Ecological Reserve is located on the east side of Highway 1, across from Bolsa Chica State Beach, just south of Warner Road in the town of Huntington Beach. There is a marked parking lot just off Highway 1.

Activities: Bird-watching, photography, hiking.

Facilities: None.

Dates: Open daily.

Fees: None.

Closest town: Huntington Beach.

For more information: Bolsa Chica Conservancy, 3842 Warner Avenue, Huntington Beach, CA 92649. Phone (714) 846-1114.

CALIFORNIA HORN SNAILS
(Cerithidea californica)
Look for these snails and their trails in mud flats.

HUNTINGTON BEACH

[Fig. 62(5)] Huntington Beach is probably the best known of southern California's towns, although most people probably think more about the activities that take place here on the beach rather than of the vibrant seaside town itself. Many people still remember the Jan and Dean hit song about Huntington Beach in the 1960s entitled *Surf City*. The nickname has stuck, but most of the old (and somewhat tacky) buildings and businesses have been replaced by new, more classy, and more expensive restaurants and shops. But, with 8.5 miles of white sandy beach along this section of coast, the focus is on the ocean and there's plenty of fun, sun, sand, and surf here for everyone.

The town is named after Henry E. Huntington who brought the Redline-Pacific Electric Railway to what was then a small seaside resort. With the railroad came more people, and the fledgling city was incorporated in 1909. After oil was discovered in the area in 1920, the population grew rapidly.

Just a few blocks from the beach is the restored home of one of the area's early settlers. The **Newland House Museum** (714-962-5777) originally belonged to William and May Newland, who moved west from Illinois during Los Angeles' "Boom of the Eighties." A few years later, in 1898, they moved southward and built their Victorian farmhouse where they lived for more than 50 years. The Newlands purchased the land around present day Beach Boulevard and an additional 500 acres of rich peat land in an area called the "Gospel Swamp." They drained the "swampland" and continued their farming activities.

The Newland House, located at 19820 Beach Boulevard, Huntington Beach, has been restored and is now open to the public on Wednesdays, Thursdays, and weekends.

The Huntington Beach International Surfing Museum (714-960-3483) exhibits photo displays showing the history of surfing in the area, including pictures of world championship surfing competitions held here. There are also old surfboards and other memorabilia. The museum is at 411 Olive Avenue, Huntington Beach.

Most people come here for the surf and sand. A good way to begin any stay is to take a walk on the **Huntington Beach Pier**. At 1,852 feet, it's the longest municipal concrete pier in California. The pier offers a different view of the surfers and body boarders working the breaking waves just north and south of the structure. There are several shops and food vendors at the very end of the pier. The pier is located at 411 Olive Avenue, Huntington Beach.

There are actually two beaches here, **Huntington City Beach** and **Huntington State Beach**, although most would be hard pressed to tell the difference between the two. Both have the same sandy beach, volleyball courts, fire rings, and a connecting bike trail running along their lengths. There generally is plenty of parking between the day-use lots and street parking meters. Huntington State Beach offers an "en route" campground that allows self-contained motorhomes, campers, and trailers to stay for one night only for a fee.

Directions: Huntington Beach is on Highway 1 about 20 miles south of Long Beach.

Activities: Swimming, surfing, beachcombing, fishing, bicycling, dining.

Facilities: Shops, beach equipment rentals.

Dates: Open daily.

Fees: There is a fee for beach parking, either in the lots or parking meters.

For more information: Huntington Beach Conference and Visitors Bureau, 417 Main Street, Huntington Beach, CA 92648, phone (714) 969-3492. Huntington State Beach, 18331 Enterprise Lane, Huntington Beach, CA 92648. Phone (714) 536-1454.

HUNTINGTON BEACH DINING

Chimayo at the Beach. 315 Pacific Coast Highway, Huntington Beach. This jazzy Latin-influenced restaurant is located at the foot of the Huntington Beach Pier. Beef and fish are featured menu items at this classy but casual eatery. Reservations are suggested. *Inexpensive to moderate. Phone (714) 374-7273.*

Duke's Huntington Beach. 317 Pacific Coast Highway, Huntington Beach. Sitting at the foot of the pier next to Chimayo at the Beach, Duke's offers fish, chicken, and beef menu items. Most tables offer nice views of the ocean and beach. The dining is casual and reservations are suggested. *Inexpensive to moderate. Phone (714) 374-6446.*

Palm Court. 21100 Pacific Coast Highway, Huntington Beach. Located in the Waterfront Hilton Beach Resort, this acclaimed restaurant overlooking the ocean serves a variety of Continental menu items. *Inexpensive to moderate. Phone (714) 960-7873.*

🔅 HUNTINGTON BEACH LODGING

Beach Inn. 18112 Beach Boulevard, Huntington Beach. Contrary to its name, Beach Inn is not near the beach. It's located about 4 miles inland, but that's what makes it more affordable. *Moderate. Phone (714) 841-6606.*

Sun 'N' Sands Motel. 1102 Pacific Coast Highway, Huntington Beach. From the hotel, it's a short 5-block walk to the pier, while the beach is just across the highway. It has a pool for those not wishing to soak in salt water. *Moderate to expensive. Phone (714) 536-2543.*

Hilton Waterfront Beach Resort. 21100 Pacific Coast Highway, Huntington Beach. Almost every room in this large resort hotel offers views of the Pacific Ocean. There's also a restaurant and gift shop. *Expensive. Phone (714) 960-7873.*

Huntington Surf Inn. 720 Pacific Coast Highway, Huntington Beach. This small, 9-room inn is located across the street from the beach and about 2 blocks from the pier. *Moderate. Phone (714) 536-2444.*

🔅 NEWPORT BEACH

[Fig. 62(6)] This picturesque town began as a shipping point built by Captain S.S. Dunnells and D.M. Dorman in 1872. Over the years, as new people entered the local scene it was given different names: Newport Landing, McFadden's Landing, Port Orange, and the Old Landing. It finally became known as Newport Beach after the town's streets were laid out in 1892. This was the same year that the *Santa Ana and Newport Railroad* chose the original wharf constructed here in 1888 as its terminus. The railroad and the port served as the primary movers of products and produce from Orange, San Bernardino, and Riverside counties.

Within Newport Beach is **Balboa Beach**, which is a long and narrow peninsula of sand that stretches for about 5 miles and protects Newport Harbor and the bay. On the bay side of Balboa Beach is the impressive **Balboa Pavilion**, a unique domed structure that the Newport Bay Investment Company built in 1905. It was designed to attract investors to the new town. The pavilion later became the southern terminus for the famous Red Cars of the *Pacific Electric Railway*.

The **Newport Pier** is a good place to begin a morning visit to the beach. Anglers line the pier and surfers ride the waves along the shoreline nearby. The Newport Dory Fishing Fleet returns to the north side of the pier at about 9:30 a.m. each day to sell its catch along the beach. There's also a restaurant at the end of the pier.

Within the protected waters of picturesque Newport Harbor is **Balboa Island**, a shoppers paradise. Among the numerous Cape Cod and their contrasting modern-style homes are some 70 gift shops, art galleries, and restaurants. Very expensive yachts line the North Bay walkway; Marine Avenue is home to many of the shops and restaurants. Choose from sidewalk cafes or award-winning restaurants. The island can be accessed by way of the bridge at the end of Jamboree Road or from Balboa Peninsula by ferry. Parking is at a premium on the island, so taking the ferry over and walking is the best way to go. The Balboa Ferry can be boarded at Agate Avenue on the South Bay.

Newport Harbor is one of the largest small craft harbors in the world. There are 1,230 residential piers, 2,219 commercial slips, 1,221 bay moorings, and all the commercial support facilities needed to service several thousand boats ranging from small sailboats to multimillion-dollar yachts.

Directions: Newport Beach is located on Highway 1 and State Highway 55.

Activities: Shopping, swimming, surfing, fishing, beachcombing, boating, dining.

Facilities: Stores, restaurants, marine supplies.

Closest town: Costa Mesa, 3 miles.

For more information: Newport Harbor Area Chamber of Commerce, 1470 Jamboree Road, Newport Beach, CA 92660. Phone (949) 729-4400.

CRYSTAL COVE STATE PARK

[Fig. 62(7)] Drive through the Los Angeles megalopolis heading south and several miles past the popular and often crowded Huntington and Bolsa Chica state beaches, and the heavily developed hillsides quickly give way to an open land that still harbors rare native plants and 3 miles of coastline. Crystal Cove State Park actually contains three very different areas, meeting the diverse recreational needs of inland hikers, beach-goers, and scuba divers.

Most of the park's 2,000 acres rise steeply from the beach and are located on the east side of Highway 1. Inland trails wind along deep and treacherous canyons and pass colorful spring wildflower shows. The trails also allow access to the park's hike-in campsites. Moro Canyon is one of the more popular destinations. During California's mission period, cattle from Mission San Juan Capistrano were grazed in the canyon. Today, it's popular with mountain bikers and hikers. There also are opportunities to see the wildlife that inhabit the area. While raccoons (*Procyon lotor*), coyotes (*Canis latrans*), and bobcats (*Felis rufus*) live in the park, it is more likely that birds, an occasional cottontail rabbit, and ground squirrels will be seen. It's a good idea to watch for either of the park's two rattlesnakes, the western diamondback (*Crotalus viridis*) or the red diamondback (*Crotalus* sp.), especially early in the morning or late evening. This is when they tend to stretch out on trails and roads, trying to soak up the warmth given off by the ground. Ticks, including the 1 percent that can cause Lyme disease, are also found in the park, so check yourself closely during and after hiking or bike riding.

As in all wild areas along this portion of California's coast, poison oak (*Toxicodendron diversilobum*) is common among the chaparral and coastal sage scrub plants. In the canyons and riparian areas, sycamores (*Platanus racemosa*) and oaks (*Quercus* sp.) are prevalent.

Cross to the west side of Highway 1 and there are several beaches that welcome swimmers, sunbathers, divers, and surfers. The beaches, most of which are sand with occasional rocky tidepool areas, are at the base of a 50-to 80-foot-tall coastal bluff. These bluffs are the eroded remnants of an ancient marine terrace uplifted to its present level by tectonic plate movement and are primarily leftover sandstone and limestone scrapings from the top of the Pacific Plate as it dove into the subduction zone beneath the North American Plate.

The park extends into offshore waters out to a depth of 120 feet. Within this 1,240-acre ocean protection zone, the only fishing allowed is for game fish and lobsters when they're in season. The park's waters are a favorite anchoring spot for boat fishing enthusiasts. Shore fishing is also very popular, with anglers tending to favor the beach near Pelican Point.

Everyone wishing to escape the crowds at the more popular swimming beaches to the north comes here, especially to the broader, more southerly beach located at Reef Point. Near the north end of the park the beach tends to be much more narrow, often disappearing completely during high tides as the waves wash against the base of the coastal terrace cliff. While swimming in the 50-degree Fahrenheit waters during winter requires a wetsuit, in the summer the water temperature generally reaches a much more comfortable 70 degrees Fahrenheit.

Directions: Highway 1 (Pacific Coast Highway) bisects the park, which is located between Corona del Mar and Laguna Beach. There are parking lots marked along the 3.2 miles of highway that pass through the park at Reef Point, Pelican Point, and Los Trancos.

Activities: Fishing, swimming, snorkeling, and scuba diving, beachcombing, hiking, camping.

Facilities: Primitive hike-in campsites.

Dates: Open year round.

Fees: There are camping and day-use fees.

Closest town: Laguna Beach, 2 miles.

For more information: Orange Coast State Parks District Office, 8471 Pacific Coast Highway, Laguna Beach, CA 92651. Phone (949) 494-3539.

MISSION SAN JUAN CAPISTRANO

[Fig. 63(1)] The first time that the Spanish padres attempted to establish the mission in 1775, an Indian uprising in San Diego caused them to abandon their effort. They returned the following year to find the mission bells where they had left them; this time they were successful. This was California's grandest mission when construction was

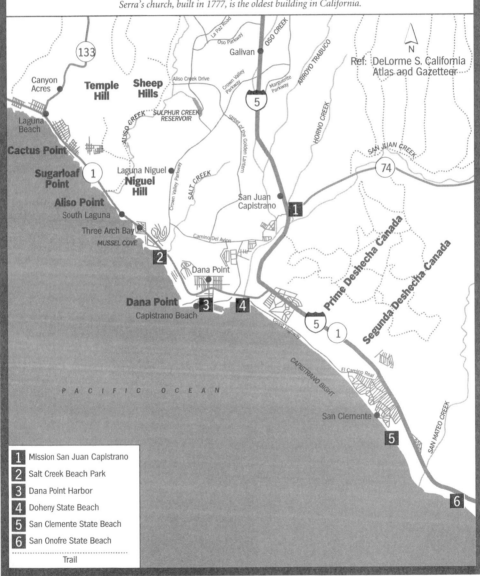

Mission San Juan Capistrano Area

Serra's church, built in 1777, is the oldest building in California.

Ref: DeLorme S. California Atlas and Gazetteer

1 Mission San Juan Capistrano
2 Salt Creek Beach Park
3 Dana Point Harbor
4 Doheny State Beach
5 San Clemente State Beach
6 San Onofre State Beach
····· Trail

completed in 1806, but the earthquake that struck in 1812 destroyed much of the mission and the church and killed 40 "neophytes," as the mission Indians were known.

A few partial restoration efforts were attempted over the years, but most of the church remains in ruins. Among the crumbling walls and restored buildings are lovely gardens and fountains. One building that is still intact today is Serra's church, which is located on the east side of the restored arched corridors. Serra's church was built in 1777, making it the oldest building still standing in California. It also is the only remaining church in the state where Father Serra said Mass.

San Juan Capistrano is just up the highway a short distance from former President Richard Nixon's home in San Clemente. President Nixon often visited **El Adobe de Capistrano's** two adobes, the oldest of which dates from 1778 and was transformed into a restaurant. Today, the mission complex is undergoing a $20 million stabilization and restoration program.

One of San Juan Capistrano's most famous attractions is the return of the swallows on St. Joseph's Day each year, marking the end of winter. It seems that swallows do indeed arrive each year, generally on the day they're scheduled, March 19. The swallows begin their annual migration to San Juan Capistrano from Santa Elena, a town of 15,000 located in Argentina's Entre Rios Province. San Juan Capistrano's Swallows Festival is celebrated each year in mid-March.

Directions: The mission is located on Ortega Highway, 2.5 blocks west of Interstate 5 in the city of San Juan Capistrano.

Activities: Tours.

Facilities: Gift shop, exhibits.

Fees: There is a small entrance fee.

Dates: Open daily. Closed Thanksgiving, Christmas, and Good Friday afternoon.

For more information: Mission San Juan Capistrano, PO Box 697, San Juan Capistrano, CA 92693. Phone (949) 248-2048.

SOUTHERN ORANGE COUNTY SIDE TRIPS

Salt Creek Beach Park [Fig. 63(2)] (949-661-7013) is located just north of Dana Point off Highway 1 via Ritz Carlton Drive. It's as popular with surfers as the 7-acre Bluff Park situated just above the beach is with picnickers. There are several stairways and a paved trail that lead down to the beach.

Dana Point Harbor [Fig. 63(3)] is named for Richard Henry Dana, author of *Two Years Before the Mast*, among other works. The harbor was originally much smaller, having only to tend to the needs of nineteenth century sailing ships. It was expanded in the late 1960s and early 1970s to meet private pleasure boaters' needs for improved and expanded marine facilities. Today, in addition to the boating facilities, there is a grassy picnic area, shops, restaurants, and the Orange County Marine Institute all located within the marina area. Phone (949) 496-2242 for harbor information. For boating trips, phone (949) 496-5794.

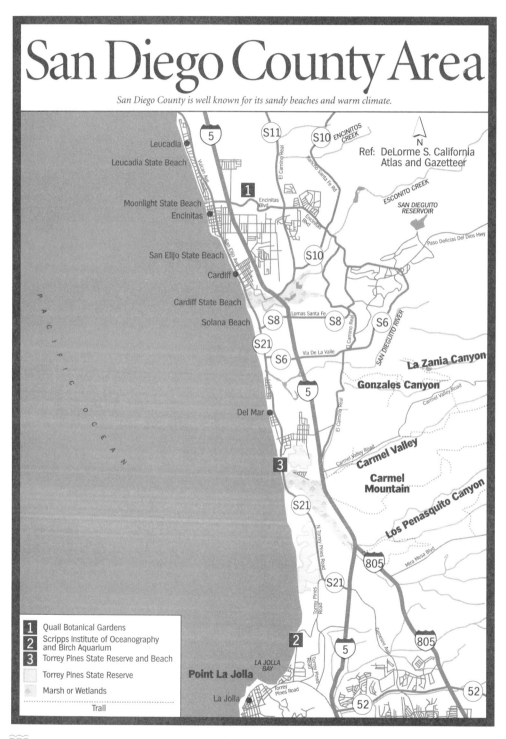

San Diego County Area

San Diego County is well known for its sandy beaches and warm climate.

Leucadia
Leucadia State Beach

S11   S10   ENCINITOS CREEK

Ref: DeLorme S. California
Atlas and Gazetteer

N

1   Encinitas Blvd

ESCONITO CREEK

SAN DIEGUITO RESERVOIR

Moonlight State Beach
Encinitas

Encinitas Blvd

Paso Delicias Del Dios Hwy

San Elijo State Beach

S10

Cardiff

Cardiff State Beach
Solana Beach

Lomas Santa Fe

S8   S8   S6

SAN DIEGUITO RIVER

S21

S6   Via De La Valle

La Zania Canyon

Gonzales Canyon

5   Carmel Valley Road

Del Mar

Carmel Valley

3   Carmel Mountain

S21   Los Penasquito Canyon

805   Mira Mesa Blvd

S21

LA JOLLA BAY   5   805   52

Point La Jolla

La Jolla   52   52

P A C I F I C   O C E A N

1   Quail Botanical Gardens
2   Scripps Institute of Oceanography
    and Birch Aquarium
3   Torrey Pines State Reserve and Beach

    Torrey Pines State Reserve

    Marsh or Wetlands

    Trail

Doheny State Beach [Fig. 63(4)] (949-496-6172), in addition to having a great beach and picnic area, also has a campground with 120 campsites. The campground is especially popular during the summer, so reservations are almost always needed to get in. The beach park also has a visitor center with exhibits and a touch tidepool. For camping reservations phone (800) 444-7275.

San Clemente State Beach [Fig. 63(5)] (949-492-3156) is another popular camping, picnicking, swimming, and surfing area. Nearly half of the 160 campsites have full hook-ups for RVs. The campground is on the coastal terrace, and there are trails down to the beach.

San Diego County

SAN ONOFRE STATE BEACH

[Fig. 63(6)] This 3,000-acre beach surrounds the San Onofre Nuclear Generating Station, which can create a strange feeling when one passes the emergency evacuation signs while driving through the beach. The state beach is comprised of three sections: San Onofre State Beach, which includes a campground; San Onofre Surf Beach, a day use area; and San Mateo Campground, which is located inland from the coast. A trail that passes under Highway 1 offers access to a day-use beach.

The majority of the state beach parallels Highway 1 for about 3.5 miles. The Marine Corps' Camp Pendleton is located across Highway 1, making it quite common to see tanks and helicopters being used in training exercises while driving either on the highway or in the park.

San Onofre State Beach's coastal campground is actually a series of parking spaces that parallel the bluff above the beach. Many are designed for RVs, while others allow space for tents. This beach is extremely popular with surfers. The area known as Trestles Beach is rumored to have some of the best breaking waves in California, or at least in San Diego County. There are several paths leading from the sandstone bluff parking and campground areas to the beach. From the inland San Mateo Campground there is a 1.5 mile bike trail to the ocean.

Directions: The beach park is located 3 miles south of San Clemente on I-5 at Basilone Road.

Activities: Camping, surfing, swimming, beachcombing, fishing, picnicking.

Facilities: Campground.

Dates: Open year round.

Fees: There are camping and day-use fees.

Closest town: San Clemente, 3 miles.

For more information: Orange Coast State Parks District Office, 3030 Avenida del Presidente, San Clemente, CA 92672. Phone (949) 492-0802.

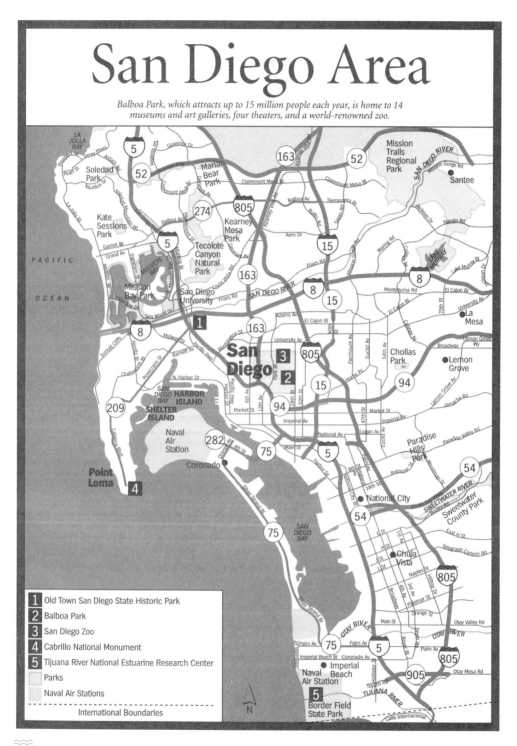

San Diego Area

Balboa Park, which attracts up to 15 million people each year, is home to 14 museums and art galleries, four theaters, and a world-renowned zoo.

1 Old Town San Diego State Historic Park
2 Balboa Park
3 San Diego Zoo
4 Cabrillo National Monument
5 Tijuana River National Estuarine Research Center
Parks
Naval Air Stations
International Boundaries

QUAIL BOTANICAL GARDENS

[Fig. 64(1)] In the hills of Encinitas there is a sprawling, park-like garden that, prior to 1957, was a private residence. It is a quiet place to walk and enjoy literally a world of plants. There are gardens representing different regions and climates of the world, including the Baja desert with its cacti and succulents and South Africa and Madagascar, with their drought-adapted plants. In one area the dragon tree (*Dracea draco*) grows, a curious-looking plant that the garden uses in its logo.

Numerous short footpaths meander through the gardens and waterfalls. Tropical and subtropical plants from Central and South America, such as Peru's Cantua (*Cantua cuzcoensis*), can be found in bloom during California's winter months. There are also flowers from the Canary Islands, such as bicacaro (*Canarina canariensis*), with its beautiful red blooms, and the purple flowers of Echium (*Echium nervosum*), which is thought to be pollinated by lizards. A plant from Iran, broom almond (*Prunus scoparia*), is grown from seed and found in the garden's Middle Eastern Desert plant collection. One of the New Zealand representatives is known as "*puriri*" to the native Maoris; botanists know it as *Vitex lucens*.

Directions: In Encinitas from Interstate 5, take the Encinitas Boulevard Exit and drive east 0.5 mile and turn left on Quail Gardens Drive. The entrance is on the left.

Activities: Tours, workshops, lectures.
Facilities: Gift shop, exhibits.
Dates: Open daily except Thanksgiving, Christmas, and New Year's Day.

Kelp Harvesting

The expansive beds of kelp lying just offshore along much of California's central and south coasts provide essential ingredients for hundreds of common products sold around the world. Giant kelp (*Macrocystis pyrifera*) is an alga that begins as spores. They attach to rocks below the water's surface, where they germinate and grow into separate, microscopic, thread-like male and female plants. Sperm from these microscopic male plants fertilize eggs from the female plants and new young kelp plants begin to develop, doubling in size about every three weeks, eventually reaching up to 100 feet long.

In California, specially designed barges harvest as much as 300 tons of the surface kelp on each trip, cutting it to a depth of 4 feet below the surface. Kelp stalks quickly replenish the crop, growing up to 2 feet each day, as the entire plant stalk is able to feed on passing nutrients in the ocean water.

Kelp is also valuable as food, containing large amounts of iodine, vitamins, minerals, and carbohydrates. But it's the algin that is most important to the commercial kelp harvesters. This substance is used in ice cream to help prevent large ice crystals from forming, and as a thickener and stabilizer in various latex products. Algin is currently used in over 100 other products, ranging from antibiotics to paints.

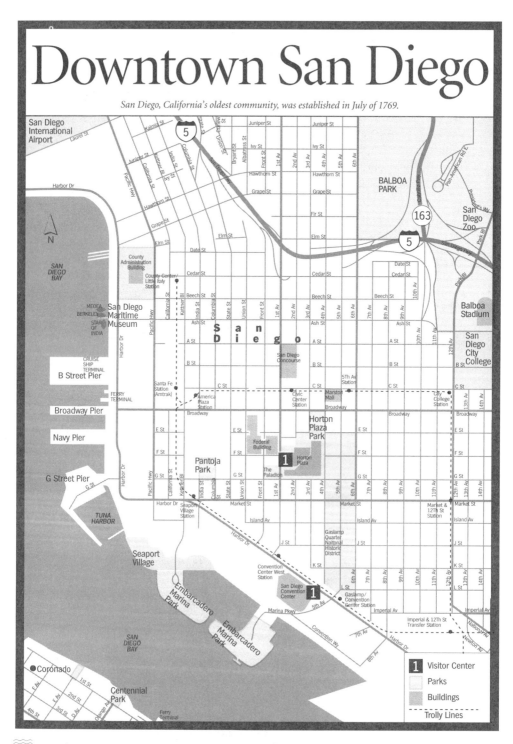

Downtown San Diego

San Diego, California's oldest community, was established in July of 1769.

Fees: There is an entry fee.

For more information: Quail Botanical Gardens Foundation, 230 Quail Gardens Drive, Encinitas, CA 92024. Phone (760) 436-3036.

SCRIPPS INSTITUTE OF OCEANOGRAPHY AND BIRCH AQUARIUM

[Fig. 64(2)] The Birch Aquarium serves as the public education arm of the University of California at San Diego's Scripps Institute of Oceanography. Its outside entrance area is dramatic, with a large fountain sculpture of spy-hopping whales. While the Birch Aquarium may be smaller

Quail Botanical Gardens.

than some of California's other aquariums, its exhibits make up for its size and are a wonderful opportunity to experience underwater domains from around the world.

The aquarium's passageway first leads past the Northwest Coast and the Southern California tanks filled with animals ranging from a giant Pacific octopus (*Octopus dofleini*) and wolf eels (*Anarrhicthys ocellatus*) to round stingrays (*Urolophus mylio-batiformes*) and shiner seaperch (*Cymatogaster aggregata*). The giant kelp forest and its typical fish inhabitants are housed in a 70,000-gallon tank. Nearby, purple-striped jellies (*Pelagia colorata*) float with the currents in their tank and intriguing giant shallow bay sea horses (*Hippocampus ingens*) swim about their own private home. There's also a tank featuring tropical ocean animals, such as bicolor goatfish (*Parupeneus barberinoides*) and surgeon fish (*Acanturidae* sp.).

The aquarium's opposite wing features an interactive exhibit hall that encourages visitors to learn more about oceanography by studying how waves work and the general properties of water. There is also an earthquake machine and seismograph. A large exhibit shows how much humans depend on the ocean for food and products common to everyday life.

Unlike most large aquariums, which are built near their water sources, the Birch Aquarium is located high on the hillside, so the aquarium's outside plaza offers a beautiful and expansive view of the Pacific Ocean in the distance. The plaza also has a model tidepool inhabited by local marine plants and animals. This is a great place to sit and enjoy the view or watch the scheduled tidepool talks given by aquarium volunteers.

Directions: From Interstate 5 in La Jolla, take the La Jolla Village Drive Exit (which becomes North Torrey Pines Road) and drive west 1 mile. Turn left onto Expedition Way and drive 0.5 mile, following the signs to the aquarium parking lot.

Activities: Self-guided tours, demonstrations.

Facilities: Gift shop, museum exhibits.

Dates: Open daily, except Thanksgiving, Christmas, and New Year's Day.

Fees: There is a parking fee and an aquarium entrance fee.

For more information: Birch Aquarium at Scripps, 2300 Expedition Way, La Jolla, CA 92037. Phone (619) 534-FISH.

TORREY PINES STATE RESERVE AND BEACH

[Fig. 64(3)] This reserve protects the Torrey pine (*Pinus torreyana*), the rarest pine tree in the United States. These relatively small, often wind-sculpted pines live only in the park and on Santa Rosa Island, offshore farther north near Santa Barbara. Disease, climate changes, and development have combined forces to reduce the once larger numbers and ranges of the tree to its remaining two small domains.

While the park's namesake is the Torrey pine, which grows primarily on the ancient terrace above the beach, there is also a major saltwater marsh area lying just to the north. With saltwater marshes nearly extinct in Southern California, this area is a vital link in the Pacific Flyway for migrating birds. Surrounded by houses and other development on both sides, the marsh is an island paradise for wildlife.

From the park's entry gate at the beach level, it's a short, but steep walk, bicycle ride, or drive to the top of the terrace, where trailheads and a small visitor center are located. The visitor center is inside the pueblo-style house that was originally built in 1923 as a restaurant. Today it houses exhibits on the park's natural and cultural history, in addition to a small gift shop. There is also a garden of native plants, each identified with both common and scientific names, in front of the house. Wonderful easterly views can be seen from the bluff behind the visitor center.

The trails are relatively short and several drop down between the steeply carved gullies and lead to the beach along the face of the bluff. Look closely at the bluff and fossils of ancient marine creatures can occasionally be found imprinted in the soft rocks. The park is protected, so digging in the bluff is not allowed, but high tides and winter wave action often uncover new rock.

The reserve and the beach are open for day use only. There is no camping in either. When walking the trails, please do not take shortcuts up or down the switchbacks, which tend to increase erosion rates. Picnicking is not allowed in the reserve, but food may be taken down to the beach. Because of the high fire danger, smoking is not permitted in the reserve. For those who do not wish to hike the trails to the beach, there is a parking lot next to the reserve and a beach entry kiosk, which is at sea level and only a few yards from the beach.

Directions: The parks are located between La Jolla and Del Mar. From Hwy 5, exit on Carmel Valley Road and drive west for about 1.5 miles, turning left (south) onto US 101. Drive about 1 mile to the park entrance, which is on the ocean side of the highway.

Activities: Hiking, swimming, fishing, surfing, beachcombing, beach picnics.

Facilities: Visitor center, gift shop.

California's Missions

First by way of Spain's insistence, then continued under the Mexican government, the Franciscan padres built 21 missions in California. In part they were a political ploy designed to claim California in an effort to keep the encroaching Russians, English, and finally, the Americans at bay.

At age 56, Padre Junipero Serra, appointed as *Padre Presidente* began his monumental task, establishing the first mission in San Diego in 1769. With no formal building experience and using Native American laborers who had never before seen buildings, he and those who followed in his footsteps constructed 21 missions in just 54 years. The missions were sited about 40 miles apart, the distance that could be traveled in a single day. The path that developed connecting the missions that stretched 600 miles north to Sonoma and became known as *El Camino Real*, The King's Highway. Today US 101 follows much of that original pathway.

The missions were designed to be self-supporting. Indians, converted to Christianity, raised cattle and sheep and grew and harvested crops. The missions were quite successful, although they forever changed the lives and cultures of Native Americans. Many thousands of Indians died of European diseases, from which they had no immunity. The padres insisted that they no longer practice their own native cultural rites and celebrations. As older generations of Native Americans died, so did their cultures and understanding of their origins.

The mission system began to crumble following secularization of the church's mission lands. In 1835 the Mexican government forced the church to return lands it had taken from the Indians. Few mission Indians benefited from land return though, most being cheated by hustlers. With economic support systems gone, many of the churches had to be abandoned and were allowed to crumble. Today many of the missions have been restored. The Catholic church still owns most of the old mission churches and holds regular worship services.

Dates: Open daily, day use only.

Fees: There is a day use fee.

For more information: San Diego Coast District State Parks, 9609 Waples Street, Suite 200 San Diego, CA 92121. Phone (858) 755-2063 or (619) 642-4200.

OLD TOWN SAN DIEGO STATE HISTORIC PARK

[Fig. 65(1)] Though San Diego is California's oldest community, established in July 1769, Spain placed little importance on it and provided only intermittent support. There were far richer treasures to be had from Spain's long-established colonies in Mexico. Spain's impetus for settling Alta (Upper) California was to create a reasonably defendable boundary that might discourage the Russians, English, and

LONG-BILLED CURLEW
(Numenius americanus)

This bird is cinnamon-brown above and buff below and can be recognized by its call, a loud, musical, ascending "cur-lee."

others from invading its Mexican colonies.

Fray (Father) Junipero Serra was given the primary task of making the new mission system in California effective and efficient. His efforts went into gathering the local Indians, converting them to Christianity, and teaching them farming and ranching skills, ending their native way of life. The purpose of the mission program was to create loyal Spanish citizens who ultimately might aid in defending California, or at least wouldn't join in any attacks on the new Spanish colonies.

Father Serra founded California's first mission, *San Diego de Alcalá*, and began his life-long endeavor of gathering Indians and converting them to Christianity. The mission fathers required that the Indians live at the mission, even though there was seldom enough food available. Indians were severely punished for "misbehaviors." Often the Indians "misbehaviors" were actions related to their own customs, actions they did not understand were unacceptable to the Spanish. Lonely soldiers molested Indian women and European diseases decimated Indian populations. All of this finally resulted in the Indians attacking and burning the San Diego Mission in 1775.

Even though San Diego's Indians continued their intermittent and often strong resistance to the changes that the mission's fathers demanded, by 1800 there were about 1,500 "neophytes" living on mission lands. But the Indians never benefited from their conversion to Christianity and European ways, remaining in poverty even after Mexico gained control and released the church-controlled lands back to them. Their situation did not change for the better when the United States finally gained control of California.

Walk the roads of Old Town San Diego today and it takes a bit of work to imagine what it was like here more than 200 years ago. The historic adobes have been restored and many are being used for museums, gift shops, stores, and restaurants. There's a plaza near the center of the historic park and the streets no longer turn to mud during San Diego's very infrequent rainy days.

In spite of, or maybe because of, Old Town's reformation from near ruin when it became a state historic park in 1968, this is an incredibly fun and informative place to spend several hours. For history buffs, there are nearly two dozen historic buildings, some of which have been restored and refurbished. Others are now museums that exhibit hundreds of early San Diego artifacts.

La Casa de Estudillo is the centerpiece of the park. Captain Jose Maria de Estudillo built the adobe in 1827-29, but was only able to enjoy his new home for a year. Estudillo died in 1830, and the home passed to his children and then, unfortunately, to a caretaker who sold many of its fixtures. Building restoration began in 1910, along with efforts to refurnish the home. Today it provides a wonderful look at how these early Spanish and Mexican settlers lived.

La Casa de Bandini was constructed in 1829 by Juan Bandini, Jose Estudillo's son-in-law. Bandini was always a step ahead politically, holding offices under the Mexican government's control, then providing supplies and his home to the U.S. Navy's Commodore Stockton when the Americans took over. In 1850 Bandini sold his home to Albert Seeley, who added the second floor and turned it into the Cosmopolitan Hotel. Today it is a colorful Mexican restaurant with a beautiful outdoor garden seating area in addition to its indoor tables.

The Seeley Stable belonged to Albert Seeley who owned the San Diego-Los Angeles Stage Line and ran his Concord stages over the 130-mile trip in less than 24 hours. The Southern Pacific Railroad ran Seeley out of business in 1887. Today the stable and barn hold an extensive horse-drawn carriage collection and exhibits of Western memorabilia, including saddles and Indian artifacts.

Bazaar del Mundo is where nearly everyone who comes to Old Town San Diego ends up. It's a large cluster of buildings in the corner of the historic park that greets everyone with its multitude of brightly-colored flowers. The walkways pass shops filled with treasures, from fine jewelry and clothes to china and paintings, mostly from Central and South America. There are also several restaurants serving a variety of foods, but Mexican cuisine is the specialty; it seems only appropriate while in this historic Spanish-Mexican town.

Directions: From Interstate 5 in San Diego, take the Old Town Avenue Exit and drive east. Turn left on San Diego Avenue, which leads to the park.

Activities: Shopping, dining, historic tours.

Facilities: Shops, restaurants, museums, historic buildings.

Dates: Open daily, except Thanksgiving, Christmas, and New Year's Day.

Fees: There is an entrance fee for Seeley Stables and La Casa de Estudillo.

For more information: San Diego Historic Park, 4002 Wallace Street, San Diego, CA 92110. Phone (619) 220-5424 or (619) 220-5422.

▒ BALBOA PARK

[Fig. 65(2)] Named one of the best urban parks in the United States, Balboa Park's 1,400 acres are home to 14 museums and art galleries, four theaters, and a world-renowned zoo. The park attracts up to 15 million people each year. Although officially established in 1868 by the City of San Diego, the park began to establish its reputation in 1915 when it teamed with San Francisco in trying to be named the site of the 1915 California-Panama Exposition. Twenty years later San Diego officially hosted the California Pacific International Exposition in 1935, bringing additional new buildings to what was still simply known as City Park.

The **San Diego Museum of Man** (619-239-2001) is housed inside the California Building, which was constructed during the city's 1915 attempt to win the Exposition. Beneath its bright blue dome are numerous permanent exhibits focusing on educating people about the science of anthropology. One of the museum's permanent exhibits includes *Life and Death on the Nile: Sungods and Mummies in Ancient Egypt*, which features 3,000-year-old Egyptian artifacts.

For those more interested in local human history, *Kumeyaay: Indians of San Diego* is an exhibit that presents the lifestyle of the local Native American population. *Early Man* uses fossils, tools, and models to demonstrate evolution, while *Life Cycles and Ceremonies* is about human reproduction, birth, and the life-related rituals with which we surround ourselves in our daily lives.

The Museum of Man is located at 1350 El Prado, in San Diego's Balboa Park. It's open daily except Thanksgiving, Christmas, and New Year's Day. There is an entry fee.

Two other museums worth visiting while in Balboa Park include the **San Diego Natural History Museum**, which is open daily and is located at 1788 El Prado, phone (619) 232-3821, and the **Museum of San Diego History**, located at 1649 El Prado, phone (619) 232-6203. The latter is closed on Mondays, Thanksgiving, Christmas Eve, Christmas, and New Year's Day.

Directions: Balboa Park is located near mid-San Diego and there are numerous access points. The easiest is near the junction of Interstate 5 and Highway 163. Well-marked exits from both highways lead to Park Boulevard, which passes through the park nearest its main museum attractions and the zoo.

Activities: Picnicking, bicycling, swimming, golf, jogging.

Facilities: Museums, zoo, golf course, gardens.

Dates: The park is open daily, but some of its museums and other facilities may be closed on holidays.

Fees: The park is free. There is a fee for most of the facilities.

For more information: Balboa Park Visitors Center, 2125 Park Blvd, San Diego 92101. Phone (619) 239-0512.

SAN DIEGO ZOO

From pandas to prairie dogs, this is one of California's best zoos, featuring 4,000 animals representing 800 species from around the world. Its design allows for easy walking around the heavily vegetated 100-acre park. For those unable or unwilling to spend the day walking, there is the Kangaroo Bus Tour that constantly drives around the zoo, making stops at nearly all of the major exhibits. Skyfari Aerial Tram also travels across the zoo, offering great views.

The zoo's numerous exhibits are designed to allow the animals to live in what is as close as possible to their natural habitat, while still allowing visitors great views of the animals. One example is what appears to be a large pond fronted by a 100-foot-long glass viewing window. Behind the window, river hippos, which when fully grown can weigh 8,000 pounds, swim underwater, surfacing occasionally and opening their mouths to reveal their large teeth. The hippos eat about 100 pounds of various vegetables, fruit, and hay each day; not quite a natural diet of grass and river vegetation, but quite nutritious.

Gorilla Tropics is a 2.5-acre re-creation of an African rain forest. It features four aviaries of African birds and seven gorillas, all surrounded by native African plants, and even the authentic sounds of Africa's jungle environment. Alvila, a 32-year-old female gorilla, is the first gorilla to be born in the San Diego Zoo.

The large Polar Bear Plunge exhibit is the one of the largest polar bear exhibits in the world, although it seems a bit strange to have an arctic tundra environment in warm and humid San Diego. The zoo's polar bears are neighbors with Siberian reindeer, arctic foxes, and numerous ducks and birds from the far north. A two-level indoor underwater viewing area lets you meet the bears face-to-face through a bear-proof, 5-inch-thick acrylic window. Here's an opportunity to see the bears in action, much closer than you'd ever want to see them in the wild.

A relatively new exhibit is the Pygmy Chimps at Bonobo Road, which, much like Gorilla Tropics, also replicates an African rain forest. Also called bonobos, pygmy chimpanzees are a separate species that have genes, behavior, and intelligence more closely related to the human primate than do their larger and more common chimp cousins. Bonobos weren't even discovered by Western scientists until the 1930s and studies of them in their native Zaire didn't begin until the 1970s. Like many African animals, their populations are being impacted by human actions.

Among the hundreds of exotic animals housed in the zoo there are also pygmy chimpanzees, Angolan colobus monkeys, rare African crowned eagles, and Garnett's galagos. Galagos are primates from Africa that are both arboreal and nocturnal. For those who have tarantulas for pets, the zoo keeps its pet baboon tarantula, a baby at only 5 inches across, in a large log exhibit. They can grow to 9 inches.

Plan to spend most of the day in the zoo. And if you want to see the pandas, get to their enclosure early in the day. The line to see these cute critters gets longer later in the day.

Directions: The San Diego Zoo is located at 2920 Zoo Drive in Balboa Park. From I-5 south, take Highway 163 north and then the Zoo/Museums Exit. From 163 North, exit at University. Go east on University to Balboa Park.

Activities: Exhibits, bus tours.
Facilities: Gift shop, food vendors.
Dates: Open daily.
Fees: There is an entrance fee.
For more information: San Diego Zoo, PO Box 551, San Diego, CA 92112-0551. Phone (619) 234-3153.

CABRILLO NATIONAL MONUMENT

[Fig. 65(4)] The monument memorializes Juan Rodriquez Cabrillo, the first European to land on what would become the West Coast of the United States just over 400 years later. Cabrillo spent less than a week here before continuing his exploration north along the coast. Today on the grounds of Cabrillo National Monument, rather than the isolation and the Native Americans that Cabrillo and his crew would have encountered, there is a museum, the **Point Loma Lighthouse**, the remains of **Fort Rosecrans**, and spectacular views of the city of San Diego and its sprawling harbor.

Cabrillo National Monument has become a popular daytime destination for thousands of people each year. From inside the glass-enclosed museum, the mountains can be seen to the east, as well as Tijuana, Mexico to the south. Besides the museum, with its displays about the Spanish exploration of California, there are tidepools to explore and whale watching for migrating gray whales during winter.

On the closest weekend to September 28, the day that Cabrillo landed, the annual Cabrillo Festival is held, with a re-enactment of his landing and plenty of food and cultural dances to keep everyone active and satisfied. The third weekend in January is also Whale Watch Weekend, with lots of marine related programs, demonstrations, and whale watching at the peak of the gray whales' southern migration.

In addition to the films shown in the visitor center, rangers lead tours of the tidepools and coastal scrub plant community. The Point Loma Lighthouse, restored and furnished as an 1880s lighthouse, is open daily for tours. There is also a self-guided trail with interpretive panels along the way that tell the natural and cultural history of Point Loma.

While exploring the park, visitors are required to stay on established trails in order to protect the fragile coastal sage scrub ecosystem. The cliff edge is very unstable and crumbles easily, so visitors are advised to remain well away.

Directions: From near the intersection of Interstate 5 and Interstate 8 in San Diego, take Highway 209 south about 7 miles to its end at the monument.
Activities: Hiking, fishing, picnicking.
Facilities: Visitor center, gift shop, museum.
Dates: Open daily.
Fees: Fees are charged to enter the park.
Closest town: San Diego, 7 miles.

For more information: Superintendent, Cabrillo National Monument, 1800 Cabrillo Memorial Drive, San Diego, CA 92106-3601. Phone (619) 557-5450.

SAN DIEGO DINING

Casa de Bandini. 2754 Calhoun Street, San Diego. Located in the heart of San Diego State Historic Park, this historic adobe-turned-restaurant has both inside and outside garden dining. The menu features Mexican and seafood. Everything is casual. The restaurant gets busy on weekends and reservations generally aren't taken. *Inexpensive. Phone (619) 297-8211.*

Harbor House Restaurant. 831 W. Harbor Drive, San Diego. Featuring fresh seafood and a children's menu, the restaurant is located in popular Seaport Village, so there are good views of the harbor. Dress casually. Reservations are suggested. *Inexpensive. Phone (619) 232-1141.*

Lino's Italian Restaurant. 2754 Calhoun Street, San Diego. Another restaurant in Old Town San Diego, this small, quiet Italian eating place is tucked into colorful Bazaar Del Mundo. They serve traditional Italian food in a casual dress atmosphere, with outdoor seating also available. Reservations are not taken. *Inexpensive. Phone (619) 299-7124.*

Mister A's. 2550 Fifth Avenue, San Diego. Here is an opportunity to dress a little fancier as semiformal attire is suggested. The restaurant sits on the top floor of the Fifth Avenue Financial Center so the views of the city and bay are exceptional. They menu is traditional Continental. Reservations are suggested. *Moderate. Phone (619) 239-1377.*

SAN DIEGO LODGING

Balboa Park Inn. 3402 Park Boulevard, San Diego. Located near Balboa Park, with gardens and a courtyard. A few of the 26 rooms have fireplaces. *Moderate to Expensive. Phone (619) 298-0823.*

Hacienda Hotel Old Town. 4041 Harney Street, San Diego. Situated on a hill above Old Town San Diego, the hotel is within walking distance of dozens of shops, restaurants, and museums. It's also just a short drive to Sea World. *Expensive. Phone (619) 298-4707.*

Island Palms Hotel & Marina. 2051 Shelter Island Drive, San Diego. The hotel fronts San Diego Bay and is within about ten minutes driving time from most of the city's attractions, including the zoo, Sea World, and Old Town San Diego State Historic Park. Some rooms have kitchens and most rooms have views of the bay or harbor. *Expensive. Phone (619) 222-0561 or (800) 345-9995.*

Holiday Inn (Mission Bay Sea World Area). 3737 Sports Arena Boulevard, San Diego. For walkers, the hotel is just a mile from Old Town, Sea World, and Mission Bay, or it's just a quick drive to these and other destinations. *Moderate. Phone (800) 405-9098.*

TIGER SALAMANDER
(Ambystoma tigrinum)

Hyatt Regency San Diego. One Market Place, San Diego. This is one of the city's many skyscrapers, with 40 stories and almost 900 rooms. It's on the waterfront and all rooms have bay views. The full-service hotel is located near Seaport Village and the convention center. *Expensive. Phone (619) 232-1234.*

TIJUANA RIVER NATIONAL ESTUARINE RESEARCH RESERVE

[Fig. 65(5)] Within view of Mexico, the Tijuana River National Estuarine Research Reserve has brought together three partners, California State Parks, the U.S. Fish and Wildlife Service, and the National Oceanic and Atmospheric Administration, in order to protect 2,500 acres of wetlands. Tijuana Slough National Wildlife Refuge, Borderfield State Park, and Tijuana River Valley County Park are included within the Reserve's boundary.

With development having filled more than 90 percent of California's coastal wetlands, the reserve has become a critical resting and feeding stop for millions of migrating birds each year. Within the reserve, numerous trails meander among the tules and rushes and around the open and protected waters of the estuary that lie just north of the border that separates the U.S. and Mexico's Baja, California.

Established in 1982, the Tijuana River Estuary is one of only 22 national estuarine research reserves in the nation. The estuary is jointly managed by the U.S. Fish and Wildlife Service and California State Parks. **Border Field State Park** lies in the far southwest corner of the estuary, with a view of the bull ring on the Mexican side of the border. There is a marker here that was placed on the site in 1851 following the treaty of Guadalupe Hidalgo that identifies the international border.

Part of what makes the estuary and the neighboring state park so attractive is the diverse natural habitats that they encompass. But the reserve has not always been so pristine. Walk the **McCoy Trail** from the visitor center and you're walking on a dike built before World War II, when the area was divided into sections used as sewage settling ponds. The dikes were breached in the 1980s and the natural tidal flow was restored to the area.

Riparian, coastal sage scrub, open beaches, salt marsh, and mud flats provide the diversity of food and safe havens for over 370 species of migratory and native birds. At least six endangered species are seen here: California least tern (*Sterna antillarum*), California brown pelican (*Pelecanus occidentalis*), the light-footed clapper rail (*Rallus longirostris levipes*), western snowy plover (*Charadrius alexandrinus*), least Bell's vireo (*Vireo bellii pusillus*), and Belding's savannah sparrow (*Passerculus sandwichensis beldingi).* In addition to the endangered species, plenty of non-endangered birds also can be seen throughout the two areas. American kestrels (*Falco sparverius*), peregrine falcons (*Falco peregrinus*), sandpipers (*Calidris minutilla*), black-necked stilts (*Himantopus mexicanus*), hummingbirds, and snowy egrets (*Egretta thula*) are only a few of the more commonly observed birds.

The animals here depend on the different plant habitats scattered around the reserve. Dunes, salt marsh, mud flat, vernal pool, brackish pond, and coastal sage scrub are the most common, with the presence or absence of saltwater significantly changing the types of plants that can inhabit any area. For example, in the upper marsh, salt marsh bird's beak (*Cordylanthus maritimus*), a federally listed plant, grows just above the high tide line. The reserve is one of the few places in the world where the plant is able to survive.

There are several miles of trail that cross the relatively flat terrain, offering access to prime bird-viewing areas and a path down to the mouth of the Tijuana River, where it empties into the Pacific Ocean. The river drains over 1,700 square miles of watershed along the California and Mexican border.

There is a visitor center that features exhibits on the area's plants and animals, a research library, interpretive programs, special trips, and videos. Outside the visitor center is a garden filled with indigenous plants from the area. There's also a painted version of the reserve on the sidewalk.

Directions: To reach the National Estuarine Reserve from Interstate 5, approximately 10 miles south of San Diego, take the Coronado Avenue Exit and drive west for 2.5 miles. Turn left on Third Street which turns to the left and becomes Caspian Way, leading into the reserve's gravel parking lot. To reach Border Field, take the Coronado Avenue Exit and go west, turning left (south) on Hollister Road for 2.2 miles. Turn right on Monument Road and drive about 2.7 miles to the parking area.

Activities: Hiking, bird-watching, beachcombing, horseback riding.

Facilities: Visitor center, picnic facilities.

Dates: Open daily.

Fees: None.

Closest town: Imperial Beach.

For more information: Tijuana Slough National Wildlife Refuge, 301 Caspian Way, Imperial Beach, CA 91932. Phone (619) 575-2704 or (619) 575-3613.

Appendices

A. Books and References

Alcatraz, Island of Change by James P. Delgado, Golden Gate National Park Association, San Francisco, CA 1991.

The Audubon Society Nature Guides: Pacific Coast by Baynard H. McConnaughey and Evelyn McConnaughey, Alfred A. Knopf, New York, NY 1990.

California Butterflies by John S. Garth and J.W. Tilden, University of California Press, Berkeley, CA 1986.

California Coastal Access Guide, California Coastal Commission, University of California Press, Berkeley and Los Angeles, CA 1983.

California Coastline Explore Series, U.S. Army Corps of Engineers, Public Affairs Offices, San Francisco District, CA 1980-81.

The California Indians: A Source Book, compiled and edited by R.F. Heizer and M.A. Whipple, University of California Press, Los Angeles and Berkeley, CA 1971.

California Landscape: Origin and Evolution by Mary Hill, University of California Press, Berkeley and Los Angeles, CA 1984.

Coast Walks: 101 Adventures Along the California Coast by John McKinney, Olympus Press, Santa Barbara, CA 1999.

Gray Whales by David G. Gordon and Alan Baldridge, Monterey Bay Aquarium Foundation, Monterey, CA 1991.

Historic Spots in California by Mildred Brooke Hoover, Hero Eugene Rensch, Ethel Grace Rensch, William N. Abeloe, revised by Douglas E. Kyle, Stanford University Press, Stanford, CA 1990.

The Jepson Manual: Higher Plants in California by James C. Hickman, Editor, University of California Press, Los Angeles and Berkeley, CA 1993.

Marin Headlands: Portals of Time by Harold and Ann Lawrence Gilliam, Golden Gate National Park Association, San Francisco, CA 1993.

Monterey Bay Aquarium by Michael Rigsby, Hank Armstrong, Ken Peterson, and Judy Rand, Monterey Bay Aquarium, Monterey, CA 1992.

The Nature of California by James Kavanagh, Waterford Press, San Francisco, CA 1994.

Natural History of the Monterey Bay National Marine Sanctuary by the Monterey Bay Aquarium in cooperation with the National Oceanic and Atmospheric Administration Sanctuaries and Reserves Division, Monterey Bay Aquarium Foundation, Monterey, CA 1997.

Roadside Geology of Northern California by David D. Alt and Donald W. Hyndman, Mountain Press Publishing Co., Missoula, MT 1975.

Water Birds of California by Howard L. Cogswell, Illustrations by Gene Christman, University of California Press, Berkeley, CA 1977.

B. Conservation Organizations

The following are some of the more prominent nonprofit organizations dedicated to the preservation and/or enjoyment of California's rich natural and cultural resources.

California Native Plant Society, 1722 J Street, Suite 17, Sacramento, CA 95814. Phone (916) 447-2677. http://www.cnps.org. A statewide organization of amateur and professional botanists that seeks to increase understanding of California's native flora and to preserve this rich resource for future generations.

California State Parks Foundation, PO Box 548, Kentfield, CA 94914. Phone (415) 258-9975. http://www.calparks.org. This nonprofit membership organization is dedicated to protecting and enhancing the rich natural, cultural, and historical resources found within California's state parks; improving visitor experiences, facilities, and services; promoting volunteerism and stewardship; advocating on behalf of state parks; and developing educational programs.

Center for Marine Conservation, 1725 DeSales Street, Suite 600, Washington, DC 20036. Phone (202) 429-5609. http://www.cmc-ocean.org. This is the nation's leading nonprofit organization dedicated solely to protecting marine life in all its abundance and diversity. It is at the forefront of every major issue affecting this great "blue planet": preventing pollution, protecting dolphins, whales, sea turtles, and all marine species, preserving critical marine habitat, and ensuring the healthy future of our nation's fisheries.

Friends of the Sea Otter, 2150 Garden Road, Monterey, CA 93940. Phone (831) 831-373-2747. http://www.seaotter.org. This nonprofit is dedicated to protecting the rare and endangered southern sea otter, as well as sea otters throughout their north Pacific range and throughout the world.

National Audubon Society, Audubon-California, 555 Audubon Place, Sacramento, CA 95825. Phone (916) 481-5332. http://www.audubon.org. The society strives to conserve and restore natural ecosystems, focusing on birds and other wildlife for the benefit of humanity and the earth's biological diversity.

The Nature Conservancy, California Regional Office, 201 Mission Street, 4th Floor, San Francisco, CA 94105. Phone (415) 777-0487. http://www.tnc.org. The Nature Conservancy was founded in 1951 and today is the world's leading private, international conservation group. It preserves habitats and species by saving the lands and waters they need to survive. The conservancy manages 1,340 preserves, the largest system of private nature sanctuaries in the world.

Oceanic Society, Fort Mason Center, Building E, San Francisco, CA 94123. Phone (800) 326-7491. http://www.oceanic-society.org. The Oceanic Society is a nonprofit organization working to protect marine mammals and the marine environment through conservation-based research and environmental education.

Planning and Conservation League, 926 J Street, Suite 612 Sacramento, CA

95814. Phone (916) 444-8726. http://www.pcl.org. The Planning and Conservation League is a nonprofit, statewide alliance of nearly 10,000 citizens and more than 120 conservation organizations that are united to protect wildlife and restore the quality of California's environment through legislative and administrative action.

Save the Redwoods League, 114 Sansome Street Room 605, San Francisco, CA 94104-3814. Phone (415) 362-2352. http://www.savetheredwoods.org. Since 1918 the league has been preserving California's redwood forests by purchasing redwood forest land, which is then turned over to one of the 37 California Redwood State Parks, to Redwood or Sequoia National Park, or to another public park or reserve, where the redwoods provide education and enjoyment today and are protected for tomorrow.

Sierra Club, 85 Second Street, Second Floor, San Francisco, CA 94105-3441. Phone (415) 977-5500. http://www.sierraclub.org. **Sierra Club Offices: Angeles Chapter Headquarters Office**, 3435 Wilshire Blvd #320, Los Angeles, CA 90010-1904. Phone (213) 387-4287. **Mother Lode Chapter Sierra Club**, 1414 K Street, Suite 300, Sacramento CA 95814. Phone (916) 557-1100 ext. 108. This grassroots organization endeavors to preserve irreplaceable wildlands, save endangered and threatened wildlife, and protect the earth's fragile environment.

The Trust for Public Land, Western Regional Office, 116 New Montgomery Street, 3rd Floor, San Francisco, CA 94105. Phone (415) 495-5660. http://www.tpl.org. The Trust for Public Land offers consultation services to public and private landowners seeking to create parks, maintain open space, protect waterways, and establish city greenways.

The Wilderness Society, 900 17th Avenue NW, Washington DC 90006. Phone (800) 843-9453. **California/Nevada Region of The Wilderness Society**, Presidio Building 1016, PO Box 29241, San Francisco, CA 94129-0241. Phone (415) 561-6641. http://www.wilderness.org. The society was formed in 1935 in order to develop a nationwide network of wildlands through public education, scientific analysis, and advocacy.

WESTERN HARVEST MOUSE
(Reithrodontomys megalotus)
This mouse frequently makes use of ground runways
of other rodents and is a nimble climber.

C. Special Events, Fairs, and Festivals

Before making plans to attend any event, please call for dates, times, and specific locations.

▓ JANUARY

Sea Lion Arrival at Pier 39, San Francisco. Each year hundreds of marine mammals return to San Francisco Bay for the plentiful herring supply. Mid-January. Phone (415) 705-5500.

Whale Watching, Oxnard and Ventura. Daily, January through March. Coastal whale-watching boat trips to observe gray whales' annual migration are available. Whales can also be seen from shore during this time. Contact Island Packers. Phone (800) 474-1361 or (805) 382-1779.

Winter Bird Festival, Morro Bay. Guided tours of estuary and surrounding areas; bird watching. Mid-January. Phone (800) 231-0592 or (805) 772-4467.

Tournament of Roses Parade, Pasadena. World-renowned parade of flower-covered floats and marching bands. January 1. Phone (626) 449-4100.

Reenactment of 1847 American Military Occupation of Mission San Luis Rey, Oceanside. A living history event that includes period costumes, docent-led tours, and infantry drills. Mid-January. Phone (760) 757-3651.

▓ FEBRUARY

World Championship Crab Races, Crescent City. A day of Dungeness crab races, crab feeds, children's games, and an art fair. Mid-February. Phone (800) 343-8300 or (707) 464-3174.

Fireman's Games, Ferndale. A day filled with various volunteer firefighters' competitions including a bucket brigade, hose coupling, and water polo. Mid-February. Phone (707) 786-9909.

▓ MARCH

Mendocino Whale Festival, Mendocino. Whale-watching walks and excursions, along with wine and clam chowder tastings. First weekend in March. Phone (707) 961-6300.

Chinese New Year's Parade, San Francisco. Celebrate the Chinese New Year at the largest Chinese New Year festival in the U.S. Parade with lion dancing and marching bands. Mid-February. Phone (415) 982-3000.

A Day of Romance in Old Monterey, Monterey. Living history performances that feature romantic stories from nineteenth century Monterey. Includes food and music. Saturday nearest Valentine's Day. Phone (831) 647-6204.

Steinbeck Birthday Celebration, Salinas. Celebration of the life and literary works of author John Steinbeck. Late February. Phone (831) 796-3833.

Festival of Whales Street Faire, Dana Point. Included are more than 100 arts and craft vendors, amusement rides, a petting zoo, games and entertainment, and free child finger-printing. Late February. Phone (800) 290-DANA or (949) 496-1555.

Aleutian Goose Festival, Crescent City. Celebrate the rebirth of this once-endangered goose; workshops and field trips featuring birds, plants, and whales; ocean, river, and coastal lagoon trips. One weekend in late March. Phone (800) 343-8300 or (707) 465-0888.

Whales, Wildlife & Wildflowers, Point Reyes. View elephant seals, great blue heron, egrets, and gray whales or go on wildflower walks, enjoy art exhibits, and tour the historic lighthouse. Late March through early April. Phone (415) 499-5000.

Hearst Castle Evening Tours, San Simeon. Living history programs feature docents in period attire. March through May. Phone (800) 444-4445 or (805) 927-2093.

Fat Tuesday Mardi Gras on Cannery Row, Monterey. Monterey Doo Dah Parade, music, and street dancing. Early March. Phone (831) 649-6690.

Return of the Swallows Celebration, San Juan Capistrano. This annual celebration begins with the traditional ringing of the historic Mission San Juan Capistrano bells at dawn, which is followed by lively entertainment, food, and displays. March 19. Phone (949) 248-2048.

APRIL

Godwit Days Spring Migration Bird Festival, Arcata. This month-long festival for local and visiting bird watchers includes bird-watching tours, workshops, and keynote speakers. Phone (707) 822-3619.

Passport to the Wineries of the Santa Cruz Mountains, Santa Cruz County. Here's an opportunity to purchase limited production, award-winning wines. Mid-April. Phone (831) 479-WINE.

Presidio Day, Santa Barbara. This celebration of California's early arts, crafts, and music takes place at the historic 1782 presidio. Mid-April. Phone (805) 965-0093.

Big Sur International Marathon, Big Sur. Probably the most spectacular marathon course in the country, the route follows along the Pacific Coast Highway from Big Sur to Carmel. Late April. Phone (831) 625-6226.

MAY

Kinetic Sculpture Race, Arcata/Ferndale. Wild and crazy people-powered sculptures race for three days across land, sand, and sea to the Victorian village of Ferndale. Late May. Phone (707) 786-9259.

Mountain Play, Mill Valley. This popular Shakespearean play is presented annually in a unique outdoor amphitheater atop beautiful Mount Tamalpais. Advance ticket purchase is advised. Sundays, May-June. Phone (415) 383-1100.

California Strawberry Festival, Oxnard. Lots of fresh strawberries from local fields, music, and more than 300 arts and crafts booths. Mid-May. Phone (888) 288-9242 or (805) 385-7578.

Art Under The Arches, Solvang. This arts and crafts show celebrates the history and culture of Mission Santa Inés, with works ranging from traditional Chumash and Mission period to contemporary. Late May. Phone (805) 688-4815.

Buds 'N Bloom, A Floral Fiesta In Balboa Park, San Diego. Tour gardens, see special exhibits, and enjoy musical and dramatic presentations. May 1-30. Phone (619) 239-0512 or (619) 235-1000.

Fiesta Cinco de Mayo, San Diego. This annual celebration features continuous entertainment including mariachi music and folkloric dancing. Early May weekend. Phone (619) 296-3161 or (619) 220-5422.

JUNE

Pony Express Days, McKinleyville. Features a parade, arts and crafts fair, barbecue, pony rides, and more. Phone (707) 839-2449.

Arcata Bay Oyster Festival, Arcata. This festival features oyster delicacies prepared by local chefs and an oyster-calling contest. Mid-June. Phone (707) 822-4500.

The Great Cannery Row Sardine Festival & Frog Jump, Monterey. Enjoy a frog jumping contest, a sardine-eating contest, Steinbeck exhibits, multicultural presentations, music, and dancing. Phone (831) 649-6690.

Santa Catalina Island Adventure Challenge, Avalon. Watch or participate in trail running, ocean kayaking, mountain biking, and swimming team competitions. Mid-June. Phone (714) 978-1528.

JULY

Harvest Century Bicycle Tour, Healdsburg. Enjoy a guided bicycle tour of scenic Sonoma wine country. Mid-July. Phone (800) 648-9922 or (707) 433-6935.

Native American Big-Time Celebration, Point Reyes Station. This celebration features many Native American demonstrations, arts, and crafts, dancing, bead drilling, flint knapping, and basketry. Mid-July. Phone (415) 663-1092.

Sloat Landing Living History Festival, Monterey. This living history program commemorates the U.S. takeover of California and includes historic military units and live cannon fire. Early July. Phone (831) 647-6204.

Lotus Festival, Los Angeles. This celebration of Asian-Pacific cultures includes entertainment, art exhibits, and ethnic foods. Early July. Phone (213) 485-1310.

Open Sandcastle Competition, Imperial Beach. This sandcastle competition is capped off by the mayor's breakfast, the Sandcastle Ball, a parade, and fireworks. Late July. Phone (619) 424-3151.

AUGUST

Salmon Festival, Klamath. Yurok Indians celebrate their culture with a traditional salmon barbecue, demonstrations, Indian stick games, and Indian music. Mid-August. Phone (707) 444-0433.

Historic Homes Tour, Angel Island. Tours of historic homes highlight the lives of former residents. Food and wine tastings are also part of the event. Early August. Phone (415) 435-3522.

PowWow, Costa Mesa. This annual powwow features American Indian dancers, singers, arts and crafts, and food. Early August. Phone (714) 663-1102.

Longboard Surfing Contest, Oceanside. Here the legends of surfing participate in the original surfing contest. Phone (800) 350-7873 or (760) 721-1101.

SEPTEMBER

Paul Bunyan Days, Fort Bragg. Enjoy a parade, craft fair, logging show, water fight, and square dance. Early September. Phone (707) 961-6300.

Hearst Castle Evening Tours, San Simeon. It's a living history program that features docents in period attire. September through December. Phone (800) 444-4445 or (805) 927-2093.

California Beach & Music Festival, Ventura. This end-of-summer party features entertainment, food, multicultural music, and arts and crafts. Mid-September. Phone (661) 260-3000.

California Avocado Festival, Carpinteria. This festival features the World's Largest Bowl of Guacamole, arts and crafts, food, contests, and entertainment. Late September, early October. Phone (805) 684-0038.

Sandcastle Contest, Newport Beach. This popular event draws participants from all levels of experience to build their beach creations. Mid-September. Phone (949) 729-4400.

▓ OCTOBER

Fleet Week, San Francisco. This annual event celebrates the U.S. Navy with air shows, the Blue Angels, a parade of ships, and ship tours. Early October. Phone (415) 705-5500.

Monterey Bay Bird Festival, Moss Landing. Enjoy bird-watching, children's activities, and non-birding activities. Early October. Phone (831) 728-5939.

Harbor Festival, Morro Bay. The event honors National Seafood Month and includes seafood and wine tastings, maritime heritage events, entertainment, arts and crafts, and exhibits. Early October. Phone (800) 366-6043.

Clam Festival, Pismo Beach. This festival features food, entertainment, a carnival, a parade, a beauty pageant, sandcastle building, and arts and crafts. Mid-October. Phone (800) 443-7778 or (805) 773-4382.

▓ NOVEMBER

Solvang Prelude, Solvang. Scenic bike rides through Santa Ynez Valley sponsored and led by the local bike club, SCOR; 25, 50, and 63 miles. First Saturday in November. Phone (800) 548-4447 (562) 690-3735.

Intertribal Marketplace, Los Angeles. More than 150 nationally known American Indian artists, traditional dancers, and storytellers offer demonstrations and sell Native American crafts items. Early November. Phone (323) 221-2164.

▓ DECEMBER

Christmas Home Tour, Ferndale. Here's an opportunity to tour Ferndale's loveliest homes decorated in their holiday finery. Early December. Phone (707) 786-4466.

Lighted Boat Parade, Morro Bay. Lighted boats of all sizes cruise the harbor. Early December. Phone (805) 772-6278.

Christmas in the Adobes, Monterey. For these special evening tours the historic adobe buildings are illuminated with candlelight and period decorations and tours include entertainment and costumed docents. Early December. Phone (831) 649-7118.

Parade of Lights, Oxnard. Lighted boats illuminate Channel Islands Harbor, while entertainment, visits with Santa Claus, and boat rides are also offered. Early December. Phone (805) 985-4852.

Newport Harbor Christmas Boat Parade, Newport Beach. More than 200 illuminated and decorated boats cruise the harbor. Mid-December. Phone (800) 94-COAST or (949) 722-1611.

D. California Fishing Regulations

In general, everyone age 16 or older is required to carry a fishing license, unless he or she is fishing from a public pier in the ocean. There are specific seasons and species size and catch limits that vary along the coast. If you're unfamiliar with California's extensive fishing regulations it's always best to consult with either agents who sell fishing licenses or with any Department of Fish and Game office. Contact the department's Web site www.dgf.ca.gov for complete fishing information, including license fees and the full text of all regulations.

For specific information contact the following California Department of Fish and Game offices:

NORTHERN CALIFORNIA AND NORTH COAST REGION
619 Second Street, Eureka 95501. Phone (707) 445-6493.

CENTRAL COAST REGION
7329 Silverado Trail, Yountville 94558. Phone (707) 944-5500

MARINE REGION
20 Lower Ragsdale Drive, Suite 100, Monterey 93940. Phone (831) 649-2870.
411 Burgess Drive, Menlo Park 94025. Phone (650) 688-6340.
330 Golden Shore, Suite 50, Long Beach 90802. Phone (562) 590-5117.

SOUTH COAST REGION
4949 Viewridge Avenue, San Diego 92123. Phone (619) 467-4201.
Ocean Salmon Hotline, phone (707) 431-4341.

E. Outfitters and Guides

The following guides, sport-fishing providers, outdoor equipment providers, and outfitters are listed alphabetically by county and the counties are listed from Northern to Southern California:

DEL NORTE COUNTY

Lunker Fish Trips Bait and Tackle. Ocean fishing trips and supplies. 2095 Highway 199, Crescent City, CA 95531. Phone (707) 458-4704.

Rivers West Outfitters. Full-service guide service for trout, steelhead, and salmon fishing on the North Coast and on Northern California and Southern Oregon rivers. 70 Cedar Lane, Klamath, CA 95548. Phone (707) 482-5822.

HUMBOLDT COUNTY

Hum-Boats Sail Canoe & Kayak Center. Kayak sales, rentals, and lessons. 423 1st Street, Eureka, CA 95501. Phone (707) 443-5157.

King Salmon Charters. Ocean fishing trips. 1875 Buhne Drive #7, Eureka, CA 95503. Phone (707) 442-3474.

🔲 MENDOCINO COUNTY

Adventure Rents. Kayak rentals and classes. 45450 Pacific Woods Road, Gualala, CA 95445. Phone (707) 884-4386.

🔲 SONOMA COUNTY

Bodega Bay Sportfishing Center. Ocean fishing trips for rock and ling cod, halibut, salmon, and crab. 1500 Bay Flat Road, Bodega Bay, CA 94923. Phone (707) 875-3344.

Jaws Sportfishing. Ocean fishing trips. PO Box 1148, Bodega Bay, CA 94923. Phone (707) 875-3495.

🔲 MARIN COUNTY

Blue Waters Kayaking. Sea kayak tours, rentals, and lessons. 12938 Sir Francis Drake Boulevard, Inverness, CA 94937. Phone (415) 669-2600.

Stinson Beach Health Club and Kayak Rental. Kayak, canoe, and bike rentals. 3605 State Route 1, Stinson Beach, CA 94970. Phone (415) 868-2739.

Tamal Saka Tomales Bay Kayaking. Kayak rentals, lessons, and tours. PO Box 833, Marshall (Point Reyes), CA 94940. www.tamalsaka.com. Phone (415) 663-1743.

West Marin Ocean Kayak. Kayak rentals. 15 Calle Del Mar, Stinson Beach, CA 94970. Phone (415) 868-9445.

🔲 SAN FRANCISCO COUNTY

Butchie B Sport Fishing. Fishing party boat rentals and trips. Fisherman's Wharf, San Francisco, CA 94117. Phone (415) 457-8388.

Hot Pursuit Sportfishing. Fishing party boat rentals and trips. Berth #1, Fisherman's Wharf, San Francisco, CA 94117. Phone (650) 965-3474.

🔲 ALAMEDA COUNTY

Berkeley Marina Sport Center and the Golden Eye Charter Boat. Fishing party boat rentals. 225 University Avenue, Berkeley, CA 94710. Phone (510) 849-2727.

California Canoe & Kayak. Sales, rentals, classes, and trips. Jack London Square, 409 Water Street, Oakland, CA 94607. Phone (510) 893-7833.

🔲 SAN MATEO COUNTY

Capt. Joe's Pacific Sport Fishing Charters LLC. Fishing boat charters for salmon and rockfish. Half Moon Bay, CA 94019. Phone (650) 752-5886.

Captain John's Deep Sea Fishing. Deep-sea and rock fishing party boats. PO Box 155, Half Moon Bay, CA 94019. Phone (650) 726-2913.

🔲 SANTA CRUZ COUNTY

Dive Crazy Adventures. Kayak rentals, scuba diving boat charters and equipment, whale-watching trips. 33621 Albion River North Side Road, Albion, CA 95410. www.divecrazy.com. Phone (707) 937-3079.

Venture Quest Kayaking. Kayak rentals and classes. 125 Beach Street, Santa Cruz, CA 95060. Phone (831) 427-2267.

🔲 MONTEREY COUNTY

Adventures by the Sea. Kayak rentals, classes, and guide-led trips. 299 Cannery Row, Monterey, CA 93940. Phone (831) 372-1807.

Chris' Fishing Trips. Ocean fishing trips. #48 Fisherman's Wharf, Monterey, CA 93940. (831) 375-5951.

Monterey Express Charters. Dive boat charters. PO Box 2600, Monterey, CA 93942. Phone (888) 422-2999.

Monterey Sport Fishing. Fishing trips, whale watching. 96 Fisherman's Wharf, Monterey, CA 93940. Phone (831) 372-2203.

Twin Otters Inc. Dive boat charters. Wharf #2, Monterey, CA 93943. Phone (831) 394-4235.

SAN LUIS OBISPO COUNTY

Central Coast Kayaks. Kayak rentals, lessons, and guided tours. 1879 Shell Beach Road, Shell Beach, CA 93449. Phone (805) 773-3500.

Kayaks of Morro Bay. Kayak rentals and classes. 699 Embarcadero #9, Morro Bay, CA 93442. Phone (800) 92-KAYAK.

Patriot Sport Fishing. Ocean fishing for salmon, halibut, and albacore. Whale watching from December through April. Pier #3, Port San Luis, Avila Beach, CA 93424. Phone (805) 595-7200.

Scuba Adventures. Scuba equipment sales and rentals, lessons, and vacation packages. 1039 Grand Avenue, Arroyo Grande, CA 93420. Phone (805) 473-1111.

Trade Winds Dive & Travel. Scuba equipment sales and rentals, lessons, and scuba and snorkeling trips. 1355 Grand Avenue, Arroyo Grande, CA 93420. Phone (800) 88-SCUBA.

Virg's Fishin. Ocean fishing for rockcod, salmon, halibut, and albacore. 1215 Embarcadero, Morro Bay, CA 93442. Phone (805) 772-1222.

SANTA BARBARA COUNTY

Cisco Sportfishing. Ocean fishing charters to the Channel Islands. Whale watching from January through March. Channel Islands Harbor, 4151 S. Victoria Avenue, Oxnard, CA 93035. www.ciscos.com. Phone (805) 985-8511.

Hornet Sport Fishing. Ocean fishing boat charter service. 125 Harbor Way #4, Santa Barbara, CA 93109. Phone (805) 966-2212.

Jandd Mountaineering. Kayak rentals; mountaineering shop offering backpacking, hiking, and outdoors equipment and clothing, kayak and canoe sales. 30 South Salsipuedes, Santa Barbara, CA 93103. Phone (805) 882-1195.

Paddle Sports. Kayak rentals and sales. Lessons and trips to the Channel Islands. 100 State Street, Santa Barbara, CA 93101. Phone (805) 899-4925.

Sea Landing. Boat charters for ocean fishing, whale watching, scuba diving, and Channel Island excursions. Across Cabrillo Boulevard at the end of Bath Street, Santa Barbara, CA 93103. Phone (805) 963-3564.

Truth Aquatics. Boat transportation to the Channel Islands along with single- or multiple-day kayaking, scuba diving, whale watching, bird-watching, and snorkeling trips. 301 West Cabrillo Boulevard, Santa Barbara, CA 93101-3886. www.truthaquatics.com. Phone (805) 962-1127 or (805) 963-3564.

VENTURA COUNTY

Captain Hook's Sport Fishing. Single- and multiple-day fishing trips to the Channel Islands. 3600 South Harbor, Oxnard, CA 93035. Phone (805) 382-6233.

Channel Islands Kayak Center. Kayak rentals and lessons. 3600 South Harbor Boulevard, Oxnard, CA 93035. Phone (805) 984-5995.

Channel Islands Scuba. Equipment rentals and sales, lessons. 4255-4 East Main, Ventura, CA 93003. Phone (805) 644-3483.

Spectre-Liberty. Scuba diving trips. 1567 Spinnaker Drive #203-75, Ventura, CA 93001. Phone (805) 483-6612.

Island Packers. Channel Island excursions, including boat transportation, hiking, camping, kayaking, snorkeling, and whale watching. 1867 Spinnaker Drive, Ventura, CA 93001-4353. Phone (805) 642-1393.

LOS ANGELES COUNTY

Belmont Pier Sport Fishing. Day sport-fishing, whale-watching, and Long Beach Harbor cruises. Ocean Boulevard and 39th Place, Long Beach, CA 90802. Phone (562) 434-6781.

Eurosail Charters. Boat rentals, day charters to Catalina Island, charters to Mexico, champagne whale-watching trips, and sailing school. Berth 75 Ports O'Call, San Pedro, CA 90731. Phone (310) 831-2363.

Long Beach Windsurf & Kayak Center. Ocean kayak rentals. 3850 East Ocean Boulevard, Long Beach, CA 90803. Phone (562) 433-1014.

Malibu Kayak Rentals. Kayak rentals. 22935-½ Pacific Coast Highway, Malibu, CA 90265. Phone (310) 456-6302.

Offshore Water Sports. Parasailing and Jet Ski and boat rentals. 128 East Shoreline Drive, Long Beach, CA 90802. Phone (562) 436-1996.

Pierpoint Landing. Offers whale-watching, scuba diving, and ocean fishing excursions ranging from half-day trips to overnighters. 200 Aquarium Way, Long Beach, CA 90802. Phone (562) 983-9300.

Long Beach Marina Sport Fishing. Offers half- and three-quarter-day ocean fishing trips. 140 Marina Drive, Long Beach, CA 90802. Phone (562) 598-6649.

ORANGE COUNTY

Dana Point Sport Fishing. Half- to full-day ocean fishing trips. Whale watching from December through April. 34675 Golden Lantern, Dana Point, CA 92629. Phone (949) 496-5794.

Davey's Locker. Sport-fishing and whale-watching trips. 400 Main Street, Newport Beach, CA 92661. Phone (949) 673-1434.

Liburdi's Scuba Center. Scuba lessons, equipment rentals, and repairs. 15315 Culver Drive, Irvine, CA 92604. www.liburdisscuba.com. Phone (877) 808-9428.

Pacific Wilderness. Scuba diving equipment rentals and sales. Lessons and boat charters. 1132 East Katella Avenue, Orange, CA 92867. www.pacificwilderness.com. Phone (714) 997-5506.

Paddle Power. Kayak, canoe, and surf ski (open-decked plastic kayaks) rentals, sales, and lessons. 1500 West Balboa Boulevard, Newport Beach, CA 92663. Phone (949) 675-1215.

Southwind Kayak Center. Kayak and canoe rentals and sales for ocean, lake, and river use. Lessons and tours available. 17855 Sky Park Circle, Irvine, CA 92614. Phone (949) 261-0200.

SAN DIEGO COUNTY

Aqua Adventures Kayak School. Kayak instruction and rentals, with ocean and river tours. 4901 Morena Boulevard, San Diego, CA 92117. www.aqua-adventures.com. Phone (800) 269-7792.

Explorer Dive & Travel. Scuba diving lessons, nature tours, whale watching, and kayak rentals. 7524 La Jolla Boulevard, La Jolla, CA 92037. Phone (858) 551-8324.

Islandia Sportfishing. Deep-sea fishing cruises. 1551 West Mission Bay Drive, San Diego, CA 92109. www.islandiasport.com. Phone (619) 222-1164.

La Jolla Kayak & Co. Guided tours of La Jolla's shoreline cliffs and caves. Kayak lessons and rentals, snorkeling. 2199 Avenida De La Playa, La Jolla, CA 92037. Phone (858) 459-1114.

Ocean Enterprises. Scuba diving classes and trips, equipment rental and sales. 7710 Balboa Avenue, San Diego, CA 92111. Phone (858) 565-6054.

Point Loma Sport Fishing. Half-day to overnight ocean fishing and whale-watching trips from January through March. 1403 Scott Street, San Diego, CA 92106. www.pointlomasportfishing.com. Phone (619) 223-1627.

Southwest Kayaks. Kayak rentals, basic and advanced lessons, and guided trips. 2590 Ingraham Street, San Diego, CA 92109. Phone (619) 222-3616.

Windsport. Kayak and windsurfing equipment sales, rentals, and lessons. 844 West Mission Bay Drive, San Diego, CA 92109. Phone (858) 488-4642.

F. Glossary

Algae—Simple non-seed-bearing plants that include multicellular seaweeds and one-celled diatoms (singular: alga).

Algin—A carbohydrate extracted from brown marine algae such as kelp. It is used as a commercial thickening and emulsifying agent in many food products.

Arthropod—Animals that wear a segmented shell and have segmented legs are arthropods, such as insects and crustaceans.

Basalt—A dark, fine-grained volcanic rock composed primarily of pyroxene and calcic plagioclase that may or may not include olovine. It commonly occurs in sheet-like lava flows.

Bedrock—Any solid rock that underlies unconsolidated surface deposits such as sand.

Bivalve—The taxonomic group (Class Bivalvia) of mollusks that have two shells hinged together, such as mussels, clams, and oysters.

Chert—A compact siliceous rock formed from opaline silica or chalcedony.

Crustacean—Crustaceans are arthropods that live in the water and breathe by gills, such as lobsters, barnacles, crabs, and shrimp.

Delta—A deposit of sediment near the mouth of a river.

Eelgrass—A grass-like, aquatic, seed-bearing plant.

Estuary—A submerged river valley, usually found along the seacoast, forming an inlet or narrow bay and whose waters are influenced by oceanic tides.

Fault—A fracture or fracture zone along which there has been movement of rocks on one side relative to the other.

Fault zone—A belt of various widths consisting of numerous interlaced or crossing faults.

Fossil—Plant or animal remains or impressions that are preserved in the earth's crust by natural methods.

Holdfast—The part of a seaweed that secures a plant to a firm underwater surface with root-like structures called haptera.

Igneous—A class of rock formed by the solidification of molten or partially molten parent materials.

Intertidal—The area of shore that lies between the high and low tide zones.

Landslide—A downward movement of soil or rock, propelled by gravity, often using water as a starting lubricant.

Littoral—That which is on or along the coastline. Often associated with currents or sand movements along the coast.

Metamorphic rock—Rock formed from its already solid state as a result of reaction to pressure, temperature, or chemicals.

Midden—Generally a dump or refuse pile of shells and other food items left by Native Americans.

Mud flat—A sandy or muddy coastal strand that is regularly inundated by high tides.

Nocturnal—Primarily active at night.

Pelagic—On or of the open ocean.

Pinniped—Any member of the taxonomic group of marine mammals with fin-like feet or flippers (Suborder Pinnipedia), such as seals and sea lions.

Salt marsh—The transition zone between terrestrial and marine ecosystems.

Sandstone—Cemented or compacted sediment composed primarily of sand-sized grains.

Sediment—The matter that settles to the bottom of a body of water.

Sedimentary rock—Rock formed by tremendous pressures placed on layers of sediment over long periods of time.

Subduction zone—As related to Plate Tectonics it is the block of the earth's crust, usually the oceanic block, that is diving beneath an adjacent block or plate, usually the continental.

Tidepool—The pool of water that is left in rocky areas of a coastline as the tide falls.

Tombolo—An island near shore that is tied to the mainland by a sand bar.

Wetlands—Lands that contain high levels of moisture, such as mud flats or swamps.

Index